Sun® Certified Security Administrator for Solaris™ 9 & 10 Study Guide

Sun® Certified Security Administrator for Solaris™ 9 & 10 Study Guide

John Chirillo
Edgar Danielyan

McGraw-Hill/Osborne

New York Chicago San Francisco Lisbon London Madrid
Mexico City Milan New Delhi San Juan Seoul Singapore Sydney Toronto

The *McGraw-Hill* Companies

McGraw-Hill/Osborne
2100 Powell Street, 10th Floor
Emeryville, California 94608
U.S.A.

To arrange bulk purchase discounts for sales promotions, premiums, or fund-raisers, please contact **McGraw-Hill**/Osborne at the above address. For information on translations or book distributors outside the U.S.A., please see the International Contact Information page immediately following the index of this book.

Sun® Certified Security Administrator for Solaris™ 9 & 10 Study Guide

1234567890 DOC DOC 0198765

Book p/n 0-07-225424-6 and CD p/n 0-07-225425-4
parts of
ISBN 0-07-225423-8

Acquisitions Editor Tim Green	**Copy Editor** Lisa Theobald	**Illustration** International Typesetting & Composition
Project Editor Jody McKenzie	**Proofreader** Mike McGee	**Series Design** Roberta Steele and Peter Hancik
Acquisitions Coordinator Jennifer Housh	**Indexer** Jack Lewis	**Cover Series Design** Peter Grame
Technical Editor Tom Brays	**Composition** International Typesetting & Composition	

This book was composed with Adobe® InDesign®.

Information has been obtained by **McGraw-Hill**/Osborne from sources believed to be reliable. However, because of the possibility of human or mechanical error by our sources, **McGraw-Hill**/Osborne, or others, **McGraw-Hill**/Osborne does not guarantee the accuracy, adequacy, or completeness of any information and is not responsible for any errors or omissions or the results obtained from the use of such information.

ABOUT THE CONTRIBUTORS

About the Author

John Chirillo, CISSP, ISSAP, ASE, CCDA, CCNA, CCNP, SCSECA, is a Senior Internetworking Engineer at ValCom and the author of several computer security books. John has also achieved certifications in numerous programming languages and is responsible for dozens of published security exploits and alerts throughout numerous listings. He has actively participated in core security developments of various UNIX flavors under the GNU. John can be reached at tiger1@tigertools.net.

About the Co-Author

Edgar Danielyan, CISSP, ISSAP, ISSMP, CISA, MBCS, SCSA, SCNA, is Information Systems Audit Manager with Deloitte & Touche in the city of London. Before joining Deloitte, he had been an independent security consultant since 1999. He is also the author of *Solaris 8 Security* (New Riders, 2001) and technical editor of a number of books on Solaris, security, UNIX, and internetworking. His personal web site can be found at www.danielyan.com.

About the Technical Editor

Tom Brays, SCSA, SCNA, SCSECA, MCP, is a network administrator for a large telecommunications firm and the technical editor and contributing author of several computer books. He can be reached at tombrays@techie.com.

About LearnKey

LearnKey provides self-paced learning content and multimedia delivery solutions to enhance personal skills and business productivity. LearnKey claims the largest library of rich streaming-media training content that engages learners in dynamic media-rich instruction complete with video clips, audio, full motion graphics, and animated illustrations. LearnKey can be found on the Web at www.LearnKey.com.

CONTENTS AT A GLANCE

CONTENTS

Part I
General Security Concepts

Part II
Detection and Device Management

4 Logging and Process Accounting 95

5 Solaris Auditing, Planning, and Management 121

Part IV
File and System Resources Protection

ACKNOWLEDGMENTS

W e would like to thank the following people:

- Everyone at Osborne: Tim Green, Jody McKenzie, Jane Brownlow, Jennifer Housh, and Jessica Wilson for all their hard work.
- The best literary agent in the business, David Fugate at Waterside.
- The fine people at Sun Microsystems for their support and contributions, especially contributing authors Stephen Moore and Tom Brays.
- Our families for their unconditional love, support, and understanding especially during those endless evenings.

This book is organized in such a way as to serve as an in-depth review for the
Sun Certified Security Administrator for the Solaris Operating System 9 and 10
certifications for candidates with 6 to 12 months of experience administering security
in a Solaris Operating System. Each chapter covers a major aspect of the exam, with an emphasis
on the "why" as well as the "how to" of working with, and supporting, Solaris 9 and 10 as a security
administrator or engineer.

On the CD

The CD-ROM contains interactive study tools and a repository of online study
material, including web-based ePractice exams and the Sun Career Accelerator
Packages.

Exam Readiness Checklist

At the end of the Introduction, you will find an Exam Readiness Checklist. This table
has been constructed to allow you to cross-reference the official exam objectives with
the objectives as they are presented and covered in this book. The checklist also allows
you to gauge your level of expertise on each objective at the outset of your studies.
This should allow you to check your progress and make sure you spend the time you
need on more difficult or unfamiliar sections. References have been provided for the
objective exactly as the vendor presents it, the section of the study guide that covers
that objective, and a chapter and page reference.

In Every Chapter

We've created a set of chapter components that call your attention to important items,
reinforce important points, and provide helpful exam-taking hints. Take a look at what
you'll find in every chapter:

■ Every chapter begins with the **Certification Objectives**—what you need to
know in order to pass the section on the exam dealing with the chapter topic.

The Objective headings identify the objectives within the chapter, so you'll always know an objective when you see it!

■ **Exam Watch** notes call attention to information about, and potential pitfalls in, the exam. These helpful hints are written by authors who have taken the exams and received their certification. (Who better to tell you what to worry about?) They know what you're about to go through!

■ **Practice Exercises** are interspersed throughout the chapters. These are step-by-step exercises that allow you to get the hands-on experience you need in order to pass the exams. They help you master skills that are likely to be an area of focus on the exam. Don't just read through the exercises; they are hands-on practice that you should be comfortable completing. Learning by doing is an effective way to increase your competency with a product.

■ **On the Job** notes describe the issues that come up most often in real-world settings. They provide a valuable perspective on certification- and product-related topics. They point out common mistakes and address questions that have arisen during on-the-job discussions.

■ **Inside the Exam** sidebars highlight some of the most common and confusing problems that students encounter when taking a live exam. Designed to anticipate what the exam will emphasize, getting inside the exam will help ensure you know what you need to know to pass the exam. You can get a leg up on how to respond to those difficult-to-understand questions by focusing extra attention on these sidebars.

■ The **Certification Summary** is a succinct review of the chapter and a restatement of salient points regarding the exam.

■ The **Two-Minute Drill** at the end of every chapter is a checklist of the main points of the chapter. It can be used for last-minute review.

■ The **Self Test** offers questions similar to those found on the certification exams. The answers to these questions, as well as explanations of the answers, can be found at the end of each chapter. By taking the Self Test after completing each chapter, you'll reinforce what you've learned from that chapter while becoming familiar with the structure of the exam questions.

■ The **Lab Question** at the end of the Self Test section offers a unique and challenging question format that requires the reader to understand multiple chapter concepts to answer correctly. These questions are more complex and more comprehensive than the other questions, as they test your ability to take all the knowledge you have gained from reading the chapter and apply it to complicated, real-world situations. These questions are aimed to be more difficult than what you will find on the exam. If you can answer these questions, you have proven that you know the subject!

Some Pointers

Once you've finished reading this book, set aside some time to do a thorough review. You might want to return to the book several times and make use of all the methods it offers for reviewing the material. The following are some suggested methods of review.

1. *Re-read all the Two-Minute Drills, or have someone quiz you.* You also can use the drills as a way to do a quick cram before the exam. You might want to take some 3×5 index cards and write Two-Minute Drill material on them to create flash cards.

2. *Re-read all the Exam Watch notes.* Remember that these notes are written by authors who have taken the exam and passed. They know what you should expect—and what you should be on the lookout for.

3. *Retake the Self Tests.* Taking the tests right after you've read the chapter is a good idea because the questions help reinforce what you've just learned. However, it's an even better idea to go back later and do all the questions in the book in one sitting. In this instance, pretend you're taking the live exam. (When you go through the questions the first time, mark your answers on a separate piece of paper. That way, you can run through the questions as many times as you need to until you feel comfortable with the material.)

4. *Complete the Exercises.* Did you do the exercises when you read through each chapter? If not, do them! These exercises are designed to cover exam topics, and there's no better way to get to know this material than by practicing. Be sure you understand why you're performing each step in each exercise. If there's something you're not clear on, re-read that section in the chapter.

5. *Review the Final Test Study Guide and take the Final Test in the appendixes.* You should retake this test until you can answer all questions correctly before taking Sun's exam.

INTRODUCTION

The Sun Certified Security Administrator for the Solaris Operating System exam is for those candidates with 6 to 12 months of experience administering security in a Solaris Operating System (Solaris OS). It is recommended that candidates have at least 6 to 12 months security administration job-role experience and have previous Solaris OS and network administration certification.

About the Exam

The examination will include multiple choice scenario-based questions, matching, drag-drop, and free-response question types and will require in-depth knowledge on security topics such as general security concepts, detection and device management, security attacks, file and system resources protection, host and network prevention, network connection access, authentication, and encryption.

Testing Objectives

Working with Sun, we put together the following general collective testing objectives—all contained in this book—which cover the material for both Sun Certified Security Administrator for the Solaris 9 and 10 Operating System exams:

Section 1: Fundamental Security Concepts

- Describe accountability, authentication, authorization, privacy, confidentiality, integrity, and non-repudiation
- Explain fundamental concepts concerning information security and explain what good security architectures include (people, process, technology, defense in depth)

Section 2: Attacks, Motives, and Methods

- Describe concepts of insecure systems, user trust, threat, and risk
- Explain attackers, motives, and methods
- Describe how the attackers gain information about the targets and describe methods to reduce disclosure of revealing information

Section 3: Security Management and Standards

- Identify the security life cycle (prevent, detect, react, and deter) and describe security awareness, security policies and procedures, physical security, platform security, network security, application security, and security operations and management
- Describe the benefits of evaluation standards

Section 4: Logging and Process Accounting

- Identify, monitor, and disable logins
- Configure syslog, customize the system logging facility, and monitor and control superuser

Section 5: Solaris Auditing, Planning, and Management

- Configure Solaris auditing and customize audit events
- Generate an audit trail and analyze the audit data

Section 6: Device, System, and File Security

- Control access to devices by configuring and managing device policy and allocation
- Use the Basic Audit Reporting Tool to create a manifest of every file installed on the system and check the integrity of the system

Section 7: Denial of Service Attacks

- Differentiate between the types of host-based denial of service attacks and understand how attacks are executed
- Establish courses of action to prevent denial of service attacks

Section 8: Remote Access Attacks

- Identify, detect, and protect against Trojan horse programs and backdoors
- Explain rootkits that exploit loadable kernel modules

Section 9: User and Domain Account Management with RBAC

- Describe the benefits and capabilities of Role-Based Access Control (RBAC)
- Explain how to configure and audit RBAC

Section 10: Fundamentals of Access Control

- Use UNIX permissions to protect files
- Use access control lists to set file permissions

Section 11: Using Cryptographic Services

- Explain how to protect files using the Solaris cryptographic framework
- Administer the Solaris cryptographic framework

Section 12: Secure RPC Across NFS and PAM

- Explain and configure secure RPC to authenticate a host and a user across an NFS mount
- Use the PAM framework to configure the use of system entry services for user authentication

Section 13: SASL and Secure Shell

- Explain the Simple Authentication and Security Layer (SASL) in Solaris
- Use Solaris Secure Shell to access a remote host securely over an unsecured network

Section 14: Sun Enterprise Authentication Mechanism

- Define the Sun Enterprise Authentication Mechanism and configuration issues
- Configure and administer the Sun Enterprise Authentication Mechanism

Purchasing, Scheduling, and Taking the Exam   When you're ready to take the actual exam, you must first purchase an exam voucher online from www.sun.com/training/certification/objectives/index.html. Once exam vouchers are purchased, you have up to one year from the date of purchase to use it. Each voucher is valid for one exam and may only be used at an Authorized Prometric Testing Center in the country for which it was purchased. Please be aware that exam vouchers are not refundable for any reason.

After you have purchased your exam, contact your Authorized Prometric Testing Center at www.2test.com to schedule your exam date, time, and location. All exams take place at Authorized Prometric Testing Centers.

You also must agree to maintain test confidentiality and sign a Certification Candidate Pre-Test Agreement. You can review this document and other certification policies and agreements before taking your exam at www.sun.com/training/certification/register/policies.html.

You will receive your results immediately following the exam. Exam information is also available from Sun's CertManager online at www.sun.com/training/certification/certmanager/index.html. Please allow three to five working days after you take the exam for the information to be posted there.

The Sun Exam Preparation Course

Getting trained and certified as a Solaris Operating System (Solaris OS) system, network or security administrator is a great way to invest in your professional development. Sun certification can help you become a more valuable member of your IT organization and boost your career potential. IT managers know that the skills verified during the certification process are the same skills that can help lead to decreased time-to-market, increased productivity, less system failure, and higher employee satisfaction.

As we know that any IT certification path can be confusing and costly, Sun offers comprehensive Career Accelerator Packages (CAPs) that take the guesswork out of preparing for certification. Offered at little more than the instructor-led component sold individually, these packages provide an excellent value for your educational investment.

The Sun Career Accelerator Package for Advanced Security Administrators

Sun CAPs can help ease the certification process by providing the right combination of classroom training, online training, online practice certification exams, and actual certification exams. The Administering Security on the Solaris Operating System course provides students with the skills to implement, administer, and maintain a secure Solaris Operating System (Solaris OS).

Students who can benefit from this course are system administrators or security administrators who are responsible for administering one or more homogeneous Solaris OSes or administering security on one or more Solaris OSes.

Prerequisites and Skills Gained   To succeed fully in this course, students should be able to:

- Demonstrate basic Solaris OS and network administration skills
- Install the Solaris OS
- Administer users, printers, file systems, networks, and devices on the Solaris OS
- Demonstrate a basic understanding of Transmission Control Protocol/ Internet Protocol (TCP/IP) networking

Upon completion of this course, students should be able to:

- Describe security terminology and common forms of security attack
- Use Solaris OS logging and auditing to identify actual and potential security attacks
- Secure a Solaris OS host against user and network attacks
- Use tools, such as Solaris Security Toolkit (SST), to improve system security

Course Content

Module 1: Exploring Security

- Describe the role of system security
- Describe security awareness
- Describe historical examples of break-ins
- Define security terminology
- Classify security attacks
- Examine the motivations of an attacker
- Identify data gathering methods
- Run an intrusion detection system
- Define a security policy
- Use open-source security tools

Module 2: Using Solaris OS Log Files

- Explore the standard Solaris OS log files
- Configure and use the system logging utility
- Monitor log files using the swatch tool
- Describe the process monitoring tools
- Collect information using the Solaris OS accounting package

Module 3: Examining the Solaris OS Basic Security Module (BSM)

- Configure Basic Security Module (BSM) auditing
- Start and stop the BSM
- Create an audit trail using the BSM
- Generate an audit trail
- Interpret and filter audit data
- Implement BSM device management

Module 4: Preventing Security Attacks

- Recognize Trojan horses
- Identify backdoor attacks
- Detect and prevent Trojan horse and backdoor attacks
- Explain how rootkits can hide attackers
- Identify DoS attacks

- Configure the SAINT network analysis tool
- Interpret SAINT reports
- Detect network analyzer attacks

Module 13: Securing Network Services

- Restrict network services
- Defend network services
- Use Berkeley r commands for remote connections
- Secure services with the chroot command
- Integrate services using PAM
- Describe the SEAM

Module 14: Automating Server Hardening

- Describe system hardening
- Describe system hardening using the Solaris Security Toolkit (SST)
- Set up the SST

Module 15: Authenticating Network Services

- Describe network authentication using TCP wrappers
- Configure host access control
- Use banners with TCP wrappers

Module 16: Securing Remote Access

- Describe the benefits of Secure Shell
- Configure Secure Shell

Module 17: Securing Physical Access

- Assess the risk from physical intrusion
- Apply physical security measures

Module 18: Connecting the Enterprise Network to the Outside World

- Design the network to improve security
- Run enterprise security audits
- Explain the role of security audits
- Identify common sources of security information

You can check availability and request a class online at www.sun.com/training/catalog/accelerator_solaris.html.

Certification ePractice Exam

For $75, Sun also offers the ePractice Certification Exam for the Sun Certified Security Administrator that provides students with preparation for Sun certifications by acquainting them with the format of the exam and its questions, providing instant feedback regarding skill levels and gaps, and suggesting specific Sun Educational Services training to fill those gaps. The exam includes sample test questions, the correct answers including explanations, and suggestions for future study.

The subscription duration for accessing the online ePractice exam is 180 days. You can find out more and order an online subscription at www.sun.com/training/certification/resources/epractice.html.

Sun Certified Security Administrator for the Solaris Operating System

Official Objective	Certification Objective	Ch #	Pg #	Beginner	Intermediate	Expert
General Security Concepts		1–3				
Explain fundamental concepts concerning information security and explain what good security architectures include (people, process, technology, defense in depth).	Describe Principles of Information Security — Explain Information Security Fundamentals and Define Good Security Architectures	1	4, 13			
Identify the security life cycle (prevent, detect, react, and deter) and describe security awareness, security policies and procedures, physical security, platform security, network security, application security, and security operations and management.	Identify the Security Life Cycle and Describe Best Security Practices	3	66			
Describe concepts of unsecure systems, user trust, threat, and risk.	Describe Concepts of Insecure Systems, User Trust, Threat, and Risk	2	36			
Explain attackers, motives, and methods.	Explain Attackers, Motives, and Methods	2	43			
Describe accountability, authentication, authorizations, privacy, confidentiality, integrity, and non-repudiation.	Describe Principles of Information Security — Explain Information Security Fundamentals and Define Good Security Architectures	1	4, 13			

Sun Certified Security Administrator for the Solaris Operating System

Official Objective	Certification Objective	Ch #	Pg #	Beginner	Intermediate	Expert
Describe the benefit of evaluation standards and explain actions that can invalidate certification.	Describe the Benefits of Evaluation Standards	3	77			
Describe how the attackers gain information about the targets and describe methods to reduce disclosure of revealing information.	Describe How Attackers Gain Information, and Describe Methods to Reduce Disclosure	2	51			
Detection and Device Management		4–6				
Given a scenario, identify and monitor successful and unsuccessful logins and system log messages, and explain how to configure centralized logging and customize the system logging facility to use multiple log files.	Identify, Monitor, and Disable Logins Configure syslog, Customize the System Logging Facility, and Monitor and Control Superuser	4	96, 106			
Describe the benefits and potential limitations of process accounting.	Configure syslog, Customize the System Logging Facility, and Monitor and Control Superuser	4	106			
Configure Solaris BSM auditing, including setting audit control flags and customizing audit events.	Configure Solaris Auditing and Customize Audit Events	5	122			
Given a security scenario, generate an audit trail and analyze the audit data using the auditreduce, praudit, and audit commands.	Generate an Audit Trail and Analyze the Audit Data	5	136			
Explain the device management components, including device_maps and device_allocate file, device-clean scripts, and authorizations using the auth_attr database, and describe how to configure these device management components.	Control Access to Devices by Configuring and Managing Device Policy and Allocation	6	152			

Sun Certified Security Administrator for the Solaris Operating System						
Official Objective	**Certification Objective**	**Ch #**	**Pg #**	**Beginner**	**Intermediate**	**Expert**
Security Attacks		7–8				
Differentiate between the different types of host-based denial of service (DoS) attacks, establish courses of action to prevent DoS attacks, and understand how DoS attacks are executed.	Differentiate Between the Types of Host-Based Denial of Service Attacks and Understand How Attacks Are Executed	7	180			
Demonstrate privilege escalation by identifying Trojan horses and buffer overflow attacks. Explain backdoors, rootkits, and loadable kernel modules, and understand the limitations of these techniques.	Identify, Detect, and Protect Against Trojan Horse Programs and Backdoors Explain Rootkits that Exploit Loadable Kernel Modules	8	218, 236			
Given a security scenario, detect Trojan horse and back door attacks using the find command, checklists, file digests, checksums, and the Solaris Fingerprint Database. Explain trust with respect to the kernel and the OpenBoot PROM and understand the limitations of these techniques.	Identify, Detect, and Protect Against Trojan Horse Programs and Backdoors	8	218			
File and System Resources Protection		4, 9, 10, and 12				
Given a security scenario: (1) manage the security of user accounts by setting account expiration, and restricting root logins; (2) manage dormant accounts through protection and deletion; and (3) check user security by configuring the /etc/default/su file, or classifying and restricting non-login accounts and shells.	Identify, Monitor, and Disable Logins	4	96			
Describe the implementation of defensive password policies and understand the limitations of password authentication.	Identify, Monitor, and Disable Logins	4	96			

Sun Certified Security Administrator for the Solaris Operating System

Official Objective	Certification Objective	Ch #	Pg #	Beginner	Intermediate	Expert
Describe the function of a Pluggable Authentication Module (PAM), including the deployment of PAM in a production environment, and explain the features and limitations of Sun Kerberos.	Use the PAM Framework to Configure the Use of System Entry Services for User Authentication	12	341			
Describe the benefits and capabilities of Role-Based Access Control (RBAC), and explain how to configure profiles and executions including creating, assigning, and testing RBAC roles.	Describe the Benefits and Capabilities of Role-Based Access Control

Explain How to Configure and Audit Role-Based Access Control | 9 | 256, 261 | | | |
| Given a scenario, use access control lists including setting file system permissions, the implications of using lax permissions, manipulating the set-user-ID and set-group-ID, and setting secure files using access control lists. | Use UNIX Permissions to Protect Files

Use Access Control Lists to Set File Permissions | 10 | 282, 293 | | | |
| **Host and Network Prevention** | | 1 | | | | |
| Explain fundamental concepts concerning network security, including firewall, IPSEC, network intrusion and detection. Describe how to harden network services by restricting run control services, inetd services, and RPC services. Understand host hardening techniques described in Sun security blueprints. | Describe Principles of Information Security

Explain Information Security Fundamentals and Define Good Security Architectures | 1 | 4, 13 | | | |
| **Network Connection Access, Authentication, and Encryption** | | 11 and 13 | | | | |
| Explain cryptology concepts including secret-key and public-key cryptography, hash functions, encryption, and server and client authentication. | Explain How to Protect Files Using the Solaris Cryptographic Framework

Administer the Solaris Cryptographic Framework | 11 | 307, 315 | | | |
| Given a security scenario, configure Solaris Secure Shell. | Use Solaris Secure Shell to Access a Remote Host Securely Over an Unsecured Network | 13 | 358 | | | |

Part I

General Security Concepts

1

Fundamental
Security Concepts

Ｗe'll begin Part I of the book with the discussion of fundamental concepts and principles of information security. These general concepts and principles are relevant in all computing environments and serve as the foundation upon which all security mechanisms and controls are designed and implemented, regardless of the particular hardware platform, operating system, or application.

CERTIFICATION OBJECTIVE 1.01

Describe Principles of Information Security

First, let's define information security. If ten different people were asked to define information security, we might well receive ten different answers, but what is surprising is that they might all be correct. Nevertheless, the universal, classic definition of information security is brief and simple:

> Information security is the confidentiality, integrity, and availability of information.

Indeed, all the principles, standards, and mechanisms you will encounter in this book are dedicated to these three abstract but fundamental goals of confidentiality, integrity, and availability of information and information processing resources—also referred to as the *C-I-A triad* or *information security triad*.

Confidentiality

In the context of information security, *confidentiality* means that information that should stay secret stays secret and only those persons authorized to access it may receive access. From ancient times, mankind has known that information is power, and in our information age, access to information is more important than ever. Unauthorized access to confidential information may have devastating consequences, not only in national security applications, but also in commerce and industry. Main mechanisms of protection of confidentiality in information systems are cryptography and access controls. Examples of threats to confidentiality are malware, intruders, social engineering, insecure networks, and poorly administered systems.

Integrity

Integrity is concerned with the trustworthiness, origin, completeness, and correctness of information as well as the prevention of improper or unauthorized modification of information. Integrity in the information security context refers not only to integrity of information itself but also to the origin integrity—that is, integrity of the source of information. Integrity protection mechanisms may be grouped into two broad types: preventive mechanisms, such as access controls that prevent unauthorized modification of information, and detective mechanisms, which are intended to detect unauthorized modifications when preventive mechanisms have failed. Controls that protect integrity include principles of least privilege, separation, and rotation of duties—these principles are introduced later in this chapter.

Availability

Availability of information, although usually mentioned last, is not the least important pillar of information security. Who needs confidentiality and integrity if the authorized users of information cannot access and use it? Who needs sophisticated encryption and access controls if the information being protected is not accessible to authorized users when they need it? Therefore, despite being mentioned last in the C-I-A triad, availability is just as important and as necessary a component of information security as confidentiality and integrity. Attacks against availability are known as *denial of service (DoS)* attacks and are discussed in Chapter 7. Natural and manmade disasters obviously may also affect availability as well as confidentiality and integrity of information, though their frequency and severity greatly differ—natural disasters are infrequent but severe, whereas human errors are frequent but usually not as severe as natural disasters. In both cases, business continuity and disaster recovery planning (which at the very least includes regular and reliable backups) is intended to minimize losses.

Now that the cornerstone concepts of confidentiality, integrity, and availability have been discussed, let's take a look at identification, authentication, and authorization processes and methods, which are some of the main controls aimed at protecting the C-I-A triad.

Identification

Identification is the first step in the identify-authenticate-authorize sequence that is performed every day countless times by humans and computers alike when access to information or information processing resources are required. While particulars of identification systems differ depending on who or what is being identified, some intrinsic properties of identification apply regardless of these particulars—just three of these properties are the *scope, locality,* and *uniqueness* of IDs.

Identification name spaces can be local or global in scope. To illustrate this concept, let's refer to the familiar notation of Internet e-mail addresses: while many e-mail accounts named *jack* may exist around the world, an e-mail address *jack@company.com* unambiguously refers exactly to one such user in the company .com locality. Provided that the company in question is a small one, and that only one employee is named Jack, inside the company everyone may refer to that particular person by simply using his first name. That would work because they are in the same *locality* and only one Jack works there. However, if Jack were someone on the other side of the world or even across town, to refer to *jack@company.com* as simply *jack* would make no sense, because user name *jack* is not *globally unique* and refers to different persons in different *localities*. This is one of the reasons why two user accounts should never use the same name on the same system—not only because you would not be able to enforce access controls based on non-unique and ambiguous user names, but also because you would not be able to establish accountability for user actions.

To summarize, for information security purposes, unique names are required and, depending on their scope, they must be locally unique and possibly globally unique so that access control may be enforced and accountability established.

Authentication

Authentication, which happens just after identification and before authorization, verifies the authenticity of the identity declared at the identification stage. In other words, it is at the authentication stage that you prove that you are indeed the person or the system you claim to be. The three methods of authentication are *what you know, what you have,* or *what you are.* Regardless of the particular authentication method used, the aim is to obtain reasonable assurance that the identity declared at the identification stage belongs to the party in communication. It is important to note that *reasonable assurance* may mean different degrees of assurance, depending on the particular environment and application, and therefore may require different approaches to authentication: authentication requirements of a national security–critical system naturally differ from authentication requirements of a small company. Because different authentication methods have different costs and properties as well as different returns on investment, the choice of authentication method for a particular system or organization should be made after these factors have been carefully considered.

What You Know

Among *what you know* authentication methods are passwords, passphrases, secret codes, and personal identification numbers (PINs). When using *what you know*

authentication methods, it is implied that if you know something that is supposed to be known only by X, then you must be X (although in real life that is not always the case). *What you know* authentication is the most commonly used authentication method thanks to its low cost and easy implementation in information systems. However, *what you know* authentication alone may not be considered strong authentication and is not adequate for systems requiring high security.

What You Have

Perhaps the most widely used and familiar *what you have* authentication methods are keys—keys we use to lock and unlock doors, cars, and drawers; just as with doors, *what you have* authentication in information systems implies that if you possess some kind of token, such as a smart card or a USB token, you are the individual you are claiming to be. Of course, the same risks that apply to keys also apply to smart cards and USB tokens—they may be stolen, lost, or damaged. *What you have* authentication methods include an additional inherent per-user cost. Compare these methods with passwords: it costs nothing to issue a new password, whereas per-user *what you have* authentication costs may be considerable.

What You Are

What you are authentication refers to biometric authentication methods. A *biometric* is a physiological or behavioral characteristic of a human being that can distinguish one person from another and that theoretically can be used for identification or verification of identity. Biometric authentication methods include fingerprint, iris, and retina recognition, as well as voice and signature recognition, to name a few. Biometric authentication methods are less well understood than the other two methods but when used correctly, in addition to *what you have* or *what you know* authentication, may significantly contribute to strength of authentication. Nevertheless, biometrics is a complex subject and is much more cumbersome to deploy than *what you know* or *what you have* authentication. Unlike *what you know* or *what you have* authentication methods, whether or not you know the password or have the token, biometric authentication systems say how much you are like the subject you are claiming to be; naturally this method requires much more installation-dependent tuning and configuration.

Authorization

After declaring identity at the identification stage and proving it at the authentication stage, users are assigned a set of *authorizations* (also referred to as rights, privileges, or permissions) that define what they can do on the system. These authorizations are most commonly defined by the system's security policy and are set by the security or system administrator. These privileges may range from the extremes of "permit nothing" to "permit everything" and include anything in between.

As you can see, the second and third stages of the identify-authenticate-authorize process depend on the first stage, and the final goal of the whole process is to enforce *access control* and *accountability*, which is described next. User account management and access control in Solaris 10 are described in more detail in Chapters 9 and 10.

Authorization is the process of ensuring that a user has sufficient rights to perform the requested operation and preventing those without sufficient rights from doing the same. At the same time, authorization is also the process which gives rights depending on the identity of the user—be it a human or another system.

Accountability

Accountability is another important principle of information security that refers to the possibility of tracing actions and events back in time to the users, systems, or processes that performed them, to establish responsibility for actions or omissions.

A system may not be considered secure if it does not provide accountability, because it would be impossible to ascertain who is responsible and what did or did not happen on the system without that safeguard. Accountability in the context of information systems is mainly provided by *logs* and the *audit trail*.

Logs

System and application logs are ordered lists of events and actions and are the primary means of establishing accountability on most systems. However, logs (as well as the audit trail, which is described next) may be considered trustworthy only if their *integrity* is reasonably assured. In other words, if anyone can write to and/or erase logs or the audit trail, they would not be considered dependable enough to serve as the basis for accountability. Additionally, in case of networked or communication systems, logs should be correctly timestamped and time should be synchronized across the network so events that affect more than one system may be correctly correlated and attributed.

Audit Trail

The difference between the audit trail and logs is not clearly defined. However, we may say that logs usually show high-level actions, such as an e-mail message delivered or a web page served, whereas audit trails usually refer to lower-level operations such as opening a file, writing to a file, or sending a packet across a network. While an audit trail provides more detailed information about the actions and events that took place on the system, it is not necessarily more *useful*, in a practical sense of the word, than logs, simply because abundance of detail in an audit trail makes it more resource and time consuming to generate, store, and analyze. Another aspect by which logs and audit trails differ is their source: logs are usually and mostly generated by particular system software or applications, and an audit trail is usually kept by the operating system or its auditing module. Auditing and audit analysis in Solaris 10 are covered in detail in Chapter 5.

Functionality vs. Assurance

Having introduced the concept of accountability and how it is implemented on most systems, it's time to look at perhaps one of the most challenging issues of information security: the issue of *functionality versus assurance*. The best way to illustrate this is to refer to your own first-hand experience with computers: how many times has a computer failed to do something that you expected of it, and how many times did it do something you didn't want it to do? It is this difference between our expectations (as well as vendors' advertising of product features) and what happens in fact that is referred to as functionality versus assurance.

A particular system may claim to implement a dozen smart security features, but this is very different from being able to say with a high degree of confidence that it indeed implements them, implements them correctly, and will not behave in an unexpected manner. Another way of looking at the functionality versus assurance issue is that functionality is about what a system *can do* and assurance is about what a system *will not do*.

Although no quick and easy solutions are available in this case, we will discuss functionality and assurance issues in more detail in Chapter 3 of this book with regard to standards, certification, and accreditation.

Privacy

Privacy in the information security context usually refers to the expectation and rights of individuals to privacy of their personal information and adequate, secure handling of this information by its users. *Personal information* here usually refers to information that directly identifies a human being, such as a name and address, although the details may differ in different countries.

In many countries, privacy of personal information is protected by laws that impose requirements on organizations processing personal data and set penalties for noncompliance. The European Union (EU) in particular has strict personal data protection legislation in place, which limits how organizations may process personal information and what they can do with it. The U.S. Constitution also guarantees certain privacy rights, although the approach to privacy issues differs between the United States and Europe.

Since privacy is not only a basic human need but also a legally protected right in most countries, organizations should take necessary precautions to protect the confidentiality and integrity of personal information they collect, store, and process. In particular, organizations' information security policies should define how personal information is to be collected and processed. Because of these requirements, although not in the C-I-A triad, privacy is also an inseparable part of information security and must be addressed in all information security policies as part of the information security requirements.

Non-repudiation

Non-repudiation in the information security context refers to one of the properties of cryptographic digital signatures that offers the possibility of proving whether a particular message has been digitally signed by the holder of a particular digital signature's private key. Non-repudiation is a somewhat controversial subject, partly because it is an important one in this day and age of electronic commerce, and because it does not provide an absolute guarantee: a digital signature owner, who may like to repudiate a transaction maliciously, may always claim that his or her digital signature key was stolen by someone and that someone actually signed the digital transaction in question, thus repudiating the transaction. The following types of non-repudiation services are defined in international standard ISO 14516:2002, *Guidelines for the use and management of trusted third party services.*

Approval   Non-repudiation of approval provides proof of who is responsible for approval of the contents of a message.

Sending   Non-repudiation of sending provides proof of who sent the message.

Origin   Non-repudiation of origin is a combination of approval and sending.

Submission   Non-repudiation of submission provides proof that a delivery agent has accepted the message for transmission.

Transport   Non-repudiation of transport provides proof for the message originator that a delivery agent has delivered the message to the intended recipient.

Receipt   Non-repudiation of receipt provides proof that the recipient received the message.

Knowledge   Non-repudiation of knowledge provides proof that the recipient recognized the content of the received message.

Delivery   Non-repudiation of delivery is a combination of receipt and knowledge, as it provides proof that the recipient received and recognized the content of the message.

There is also a difference between the legal concept of non-repudiation and non-repudiation as an information security/cryptographic concept. In the legal sense, an alleged signatory to a paper document is always able to repudiate a signature that has been attributed to him or her by claiming any one of the following:

- Signature is forged
- Signature is a result of fraud by a third party
- Signature was unconscionable conduct by a party to transaction
- Signature was obtained using undue influence by a third party

In the information security context, one should keep in mind that the cryptographic concept of non-repudiation may, and often does, differ from its legal counterpart. Moreover, in some countries there is a trend of moving the burden of proof from the party relying on the signature (which is applicable to regular on-paper signatures) to the alleged signatory party, who would have to prove that he or she *did not* sign something. Chapter 11 of this book looks at cryptography in more detail.

INSIDE THE EXAM

General Security Concepts

The Sun Certified Security Administrator for Solaris exam consists of 60 multiple-choice, drag-drop, and matching questions to be answered in 90 minutes. The passing score for the entire exam is 60 percent. Of these 60 questions, approximately ten questions cover "Section 1 – General Security Concepts" of the official exam objectives and include the following items:

1. Explain fundamental concepts concerning information security and explain what good security architectures include (people, process, technology, defense in depth).

2. Describe accountability, authentication, authorizations, privacy, confidentiality, integrity, and non-repudiation.

3. Identify the security life cycle (prevent, detect, react, and deter) and describe security awareness, security policies and procedures, physical security, platform security, network security, application security, and security operations and management.

4. Describe concepts of insecure systems, user trust, threat, and risk.

5. Explain attackers, motives, and methods.

6. Describe the benefit of evaluation standards and explain actions that can invalidate certification.

7. Describe how attackers gain information about the targets, and describe methods to reduce disclosure of revealing information.

The first two exam objectives in this list are covered in this chapter. The purpose of Section 1 of the exam objectives is to test your understanding of the general security concepts and principles. Unlike other sections of the exam, Section 1 tests your knowledge of abstract matters that are universally applicable and are not specific to the Solaris operating environment. To perform well on the exam, you must have a clear understanding of the material presented in this chapter; the self-test questions at the end of the chapter should help you to check and reinforce the most important concepts.

CERTIFICATION OBJECTIVE 1.02

Explain Information Security Fundamentals and Define Good Security Architectures

Now that we have armed ourselves with the fundamental concepts of information security, let's consider some of the universal security principles, such as principles of least privilege, minimization, and compartmentalization.

Least Privilege

The principle of *least privilege* stipulates, "Do not give any more privileges than absolutely necessary to do the required job." This principle applies not only to privileges of users and applications on a computer system, but also to other non-information systems privileges of an organization's staff. The principle of least privilege is a preventive control, because it reduces the number of privileges that may be potentially abused and therefore limits the potential damage. Like most good principles, the principle of least privilege is applicable in all information systems environments. Some examples of application of this principle include the following:

- Giving users only read access to shared files if that's what they need, and making sure write access is disabled
- Not allowing help desk staff to create or delete user accounts if all that they may have to do is to reset a password
- Not allowing software developers to move software from development servers to production servers

Defense in Depth

The principle of *defense in depth* is about having more than one layer or type of defense. The reasoning behind this principle is that any one layer or type of defense may be breached, no matter how strong and reliable you think it is, but two or more layers are much more difficult to breach. Defense in depth works best when you combine two or more different types of defense mechanisms—such as using a firewall between the Internet and your LAN, plus the IP Security Architecture (IPSEC) to encrypt all sensitive traffic on the LAN. In this scenario, even if your firewall is compromised, the attackers still have to break IP Security to get to your data flowing across the LAN.

Generally, different types of controls should be used together: first, preventive controls should be in place to try and prevent security incidents from happening at all; second, detective controls are necessary so that you can know whether preventive controls are working or have failed; and third, corrective controls are needed to help you respond effectively to security incidents and contain damage. However, the defense in depth principle does not mean that you should indiscriminately apply all the controls and security measures you can get your hands on: balance has to be found between security provided by the defense in depth approach and the financial, human, and organizational resources you are willing to expend following it. This balance is addressed by the cost-benefit analysis, introduced later on in this chapter.

Minimization

The *minimization* principle is the cousin of the least privilege principle and mostly applies to system configuration. The minimization principle says "do not run any software, applications, or services that are not strictly required to do the entrusted job." To illustrate, a computer whose only function is to serve as an e-mail server should have only e-mail server software installed and enabled. All other services and protocols should either be disabled or not installed at all to eliminate any possibility of compromise or misuse. Adherence to the minimization principle not only increases security but usually also improves performance, saves storage space, and is a good system administration practice in general.

Cost-Benefit Analysis

Although not strictly a principle, the *cost-benefit analysis* is a must when considering implementation of any security measure. It says that the overall benefits received from a particular security control or mechanism should clearly exceed its total costs; otherwise, implementing it would make no sense. Cost-benefit analysis directly affects return on investment (ROI). This may sound like simple common sense, and it probably is; nevertheless, this is an important and often overlooked concern. When doing cost-benefit analysis, one should consider all costs and all benefits over a period of time, for example from one to five years, to have a complete picture.

Risk-Control Adequacy

We will discuss risk analysis and management in more detail in Chapter 2. For now, suffice to say that controls should match the risks they are expected to control and should not be implemented just for the sake of having them. This is yet another common-sense principle that is often neglected.

Compartmentalization

Compartmentalization, or the use of compartments (also known as zones, jails, sandboxes, and virtual areas), is a principle that limits the damage and protects other compartments when software in one compartment is malfunctioning or compromised. It can be best compared to compartments on ships and submarines, where a disaster in one compartment does not necessarily mean that the entire ship or submarine is lost. Compartmentalization in the information security context means that applications run in different compartments are isolated from each other. In such a setup, the compromise of web server software, for example, does not take down or affect e-mail server software running on the same system but in a separate compartment. Zones in Solaris 10 implement the compartmentalization principle and are powerful security mechanisms.

Keep Things Simple

Complexity is the worst enemy of security. Complex systems are inherently more insecure because they are difficult to design, implement, test, and secure. The more complex a system, the less assurance we may have that it will function as expected. Although complexity of information systems and processes is bound to increase with our increasing expectations of functionality, we should be very careful to draw a line between avoidable and unavoidable complexity and not sacrifice security for bells and whistles, only to regret it later. When you have to choose between a complex system that does much and a simple system that does a bit less but enough, choose the simple one.

Fail Securely

Although *fail securely* may sound like an oxymoron, it isn't. Failing securely means that if a security measure or control has failed for whatever reason, the system is not rendered to an insecure state. For example, when a firewall fails, it should default to a "deny all" rule, not a "permit all." However, *fail securely* does not mean "close everything" in all cases; if we are talking about a computer-controlled building access control system, for example, in case of a fire the system should default to "open doors" if humans are trapped in the building. In this case, human life takes priority over the risk of unauthorized access, which may be dealt with using some other form of control that does not endanger the lives of people during emergency situations.

Secure the Weakest Link

To people new to information security, many information security principles and approaches may sound like little more than common sense. Although that may well be the case, it doesn't help us much, because very often we still fail to act with common sense. The principle of securing the weakest link is one such case: look around and you will likely see a situation in which instead of securing the weakest link, whatever it may be, resources are spent on reinforcing already adequate defenses.

Use Choke Points

Security is very much about control, and control is so much more effective and efficient when you know all ways in and out of your systems or networks. *Choke points* are logical "narrow channels" that can be easily monitored and controlled. An example of a choke point is a firewall—unless traffic can travel only via the firewall, the firewall's utility is reduced to zero. Consider the example of controlled entrances to buildings or facilities of high importance, such as perimeter fencing and guard posts.

Leverage Unpredictability

Just as states don't publicize the specifics of their armaments, exact locations, or numbers of armed forces, you should not publicize the details of your security measures and defenses. This principle should not be seen as contradicting deterrent security controls—controls that basically notify everyone that security mechanisms are in place and that violations will be resisted, detected, and acted upon. The important difference here is that deterrent controls don't provide details of the defenses but merely announce their existence so as to deter potential attackers without giving them detailed information that later may be used against the defenders. In practical terms, this means you can, for example, announce that you are using a firewall that, in particular, logs all traffic to and from your network, and these logs are reviewed by the organization—there is no need to disclose the type, vendor, or version number of the firewall; where it is located; how often logs are reviewed; and whether any backup firewalls or network intrusion detection systems are in place.

Segregation of Duties

The purpose of the segregation (or separation) of duties is to avoid the possibility of a single person being responsible for different functions within an organization, which when combined may result in a security violation that may go undetected. Segregation of duties can prevent or discourage security violations and should be practiced when possible. Although the actual job titles and organizational hierarchies may differ greatly, the idea behind the principle of separation of duties stays the same: no single person should be able to violate security and get away with it. Rotation of duties is a similar control that is intended to detect abuse of privileges or fraud and is a practice to help your organization avoid becoming overly dependent on a single member of the staff. By rotating staff, the organization has more chances of discovering violations or fraud.

Types of Controls

Central to information security is the concept of controls, which may be categorized by their *functionality* (preventive, detective, corrective, deterrent, recovery, and compensating, in this order) and *plane of application* (physical, administrative, or technical). Physical controls include doors, secure facilities, fire extinguishers, flood protection, and air conditioning. Administrative controls are the organization's policies, procedures, and guidelines intended to facilitate information security. Technical controls are the various technical measures, such as firewalls, authentication systems, intrusion detection systems, and file encryption, among others.

Preventive Controls

Preventive controls are the first controls met by the adversary. Preventive controls try to prevent security violations and enforce access control. Like other controls, preventive controls may be physical, administrative, or technical: doors, security procedures, and authentication requirements are examples of physical, administrative, and technical preventive controls, respectively.

Detective Controls

Detective controls are in place to detect security violations and alert the defenders. They come into play when preventive controls have failed or have been circumvented and are no less crucial than detective controls. Detective controls include cryptographic checksums, file integrity checkers, audit trails and logs, and similar mechanisms.

Corrective Controls

Corrective controls try to correct the situation after a security violation has occurred. Although a violation occurred, not all is lost, so it makes sense to try and fix the situation. Corrective controls vary widely, depending on the area being targeted, and they may be technical or administrative in nature.

Deterrent Controls

Deterrent controls are intended to discourage potential attackers and send the message that it is better not to attack, but even if you decide to attack we are able to defend ourselves. Examples of deterrent controls include notices of monitoring and logging as well as the visible practice of sound information security management.

Recovery Controls

Recovery controls are somewhat like corrective controls, but they are applied in more serious situations to recover from security violations and restore information and information processing resources. Recovery controls may include disaster recovery and business continuity mechanisms, backup systems and data, emergency key management arrangements, and similar controls.

Compensating Controls

Compensating controls are intended to be alternative arrangements for other controls when the original controls have failed or cannot be used. When a second set of controls addresses the same threats that are addressed by another set of controls, the second set of controls are compensating controls.

Access Control Models

Logical *access control models* are the abstract foundations upon which actual access control mechanisms and systems are built. Access control is among the most important concepts in computer security. Access control models define how computers enforce access of subjects (such as users, other computers, applications, and so on) to objects (such as computers, files, directories, applications, servers, and devices). Three main access control models exist: the discretionary access control model, the mandatory access control model, and the role-based access control model.

Discretionary Access Control (DAC)

The discretionary access control model is the most widely used of the three models. In the DAC model, the owner (creator) of information (file or directory) has the discretion to decide about and set access control restrictions on the object in question—which may, for example, be a file or a directory. The advantage of DAC is its flexibility: users may decide who can access information and what they can do with it—read, write, delete, rename, execute, and so on. At the same time, this flexibility is also a disadvantage of DAC because users may make wrong decisions regarding access control restrictions or maliciously set insecure or inappropriate permissions. Nevertheless, the DAC model remains the model of choice for the absolute majority of operating systems today, including Solaris.

Mandatory Access Control (MAC)

Mandatory access control, as its name suggests, takes a stricter approach to access control. In systems utilizing MAC, users have little or no discretion as to what access permissions they can set on their information. Instead, mandatory access controls specified in a system-wide security policy are enforced by the operating system and applied to all operations on that system. MAC-based systems use data classification levels (such as public, confidential, secret, and top secret) and security clearance labels corresponding to data classification levels to decide, in accordance with the security policy set by the system administrator, what access control restrictions to enforce. Additionally, per-group and/or per-domain access control restrictions may be imposed—that is, in addition to having the required security clearance level, subjects (users or applications) must also belong to the appropriate group or domain. For example, a file with a confidential label belonging only to the research group may not be accessed by a user from the marketing group, even if that user has a security clearance level higher than confidential (for example, secret or top secret). This concept is known as *compartmentalization* or *need to know*.

Although MAC-based systems, when used appropriately, are thought to be more secure than DAC-based systems, they are also much more difficult to use and administer because of the additional restrictions and limitations imposed by the operating system. MAC-based systems are typically used in government, military, and financial environments, where higher than usual security is required and where the added complexity and costs are tolerated. MAC is implemented in Trusted Solaris, a version of the Solaris operating environment intended for high-security environments.

Role-Based Access Control (RBAC)

In the role-based access control model, rights and permissions are assigned to roles instead of individual users. This added layer of abstraction permits easier and more flexible administration and enforcement of access controls. For example, access to marketing files may be restricted to the marketing manager role only, and users Ann, David, and Joe may be assigned the role of marketing manager. Later, when David moves from the marketing department elsewhere, it is enough to revoke his role of marketing manager; no other changes would be necessary. When you apply this approach to an organization with thousands of employees and hundreds of roles, you can see the added security and convenience of using RBAC. Solaris has supported RBAC since release 8.

Centralized vs. Decentralized Access Control

Further distinction should be made between centralized and decentralized (distributed) access control models. In environments with centralized access control, a single, central entity makes access control decisions and manages the access control system; whereas in distributed access control environments, these decisions are made and enforced in a decentralized manner. Both approaches have their pros and cons, and it is generally inappropriate to say that one is better than the other. The selection of a particular access control approach should be made only after careful consideration of an organization's requirements and associated risks.

Information Security Architectures

In the rest of this chapter we will discuss information security architectures and best practices. You will see that information security is not only a technological challenge but a human challenge as well and needs human solutions first and foremost. We will also try to identify the most common shortcomings and pitfalls that result in inefficient or insufficient information security and see what can be done to minimize their impact and the rate of occurrence.

We begin with an overview of information systems governance and how good governance practices improve information systems security during planning, design, implementation, use, and maintenance stages of information systems.

Information Systems Governance

Information security is a part of *information systems governance*. With our exponentially increasing dependence on information systems in all areas of human life, information systems affect nearly everyone. How we build and use information systems affects our national security, our competitiveness, and our economy. Information systems governance is the foundation that determines whether these information systems are aligned with our objectives and serve our needs. Therefore, good information systems governance practices are vital for every organization, and these practices or their absence directly affect security of information systems.

Information systems governance is mainly concerned with two responsibilities: making the most of available information systems resources and at the same time managing risks associated with use of these information systems. Ultimately, information systems governance is the responsibility of an organization's highest governing bodies, which are usually the board of directors or trustees. The board of directors is responsible for understanding the role and impact of information systems on the organization, defining high-level policies, measuring performance of information systems, and delegating management of information systems risks. Regretfully, information security is often mistakenly viewed as a technology issue only, with little consideration given to business priorities and requirements, although research indicates that it is first and foremost a business issue. Responsibility for governing and managing the improvement of information security has been mostly limited to technical management and IT staff. However, for information security to be managed properly, understanding and involvement of the board of directors and executive management is necessary. In particular, the board of directors should do the following:

- Be informed about information security
- Set policy and strategy
- Provide resources for information security
- Assign responsibilities to management and set priorities

Executive management, in turn, should assume responsibility for the following aspects of information systems governance and be proactive in their management:

- Setting information security policy
- Assigning responsibilities to staff
- Assessing, analyzing, and managing risks associated with information systems
- Defining the information security management framework
- Implementing security awareness training of all staff

To assess information systems governance effectively in an organization, an information security governance maturity model defined by the Information

Technology Governance Institute (ITGI) as part of the Control Objectives for Information Technology (COBIT) framework may be used. COBIT defines the following as information systems governance criteria:

- Effectiveness
- Efficiency
- Confidentiality
- Integrity
- Availability
- Compliance
- Reliability

The information technology includes the people, technology, applications, facilities, and data of the organization. This model defines six levels of information systems and security governance, ranging from nonexistent to optimized. Although surveys show that very few organizations find themselves at these polar levels, the absolute majority of organizations have a way to go to reach higher levels of information systems governance.

The six levels of the information systems governance maturity model are as follows:

- **Level 0**   Nonexistent
- **Level 1**   Initial
- **Level 2**   Repeatable
- **Level 3**   Defined
- **Level 4**   Managed
- **Level 5**   Optimized

Nonexistent   Information systems governance and security management processes are nonexistent. The board of directors and management are breaching their fiduciary duties to the organization's stockholders by not fulfilling their responsibilities with regard to the governance and protection of the organization's information systems and assets.

Initial   Although existing, information systems governance and security management are mostly ad hoc and not well organized. Policies are not well founded. Standards and procedures are either unknown or are not being applied in an appropriate manner. Governance and management may be said to be in their embryonic form.

Repeatable   At this level, although it is understood that information systems governance and security management are important to the organization, the actual implementation of information systems governance practices is not adequate. Security awareness is fragmented, and information security management is not effective. This is the level of information systems governance and security management at most organizations.

Defined   Information systems governance processes are documented and they are communicated to all relevant parties. Risk-management policy exists and it is communicated to responsible staff. Information security policies exist and they are communicated to staff. Security awareness is facilitated, and information security responsibilities are defined and delegated.

Managed   Information systems governance processes are not only documented and communicated to all parties but are also monitored to ensure correct application and enforcement. Responsibilities for information security are clearly assigned, managed, and enforced. Information security risk analysis is consistently performed. Security policies and practices are complete with specific security baselines. Standards are used. Security awareness training is mandatory. Security certification of staff is encouraged and recognized.

Optimized   Best practices are followed in all aspects of information systems governance and information security management. Risk assessment has developed to the stage at which a structured process is enforced and well-managed. Information security is a joint responsibility of business and information systems management and is aligned with business objectives. Security functions are integrated in applications at the design stage, and end users are increasingly accountable for managing security. The existing processes provide for continuing self-improvement. Third-party certification or accreditation attests to the deployment of best practices in information systems governance and security.

As you can see, we have a way to go before we reach the more advanced levels of this model, but every step toward more effective and efficient information systems governance is a worthwhile investment. We will cover fundamentals of information security management in Chapter 3.

The Weakest Link

It is a widely held opinion among information security professionals that we, the humans, are the weakest link in the chain of information security. Nevertheless, we continue to suffer from our own errors and omissions, despite increasing information security risks. Until and unless we realize and accept this reality, it would be very difficult to rectify this unfortunate situation. Everyone involved with information systems—including their owners, managers, designers, administrators, and of course users—needs to do their part in being a responsible citizen of the information society. Owners and managers should accept responsibility for the overall management and governance of information systems; designers and administrators should adhere to security principles and best practices; and users should not compromise security for minute convenience.

The Information Security Process

Bruce Schneier, one of the world's most well-known experts on security, once wrote that "security is a process, not a product." Indeed, with all the changing variables and players, security is a never-ending evolutionary process, wherein defenses change in response to new threats and new threats emerge with the introduction of new systems and defenses. This view only reinforces something that has been known for a while—that you cannot buy security off the shelf. In the case of Solaris, the operating environment provides a good set of proven security features and technologies, but they are useless if not correctly used and administered as part of an encompassing security process that tries to prevent security violations, detect them when they occur, apply corrective controls, recover from the incident, and improve itself. The strength of protection against information security risks lies in the way this process is practiced: whether sufficient resources are allocated, whether qualified professionals do their jobs well, and whether management actually cares about the whole issue.

Know Your Enemy

Earlier in this chapter, we mentioned cost-benefit analysis and risk-control adequacy. It is worth revisiting this topic from a slightly more specific angle, that of knowing your enemy. No one would argue that before building defenses and getting ready for the battle, one should have at least a general idea of who may attack and, therefore, what can and cannot be done to prevent or fight against the attack. Meaningful cost-benefit and risk-control analyses are impossible or would yield incorrect results if one doesn't know his enemies and is unaware of their means and intentions. An adversary's profile determines to a great extent the type and quantity of controls that should be applied and therefore affects the cost-benefit equation in a nonlinear way. We will be discussing the attackers and their motives in more detail in the next chapter; for the purposes of this chapter, let's note that before erecting defenses, you should understand from whom you are trying to protect your organization's information assets and resources.

CERTIFICATION SUMMARY

In this chapter, we explained the fundamental information security concepts and principles, looked at what constitutes good security architectures and practices, and learned that good practices include people, processes, and technology working in concert. We also discussed the concepts of accountability, authentication, authorization, privacy, confidentiality, integrity, and non-repudiation, as well as types and functionalities of information security controls and the importance of information systems governance.

✓ TWO-MINUTE DRILL

Here are some of the key points from the certification objectives in Chapter 1.

Describe Principles of Information Security

- ❑ Information security is the confidentiality, integrity, and availability of information.
- ❑ Confidentiality is the prevention of unauthorized disclosure of information.
- ❑ Integrity is the means of ensuring that information is protected from unauthorized or unintentional alteration, modification, or deletion.
- ❑ Availability ensures that information is readily accessible to authorized viewers at all times.
- ❑ Identification is the means by which a user (human, system, or process) provides a claimed unique identity to a system.
- ❑ Authentication is a method for proving that you are who you say you are.
- ❑ Strong authentication is the use of two or more different authentication methods, such as a smart card and PIN, or a password and a form of biometrics, such as a fingerprint or retina scan.
- ❑ Authorization is the process of ensuring that a user has sufficient rights to perform the requested operation and preventing those without sufficient rights from doing the same.

Explain Information Security Fundamentals and Define Good Security Architectures

- ❑ The principle of least privilege stipulates that one should not be assigned any more privileges than those absolutely necessary to do the required job.
- ❑ The purpose of the segregation (or separation) of duties is to avoid the possibility of a single person being responsible for a variety of functions within an organization. Rotation of duties is a similar control that is intended to detect abuse of privileges or fraud and is a practice that helps the organization avoid becoming overly dependent on a single member of staff. By rotating staff, the organization has more chances of discovering violations or fraud.

SELF TEST

The following questions will help you measure your understanding of the material presented in this chapter. Read all the choices carefully because there might be more than one correct answer. Choose all correct answers for each question.

Describe Principles of Information Security

1. What is the purpose of audit trails and logs?
    A. They record events as they happen.
    B. An audit trail can be used in court proceedings but logs cannot.
    C. They serve to establish accountability.
    D. They may be used in place of deterrent controls.
    E. All of the above

2. Fingerprints can be used for
    A. *What you have* authentication
    B. *What you are* authentication
    C. Biological identification
    D. Keeping things simple
    E. All of the above

3. What type of control is intended to offset deficiencies of other controls?
    A. Preventive
    B. Defensive
    C. Compensating
    D. Recovery
    E. All of the above

4. What is strong authentication?
    A. Strong authentication uses long passwords.
    B. Strong authentication requires smart cards.
    C. Strong authentication requires the use of at least two different authentication methods.
    D. Strong authentication is provided via biometrics.
    E. All of the above

5. The principle of least privilege applies only to user accounts.
   A. True
   B. False
   C. True, but only on non-Solaris systems.
   D. True, provided users use good passwords.

6. The principle of isolating process spaces from each other is known as
   A. Virtualization
   B. Separation
   C. Defense in depth
   D. Compartmentalization
   E. All of the above

7. Surveys show that most organizations are at which level of the information security maturity model?
   A. Nonexistent
   B. Defined
   C. Detective
   D. Repeatable
   E. All of the above

8. Privacy is a concern in which of the following industries?
   A. Financial services
   B. Financial services and government
   C. Telecommunications
   D. All of the above

9. What is assurance?
   A. It is a type of insurance against security violations.
   B. It is the written security policy.
   C. It is about the trustworthiness of a system.
   D. It is provided by the mandatory access control (MAC).
   E. All of the above

10. Information security policies and procedures are a(n)

    A. Technical control

    B. Administrative control

    C. Form of access control

    D. Operational control

    E. All of the above

11. In information security context, names must be

    A. Unique locally

    B. Unique globally

    C. Standardized

    D. Secret

    E. All of the above

12. What risks apply to *what you have* authentication methods? (Choose all that apply.)

    A. Same risks as with *what you are* authentication

    B. Same risks that apply to regular keys

    C. Risks that apply to all authentication methods

    D. Certain non-assurance–related risks

    E. All of the above

Explain Information Security Fundamentals and Define Good Security Architectures

13. Who must be ultimately responsible for information security within organizations?

    A. Information security professionals

    B. Information systems auditors

    C. Top management

    D. Stockholders

    E. All of the above

14. Fundamental security principles

    A. Do not apply in all situations

    B. Apply to most information systems

    C. May be used only in enterprise systems

    D. Are system-dependent

    E. All of the above

15. Information systems governance is about what?
    A. Information security
    B. Effective and risk-aware use of information systems
    C. Risk management
    D. Corporate responsibility
    E. All of the above

16. What is the advantage of Role-Based Access Control (RBAC) over Discretionary Access Control (DAC)?
    A. RBAC has no advantages over DAC.
    B. RBAC is an improved version of DAC.
    C. RBAC improves management of access control and authorizations.
    D. RBAC is one level below Mandatory Access Control (MAC).
    E. All of the above

17. Which authentication method is the most complex to administer?
    A. *What you know*
    B. *What you have*
    C. *What you are*
    D. *Who you are*
    E. All of the above

18. What is the purpose of choke points?
    A. Choke points are used to isolate firewalls.
    B. Choke points protect confidentiality of information.
    C. Choke points may be used only on TCP/IP networks.
    D. Choke points are for control and monitoring of data flow.
    E. All of the above

19. What is the purpose of authentication?
    A. To obtain proof of claimed identity
    B. To implement access control
    C. To establish accountability
    D. To allow use of different authorizations
    E. All of the above

20. What is the benefit of cost-benefit analysis? (Choose all that apply.)

    A. It is necessary because organizations cannot reduce all risks to zero.

    B. It increases an organization's return on investment.

    C. It prevents denial of service attacks.

    D. It is a good governance practice.

    E. All of the above

SELF TEST ANSWERS

Describe Principles of Information Security

1. ☑ **C.** The purpose of the audit trail and logs is to provide accountability in information systems.
☒ **A** is correct but is not the best answer; choices **B** and **D** are wrong. The issue of whether audit trails and logs can be used in court proceedings would depend on particular jurisdiction and is outside the scope of this book; audit trails and logs are detective controls but may function as deterrent controls as well when their existence is known to potential attackers.

2. ☑ **B.** Fingerprints can be used for *what you are*, or biometric, authentication.
☒ **A** is wrong because *what you have* authentication refers to token-based authentication mechanisms. **C** is wrong because there is no such term as biological identification in information security. **D** is wrong because use of fingerprints does not simplify authentication or identification since this requires additional configuration and tuning.

3. ☑ **C.** Compensating controls offset deficiencies of other controls.
☒ There is no such term as defensive controls in information security, so that rules out **B.** Choices **A** and **D** are incorrect because preventive controls aim to prevent security violations and recovery controls are not intended to offset deficiencies of other controls.

4. ☑ **C.** At least two different authentication methods are necessary for strong authentication.
☒ Long passwords do not provide strong authentication on their own, so answer **A** is not correct. Strong authentication does not necessarily require use of smart cards, as stated in **B.** And **C** is wrong because biometrics does not necessarily provide strong authentication on its own.

5. ☑ **B.** The principle of least privilege does not only apply to user accounts but is a universally applicable principle.
☒ The answers are incorrect because the principle of least privilege has no relation to use of good passwords and is not dependent on a particular operating system or environment.

6. ☑ **D.** Compartmentalization is the isolation of process spaces from each other in order to minimize the effect of security violation in one compartment on another.
☒ Answer **A,** virtualization, is a related concept but is not the correct answer. **B** is wrong because compartmentalization is the correct term. **C** is wrong because defense in depth is about using several types and/or layers of defense.

7. ☑ **D.** Most organizations are at the repeatable level of the information security maturity model.
☒ **C** is inappropriate because it refers to a type of control. Other choices are wrong because surveys show that most organizations are at the repeatable level.

8. ☑ **D.** All of the above. Privacy is a concern in all industries, because organizations in all industries collect, process, and store personal information of employees, clients, and partners.

9. ☑ **C.** Assurance is about the trustworthiness of a system.
   ☒ **A** is wrong because there is no such type of insurance. **B** is wrong because, although written security policy is always required, it is not a guarantee of assurance. **D** is wrong because the use of MAC does not guarantee assurance.

10. ☑ **B.** Information security policies and procedures are an administrative control.
   ☒ **A** is wrong because policies and procedures are not a technical control. **C** is wrong because policies and procedures are not a form of access control. **D** is wrong because, although policies and procedures address operational controls, choice **B** is a better answer.

11. ☑ **A.** Names *must* be unique locally.
   ☒ **B** is wrong because names *may* be unique globally, but it's not necessary. **C** is wrong because names may be standardized, but that is not mandatory. **D** is wrong because names are not necessarily secret.

12. ☑ **B** and **C** are correct because *what you have* authentication methods are subject to the same risks (such as theft and damage) as regular keys, and they are subject to the same general risks that apply to all authentication methods (such as unauthorized access).
   ☒ **A** is wrong because risks of *what you are* and *what you have* authentication methods are different, and **D** is wrong because it doesn't make sense.

Explain Information Security Fundamentals and Define Good Security Architectures

13. ☑ **C.** Top management must be ultimately responsible for information security within an organization.
   ☒ **A** is incorrect because information security professionals advise management and implement management's decisions. **B** is wrong because information systems auditors report on the organization's security to the board of directors and/or the stockholders. **D** is incorrect because stockholders appoint management and are not involved in day-to-day management.

14. ☑ **B.** Fundamental security principles apply to most information systems.
   ☒ **A** is wrong because it is not the best available answer. **C** is wrong because fundamental security principles do not apply only in enterprise systems, and **D** is wrong because fundamental security principles are not system dependent.

15. ☑ **E.** All of the answers are correct.

16. ☑ **C.** RBAC improves management of access control and authorizations by introducing the concept of roles distinct from individual users.
    ☒ **A** is wrong because RBAC has advantages over DAC; **B** is wrong because RBAC is not an improved version of DAC; **D** is wrong because it doesn't make sense.

17. ☑ **C.** *What you are* (biometrics) is inherently more complex to administer than *what you have* or *what you know* authentication methods.
    ☒ **A, B,** and **D** are incorrect because none of these methods is as difficult to administer as *what you are*.

18. ☑ **D.** Choke points are logical "narrow channels" that can be easily monitored and controlled.
    ☒ **A** is wrong because choke points are not used to isolate firewalls. Choke points do not affect confidentiality of information, so **B** is wrong. And **C** is not the answer because choke points are not protocol-dependent.

19. ☑ **E.** All of the above. Authentication is needed to obtain proof of claimed identity, to implement access control, to establish accountability, and to allow for different users with different authorizations.

20. ☑ **A, B,** and **D.** Cost-benefit analysis is necessary because organizations cannot reduce all risks to zero, it increases an organization's return on investment, and it is a good governance practice.
    ☒ **C** is wrong because cost-benefit analysis is not related to, and does not prevent, denial of service attacks.

2

Attacks, Motives, and Methods

I n Chapter 1, we defined the three pillars of information security as the *confidentiality, integrity,* and *availability* of information. Unfortunately, defining what is a secure system is not as universal and as simple as defining information security itself. With that said, in this chapter we'll dissect the concept of secure systems and talk about trust, threat, and risk, and we'll look at attackers and their motives.

Describe Concepts of Insecure Systems, User Trust, Threat, and Risk

Although the expressions *secure system* and *insecure system* are frequently used in various contexts, and most of us intuitively understand what they mean, exam objectives require that you have a clear understanding of these concepts. Unlike the generally accepted definition of information security, no single generally accepted and universally applicable formal definition exists for what is a secure system, so let us formulate one for the purposes of this guide:

A secure system has certain security functionalities and provides certain assurances that it will function in accordance with and enforce a defined security policy in a known environment provided it is operated in a prescribed manner.

Let's now consider this definition part by part to see what each part means.

"A secure system has certain security functionalities…"

For a system to be secure, it should have security mechanisms in place and implement controls that, in particular, prevent, detect, and recover from security violations. At this point, it would be useful to compare the concepts of *security* and *safety*. Although these concepts are closely connected and related, they are fundamentally different in scope. Safety is about protection against unintentional, natural threats—that is, actions that are not performed by an intelligent and malicious adversary. Security, in contrast, is about protection against intentional acts of intelligent and malicious adversaries. Although in many cases security mechanisms and safety measures may overlap and support each other, they are not the same, because they guard against different threats.

"…and provides certain assurances…"

Functionality alone is useless if you cannot depend on it. A secure system provides certain assurances that it will enforce security policy and that its functionality performs as described. The degrees of assurances may, for example, be described as very high, high, medium, low, or very low, or be described in more formal terms. We briefly discussed the issue of functionality versus assurance in Chapter 1 and will also discuss some aspects of assurance as related to certification and accreditation of systems in Chapter 3.

"…that it will function in accordance with and enforce a defined security policy…"

To be described as secure, a system must have a defined security policy, because the security policy defines what is "secure" in every particular case. There can be no secure system without a security policy, because it is the security policy that says what should or should not be allowed, when this should or should not occur, and how it should or should not be allowed.

"…in a known environment…"

How and where a system is used greatly affect its security. A system that may be considered secure when used in one environment—such as an isolated, well-guarded data center operated by professionals—may not be considered secure in another environment—such as on the street corner, connected to the Internet, and operated by amateurs. This is because it is impossible to create a system that is secure in all environments and against all threats and that at the same time is functional, effective, and efficient.

"…provided it is operated in a prescribed manner."

There is no such thing as a completely automatic or foolproof system. This final requirement stipulates that a system must be professionally installed, operated, and maintained in accordance with its requirements and must not be misused.

As you can see, the definition of *secure system* includes many clarifications, restrictions, and conditions. This perhaps illustrates why it is so difficult to develop secure systems and keep them secure once deployed, because of the complex interactions that exist between various external and internal entities, requirements, and environments.

Trust

Security is basically a matter of trust, and the concept of trust has several different meanings when used in the information security context. The first is the traditional dictionary definition of trust: assured reliance on the character, ability, strength, or truth of someone or something. Another definition, attributed to the U.S. National Security Agency, relates to *trusted systems*: a trusted system or component has the power to break one's security policy. A trusted system breaking security may seem like an oxymoron—how do you trust a component that can break your security policy?—but it is not. Although it is a good engineering practice to have as few trusted components as possible (remember the principles of least privilege and minimization), it is impossible to eliminate them altogether. This means that in any system, you have to trust at least one component that may theoretically break your security policy. This also means that maximum engineering and maintenance efforts are directed at this trusted component to minimize the possibility of security violation.

Trusted path is the term used to describe the secure communication channel that exists between the user and the software (an application or the operating system itself). A trusted path exists when a mechanism is in place to assure users that they are indeed interacting with the genuine application or the operating system and not software that impersonates them. Put simply, trusted path is an assurance that the user's keystrokes are read only by the intended application, and screen output indeed comes from the intended application. Although an important feature of trusted computer systems, trusted path facilities are not widely available in general-purpose operating systems.

Trust relationships between entities follow several rules of trust, and the three most important of those are briefly summarized here:

- *Trust is not transitive*. If A trusts B, and B trusts C, it does not mean that A automatically trusts C.
- *Trust is not symmetric*. If A trusts B, it doesn't mean that B trusts A.
- *Trust is situational*. If A trusts B in situation X, it doesn't mean that A trusts B in situation Y.

User trust refers to the users' expectations of reasonable security of systems, which in practical terms is the responsibility of security administrators who enforce security policy set by management. User trust may also refer to expectations of reasonable operation of systems (hardware and software), which is closely linked to the issue of assurance. User trust is gained and maintained by definition of sound security policies and their professional implementation and enforcement.

Threats

A *threat* is anyone or anything that can exploit a vulnerability. Threats to information systems may be grouped into the following broad categories:

watch   *A threat describes the potential for attack or exploitation of a vulnerable business asset. This term defines the cost of an attack weighed against the benefit to the attacker that can be obtained through such an attack. The benefits may be financial, strategic, tactical, or indirect. It does not describe an administrator's decision to accept a specific risk.*

- **Natural threats**   Floods, earthquakes, fires, and tornadoes
- **Physical threats**   Damage, loss, theft, and destruction by humans
- **Logical threats**   Network attacks, malicious hackers, and software glitches

It is important to realize that threats come in all sizes and shapes, and they are not limited to the preceding examples. All threats, regardless of type, affect either confidentiality, integrity, or availability of information.

Vulnerabilities

Vulnerabilities are weaknesses that can be exploited by threats. As with threats, types of vulnerabilities can be very different—software bugs, uneducated staff, absence of access controls, and inadequate security management, to name a few. One thing that unites all vulnerabilities is their ability to be exploited by threats, thus posing a risk. Recalling the formula for risk, we can see that if no vulnerabilities are present, there is no risk—however, we know that in practice, any system has vulnerabilities. Although a myriad of vulnerabilities are possible, they belong to one or both of the following groups.

Vulnerability by Design

When a system is poorly designed (that is, security considerations are either not taken into account or are inadequately designed), it is vulnerable by design. Systems vulnerable by design are insecure regardless of whether or not the design in question is well-implemented. The definition of *systems* in this context is wide and includes computers, networks, protocols, devices, software, operating systems, and applications.

Vulnerability by Implementation

Vulnerability by implementation is caused by bad implementation of an otherwise well-designed system. This means that even if a system is well-designed, with security taken into account at the design stage, it may still be vulnerable because of poor implementation. Of course, systems may be vulnerable both by design and by implementation if ill-designed and ill-implemented at the same time.

Risks and Risk Management

Risk is the likelihood and cost of a threat exploiting a vulnerability. Information security management is about risk management, because in an absolute majority of cases it is either impossible or not cost-effective to eliminate all risks. In these cases, risk management comes to the rescue and helps us to understand risks and decide what risks to minimize, what risks to transfer (insure against), and what risks to accept. An integral part of risk management is risk analysis and assessment: identifying risks and assessing the possible damages that could be caused by identified risks, and deciding how to handle them. Information security risk management involves three steps:

1. Assign a value and relative importance to information assets and information processing resources.
2. Assess and analyze the risk.
3. Decide how to handle identified risks, which usually includes selecting and implementing countermeasures.

A simple formula that conveniently shows the relationship between threats, vulnerabilities, and risk is shown here:

$$\text{Threats} \times \text{Vulnerabilities} \times \text{Asset value} = \text{Risk}$$

As you can see, if either threats, vulnerabilities, or asset value equals zero, the resulting risk is also zero. That is, if the asset in question has no value, no vulnerabilities or no threats can affect the asset, resulting in no risks. In practice, risk is never zero.

Assignment of Value to Information Assets

When determining the value of information assets and information processing resources, it is important that you take into account the total value of information, which is often much higher than what may appear at first glance. The following factors, in particular, should be considered when estimating the value of information assets:

- Cost to acquire or develop information
- Cost to maintain and protect information
- Value of information to owners and users
- Value of information to adversaries
- Value of intellectual property
- Price others are willing to pay for the information
- Cost to replace information if stolen or lost
- Cost of productivity lost if information is not available
- Cost of legal and regulatory considerations
- Damage to reputation or public confidence if information is compromised or lost

Valuation of information assets is a complex and subjective exercise, where very often no single correct value exists; however, the more factors you consider for the purposes of valuation, the more accurate your valuation will be.

Risk Analysis and Assessment

Various approaches and methodologies have been developed for risk analysis and assessment; however, all these methodologies follow either qualitative, quantitative, or hybrid risk-analysis approaches. Quantitative risk analysis requires assignment of numeric/monetary values to assets and risks; as a result, it provides more objective metrics than qualitative risk analysis but at the same time is more complex to perform. Qualitative risk analysis, on the other hand, does not use numeric values but instead deals with such subjective estimates as "low," "medium," and "high" when ranking risks and value of assets. Qualitative risk analysis also heavily depends on the knowledge and experience of those performing the risk analysis, because they use their judgment to decide what values the particular risks should be assigned.

Regardless of the risk analysis method used, the results of risk analysis should in particular include the following:

- Lists of assets, threats, risks, and vulnerabilities
- Estimated rates of occurrence

■ Estimates of potential losses on a per-incident and annualized basis

■ Probability of threat occurrences

The relationship between the threats, vulnerabilities, and risks may be further expressed as follows:

1. Threat exploits vulnerability.
2. Vulnerability results in risk.
3. Risk can result in loss.
4. Exposure to loss can be counteracted by safeguards.
5. Safeguards affect the ability of threats to exploit vulnerabilities.

The output of the risk analysis and assessment is the input of the next step in risk management: deciding how to handle the risk and selecting and implementing countermeasures, mechanisms, and controls that minimize identified risks.

Selection and Implementation of Countermeasures

After information assets have been identified, their values estimated, and risks affecting them analyzed and assessed, it's time to handle the risks. Generally, you can handle risks in four ways: transfer them, reduce them, accept them, or ignore them. The first three are perfectly acceptable approaches to handling risk, but the last one—ignoring risks—is a recipe for disaster.

Reduction of risk requires selection of countermeasures, which is both a business and a technical decision, because the countermeasures should not only be appropriate from the technical viewpoint but should also make sense business-wise; this is one of the requirements of good information systems governance and management. This requirement means that the process of selection of countermeasures should involve both management and technical staff and should take into account the following diverse considerations:

■ An organization's strategy

■ Product/service/solution cost

■ Planning and design costs

■ Implementation/installation costs

■ Environment modification costs

■ Compatibility issues

■ Maintenance requirements

w a t c h *Risk assessment is a critical element in designing the security of systems and is a key step in the accreditation process, the formal acceptance of the adequacy of the system's overall security by the management of a particular organization. For more information about accreditation, see Chapter 3.*

- Testing requirements
- Repair costs
- Operational costs
- Effect on productivity of staff
- Effect on system/network performance

These are just some of the issues that must be considered before selecting a security mechanism or control to make sure it addresses the risks in question, is cost-effective, and when taken as a whole brings more benefit than hassle to the organization.

CERTIFICATION OBJECTIVE 2.02

Explain Attackers, Motives, and Methods

Three factors must be present for an attack of any type to take place and succeed: the attacker must have a motive, an opportunity, and means to carry out the attack. The goal of an organization's management and security staff is to eliminate or minimize the second component of this triangle—opportunity.

The potential attacker who may have the motive and means to attack or inflict damage should not be given the opportunity to do so, or the opportunity should require so much work that for the attacker it is no longer worth the trouble. Opportunities exist when the security policies, procedures, and mechanisms are weak or are not functioning as needed—such as misconfigured firewalls, weak passwords, unpatched software, and similar problems.

At this point, it is important to differentiate between attackers interested in a particular organization or system and attackers who don't care which organization or system they compromise. In the first case, the attackers may be after some confidential information that your company has, or their goal may be to deface your web site or affect availability of services you provide, for example. In the second case, all the attackers need is to add another victim to their ring of compromised systems to use as a launching pad or a zombie to carry out attacks against other systems or house-pirated, illegal, or obscene material. In the second case, attackers will look for vulnerable and easily exploitable systems where security mechanisms do not exist or are manifestly dysfunctional; whereas in the first case, they will have to attack whatever security mechanisms are in place. Obviously, to defend your system against specific, targeted attacks is very difficult.

Types of Attackers

To build appropriate, effective, and efficient defenses, you need to know who the potential attackers are. Of course, it is not always possible to know this in advance; nevertheless, in most cases, it is possible to define a rough profile or profiles of the most likely adversaries. Knowing the profile of likely attackers gives you an idea of the attacks they are likely to try and resources they command.

Although goals and motivations of attackers remain constant, their means and opportunities differ widely. The defenders' challenge is to defend against all attacks, while the attackers need only one successful attack to succeed. Equally, one attack may use different types of attack methods, and the same type of attack may be launched by different attackers.

A very important consideration to keep in mind is that attackers are not always "them"; they may well be "us"—company employees, managers, contractors, consultants, and other insiders constitute a higher threat than a person on the street, because insiders have much more authorization and sensitive knowledge than outsiders. In fact, risks posed by insider attacks are more substantial, require less means to mount, and may result in larger losses than risks posed by outside attackers. Inside attacks may also be more difficult to detect and recover from. Attacks from disgruntled employees are most dangerous, because these employees have the closest physical and logical access to the internal infrastructure, applications, and data. They also have a good understanding of the business and technical climate, organization, and capabilities.

Continuing and increasing blurring of corporate borders (both in terms of business organization and technical infrastructures) means that it is ever more difficult to differentiate between "us" and "them." This further indicates that the ages-old concepts of security perimeters, walls, and doors are being challenged. The question of whether the attacker is acting alone or is part of a group is another important consideration; a group can always do more damage than a single person, and if that group includes insiders, then defending against such a threat is a formidable task indeed.

Let's now take a look at the following broad types of possible attackers—script kiddies, amateur hackers, professional hackers, organized hacker groups, corporate hackers, and state-sponsored hackers—to create a rough profile of each category.

Script Kiddies

Script kiddies is a term used to describe individuals with minimal understanding of computers and security, but who nevertheless have an interest in malicious hacking and can use the attack tools and techniques available on the Internet to launch unsophisticated attacks against Internet-connected systems. Although they do not possess specialist knowledge and understanding, they may cause considerable inconvenience and disruption because of widespread vulnerabilities and widely available attack tools. Defenses against script kiddie attacks include such relatively simple controls as effective security policies and good system administration practices (such as installing software patches and updates on time, using a correctly configured firewall, and using secure network protocols).

exam

watch   *A script kiddie is a novice hacker with little experience who has access to tools and documentation. They are able to cause a moderate amount of damage using these tools but do not possess the knowledge and skills associated with more proficient hackers.*

Amateur Hackers

This group of potential attackers occupies the space between script kiddies and professional hackers. Amateur hackers have a better understanding of computer and network security than script kiddies, but hacking is not their only or main occupation and they are not doing hacking for profit.

Professional Hackers

Professional hackers are individuals whose main or only occupation is hacking for profit and who have in-depth knowledge and experience. They are specialists of the trade, and it takes much more to defend against professional hackers than against script kiddies or amateurs.

Organized Hacker Groups

Organized malicious hacker groups may exist at all levels of proficiency: script kiddie groups, amateur groups, and professional groups. Naturally, regardless of the level of the group, such groups as a whole represent a higher risk than individual members of the group on their own.

Corporate Hackers

Although no organization would confess to using hackers to attack other organizations, such as competitors, it is believed that such a practice exists. The scale and risks of such engagements is open to debate.

State-Sponsored Hackers

With the increasing reliance of societies on information systems, information warfare is an approaching reality, if not today's reality. Governments worldwide are among prime employers of information security specialists, and most industrialized nations have information warfare groups within their militaries. However, as with the preceding category, no state is likely to admit that it is using hackers against other states' information systems.

Attack Motives

Unlike means and opportunities, attack motives and crimes in general have not changed much for ages. A theft is a theft, regardless of whether it is a theft of a physical asset or information; vandalism is vandalism, regardless of whether it occurs at a shop front or on a web site. Motives may be as diverse as economic gain, revenge, a sense of satisfaction, and a desire to demonstrate one's ability to peers. What is important, however, is that motives alone are not enough: attackers also need the means and opportunities to attack.

Attack Methods

Attack methods differ widely in their sophistication, effectiveness, and other properties; however, all attacks belong to one of the two broad types of attacks: *passive* attacks or *active* attacks. Passive attacks do not directly affect or change the state of target systems. In many cases, passive attacks are difficult or impossible to detect, unlike active attacks, which directly affect the targeted systems to violate confidentiality, integrity, and/or availability of information. Different types of attacks may also be used at different attack stages; attacks may also be combined to achieve greater efficiency or scale.

Generally the following high-level attack stages are recognized:

1. **Reconnaissance/information gathering**   At this stage, the adversary is collecting information that is necessary or may be useful in the later stages of the attack.

2. **The actual attack** Using the information obtained during the reconnaissance stage, the attacker carries out the attack.

3. **Destruction of evidence** After the attack takes place, the attackers may wish to destroy any evidence that may be used against them.

For example, at stage one, eavesdropping (a passive attack) may be used to collect information about the target system—such as user names and/or passwords. Later, this information may be used to launch an active attack to obtain unauthorized access to the victim's system. Stage two may include several substages, depending on the attackers' goals and plans; for instance, the attacker may upload illegitimate/modified versions of software to replace the installed originals or install backdoors and/or Trojans to provide an easier and convenient way to return.

Let's now take a look at some of the common attack methods and consider possible ways to make attackers' work more difficult.

Eavesdropping

Eavesdropping, or *sniffing,* is secretly listening to communications that are supposedly private. Eavesdropping is a passive attack that affects confidentiality of information; it may be used alone or as part of a larger scheme. Regular Internet protocols are insecure and prone to eavesdropping attacks because they transmit unencrypted information, so passwords and other information sent across the network may easily be captured and misused. It is relatively easy to defend against eavesdropping attacks by using encryption so that even when the information is intercepted, it is of no use—unless the attacker somehow obtains the plain text of the communication.

Traffic Analysis

Traffic analysis is also a passive attack, but unlike eavesdropping it is aimed not at the actual content of communications (perhaps because they are encrypted) but at such aspects of communication as time, direction, frequency, flow, sender, and receiver. An important issue to note is that encryption does not protect against traffic analysis unless specifically designed and implemented with traffic analysis resistance.

Timing Analysis

Timing analysis is about measuring time between actions or events in information systems and networks. Although not practically very useful on its own, timing analysis may be effective when used in concert with other attack types in complex attacks. Timing analysis may be either passive or active—active timing analysis may involve generation of external stimuli and timing analysis of the target system.

Social Engineering

Social engineering involves manipulating people to do what you want them to do without them realizing your hidden agenda. Social engineering takes on different forms, but the central concept of social engineering is exploiting human qualities or weaknesses to achieve one's aim. Ego, intimidation, and sympathy are some of the human factors that can be exploited in social engineering attacks. The only defense against social engineering is having security-aware and risks-aware staff and management.

Buffer Overflows

Buffer overflow attacks are perhaps the most primitive and effective of attacks. In a buffer overflow attack, the target system or application is sent more or different data than it is designed to handle, which usually results in a crash of the target or execution of part of the sent data. The data sent to the target may contain machine code or instructions that may be executed as a result of buffer overflow, thus giving the attacker a way in or making it simpler to gain access. We as security administrators can't do much to fix buffer overflows; what we can do is design and administer systems in such a way that risks resulting from buffer overflows are understood, minimized, and controlled. Principles of compartmentalization and minimization should be followed in these situations; refer to Chapter 7 for more on buffer overflows and best preventative measures.

Denial of Service

Denial of service (DoS) attacks are directed at the availability of information and information systems. DoS attacks exhaust all available resources—be it network bandwidth, number of maximum simultaneous connections, disk space, or RAM—to prevent legitimate users from using the system. Defending against DoS attacks is particularly difficult and regrettably not very effective because of inherent vulnerabilities of the Internet and the TCP/IP suite of protocols. Chapter 7 discusses DoS in more detail, including ways to safeguard against such attacks.

Spoofing

Spoofing refers to attacks in which the source of information (such as network packets or e-mail messages) is falsified with malicious intent. Spoofing attacks are usually used to circumvent filtering and access control based on source addresses. The most effective defense against spoofing is the use of cryptographic authentication and digital signatures.

For the exam, it's very important to remember the various common attack methods. Let's recap the first six here:

■ *Eavesdropping* **A passive attack that affects confidentiality of information. It is relatively easy to defend against eavesdropping attacks by using protocols that encrypt information before transmitting it over the network.**

■ *Traffic analysis* **A passive attack aimed at such aspects of communication as time, direction, frequency, flow, sender, and receiver. Cryptographic controls such as encryption would not necessarily protect against traffic analysis unless they are specifically designed to do so.**

■ *Timing analysis* **Measuring time between actions or events in information systems and networks to understand how external events affect security properties of the**

system. **This knowledge may be useful in devising possible attack vectors. Timing analysis may be either passive or active.**

■ *Social engineering* **A way of manipulating people to do what you want them to do without them realizing your hidden, and it is assumed malicious, agenda. It is important to remember that this is a non-technological attack aimed at humans, not technology.**

■ *Buffer overflow attacks* **The target system or application is sent more or different data than it is designed to handle, which usually results in a crash of the target or execution of the part of sent data.**

■ *Denial of service attacks* **Directed at the availability of information and information systems. Such attacks exhaust all available resources. Denial of service is a general name for a number of different attacks affecting availability.**

Man-in-the-Middle Attacks

Man-in-the-middle attacks involve an attacker located physically or logically between two or more communicating parties on a network, where the attacker poses as the remote party to communication and actively engages in masquerading as the remote party. The other parties are tricked into believing that they are communicating with the intended recipient (each other), and they may act on instructions received from the attacker or divulge confidential information to the attacker in the false belief that they are communicating with the intended party. Man-in-the-middle attacks are difficult to protect against unless a well-designed and well-implemented cryptographic authentication system is in place. We'll talk more about mitigating risks to masquerading attacks such as those by man-in-the-middle throughout this text.

Replay Attacks

Replay attacks are usually directed against simple authentication mechanisms but may also be used against poorly designed or implemented cryptographic protocols. During a replay attack, the attacker intercepts and records a valid authentication session and later replays it in whole or in part to gain unauthorized access. Replay attacks are active attacks that are usually launched after successful eavesdropping or man-in-the-middle attacks.

Hijacking

Connection or session *hijacking* involves taking over an already established connection or session with assigned identity and authorizations. When an attacker hijacks a connection, he or she inherits the authorizations and access level of the user who originally set up the connection. Insecure network protocols that do not provide continuous authentication and do not use strong cryptographic algorithms to protect confidentiality and integrity of data transmissions are especially vulnerable to connection hijacking; however, vulnerabilities in design or implementation of purportedly secure protocols may also allow hijacking attacks to succeed.

Brute-Force Attacks

Brute-force (or monotonic linear exhaustive search) attacks are usually used against passwords, cryptographic keys, and other security mechanisms. In a brute-force attack, the adversary performs an exhaustive search of the set in question to find the correct password or cryptographic key. The defense against brute-force attacks is to make the amount of time and computations required to conduct an exhaustive search impossible to afford by using a sufficiently large set—that is, longer passwords and keys. For example, using existing computers to brute-force attack a 128 bits–long cryptographic key would require more time for the attacker than the age of the universe.

Dictionary Attacks

Unlike brute-force attacks, in a *dictionary* attack, the adversary uses a list (a dictionary) of possible passwords or cryptographic keys to perform a search of the set to find the correct password or key. The defense against dictionary attacks is to use passwords or keys that are unlikely to be included in such a list. That's why using regular words in any language as your password is a bad idea. Later on, we'll talk more about guidelines to follow to prevent unnecessary exposure to dictionary attacks.

Here's a review of the remaining six types of common attacks to be sure to study for the exam:

■ *Spoofing* **The source of information is falsified with malicious intent so as to appear to be from a different and/or legitimate source.**

■ *Man in the middle attacks* **Involve an attacker located physically or logically between two or more parties on a network, where the attacker poses as one or more of the remote legitimate parties to communication and actively engages in masquerading as the remote party.**

■ *Replay attacks* **Active attacks usually directed against simple authentication mechanisms but may also be used against poorly designed or implemented cryptographic protocols. In such attack, an authenticator (e.g., a password) or instruction is intercepted (e.g., by** eavesdropping) and later re-sent ("replayed") to the target system.

■ *Connection or session hijacking* **Involves taking over an already established connection or session with assigned identity and authorizations. Appropriately implemented cryptographic controls provide good defenses against connection hijacking.**

■ *Brute-force attacks* **Are usually used against passwords, cryptographic keys, and other security mechanisms. Possible defenses against brute-force attacks include detection of such attacks, appropriate response, and large sets which would require too much time or computational power to brute-force.**

■ *Dictionary attack* **In this type of attack the adversary uses a list (dictionary) of possible passwords or cryptographic keys to perform a search of the set to find the correct password or key.**

CERTIFICATION OBJECTIVE 2.03

Describe How Attackers Gain Information, and Describe Methods to Reduce Disclosure

As mentioned, the first step in any attack is reconnaissance, or information gathering. At this stage, the attacker's goal is to collect as much information as possible, because this information may come in handy at later stages—when the actual attack is carried out and thereafter to destroy the evidence and traces of the attack. The goal of the defenders is to give out as little information as possible to the attackers, while at the same time making sure the system provides required services and that authorized users are able to use them. The key here is to find the balance between these two goals and remember the security principles discussed in Chapter 1, namely the principles of minimization and least privilege.

Before we discuss how to reduce disclosure of revealing information, let's see what methods of reconnaissance exist, how they work, and what sources of information may potentially be used in an attack. In general, any information about the target organization, network, or system may be useful to an attacker. The issue is just *how useful* such information is and how difficult it is to obtain this information. The usefulness of information gathered at the reconnaissance stage would depend on the type of attack; type of target organization, network, or system; and, of course, the resources at an attacker's disposal. It is difficult to overestimate the importance of the information-gathering stage, because the success of the entire attack largely depends on what information attackers have managed to collect during reconnaissance.

Surprisingly, public databases and records provide a wealth of information that may be very useful to potential attackers in planning and carrying out an attack. Three such databases are the Domain Name System (DNS), the whois databases, and the IP address allocation databases maintained by the Regional Internet Registries (RIRs), such as the American Registry for Internet Numbers (ARIN), Reseaux IP Europeens (RIPE), or the Asia Pacific Network Information Center (APNIC). Other sources of information include more conventional public records such as yellow pages, phone and web directories, search engines, and the like.

Utilities such as traceroute, ping, and their variants and incarnations also provide a wealth of information regarding network topologies, names of network nodes and routers and their location, and other information—and this is just the publicly available information that we are talking about! Passive reconnaissance involves collection of information without directly interacting with the target system; in most cases, this means that the target organization is not even aware that the adversary is gathering information to be used later in an attack. The very nature of this publicly accessible information is that it should be available to everyone by definition; hence, there isn't much we can do to minimize information leakage at this point.

After the attackers have exhausted all passive reconnaissance opportunities, they are likely to proceed to active reconnaissance: interacting with the target organization, system, or network to obtain more information about the target. This information may include the following crucial bits and pieces:

- Systems and networks reachable from the Internet
- Protocols and services running on these systems

- Types and versions of operating systems used on these systems
- Types and versions of application software (such as web and e-mail server software) installed on these systems
- Firewall access control rules

The preceding information may then be used to deduce the following:

- What systems may be attacked and how
- What systems run obsolete or vulnerable operating systems or applications
- What bugs may be present on particular systems
- How the firewalls and routers are configured

Of course, this is not a complete list of what information may be collected during reconnaissance; the information that the attacker will be able to harvest depends on his or her creativity and skills, as well as the type, size, and industry of the target and professionalism of the people defending it. The moral is that much information is and has to be publicly available, and all of this information can be accessed in an attack, so our goal is to minimize the amount of additional information we give out that may help the attackers. This information includes the following:

- **Types and version numbers of operating systems** There is no need to announce them on your web site, for example.
- **Versions of server software you are using** Most modern software allows you to disable banners giving out such information as the version number, patch level, and operating system.
- **Details of your network topology and infrastructure** Legitimate users do not usually need to know what type of routers and switches you are using or where the network cables lay.
- **Details of your security mechanisms** Details include what firewalls and authentication systems you use.

At this point, you may be asking, "If attackers are able to find out this information themselves anyway, why bother protecting it?" The simple answer is that this is simply a race—you should make their job more difficult and more consuming of time, effort, and resources. As discussed in Chapter 1 and earlier in this chapter, you cannot eliminate all risks. The possibility that a skilled, sophisticated attacker will be able to penetrate your defenses in one way or another is always a risk, even if it's a miniscule risk. What you *can* do is to make it increasingly difficult and effortful for attackers by not providing them with information they need and having in place detective and corrective controls that would detect successful attacks and minimize their consequences.

Top 10 UNIX Vulnerabilities

Although a number of different types of attacks have been described, most security breaches are caused by a handful of specific vulnerabilities that have been known for a long time but that are still proving difficult to fix or avoid. The Systems Administration, Networking, and Security (SANS) Institute, in partnership with the U.S. Federal Bureau of Investigation, regularly publishes a list of Top 20 vulnerabilities of UNIX and Windows systems, which is available online at www .sans.org/top20.

The current Top 10 vulnerabilities of UNIX systems that also affect Solaris systems are listed here:

1. BIND domain name server software
2. Web servers
3. Authentication
4. Version control systems
5. Mail transport services
6. Simple Network Management Protocol (SNMP)
7. Open Secure Sockets Layer (OpenSSL)
8. Network Information Service (NIS)/Network File System (NFS)
9. Database management systems
10. Kernel

In practical terms, before you take care of other security issues, it is prudent to make sure that these vulnerabilities do not affect your systems.

CERTIFICATION SUMMARY

In this chapter, we discussed the concepts of risks, threats, and vulnerabilities and their relationships; defined a formula that may be used to calculate risk; and saw that risk is a product of threats, vulnerabilities, and the value of assets with which we are concerned. We also came up with a possible definition of what constitutes a secure system and what are the requirements to protect such a system. Types of attackers, their motives, and their means were discussed, along with overviews of attack methods. Outlines of risk-management and risk-analysis techniques were discussed from the viewpoint of a risk-based management approach to information security. Understanding that we cannot eliminate all risks, we must nevertheless manage them—reducing, transferring, or accepting risks as appropriate, but never ignoring or rejecting them. Finally, we took a look at how attackers gather information about their targets, which may later be used in an attack, and how we can minimize the leakage of such information.

✓ TWO-MINUTE DRILL

Here are some of the key points from the certification objectives in Chapter 2.

Describe Concepts of Insecure Systems, User Trust, Threat, and Risk

❑ A secure system is a system that has certain security functionalities and that provides certain assurance that it will function in accordance with and enforce a defined security policy in a known environment, provided it is operated in a prescribed manner.

❑ A trusted system or component has the power to break security policy. *Trusted path* is the term used to describe the secure communication channel between the user and the software (an application or the operating system itself). A trusted path exists when a mechanism is in place to assure the users that they are indeed interacting with the genuine application or the operating system, and not software that impersonates them.

❑ A threat describes a business asset that is most likely to be attacked. This term defines the cost of an attack weighed against the benefit to the attacker that can be obtained through such an attack. It does not describe when an administrator decides to accept a specific risk.

❑ A vulnerability describes how susceptible your system is to an attack and how likely you are to succumb to an attack if it occurs.

❑ Risk assessment is a critical element in designing the security of systems and is a key step in the accreditation process that helps managers select cost-effective safeguards.

Explain Attackers, Motives, and Methods

❑ Three factors must be present for an attack of any type to take place and succeed: the attacker must have a motive, an opportunity, and the means to carry out the attack.

❑ Main categories of attackers may be descibed as script kiddies, amateur hackers, professional hackers, organized hacker groups, corporate hackers, and state-sponsored hackers.

❑ Attack methods differ widely in their sophistication, effectiveness, and other properties; however, all attacks belong to one of the two broad types of attacks: *passive* attacks or *active* attacks.

❑ Attacks from disgruntled employees are most dangerous because they have the closest physical and logical access to the internal infrastructure, applications, and data. Disgruntled employees also have a good understanding of business and technical climate, organization, and capabilities.

❑ Most widely known attacks are eavesdropping, social engineering, buffer overflows, denial of service, spoofing, man in the middle, replay, hijacking, brute force, and dictionary attacks.

Describe How Attackers Gain Information, and Describe Methods to Reduce Disclosure

❑ The first step in any attack is reconnaissance, or information gathering. At this stage, the attacker's goal is to collect as much information as possible. This stage is very important because the success of the entire attack largely depends on what information attackers have managed to collect.

❑ Public databases and records provide a wealth of information that may be very useful to potential attackers in planning and carrying out an attack. Three such databases are the Domain Name System (DNS), the whois databases, and the IP address allocation databases maintained by the Regional Internet Registries (RIRs).

❑ Utilities such as traceroute, ping, and their variants and incarnations also provide information regarding network topologies, names of network nodes and routers and their location, and other information.

❑ Although much information is public, the goal is to minimize the amount of additional information given out that may help the attackers. Information that should be protected includes the following: types and version numbers of operating systems, versions of server software, details of network topology and infrastructure, and details of security mechanisms.

SELF TEST

The following questions will help you measure your understanding of the material presented in this chapter. Read all the choices carefully, because there might be more than one correct answer. Choose all correct answers for each question.

Describe Concepts of Insecure Systems, User Trust, Threat, and Risk

1. What is a trusted system? (Choose all that apply.)
 A. A trusted system is another name for a high-security system.
 B. A trusted system is a system that can break security policy if compromised.
 C. Trusted system refers to operating systems such as Trusted Solaris.
 D. Trusted systems are more rigorously designed and tested.
 E. All of the above

2. If A trusts B, and B trusts C, then:
 A. A trusts C.
 B. A does not automatically trust C.
 C. C trusts A.
 D. The trust relationship is symmetric and bidirectional.
 E. All of the above

3. User trust is
 A. Guaranteed by trusted systems
 B. Defined in security policy
 C. Gained and maintained by definition and enforcement of good security policies and their professional implementation
 D. Transitive and bidirectional
 E. All of the above

4. What is a threat? (Choose all that apply.)
 A. A threat is the absence of security mechanisms.
 B. A threat is the opposite of assurance.
 C. A threat is anything that can exploit vulnerabilities.
 D. Threats may be natural, physical, and logical.
 E. All of the above

5. Vulnerabilities are weaknesses that can be exploited by
 A. Risks
 B. Threats
 C. Hackers

    D. Software bugs

    E. All of the above

6. Why is risk management important? (Choose all that apply.)

    A. Because it is impossible to eliminate all risks.

    B. Because it is not cost effective to eliminate all risks.

    C. Because it is a good governance practice.

    D. Because it improves business performance.

    E. All of the above

7. Risk is a product of

    A. Threats – Vulnerabilities + Asset value

    B. Threats × Vulnerabilities + Asset value

    C. Threats × Vulnerabilities × Asset value

    D. Threats + Vulnerabilities × Asset value

    E. All of the above

8. Which of the following should be considered when estimating asset value? (Choose all that apply.)

    A. Cost to acquire

    B. Cost to protect and maintain

    C. Market value

    D. Value to adversaries and competitors

    E. All of the above

Explain Attackers, Motives, and Methods

9. For an attack to take place and succeed, which of the following should be present? (Choose all that apply.)

    A. Opportunity

    B. Means

    C. Motives

    D. All of the above

10. Do insiders pose a threat to information security, and if so, why?

    A. No, because they are bound by employment and confidentiality agreements.

    B. Yes, because they are not subject to access control.

    C. No, because they already have access to information.

    D. Yes, because they have more authorizations and knowledge.

    E. All of the above

11. Which of the following has changed with the advent of information systems and the Internet? (Choose all that apply.)

    A. Means

    B. Motives

    C. Opportunities

    D. Vulnerabilities

    E. All of the above

12. Which of the following may be performed by an attacker during the actual attack? (Choose all that apply.)

    A. Installation of backdoors

    B. Installation of Trojans

    C. Elevation of privileges

    D. Destruction of incriminating evidence

    E. All of the above

Describe How Attackers Gain Information, and Describe Methods to Reduce Disclosure

13. What are the public sources of information that may be useful to an attacker? (Choose all that apply.)

    A. Domain Name System

    B. Whois databases

    C. Business directories

    D. Annual reports

    E. All of the above

14. Are Internet protocols that do not include confidentiality mechanisms vulnerable to sniffing, and if so, why?

    A. Yes, because they were developed a while ago.

    B. No, because they include anti-sniffing handshakes.

    C. Yes, because they mostly transmit unencrypted information.

    D. No, because it is difficult to mount sniffing attacks on the Internet.

    E. All of the above

15. Why can't technical measures be used to defend against social engineering?

    A. Because it is basically a human problem.

    B. Because it involves subjective decisions.

    C. Social engineering is not really an issue.

    D. Because technical measures are not good enough.

    E. All of the above

16. Which security principles may be used to protect against buffer overflows? (Choose all that apply.)

    A. Principle of compartmentalization

    B. Principle of minimization

    C. Defense in depth

    D. Secure programming

    E. All of the above

17. Which of the following may protect against spoofing attacks?

    A. Encryption

    B. Cryptographic initiation

    C. Cryptographic authentication

    D. Secret addresses

    E. All of the above

18. Continuous authentication protects against

    A. Hacking

    B. Script kiddies

    C. Hijacking attacks

    D. Sniffing

    E. All of the above

19. How can you protect systems against brute-force attacks? (Choose all that apply.)

    A. Use strong authentication

    B. Make the amount of time and computations required for the attack unaffordable

    C. Use longer passwords and keys

    D. Use Role-Based Access Control

    E. All of the above

20. What is the rationale behind nondisclosure of software version numbers and other details of systems? (Choose all that apply.)

    A. Makes attackers spend more time and effort

    B. Avoids easy identification of bugs and vulnerabilities of deployed software

    C. Avoids or minimizes script kiddie attacks

    D. Complies with principles of minimization and least privilege

    E. All of the above

SELF TEST ANSWERS

Describe Concepts of Insecure Systems, User Trust, Threat, and Risk

1. ☑ **B and D.** A trusted system or component has the power to break one's security policy. Trusted systems are more rigorously designed and tested than untrusted systems.
☒ **A and C** are incorrect because a high security system is not necessarily a trusted system and trusted systems do not refer to operating systems only.

2. ☑ **B.** Trust is not transitive.
☒ **A and C** are incorrect because if A trusts B, and B trusts C, it does not mean that A automatically trusts C, or vice versa. **D** is incorrect because trust is not symmetric: if A trusts B, it doesn't mean that B trusts A.

3. ☑ **C.** User trust refers to users' expectations of the reasonable security of systems, which is the responsibility of security administrators who enforce security policy set by management. User trust may also refer to expectations of reasonable operation of systems (hardware and software).
☒ **A, B,** and **D** are incorrect because user trust is not guaranteed by trusted systems, it is not defined in security policy, and it is not transitive and bi-directional.

4. ☑ **C and D.** A threat is anyone or anything that can exploit a vulnerability. Threats to information systems may be grouped into natural, physical, and logical threats.
☒ **A and B** are incorrect because absence of security mechanisms is not a threat, and threat is not the opposite of assurance.

5. ☑ **B and C.** Vulnerabilities can be exploited by threats, and malicious hackers can pose a threat.
☒ **A and D** are incorrect because risks and software bugs do not exploit vulnerabilities—risk is the possibility of an exploit and software bugs are vulnerabilities.

6. ☑ **E.** All of the answers are correct.

7. ☑ **C.** This simple formula conveniently shows the relationship between threats, vulnerabilities, and risk.
☒ **A, B,** and **D** are incorrect because the correct formula is Threats × Vulnerabilities × Asset value = Risk.

8. ☑ **E.** All answers are correct. Valuation of information assets is a complex and subjective exercise in which very often no single value is correct; however, the more factors you consider for the purposes of valuation, the more accurate your valuation would be.

Explain Attackers, Motives, and Methods

9. ☑ **D.** All answers are correct. For an attack of any type to take place and to succeed, three factors must be present: the attacker must have a motive, an opportunity, and the means to carry out the attack.

10. ☑ **D.** Company insiders constitute a higher threat than a person on the street because they have more authorized network access and sensitive knowledge than outsiders. In fact, risks posed by insider attacks are more substantial, require less means to mount, and may result in larger losses than risks posed by outside attackers. They may also be more difficult to detect and recover from.
☒ **A, B,** and **C** are incorrect because although insiders are usually bound by employment and confidentiality agreements, that alone doesn't remove the threat. Insiders are subject to access controls, and access to information is not a threat in itself.

11. ☑ **A, C,** and **D.** Means, opportunities, and vulnerabilities have changed with the advent of computers and computer networks.
☒ **B** is incorrect because crime motives have not changed—a theft is a theft, regardless of whether it is a theft of a physical asset or information, and vandalism is vandalism, regardless of whether it occurs at a shop front or a web site.

12. ☑ **A, B,** and **C.** Attacks may include installation of backdoors, Trojans, and elevation of privileges.
☒ **D** is incorrect because destruction of evidence is usually considered a post-attack activity. After the attack took place, the attackers may wish to destroy the evidence.

Describe How Attackers Gain Information, and Describe Methods to Reduce Disclosure

13. ☑ **E.** All these sources contain information that may potentially be useful to attackers. The only issue is just *how useful* such information is and how difficult it is to obtain this information.

14. ☑ **C.** Internet protocols that do not include confidentiality mechanisms are insecure and prone to eavesdropping attacks because they transmit unencrypted information, so passwords and other information sent across the network may easily be captured and misused.
☒ **A, B,** and **D** are incorrect because when the protocol was developed does not directly affect its security, there is no such term as anti-sniffing handshakes, and it is not difficult to mount sniffing attacks on the Internet.

15. ☑ **A.** Social engineering takes on different forms, but the central concept of social engineering is exploiting human qualities or weaknesses to achieve one's aim. The only defense against social engineering is having security-aware and risks-aware staff and management—technological defenses do not protect against social engineering.
☒ **B, C,** and **D** are incorrect because social engineering is a real security issue and because technical measures simply do not address social engineering risks.

16. ☑ **A, B,** and **C.** What we can do is to design and administer systems in such a way that risks resulting from buffer overflows are understood, minimized, and controlled. Compartmentalization prevents the compromise of the entire system when one compartment is compromised; minimization reduces the potential attack targets and channels; and defense in depth guards against failure of some security controls.
    ☒ **D** is incorrect because secure programming is not a security principle. There isn't much we as security administrators can do to fix buffer overflows.

17. ☑ **C.** The most effective defense against spoofing is the use of cryptographic authentication and digital signatures.
    ☒ **A** is incorrect because encryption does not necessarily protect against spoofing. There is no such term as cryptographic initiation (**B**), and secret addresses don't make sense (**D**).

18. ☑ **C.** Continuous authentication protects against hijacking attacks.
    ☒ Answers **A** and **B** are too general. **D** is incorrect because continuous authentication does not protect against sniffing unless all traffic is encrypted.

19. ☑ **B** and **C.** The defense against brute-force attacks is to make the amount of time and computations required to conduct an exhaustive search impossible to afford by using a sufficiently large set—that is, longer passwords or keys.
    ☒ **A** and **D** are incorrect. The use of strong authentication alone would not guarantee protection against brute-force attacks, and role-based access control does not address the risk of brute-force attacks.

20. ☑ **E.** All of the answers are correct. It is important to protect software version numbers and other details of your systems in order to make attackers spend more time and effort on an attack, to avoid easy identification of bugs and vulnerabilities of deployed software, to avoid or minimize script kiddie attacks, and to comply with principles of minimization and least privilege.

3

Security Management and Standards

CERTIFICATION OBJECTIVE 3.01

Identify the Security Life Cycle and Describe Best Security Practices

"Security is a process, not a product." This statement, attributed to security guru Bruce Schneier, well introduces the process life cycle–based approach to security that is necessary to provide a living, iterative framework for information security management. The main parts of such a life cycle are prevention, detection, reaction, and deterrence. This framework is defined by security policies, procedures, guidelines, and standards. For security policies and procedures to be effectively and efficiently set and implemented, management and staff security awareness is necessary. Issues affecting physical, platform, network, applications, and operations security must be known and understood. This chapter builds on the knowledge gained from the previous two chapters and concludes Part I of this guide.

Security Management and Operations

Before we discuss the security life cycle and its constituent steps, you must remember that to secure its information and information processing resources, real commitment from an organization's top management is necessary. Security requires business-wide changes in processes, habits, and approaches that would not happen without management's full understanding, agreement, and commitment. Although it is outside the scope of this book to cover methods of building a business case for information security and obtaining management support, information security practices in the organization must be aligned with the organization's business goals. Information security should not and cannot be an isolated mission—its purpose is to protect the organization and its business from risks, taking into account the environment in which the organization operates and the specifics of its business and industry in a cost-effective manner.

Accepted standards and frameworks, such as ISO 17799 (*Code of Practice for Information Security Management*), COBIT, and others should be considered and used if appropriate, with information security management being interwoven into the fabric of business decisions and operations. This, of course, requires a good level of information security awareness throughout the organization at all levels, which may be expected only if the organization provides suitable and regular security awareness training at both management and staff levels. The security policy is the high-level document or set of documents that in particular identifies the information assets of the organization, stipulates who owns them, indicates how they may or may not be used, and sets requirements for their use along with sanctions for misuse.

Security Life Cycle

In Chapter 1, we stipulated the importance of not only preventive security controls but of detection, response, and deterrence. Without any one of these parts of the life cycle, the security controls would be incomplete and lacking. It is important to state that this life cycle approach to security is applicable in all cases, whether you are securing an enterprise by defining security policies and procedures, a network by means of authentication and access control mechanisms, or a Solaris server by using secure configuration practices and security tools. In all cases, the life cycle process is the same—prevent, detect, respond, and deter—and then the cycle repeats, keeping in mind the lessons learned.

Prevention

Preventing a problem from occurring is very often much easier than sorting it out after it has happened. However, circumstances outside of your control may make preventive measures ineffective or impossible. Preventive security controls may also negatively affect availability, performance, or staff acceptance of security measures. This all means that although preventive controls should be the first ones to be considered, they are by no means the only controls you should consider. Examples of preventive controls include firewalls, logical and physical access control systems, and security procedures that are devised to prevent violations of security policy to occur.

Detection

Detection mechanisms serve not only to detect failures of preventive security controls—which is perhaps their main function—but also to provide a degree of assurance by demonstrating when the preventive controls are indeed operating and functioning as expected. When considering detective controls, it is imperative that you realize that in certain cases, detection has its restrictions as well. In particular, with regard to software vulnerabilities (bugs), testing and verification cannot prove the absence of bugs. What they can prove is that after so much testing, only some of the bugs were found.

Obviously, because only discovered security breaches may be analyzed and countermeasures against future occurrences devised, detection controls are very important. To employ preventive security controls and ignore detection issues is unacceptable; this may result in a false sense of security, which sooner or later will be exploited. Detection controls should always follow preventive controls and include network and host intrusion detection systems, physical movement and intrusion detection systems and alarms, and cryptographic checksums on transmitted information (to detect unauthorized modifications).

Response

As with prevention and detection, detection and response are bound together. What use is detection if you do nothing about the detected events? *Incident response* is actually a subdiscipline of information security; it is the formal set of defined and approved actions based on the information security policy and best practices that are to be taken in response to a security incident. It may cover what to do in case of incident, who is to do it, how to do it, when to do it, whom to inform, what may go wrong, how not to create more problems, how to collect and preserve evidence for possible legal actions, and how to minimize damage after the incident took place. Some large organizations may benefit from an entire department, a corporate Computer Emergency Response Center (CERT), taking care of incident response issues.

Deterrence

Deterrent controls may potentially be confused with preventive controls, and although both types of controls aim to preclude security violations from happening, they try to do so at different times. While preventive security controls try to prevent a breach of security after the adversary has decided to attack but before the attack has succeeded, deterrent controls try to discourage the attacker from attacking in the first place by demonstrating that the attack is not going to succeed; and even if it does, it will be detected and dealt with. Deterrent controls may take on many different faces—such as good information security management, regular audits, security-aware staff, well-administered systems, good employee morale, and security certifications. All of these deterrent controls serve to put off potential attackers; they basically send the message that the organization is prepared, able to defend itself, and knows what to do to stop you.

The key to correct application of the security process life cycle is to realize that it has to be an iterative, feedback-driven, living process. After every step, the entire process should be evaluated to identify weaknesses, address them, document them, and proceed to the next step, in a never-ending, continuous process.

Security Awareness

In Chapter 2, we identified security awareness as the best defense against social engineering attacks. However, the benefits of having security-aware staff and management do not stop there. Needless to say, security-aware employees are the best partners of the organization and its information security efforts, while staff members who have no idea about security practices or simply don't care are not partners at all. One doesn't need determined adversaries to suffer a security breach—a clueless insider who doesn't understand the consequences may expose the organization to risks that could otherwise be avoided.

When it comes to security awareness training, remember that management and staff training resources may and usually will differ in scope and content; however, certain aspects stay the same. The most important of them is the regularity of training: security awareness should not be a one-off project but should take the form of regular (for example, quarterly) meetings that would remind the audience of risks, update them on the latest developments and events, and reinforce the organization's security policies and procedures.

Management needs a high-level, big picture of security risks, threats, and vulnerabilities, which takes into account industry specifics and regulations as well as the organization's business objectives and resources. While managers are information systems users just like others in the organization, their decision-making responsibility extends over a wider area than those of non-managerial staff; therefore, they need a greater understanding of security concerns. The format of training aimed at management also should support the goal of delivering management-oriented security awareness training that is seen as time well-spent and not as a nuisance. Staff security-awareness training, in contrast, does not need to be wide in scope but should address issues that are widely seen and pose the most risk, such as social engineering, malware, and password management. Staff should be encouraged to participate in the process by sharing their experiences and good practices.

Security Policies, Procedures, and Guidelines

There can be no information security management without defined, written, and communicated information security policies, procedures, and guidelines. It is important to understand the relationship among these documents and their objectives, as well as the significance of communicating these objectives throughout the organization. These may include such mechanisms as logging and auditing, system software maintenance, patch management, and configuration and change management.

Security Policies

Security policies are to be set by management and are high-level in nature. They specify what should and should not happen, without going into detail regarding how to reach these goals. Security policies should be sufficiently specific to convey their meaning and objectives unambiguously, but at the same time general enough not to require modification every month or after introduction of a new system or application in the organization. Security policies may be thought of as one of the mechanisms that define and convey the information security requirements of the organization's management to the staff of the organization.

Security Procedures

Security procedures are developed within the organization by subject-matter specialists with the assistance of security professionals and/or information systems auditors. Because security procedures are usually highly specific and technical in nature, they should be developed by those who appreciate these considerations. Procedures may be application-specific and/or version-specific and need to be kept current with the information systems environment of the organization. System and security administrators play a key role in developing and enforcing security procedures.

Security Guidelines

Security guidelines are nonbinding recommendations that focus on how to develop, define, and enforce security policies and procedures. Although these guidelines are nonbinding, it is customary in an organization to require explanation from those who choose not to follow them; this practice acknowledges the fact that something that is appropriate in most circumstances is not necessarily appropriate in all circumstances and that staff should have the option of not following guidelines, if justified.

Security Standards

Unlike guidelines, security standards are mandatory, either because they are dictated by the security policy, law, or regulations or because the entity in question has decided to adhere to the standard. Examples of well-known security standards are ISO 17799, *Code of Practice for Information Security Management*, and ISO 15408, *Common Criteria for Information Technology Security Evaluation*, which are discussed later in this chapter.

Physical Security

Physical security addresses the physical vulnerabilities, threats, and countermeasures used to control risks associated with physical destruction; unauthorized access; loss due to theft, fire, natural disasters (floods, earthquakes, tornados), or environmental issues (air conditioning, ventilation, humidity control); and all associated issues. Physical security is the foundation of all other aspects of security and a basic requirement that must be addressed, because without physical security, most if not all other areas of security become irrelevant. To take care of physical security properly, the following physical security issues should be considered and appropriate policies set, which may define the location of assets, what access and to whom it should be granted, and on which basis access should be granted.

Selection and Management of Facilities

When choosing a facility that will house information systems, it is important to remember some guiding principles. Although in many cases the IT or information security department of the organization has no control over such aspects of the facility as location or type of building materials used, it is nevertheless useful to know what issues affect physical security of the facility. The first issue to consider is whether the facility is potentially vulnerable to devastating natural disasters such as floods, earthquakes, or tornadoes. Risk assessment of a facility's susceptibility to these disasters should take into account the location of the facility and historic information about these disasters, such as those provided by insurance companies and weather monitoring services. Next, the surrounding area, road access, and proximity to fire, police, and medical facilities should also be considered when assessing and analyzing physical risks.

Physical Access Control and Monitoring

After a suitable facility has been chosen in which to house information systems, it should be secured to provide physical access control and monitoring. A security perimeter should be defined and indicated, which would divide the territory into "inside," "outside," and "buffer zones." Physical security, access control, and monitoring objectives should be set and implemented using appropriate controls, such as secure locks, closed-circuit cameras, and motion detectors. All these mechanisms should implement the high-level physical security policy, which may be a separate document or form part of the organization's information security policy. Procedures should be developed for such operations as granting access to a facility, changing access privileges, and terminating access. Universal security principles, such as principles of least privilege and compartmentalization, should be employed in physical security controls as well.

Fire Prevention, Detection, and Suppression

Fire is perhaps the most important physical security risk that should be assessed and controlled. Fire has the potential to destroy not only an organization's facilities, information systems, and data, but it can also affect the most important asset of any organization—the human worker. Therefore, fire prevention, detection, and suppression systems must be in place throughout the facility. Various types of fire prevention, detection, and suppression mechanisms exist; depending on the size and requirements of the facility, the organization should choose the most appropriate system. All systems should also comply with local fire regulations, and fire insurance should be in place to cover losses from fire, should the prevention and/or detection mechanisms fail.

Humidity, Ventilation, Air Conditioning, and Electrical Power

Although modern information technology equipment is not as environmentally demanding as it was several decades ago, it is still necessary to provide appropriate environmental conditions not only for the computer hardware but for its human operators and users as well. This is especially relevant for areas with relatively high humidity and/or a hot climate. Environment control should ensure that humidity stays within acceptable levels (between approximately 45 and 60 percent) and that indoor temperature is around 70 degrees Fahrenheit. Ventilation is also required for manned facilities and offices. Country-specific regulations usually govern the mandatory health and safety requirements that would apply to such facilities. Adequate mechanisms (such as line conditioners, uninterruptible power supplies, and backup generators) should also exist to shield against electrical power fluctuations and outages that may either interrupt operations or cause permanent damage to equipment. Lightning protection and grounding should also be installed and tested as appropriate.

Platform Security

Security of a particular computer platform depends on the security of its three parts, which make up the platform itself: the hardware, firmware, and operating system. Depending on the particular platform used under the Solaris 10 platform, security of the system will also vary due to differences in hardware and firmware between supported platforms.

Hardware Security

As you know, the Solaris 10 operating environment is available for SPARC (Scalable Processor Architecture), IA32, and AMD64 computer architectures.

From the beginning, SPARC was designed for multi-user, multi-processor server systems, whereas the IA32 architecture began its life as primarily a personal computer architecture. Although IA32 has seen many modifications and improvements over the years, SPARC has some features that are not provided by IA32. One of the features that directly affects security is the ability to disable the execution of code in a stack on SPARC systems.

Firmware Security

The OpenBoot firmware used on SPARC systems is a flexible, full-featured, standards-compliant firmware environment that includes two-level password protection and a user-definable maximum number of incorrect password attempts.

Operating System Security

As you will see later in this book, Solaris 10 has a solid set of security features and tools that are among the best available in modern operating systems. These include such vital functions for a multi-user network operating system as auditing, role-based access control, pluggable authentication modules, and compartmentalization.

Network Security

Network security is a term that covers a myriad of security issues, technologies, and mechanisms at the physical, data link, network, and transport layers of the ISO Open Systems Interconnection (OSI) reference model. As such, network security is not platform- or operating system–dependent but instead covers the security of protocols and network mechanisms. Although system-level security issues such as buffer overflow vulnerabilities are often described as network security issues, this is not actually the case. In the chapters that follow, you will see how to use the network security features of Solaris 10 to increase network security. One of the tools used to control TCP/IP options can be used to modify various networking stack options to suit particular environment or security requirements.

on the
job
Although Sun Certified Security Administrator certification candidates are not required to have Sun Certified System or Network Administrator certifications, they are expected to be familiar with subjects covered by their exam objectives and have at least six months of experience administering Solaris systems.

Physical Layer Security

Network security considerations at the physical layer differ for wired and wireless networks. In wired networks, physical access to cabling may be controlled; whereas in wireless networks, such as those based on the IEEE 802.11 standards, this is either impossible or infeasible because of their very nature. This means that physical security strategies in these two cases have to be different: wireless networks may not rely on physical access controls but must instead provide security at higher layers, such as the data link, network, transport, or application layer.

The concept of availability also takes on different meanings in wired and wireless networks: availability of wired networks may be affected only by cut or damaged cables, whereas availability of wireless networks is easier to compromise. Confidentiality and integrity of communications over wired networks may be affected by wiretaps. Fiber-optic cables are much more difficult to tap into than electrical cables, and they do not radiate information and are not susceptible to the noise, attenuation, or crosstalk problems that plague electrical cables; fiber-based wired networks therefore generally provide better physical layer security.

Network security at the physical layer also greatly depends on the network topology employed. The main types of network topologies are ring, bus, star, and mesh topologies. The most secure of these is the full mesh topology; because all systems are connected to each other, failure of any system or communication path will not affect communications between other systems. However, because of cost and implementation issues, full mesh networks are seldom used and may be used only in small networks. Star topology networks have a single point of failure—the hub, switch, or router—and, as you know, having single points of failure is bad for security. At the same time, having a single communications center makes the network easier to protect and manage than many distributed centers.

Data Link Layer Security

At the data link layer, network security goals are the same: confidentiality, integrity, and availability. These three goals may be affected by a number of considerations, such as the type of transmission (asynchronous or synchronous), media access technology (carrier sensing or token passing), existence of integrity checks (checksums), broadcast domains, collision domains, and whether hubs, routers, or switches are used. In switch- and router-based networks, frames are forwarded only to the destination device (unless the frame in question is a broadcast one, in which case it is broadcast in the broadcast domain). Confidentiality and availability in switched and routed networks is better protected than in hub networks for the following reasons:

- Since the frame is delivered only to the intended destination, adversaries do not see it and therefore do not have a chance to compromise the frame's confidentiality.
- Unlike hub-based networks, frames in router- or switch-based networks are not forwarded to all nodes, so network bandwidth and processing time at nodes are not wasted, improving availability.

Most modern data link layer protocols employ cyclic redundancy checksums (CRCs) to guard against data corruption in transit. Although effective against data transmission errors, CRCs do not prevent malicious modification of frames by an intelligent adversary. For these purposes, cryptographic message digest algorithms are used—namely MD5, SHA1, and HMAC.

Network Layer Security

Perhaps the most important security consideration at the network layer is the protection of integrity and availability of routing information and protocols, because routing is the main function at the network layer. Although smaller networks may use static routing and avoid using routing protocols at all, thus effectively avoiding any potential issues associated with routing security, networks of any substantial size need and use routing protocols to exchange network reachability and path information between routers.

Routing protocol security issues include the following, in particular:

- Message origin authentication
- Message integrity protection
- Malicious router detection
- Methods of checking reasonableness of routing updates

In many protocols, the first two concerns are addressed by using cryptographic message digest algorithms such as MD5 to authenticate routing update messages exchanged between routers and to detect any changes made to these messages after they have been sent by the source router. For instance, a standard and popular network layer security framework is the IP Security Architecture (IPSEC).

Because IPSEC works at the network (Internet Protocol) layer, all layers above are protected by IPSEC's confidentiality, integrity, and authentication services.

Transport Layer Security

In some situations, it is impossible or inappropriate to provide security at the network layer. In such cases, transport layer security mechanisms and protocols may be used. Two of the most widely employed transport layer security protocols are Secure Sockets Layer (SSL) and Transport Layer Security (TLS), often referred to as SSL/TLS. SSL/TLS uses strong cryptography to provide security to connection-oriented transport protocols such as the Transmission Control Protocol (TCP). Many secure protocols such as HTTPS, POP3S, and IMAPS use SSL/TLS.

Applications Security

Although security at the operating system and network levels plays an important role in any computing environment, a system may not be considered secure if the applications that run on top of these operating systems and networks are insecure. The domain of applications security is concerned with all life stages of computer applications, from defining requirements and drafting functional specifications to designing, coding, testing, installing, and maintaining applications. Increasing interconnection of previously standalone applications using technologies such as Web Services and Remote Procedure Calls (RPC) increase the need for security at the application level. In the past, applications were isolated and protected by physical and logical access controls, but today organizations are pressed to open up their systems for greater efficiency and new services.

With exponential growth of Web applications, the importance of applications security has reached new heights and requires the same process-based life cycle approach, also taking into account specifics of application development. Many standards, frameworks, toolkits, and methodologies have been developed to aid in secure software development, but as usual, good old practices, such as documenting applications and making realistic assumptions, can increase software quality and security.

The importance of applications security is further demonstrated by the fact that most security vulnerabilities in the SANS Top 10 list (shown in Chapter 2) are due to applications vulnerabilities, not weaknesses in the operating system.

CERTIFICATION OBJECTIVE 3.02

Describe the Benefits of Evaluation Standards

Evaluation standards and frameworks can be powerful and valuable tools in the information security arsenal when well understood and properly applied. They may be used to prove a professional's mastery of his or her trade (professional certifications), a system's level of assurance (Common Criteria—see the next section), or an organization's compliance with standards. In this part of the chapter, we'll take a look at some evaluation standards to outline their benefits.

e x a m

ω a t c h   *The aim of the exam objectives covered in this chapter is to test your understanding of the security process life cycle approach. As mentioned previously, the topics covered in Part I of this guide are general security concepts that are universally applicable, even though particulars of their implementations may vary. Candidates should concentrate on their understanding of the spirit rather than the letter of these approaches. Although the Sun Certified Security Administrator for Solaris examination tests your mastery of the Solaris operating environment's security features and tools first and foremost, clear appreciation of information security as a vendor-neutral discipline is necessary to pass the exam.*

The Common Criteria (ISO 15408)

The *Common Criteria for Information Technology Security Evaluation*, or *Common Criteria* for short, is the product of the cooperation between national information systems security organizations of the United States, France, Germany, the United Kingdom, the Netherlands, and Canada. It builds upon the experience gained from preceding evaluation standards: the U.S. Trusted Computing Systems Evaluation Criteria (TCSEC), Canadian Trusted Computing Products Evaluation Criteria (CTCPEC), and the European Information Technology Security Evaluation Criteria (ITSEC). The Common Criteria defines seven levels of assurance that are granted to systems after they are evaluated against one or several of the "Common Criteria Protection Profiles" by an accredited evaluation body. The granted certification is intended to be valid in all countries recognizing Common Criteria certifications. In practice, this means, for example, that a Canadian product certified to a certain evaluation assurance level in France may be used by those organizations that require Common Criteria certification in the United States and the other previously mentioned countries without unnecessary and costly reevaluation.

Evaluation Assurance Levels (EALs)

Common Criteria defines seven evaluation assurance levels that aim to reflect trustworthiness of evaluated systems, ranging from EAL1, the lowest level, to EAL7, the highest level of assurance. Although they express the assurance level of evaluated systems, evaluation assurance levels are meaningless without knowing against which Protection Profile (PP) the systems have been evaluated. To understand the meaning and impact of a Common Criteria evaluation, it is necessary to know both the evaluation assurance level and the protection profile under which it was issued.

Functionally Tested (EAL1)   EAL1 involves testing against a specification and review of system documentation. EAL1 certification provides evidence that the system functions in accordance with its documentation. This is the lowest evaluation assurance level.

Structurally Tested (EAL2)   At EAL2, a more structured approach is applied to testing against specification and review of documentation than at EAL1.

Methodically Tested and Checked (EAL3)   EAL3 is applicable in situations when there is a need for independently assured moderate security. EAL3 involves thorough examination of the system and its development environment and controls.

Methodically Designed, Tested, and Reviewed (EAL4)   EAL4 is the highest practical level of assurance that may be gained using good commercial development practices. Higher levels (EAL5–7) require special development methodologies and procedures that are expensive and not commonplace.

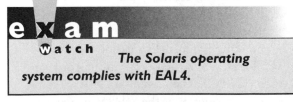

The Solaris operating system complies with EAL4.

Semiformally Designed and Tested (EAL5)   EAL5 requires analysis that includes all of the implementation. Assurance is provided by a formal model and a semiformal functional specification.

Semiformally Verified Design and Tested (EAL6)   At EAL6, specialized security engineering techniques are required and a systematic search for vulnerabilities is performed.

Formally Verified Design and Tested (EAL7)   EAL7 provides the highest level of assurance. At EAL7, white box testing and complete independent verification of test results are required. Because of extremely high costs associated with EAL7, it is appropriate only for systems requiring the highest level of assurance.

Protection Profiles

Protection Profiles (PPs) are the sets of requirements and definitions against which systems are evaluated and awarded EALs. Because different systems in different environments have distinct security requirements, different PPs are employed. In particular, Common Criteria PPs exist for the following types of systems:

- Operating systems
- Biometrics
- Certificate management
- Firewalls
- Intrusion detection systems
- Peripherals
- Public key management infrastructures
- Security tokens

Other protection profiles may be developed and used when no appropriate PPs exist.

ISO 17799

ISO 17799, *Code of Practice for Information Security Management,* is an international standard published by the International Organization for Standardization (ISO). It is based on British Standard 7799 Part 1. To describe ISO 17799, it is best to refer to the official description:

> It is intended to serve as a single reference point for identifying the range of controls needed for most situations where information systems are used in industry and commerce, and to be used by large, medium, and small organizations. The term organization is used throughout the standard to mean both profit and non-profit making organizations such as public sector organizations.
>
> Not all of the controls described in this document will be relevant to every situation. It cannot take account of local system, environmental, or technological constraints. It may not be in a form that suits every potential user in an organization.

Consequently the document may need to be supplemented by further guidance. It can be used as a basis from which, for example, a corporate policy or an inter-company trading agreement can be developed.

As a code of practice this standard takes the form of guidance and recommendations. It should not be quoted as if it were a specification, and particular care should be taken to ensure that claims of compliance are not misleading.

Despite its limitations, ISO 17799 is a useful and widely used framework for information security management. Its popularity has only increased with time. ISO 17799 covers the following ten domains of information security:

1. Security policy
   1.1. Information security policy
2. Security organization
   2.1. Information security infrastructure
   2.2. Security of third-party access
   2.3. Outsourcing
3. Asset classification and control
   3.1. Accountability for assets
   3.2. Information classification
4. Personnel security
   4.1. Security in job definition and resourcing
   4.2. User training
   4.3. Responding to security incidents and malfunctions
5. Physical and environmental security
   5.1. Secure areas
   5.2. Equipment security
   5.3. General controls
6. Communications and operations management
   6.1. Operational procedures and responsibilities
   6.2. System planning and acceptance
   6.3. Protection against malicious software
   6.4. Housekeeping

      6.5. Network management

      6.6. Media handling and security

      6.7. Exchanges of information and software

  7. Access control

      7.1. Business requirement for access control

      7.2. User access management

      7.3. User responsibilities

      7.4. Network access control

      7.5. Operating system access control

      7.6. Application access control

      7.7. Monitoring system access and use

      7.8. Mobile computing and teleworking

  8. Systems development and maintenance

      8.1. Security requirements of systems

      8.2. Security in application systems

      8.3. Cryptographic controls

      8.4. Security of system files

      8.5. Security in development and support processes

  9. Business continuity management

      9.1. Aspects of business continuity management

 10. Compliance

      10.1. Compliance with legal requirements

      10.2. Reviews of security policy and technical compliance

      10.3. System audit considerations

As you can see, ISO 17799 covers different security areas that are essential for effective information security management. It is currently being revised by an international working group, and it is expected that a new release of the standard will be published in 2005 or 2006.

Certification, Evaluation, and Accreditation

Certification is the technical evaluation of systems and issuance of an opinion regarding their compliance with a defined set of requirements, usually (but not necessarily) for the purpose of accreditation. During *evaluation*, the evaluating body may look at the requirements, specifications, design, and implementation of the system in question to ascertain whether it meets the particular requirements. The certifying body, usually an independent and qualified third party, audits a system for compliance with an established set of security requirements. *Accreditation*, in contrast, is the formal acceptance of the adequacy of the system's overall security by the management of a particular organization, according to that organization's formal requirements for accreditation, which may in particular cover questions such as how closely the system follows system specifications and whether the security controls are well implemented. Certification is a basis for accreditation, but the responsibility for the accredited system lies mainly with the management of the organization that accredits the system. Certification and accreditation are particularly important in government, military, and financial services industries.

e x a m

ⓦa t c h

It is important that you know and understand the difference between certification, evaluation, and accreditation for the exam. An evaluating body evaluates requirements, specifications, design, and implementation of the system; the system can then be certified to be in compliance; and accreditation comes last and is the formal acceptance of the organization's requirements, specifications, design, and implementation.

CERTIFICATION SUMMARY

This chapter covered two last objectives of Part I of the Sun Certified Security Administrator for Solaris examination. We discussed the process-based approach to security, including its life cycle; security awareness; applications, network, and physical security; as well as evaluation standards. The aim of the exam objectives covered in this chapter is to test your understanding of the security process life cycle approach. As mentioned previously, the topics covered in Part I of this guide are general security concepts that are universally applicable, even though particulars of their implementation may vary.

TWO-MINUTE DRILL

Here are some of the key points from the certification objectives in Chapter 3.

Identify the Security Life Cycle and Describe Best Security Practices

❑ A security policy is a high-level document or set of documents that identifies the particular information assets of the organization, stipulates who owns them, indicates how they may or may not be used, and sets requirements for their use along with sanctions for misuse.

❑ The security life cycle process is intended to prevent, detect, respond, and deter—and repeat the cycle again, keeping in mind the lessons learned.

❑ Preventive controls include firewalls, logical and physical access control systems, and security procedures that are devised to prevent the occurrence of violations of security policy.

❑ Detection controls include network and host intrusion detection systems, physical movement and intrusion detection systems and alarms, and cryptographic checksums on transmitted information (to detect unauthorized modifications).

❑ Incident response is a subdiscipline of information security; it is the formal set of defined and approved actions based on the information security policy and best practices that are to be taken in response to a security incident.

❑ Deterrent controls include good information security management, regular audits, security-aware staff, well-administered systems, good employee morale, and security certifications.

❑ Security-aware employees are the best partners of the organization and its information security efforts, while staff that have no idea about security practices or simply don't care are not partners at all. One doesn't need determined adversaries to suffer a security breach—a clueless insider who doesn't understand the consequences may expose the organization to risks that could otherwise have been avoided.

❑ Security policies are one of the mechanisms that define and convey the information security requirements of the organization's management to the staff of the organization.

❑ Security procedures are developed within the organization by subject-matter specialists with assistance of security professionals and/or information systems auditors. Procedures may be application-specific and/or version-specific and need to be kept current with the organization's latest information systems environment. System and security administrators play a key role in developing and enforcing security procedures.

❑ Security guidelines are nonbinding recommendations dealing with how to develop, define, and enforce security policies and procedures.

❑ Security standards are mandatory either because they are dictated by the security policy, law, or regulations or because the entity in question has decided to adhere to the standard.

❑ Physical security addresses the physical vulnerabilities, threats, and countermeasures used to control risks associated with physical destruction; unauthorized access; loss due to theft, fire, natural disasters (floods, earthquakes, tornados), or environmental issues (air conditioning, ventilation, humidity control); and all associated issues.

❑ Although Sun Certified Security Administrator certification candidates are not required to have Sun Certified System or Network Administrator certifications, they are expected to be familiar with subjects covered by their exam objectives and have at least six months of experience administering Solaris systems.

Describe the Benefits of Evaluation Standards

❑ Evaluation standards provide a common framework for developers, users, and evaluators to define, evaluate, and compare security functionality and assurance levels of different products, from operating systems to smart cards.

❑ Although formal evaluation of systems is a complex and expensive process, it is justified for high-security environments such as military, government, and financial.

❑ The result of evaluation is an evaluation assurance level assigned to the evaluated system which indicates the level of assurance or trust, which in turn depends on how the system was designed, implemented, and evaluated.

❑ The Solaris operating system has been evaluated to EAL4.

SELF TEST

The following questions will help you measure your understanding of the material presented in this chapter. Read all the choices carefully, because there might be more than one correct answer. Choose all correct answers for each question.

Identify the Security Life Cycle and Describe Best Security Practices

1. Why is a process life cycle–based approach to information security management appropriate?
   A. Because it is the only existing approach
   B. Because it is a good practice
   C. Because it takes into account the changing environment
   D. Because it is business-oriented
   E. All of the above

2. Security life cycle includes which of the following?
   A. Preventive controls
   B. Detection
   C. Controls that deter potential attackers
   D. Incident response
   E. All of the above

3. Why is detection an important part of the security process?
   A. Because it shows which preventive controls work and which don't.
   B. Because it serves as a quality/reliability control.
   C. Because no usable preventive control is perfect.
   D. Detection is not necessary in low-security environments.
   E. All of the above

4. What is the purpose of deterrent controls?
   A. To back up detective controls
   B. To prevent attacks from happening
   C. To discourage attackers
   D. To compensate for preventive controls
   E. All of the above

5. Why is incident response capability necessary?
   A. Because any organization may have a security incident
   B. Because detection is useless without response
   C. Because it is required by law
   D. Because correct reaction to a security incident is important
   E. All of the above

6. Why should security awareness training be an ongoing concern?
   A. Because security risks and vulnerabilities change and evolve
   B. Because people need to refresh their knowledge periodically
   C. Because an organization's information systems change over time
   D. Because people may become complacent with time
   E. All of the above

7. Documents that set high-level goals, requirements, and priorities are called
   A. Guidelines
   B. Procedures
   C. Standards
   D. Policies
   E. All of the above

8. Documents that are usually technical, detailed, and implement security policies are called:
   A. Guidelines
   B. Normative acts
   C. Procedures
   D. Standards
   E. All of the above

9. Nonbinding recommendations on how to develop, define, and enforce security policies and procedures are known as:
   A. Standards
   B. Auditing regulations
   C. Guidelines
   D. Control objectives
   E. All of the above

10. When are information security standards compulsory?
    A. When required by law
    B. When adopted by the organization
    C. Always
    D. When required for certification or accreditation
    E. All of the above

11. Physical security includes which of the following?
    A. Location of facilities
    B. Building materials
    C. Humidity, ventilation, and air conditioning
    D. Fire detection and suppression systems
    E. All of the above

12. System firmware affects the overall security of the system?
    A. True
    B. False
    C. Only on SPARC systems
    D. On all systems except SPARC systems
    E. All of the above

13. What is the difference between SSL/TLS and IPSEC?
    A. IPSEC is a transport layer and SSL/TLS is a network layer technology.
    B. SSL/TLS is a transport layer and IPSEC is a network layer technology.
    C. IPSEC secures only the network layer and SSL/TLS secures all layers.
    D. SSL/TLS provides only confidentiality and not integrity protection.
    E. All of the above

Describe the Benefits of Evaluation Standards

14. What is the purpose of Common Criteria certification?
    A. To increase security of certified operating systems
    B. To offer cost-effective systems certification
    C. To provide comparability between the results of independent security evaluations
    D. To guarantee security of evaluated systems
    E. All of the above

15. What is the highest evaluation assurance level under Common Criteria that may be reached using commonly accepted best practices in systems/software development?

A. EAL7

B. EAL5

C. EAL4

D. EAL3

E. All of the above

16. What is a Common Criteria Protection Profile (PP)?

A. It rates the strength of security of evaluated systems.

B. It specifies a system's assurance evaluation level.

C. It is a Common Criteria assessment scheme.

D. It is a set of requirements and definitions against which systems are evaluated.

E. All of the above

17. Which of the following security domains are covered by ISO 17799?

A. Security policy

B. Access control

C. Physical security

D. Solaris security

E. All of the above

18. Which of the following statements are true?

A. Certification is the technical evaluation of systems.

B. Certification is done by an organization's management.

C. Accreditation is the formal acceptance of the system and its risks.

D. Certification requires accreditation.

E. All of the above

SELF TEST ANSWERS

Identify the Security Life Cycle and Describe Best Security Practices

1. ☑ **B, C,** and **D.** A process life cycle–based approach to information security management is appropriate because it takes into account changing information systems environments, it is business-oriented, and it is considered a good practice.

   ☒ **A** is incorrect because the process life cycle-based approach is not the only existing approach to information security management.

2. ☑ **E.** All of the answers are correct. The security life cycle process consists of prevention, detection, response, and deterrence.

3. ☑ **A, B,** and **C.** Detection is an important part of the security process because it shows whether preventive controls work or not, because it serves as a quality and reliability control, and because no usable preventive control is perfect.

   ☒ **D** is incorrect because the security level of the environment has no bearing on the need for detective controls.

4. ☑ **C.** Deterrent controls are created to discourage potential attackers. Deterrent controls may potentially be confused with preventive controls, and although both types of controls aim to preclude security violations from happening, they try to do so at different times.

   ☒ **A** and **B** are incorrect because deterrent controls are not a backup for detective controls and they do not necessarily prevent attacks from happening. **D** is incorrect because, while preventive security controls try to prevent a breach of security after the adversary has decided to attack but before the attack has succeeded, deterrent controls try to discourage the attacker from attacking in the first place by demonstrating that the attack is not going to succeed and even if it does, it will be detected and dealt with.

5. ☑ **A, B,** and **D.** Computer security incidents are occurring at an ever-increasing rate; therefore, we must be prepared to respond to and investigate computer security incidents.

   ☒ **C** is incorrect because incident response is not necessarily always required by law; however, depending on the jurisdiction of company policy or industry compliancy, incident response capability may be required.

6. ☑ **E.** All answers are correct. To address all of these concerns, security awareness training should be held regularly.

7. ☑ **D.** Security policies are set by management and are high-level in nature. They specify what should and should not happen, without going into detail on how to reach these goals. Security policies should be sufficiently specific to convey their meaning and objectives unambiguously, but at the same time general enough not to require modification every month or after introduction of a new system or application in the organization.

   ☒ **A, B,** and **C** are incorrect because guidelines are recommendations for consideration, procedures are detailed step-by-step instructions, and standards are general in nature.

8. ☑ **C.** Security procedures are developed by subject-matter specialists within the organization with the assistance of security professionals and/or information systems auditors. Because security procedures are often highly specific and technical in nature, they should be developed by those who appreciate these considerations.

   ☒ **A, B,** and **D** are incorrect because guidelines, normative acts, and standards only influence procedures.

9. ☑ **C.** Security guidelines are nonbinding recommendations that deal with how to develop, define, and enforce security policies and procedures. Although guidelines are nonbinding, it is customary to require explanation from those who choose not to follow them.

   ☒ **A, B,** and **D** are incorrect because standards, auditing regulations, and control objectives are not non-binding recommendations.

10. ☑ **A, B,** and **D.** Unlike guidelines, security standards are mandatory either because they are dictated by the security policy, law, or regulations or because the entity in question has decided to adhere to the standard.

    ☒ **C** is incorrect because information security standards are not always compulsory.

11. ☑ **E.** All answers are correct. Physical security includes all aspects mentioned as well as physical access control and monitoring.

12. ☑ **A.** Although particulars may vary, a system's firmware affects the overall security of the system.

    ☒ **B** is incorrect because the statement is true. **C** and **D** are incorrect because firmware on any platform may affect the overall security of the system.

13. ☑ **B.** SSL/TLS is a transport layer and IPSEC is a network layer technology.

    ☒ **A, C,** and **D** are incorrect because both SSL/TLS and IPSEC provide confidentiality and integrity protection to all layers above them.

Describe the Benefits of Evaluation Standards

14. ☑ **C.** The purpose of Common Criteria is to provide comparability between the results of independent security evaluations of IT systems.

    ☒ **A, B,** and **D** are incorrect because evaluated systems are not necessarily more secure than other systems, evaluation usually is an expensive service, and evaluation doesn't guarantee security of evaluated systems.

15. ☑ **C.** EAL4 is considered to be the highest practical level of assurance that may be gained using good commercial development practices.

    ☒ **A** and **B** are incorrect because higher levels (EAL5–7) require special development methodologies and procedures that are expensive and not common place. **D** is incorrect of course because it is a lower level of assurance than EAL4.

16. ☑ **D.** A Protection Profile (PP) is a set of requirements and definitions against which systems are evaluated and awarded evaluation assurance levels (EALs). Because different systems in different environments have distinct security requirements, different protection profiles are in existence.

☒ **A, B,** and **C** are incorrect because PPs do not rate the strength of security of evaluated systems, do not specify systems' assurance evaluation levels, and are not a Common Criteria assessment scheme.

17. ☑ **A, B,** and **C.** ISO 17799 is a *Code of Practice for Information Security Management* and does not cover any specific products or systems such as Solaris.

☒ **D** is incorrect because ISO 17799 does not cover the Solaris operating environment specifically but is an information security management standard.

18. ☑ **A** and **C.** Certification is a technical evaluation conducted by independent and qualified third parties. Certification does not require accreditation. It is a basis for accreditation, but the responsibility for the accredited system lies mainly with the management of the organization that accredits the system.

☒ **B** is incorrect because certification is a technical evaluation conducted by third parties. **D** is incorrect because certification does not require accreditation.

Part II

Detection and Device Management

4

Logging and Process Accounting

A n estimated $59 billion is lost each year in proprietary information and intellectual property, according to *Trends in Proprietary Information Loss Survey,* by ASIS International (September 2002). The collective basis for these losses is a low level of priority for information security—especially at the user level—and lack of management support. With the rapid release of new software and hardware and the progression of technology and processing power, the threat of further loss is imminent. We simply must equally integrate security throughout the infrastructure and should not depend so much on robust perimeter security such as firewalls.

In any organization, the need for appropriate levels of security—both physical security (that is, employees and facilities) as well as information security (system and application level access)—is easily recognized. However, when it comes to practice, complacency may often take center stage, thereby introducing additional exposures, risks, threats, and vulnerabilities into the organization. These security-related issues, if unaddressed, can seriously undermine an organization and adversely impact its ability to continue its stated mission successfully.

This chapter presents discussions on identifying, monitoring, and disabling user-level logins. Furthermore, we'll look at how to configure and customize the syslog logging facility and ways to monitor and restrict remote superuser access using the switch user (su) program. Most of the techniques in this chapter are essential for the Sun Certified Security Administrator's arsenal and mandated by many enterprise information security policies.

CERTIFICATION OBJECTIVE 4.01

Identify, Monitor, and Disable Logins

Before we talk about login identification and monitoring, it's important that you understand a few standard conventions. Among the most implicated issues with regard to user-level security practices are password and login management. Following are some standardized rules that organizations use as a template for creating internal policies:

- Passwords are to be kept confidential.
- Only the individual user to whom the logon ID is assigned is to know the password. Disclosure of the password is a serious security violation and may result in loss of systems access privileges and possible disciplinary actions.

- Passwords are not to be programmed into a PC or recorded anywhere else where someone may find and use them.

- Individually assigned user IDs and personal passwords (for authentication purposes) are required for access to all of these applications.

- All user IDs must be unique and not shared.

- Assigned user IDs will be set up to include the user's first initial and full last name—for example, the user ID for employee John Smith would be jsmith.

- Passwords must be used for all access (local and/or remote). They must be changed at least once each quarter (forced system-generated expiration at 90 days, if possible) or more frequently if compromise is suspected.

- Concurrent session logins are not permitted. All requests for exceptions to this policy must be reviewed on a case-by-case basis.

- Automatic terminal timeouts (for inactivity) must be used. Use of a screen-saver lockout option, set at no more than a recommended 15 minutes, is one acceptable method.

- Failed login attempts are restricted to three consecutive attempts, followed by a "lock out" requiring a reset of the user's password after investigation of the circumstances by the administration.

- Users must safeguard their access to information and information resources from unauthorized use. This requirement extends to maintaining the confidentiality of passwords and other access tools.

In addition, here are the general Sun-required rules for creating user logins and passwords:

- The user name must
  - Be unique
  - Contain a combination of 2 to 32 letters, numerals, underscores (_), hyphens (-), and periods (.), but no spaces
  - Begin with a letter and have at least one lowercase letter
  - Be three to eight characters long for compatibility purposes
- The password must
  - Consist of between 6 and 15 letters, numbers, and special characters
  - Have at least two alphabetic characters and at least one numeric or special character within the first six

Following are some additional industry-recognized security recommendations for creating passwords:

- Passwords should be at least eight characters long.
- Passwords should contain at least
  - One alpha character (a–z, A–Z)
  - One numeric character (0–9)
  - One special character from this set:` ! @ $ % ^ & * ( ) - _ = + [ ] ; : ' " , < . > / ?
- Passwords should not contain spaces, begin with an exclamation (!) or a question mark (?), or contain the login ID.
- The first three characters of the password should not be the same, and the sequence of the first three characters should not be in the login ID.
- The first eight characters of the new password should not be the same as the previous password.

Identifying, Disabling, and Monitoring Logins

The first step with regard to login management is to identify user login status—especially for users without assigned passwords. We'll look at how to disable user logins and then how to monitor user login attempts. Before we begin, note that to perform these tasks, you need either to log in as primary administrator, which includes the primary administrator profile, or become superuser. In other words, you must log in with an account that has root privileges or use the switch user (su) command to become superuser. As superuser, you'll have full privileges that will be required. For example, to switch to the root account, simply open a terminal session, type **su root**, press ENTER, and then enter the root's password at the prompt.

Identifying User Login Status

The easiest way to determine which users are currently logged into the system is by issuing the who command at a terminal prompt with full privileges. Displaying user login status, on the other hand, is also painless with the logins command. Following is an extract from the command using the -x argument, which displays extended output:

```
# logins -x
root              0         other          1         Super-User
                            /
                            /sbin/sh
                            PS 082587 -1 -1 -1
nuucp             9         nuucp          9         uucp Admin
                            /var/spool/uucppublic
                            /usr/lib/uucp/uucico
                            LK 082587 -1 -1 -1
j_public          101       staff          10        Sales
                            /home/j_public
                            /bin/sh
                            NP 051304 -1 -1 -1
b_friedman        102       mail           6         Marketing
                            /home/b_friedman
                            /bin/sh
                            PS 051304 -1 -1 -1
nobody            60001     nobody         60001     NFS Anonymous Access User
                            /
                            /sbin/sh
                            LK 082587 -1 -1 -1
```

As shown, the output is organized in ascending order by user ID. Using the *b_friedman* account as an example, let's break down the user status details:

- b_friedman is the user's login name.
- 102 is the user ID (UID).
- mail identifies the user's primary group.
- 6 is the group ID (GID).
- Marketing is the user description (in this case, the description indicates the user's work group within the organization).
- /home/b_friedman is the user's home directory.
- /bin/sh identifies the login shell.
- PS 051304 -1 -1 -1 specifies the following password aging information: the last date that the password was changed, the number of days required between changes, the number of days before a change is required, and the warning period.

Another logins command argument you should know for the exam is the -l *username*; where *username* is the user login name. For example, to display the extended user login status for Kelly Martin, whose login name is *k_martin*, you would issue the following command:

```
logins -x -l k_martin
```

One more critical argument you can use with the `logins` command is with the -p option. With this option, you can display which users do not have assigned passwords. For example, by issuing the `logins -p` command, you get the following output:

```
# logins -p
j_public        101     staff       10      Sales
```

Here we see that user name *j_public*, part of the *staff* group, does not have an assigned password. This is typically the case when administrators set up user logins without a temporary password (that is, selecting the User Must Set Password At First Login option when adding a user). This could lead to a security breach; thus, Sun recommends actively monitoring and disabling user logins without passwords on a regular basis—or, better yet, preventing them from being created in the first place.

Finally, another method used to view user login status is by accessing the */etc/shadow* file with full privileges (since the file is owned by root). A user account is currently disabled when a user record contains *LK* in the *shadow* file, such as in the following extract:

```
j_public:*LK*:12557
```

Additionally, when an account name is followed by a *NP*, that account currently is not assigned a password, as shown here:

```
adm:*NP*:6445
```

It's important to note that only root can view the contents of the read-only */etc/shadow* file—and for good reason. User names with assigned passwords are followed by an encrypted password string, and if it were readable by anyone, intruders would have much easier access to utilize password-cracking utilities to guess them.

e x a m

ⓦ**a t c h** *For the exam, you should remember the three common ways to identify user login status—by issuing the `logins` command, using the Solaris Management Console, and viewing the /etc/shadow file. This is important in determining which accounts are locked or disabled and which do not currently have assigned passwords.*

Disabling User Logins

At times during a security investigation, or perhaps during system maintenance, you'll need to disable user logins while performing forensics or routine tasks. Keep this in mind as well when you're running the Automated Security Enhancement Tool (ASET) tasks (see Chapter 8 for more information) to keep system utilization down to a minimum by blocking user access.

In this chapter, when we edit a system file, we'll be using the operating system's visual editor (vi), a text editor that enables you to enter or modify text in a file. Fundamentally, vi supports two modes of operation: a command mode and an insert mode. By default, when you start vi, you're in the command mode. While in command mode, vi accepts commands that correspond with specific actions. Table 4-1 shows a summary of the most common commands you should know. On the other hand, while in insert mode, you're allowed to enter text. While in command mode, you can enter insert mode by pressing the I key on your keyboard. To revert back to command mode, press the ESC key.

TABLE 4-1	Command	Description
Common vi Commands	:q!	Quit now
	:wq	Write changes and quit
	:w CTRL-b	Write changes without quitting
	i	Insert
	.	Repeat last
	ESC	End insert
	CTRL-w	Erase last word
	D	Delete line
	x	Delete character
	:w	Write changes without quitting
	U	Restore line
	CTRL-b	Go back one screen
	CTRL-d	Scroll down
	CTRL-u	Scroll up
	O	Go to beginning of line
	l	Move forward one character
	h	Move backward one character
	b	Move backward one word

INSIDE THE EXAM

Manually Disabling User Logins

Following are steps for manually disabling user logins:

1. Log in with an account that has root privileges, or use the su command to become superuser.

2. Create the /etc/nologin file in your text editor by issuing the vi /etc/nologin command.

3. Insert a notification message (by pressing the I key on the keyboard) to be displayed when users attempt access by typing
Performing System Maintenance. The system will be unavailable until 10pm.

4. End insert mode by pressing the ESC key, and then save the file and exit the editor with the :wq command.

Using the vi text editor, the steps involved in disabling user logins temporarily are straightforward and relatively uncomplicated. To do so, you become superuser, create a /etc/nologin file, insert a notification message in the file (to be displayed when users attempt access), and then save and exit the file.

Alternatively, you can also disable logins by bringing down the system to *run level S* (single-user mode, as shown in Table 4-2). To do so, follow these three steps:

1. Become superuser.

2. Shut down the system with this command:
   shutdown -i *init-level* -g *grace-period* -y
   Where *init-level* is 0, 1, 2, 5, 6, or S (which is the default) and *grace-period* is the time (in seconds) before the system is shut down (default is 60 seconds). For example, to shut down the system to run level S and therefore disable all logins, you would use this command: shutdown -y

3. Enter the password for root at the system maintenance prompt request.

By issuing the init (*Run Level #*) command, you can switch between run levels to perform functions such as halting and rebooting the Solaris operating system. In essence, init is the process spawner, while a Run Level is a software configuration for a selected group of processes. As an example, to shut down the operating system and reboot the computer, you'd open a terminal session with the appropriate administrative privileges and type **init 6**.

TABLE 4-2	Level	Description
Common Run Levels	S	Single-user state for administrative functions
	0	Go into firmware maintenance mode
	2	Multi-user state where NFS is not running.
	5	Shut down
	6	Stop the operating system and reboot

Table 4-2 lists a summary of run levels that you should know.

If done correctly, when disabling user logins by bringing the system down and initiating single-user mode, you'll see output similar to the following:

```
Shutdown started. Thu May 13 11:30:32 CST 2004

Broadcast Message from root (console) on sun Thu May 13 11:30:33...
The system sun will be shut down in 1 minute
.
Broadcast Message from root (console) on sun Thu May 13 11:31:03...
The system sun will be shut down in 30 seconds
.
Broadcast Message from root (console) on sun Thu May 13 11:31:33...
The system sun IS BEING SHUT DOWN NOW!!!
.
INIT: New run level: S
The system is coming down for administration. Please wait.
Unmounting remote filesystems: /vol nfs done.
Shutting down Solaris Management Console server on port 898.
Print services stopped.
May 13 11:31:34 sun syslogd: going down on signal 15
Killing user processes: done.
INIT: SINGLE USER MODE
Type control-d to proceed with normal startup,
(or give root password for system maintenance): (you enter root password here)
Entering System Maintenance Mode ...
#
```

Lastly, you can also disable user accounts individually. The method that Sun recommends is uncomplicated and requires using the Solaris Management Console (SMC) interface. To disable accounts individually, simply follow these steps:

1. Log in with an account that has root privileges, or use the su command to become superuser.

2. Right-click on the desktop to open the Workspace menu.

3. Click the Tools/Solaris Management Console option to open the GUI interface.

4. In SMC, click to open This Computer in the Navigation panel.

5. Within This Computer, click the System Configuration option and then Users.

6. At the prompt, enter root's password and click OK.

7. Click to open the User Accounts option.

8. Click to open a particular user account and then select the Account Is Locked option at the bottom of the interface.

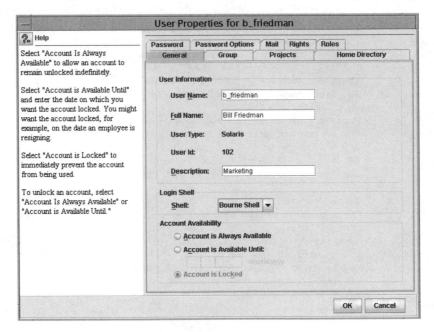

9. Click OK to disable and update the account.

10. Exit SMC.

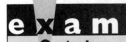

Remember how to disable all user logins with the exception of superuser. This can be done by creating a /etc/nologin file, bringing the system down to single-user mode (level S), and disabling user accounts individually using the Solaris Management Console (SMC) interface.

Monitoring Failed Terminal Session User Login Attempts

Solaris keeps track of each user login so that the next time a user logs in, the previous login is reported on the screen. Capturing unsuccessful login attempts is accomplished by creating a *var/adm/loginlog* file. The *loginlog* file should be owned by root with read and write permissions and belong to the *sys* group. Each failed login (after five unsuccessful attempts) is appended as a line entry containing the user's login name, TTY device, and time. Failed login attempts will be logged to the *loginlog* file, and therefore it should be utilized for potential intrusion detection and monitored regularly. The file contents can be viewed by issuing the `more /var/adm/loginlog` command.

The following extract displays a few entries from a *loginlog* file:

```
j_public:/dev/pts/9:Tue May 25 23:10:15 2004
j_public:/dev/pts/9:Tue May 25 23:10:17 2004
j_public:/dev/pts/9:Tue May 25 23:10:20 2004
j_public:/dev/pts/9:Tue May 25 23:10:21 2004
j_public:/dev/pts/9:Tue May 25 23:10:22 2004
b_friedman:/dev/pts/2:Tue May 25 23:14:11 2004
b_friedman:/dev/pts/2:Tue May 25 23:10:12 2004
```

INSIDE THE EXAM

Setting Up the *loginlog* File to Monitor Failed Logins

Following are five simple steps for manually setting up the *var/adm/loginlog* file to monitor failed user login attempts and then test its functionality:

1. Log in with an account that has root privileges, or use the `su` command to become superuser.

2. Create the *var/adm/loginlog* file with your vi text editor or by issuing the `touch /var/adm/loginlog` command.

3. Make the *loginlog* file part of the sys group with the `chgrp sys /var/adm/loginlog` command.

4. Set both read and write permissions for only the root user on the *loginlog* file with the `chmod 600 /var/adm/loginlog` command.

5. Test that the system is logging failed login attempts by unsuccessfully logging in to the system from terminal windows at least five times, and then view the *loginlog* file contents by issuing the `more /var/adm/loginlog` command.

You should note that the *loginlog* file records only failed login attempts from terminal sessions; therefore, it does not capture unsuccessful logins from CDE or GNOME. However, capturing all login types is possible using syslog, which is explained in the next section.

Monitoring All Unsuccessful Login Attempts   In the previous section, we used the *loginlog* file to record failed login attempts from terminal sessions; however, there are ways to monitor all unsuccessful logins as well as supervise root access whether they are from terminal sessions, CDE, or GNOME. In the next section, we'll do this by using *syslog* and *sulog* files and we'll discuss techniques to customize and control access logging and process accounting.

CERTIFICATION OBJECTIVE 4.02

Configure syslog, Customize the System Logging Facility, and Monitor and Control Superuser

Syslog is the de facto standard for event logging on UNIX systems. For years, system logging facilities have used syslog to store and manage system event notifications. This section takes logging and process accounting beyond the limitations of using the *loginlog* file for monitoring unsuccessful login attempts. In addition, we'll also look at ways to monitor and restrict superuser by means of the switch user (su) program.

Configuring syslog and Customizing the System Logging Facility

As mentioned, you can monitor all unsuccessful logins whether they are from terminal sessions, CDE, or GNOME. All failed login attempts will be stored in a *syslog* file. The *syslog* file can and should be monitored closely on a regular basis to pinpoint potential intrusion attempts and other irregularities.

The syslog daemon launcher script that controls the logging facilities is located in the */etc/init.d/* directory as *syslog*. Following is the command syntax for starting and stopping the syslog daemon:

```
/etc/init.d/syslog start
/etc/init.d/syslog stop
```

Monitoring All Failed User Login Attempts with syslog

Let's look at the steps involved in monitoring all unsuccessful login attempts with syslog.

1. With full privileges, edit the *letc/default/login* file and make sure that the SYSLOG=YES and SYSLOG_FAILED_LOGINS=0 entries are uncommented.

2. Create the log file (*/var/adm/authlog*) and assign the appropriate read/write permissions for root.

3. Change the *authlog* file group membership to *sys*.

4. Edit the *syslog.conf* file to send all failed login attempts to the *authlog* file with the following entry:

   auth.notice<TAB>/var/adm/authlog

   (Note that a tabbed-space, not a standard space, appears between the auth.notice and /var/adm/authlog attributes in this entry).

5. Stop and start the syslog daemon.

Customizing the System Logging Facility   Optionally, you can customize the System Logging Facility not only to log failed login access attempts after some predefined number of tries, but to close the login connection after some predefined number of failures as well.

The first part is accomplished by simply editing the SYSLOG_FAILED_ LOGINS=0 entry in the *letc/default/login* file to some number such as this: SYSLOG_ FAILED_LOGINS=3. At this point, the system will log access attempts only after the first three failures.

The second part involves closing connections after some number of retries—for example, after five unsuccessful login attempts. This is a common configuration for enterprises, as many security policies mandate this rule. To do so, simply uncomment the RETRIES entry in the *letc/default/login* file, and make sure the value is either set to 5 (which is the default value) or some other reasonable mandated value. Upon saving the file, the changes will take effect immediately; after five failed login

INSIDE THE EXAM

Setting Up syslog to Monitor All Failed Logins

Following are the steps for setting up syslog to monitor all failed user logins attempts:

1. Log in with an account that has root privileges or use the su command to become superuser.

```
Edit the /etc/default/login file by uncommenting the SYSLOG=YES and SYSLOG_
FAILED_LOGINS=0 entries:
#
# SYSLOG determines whether the syslog(3) LOG_AUTH facility should be used
# to log all root logins at level LOG_NOTICE and multiple failed login
# attempts at LOG_CRIT.
#
SYSLOG=YES
#
# These entries were clipped for brevity.
#
# The SYSLOG_FAILED_LOGINS variable is used to determine how many failed
# login attempts will be allowed by the system before a failed login
# message is logged, using the syslog(3) LOG_NOTICE facility.  For example,
# if the variable is set to 0, login will log -all- failed login attempts.
#
SYSLOG_FAILED_LOGINS=0
#
```

2. Create the log file in the */var/adm* directory:

   ```
   touch /var/adm/authlog
   ```

3. Assign the appropriate read/write permissions for root to the log file:

   ```
   chmod 600 /var/adm/authlog
   ```

4. Change the *authlog* file group membership to *sys*:

   ```
   chgrp sys /var/adm/authlog
   ```

5. Edit the *syslog.conf* file to send all failed login attempts to the *authlog* file:

   ```
   auth.notice     /var/adm/authlog
   ```

6. Stop and start the syslog daemon.
   To stop

   ```
   /etc/init.d/syslog stop
   ```

   To start

   ```
   /etc/init.d/syslog start
   ```

   You can test to determine whether the system is logging failed login attempts by unsuccessfully logging in to the system and then viewing the */var/adm/authlog* file contents by issuing this command:

   ```
   more /var/adm/authlog
   ```

attempts in the same session, the system will close the connection. Following is an extract of this entry:

```
#
# RETRIES determines the number of failed logins that will be
# allowed before login exits.
#
RETRIES=5
#
```

Monitoring and Controlling Superuser Access

Role-Based Access Control (RBAC), which we'll visit later in Chapter 9, is Sun's recommended alternative to using the switch user (su) program and the superuser account. With superuser access permissions, a user will have full control over the system commands and functionality. With full privileges, superusers can wreak havoc on the integrity of the operating system and potentially damage critical data. Therefore, monitoring and controlling superuser access is critical. In this section, we'll look at steps to use not only to monitor who is using the su program but also how to control superuser access.

Monitoring the su Program

The su program usage, by default, is already monitored through the */etc/default/su* file as `SULOG=/var/adm/sulog`, and the syslog logging facility will determine whether or not all su attempts are logged with the `SYSLOG=YES` entry. As a result, monitoring the output is as simple as running the command `more /var/adm/ sulog` from the terminal. The su logging in the */var/adm/sulog* file entries display useful information including the date and time that the command was executed, whether or not the su attempt was successful (+ means success, - means failure), the port from which the su program was executed, and the user name that ran the program as well as the user name to which the user switched.

The su program is monitored by default. The configuration can be found in the /etc/default/su file.

Following is an extract from the *sulog* file with regard to superuser (root) account access:

```
SU 05/26 10:18 + pts/0 j_public-root
SU 05/26 12:02 + pts/0 j_chirillo-root
SU 05/26 15:09 + pts/0 j_public-root
SU 05/26 15:43 + pts/0 b_friedman-root
SU 05/26 16:52 - pts/0 guest-root
```

This file should be monitored on a regular basis to pinpoint potential malicious access attempts.

Displaying Superuser Access Attempts   Optionally, for hands-on monitoring, you can set up the system so that it will detect and display superuser access attempts directly on the console. To do so, follow these steps:

1. Log in with an account that has root privileges, or use the su command to become superuser.

2. Edit the */etc/default/su* file by uncommenting this entry: CONSOLE=/dev/ console

3. Save and exit, and then log in as superuser again using the su command.

After issuing the su command to become superuser, a message will appear on the console. This is a granular approach to monitoring and is typically used when administrators are actively monitoring superuser access attempts. Also, security professionals often deploy this technique, among others, when observing a real-time attack against the operating system.

Controlling Remote Superuser Access

When you install the Solaris operating system, by default, remote superuser (root) logins are disabled. In other words, users typically have to log in as some user account (other than root) and then issue the su command to become a superuser with full privileges. However, if you detect that remote superuser login access is enabled, follow these steps to mitigate risks associated with it:

1. Log in with an account that has root privileges, or use the su command to become superuser.

2. Edit the */etc/default/login* file by uncommenting this entry: CONSOLE=/dev/ console

3. Save and exit, and then attempt to log in as superuser remotely.

At this point, remote superuser login access should be denied. Subsequently, to become superuser remotely, simply log in with a standard user account and then issue the su command followed by root's password.

✓ TWO-MINUTE DRILL

Here are some of the key points from the certification objectives in Chapter 4.

Identify, Monitor, and Disable Logins

❑ Issue the `logins` command and view the *etc/shadow* file to determine which accounts are locked or disabled and which do not currently have assigned passwords. These techniques are useful when identifying user login status.

❑ You can disable user logins by either creating a *etc/nologin* file, bringing the system down to single-user mode with the command `init S`, or disabling user accounts from the Solaris Management Console (SMC) interface.

Configure syslog, Customize the System Logging Facility, and Monitor and Control Superuser

❑ Solaris keeps track of each terminal session user login and records login attempts in the *var/adm/loginlog* file if it exists and has the correct permissions.

❑ Failed login attempts from terminal sessions are stored in the *var/adm/loginlog* file.

❑ Syslog can monitor all unsuccessful login attempts. To make this happen, edit the *etc/default/login* file and make sure that the `SYSLOG=YES` and `SYSLOG_FAILED_LOGINS=0` entries are uncommented.

❑ You can customize the System Logging Facility to log failed login access attempts after a predefined number of tries by editing the `SYSLOG_FAILED_LOGINS=0` entry in the *etc/default/login* file to some number such as this: `SYSLOG_FAILED_LOGINS=3`. At this point, the system will log access attempts only after the first three failures.

❑ You can customize the System Logging Facility to close the login connections after some predefined number of failures by uncommenting the `RETRIES` entry in the *etc/default/login* file (make sure the value is set to some number; 5 is the default value). By default, after five failed login attempts in the same session, the system will close the connection.

❑ The su program usage is monitored through the *etc/default/su* file as `SULOG=/var/adm/sulog`, and the syslog logging facility will determine whether or not to log all su attempts with the `SYSLOG=YES` entry.

❑ In real time, you can display superuser access attempts on the console by uncommenting the `CONSOLE=/dev/console` entry in the *etc/default/su* file.

❑ To disable remote superuser login access attempts (which is disabled by default), simply uncomment the `CONSOLE=/dev/console` entry in the *etc/default/login* file.

SELF TEST

The following questions will help you measure your understanding of the material presented in this chapter. Read all the choices carefully, because there might be more than one correct answer. Choose all correct answers for each question.

Identify, Monitor, and Disable Logins

1. Which of the following techniques is used to identify user login status with regard to logins without assigned passwords?
   A. Issue the command `logins`
   B. Issue the command `logins -x`
   C. Issue the command `logins -p`
   D. Access the /var/adm/loginlog file with superuser privileges.
   E. All of the above

2. Which of the following are part of Sun's required password policy?
   A. The password should be at least 8 characters long.
   B. The password must be composed of between 6 and 15 letters, numbers, and special characters.
   C. The password must have at least 2 alphabetic characters and at least 1 numeric or special character within the first 6 characters.
   D. The first 8 characters of the password should not be the same as the previous password.
   E. All of the above

3. Failed login attempts from terminal sessions are stored in which file?
   A. /etc/default/login
   B. /etc/nologin
   C. /etc/shadow
   D. /var/adm/loginlog
   E. All of the above

4. Which of the following techniques can be used to identify current user login status?
   A. Accessing the /etc/shadow file with superuser privileges
   B. Issuing the command `logins`
   C. Issuing the command `init s`
   D. Accessing the /var/adm/loginlog file with superuser privileges
   E. All of the above

5. Which of the following commands can be executed to switch between run levels and to perform functions such as halting and rebooting the Solaris operating system?

    A. `shutdown -y`

    B. `init (Run Level #)`

    C. `shutdown -i init-level -g grace-period -y`

    D. All of the above

6. Which of these commands can be executed to display only the extended user login status for Becky Blake, whose login name is *b_blake*?

    A. `logins`

    B. `logins b_blake`

    C. `logins -p`

    D. `logins -x -l b_blake`

    E. All of the above

7. Which of these is a common run level used to stop the operating system and reboot?

    A. S

    B. 0

    C. 2

    D. 5

    E. 6

    F. All of the above

8. Which of these is a common run level used to go into single-user state for administrative functions?

    A. S

    B. 0

    C. 2

    D. 5

    E. 6

    F. All of the above

9. To perform system maintenance, you must bring system resources down to minimum levels. Which of these techniques can be used to disable user logins?

    A. Bring the system down to single-user mode.

    B. Issue the `shutdown -g 120 -y` command.

    C. Issue the `init S` command.

    D. Create a */etc/nologin* file.

E. Disable user accounts individually with the Solaris Management Console.

F. All of the above

Configure syslog, Customize the System Logging Facility, and Monitor and Control Superuser

10. The switch user (su) program usage (by default) is monitored.

A. True

B. False

11. Which of these techniques is used to detect and display superuser access attempts actively on the console?

A. Commenting out the CONSOLE=/dev/console entry in the /etc/default/login file

B. Uncommenting the CONSOLE=/dev/console entry in the /etc/default/su file

C. Uncommenting the CONSOLE=/dev/console entry in the /etc/default/login file

D. Commenting out the CONSOLE=/dev/console entry in the /etc/default/su file

E. All of the above

12. The syslog daemon is located in which directory?

A. /etc

B. /etc/init.d

C. /usr/local

D. /usr/asset

E. /devices

F. All of the above

13. Which of these techniques can be used to capture unsuccessful login attempts?

A. Edit the /etc/default/login file and uncomment the RETRIES entry.

B. Create a var/adm/loginlog file.

C. Edit the /etc/default/login file and uncomment the SYSLOG=YES and SYSLOG_FAILED_LOGINS=0 entries.

D. All of the above

LAB QUESTION

ABCD Inc. is a chemical distribution firm that hired you to set up syslog on its Solaris 10 server to monitor all failed user login attempts as well as monitor uses of the switch user (su) program. What steps would you perform to provide the requested services?

SELF TEST ANSWERS

Identify, Monitor, and Disable Logins

1. ☑ **C.** The `logins` command with the `-p` option is used to display which users do not have assigned passwords.

   ☒ **A** is wrong because the `logins` command will display general information concerning all login accounts organized in ascending order by user ID. **B** is incorrect because the `-x` argument will display extended information regarding all login accounts. **D** is wrong because Solaris keeps track of each user login and records login attempts in the *var/adm/loginlog* file.

2. ☑ **B and C.** Sun's policy mandates that passwords must be composed of between 6 and 15 letters, numbers, and special characters, and must have at least 2 alphabetic characters and at least 1 numeric or special character within the first 6 characters.

   ☒ **A and D** are wrong because they are part of industry-recognized security recommendations for creating passwords and are not mandated by Sun's password policy.

3. ☑ **D.** Solaris keeps track of each terminal session login attempt in the *var/adm/loginlog* file.

   ☒ **A** is wrong because */etc/default/login* involves syslog and monitoring *all* unsuccessful login attempts. **B** is wrong because */etc/nologin* is used when disabling user logins. **C** is incorrect because the */etc/shadow* file can be accessed to determine which accounts are locked or disabled and which do not currently have assigned passwords.

4. ☑ **A and B.** Identifying user login status—by issuing the `logins` command and viewing the */etc/shadow* file—is important for determining which accounts are locked or disabled and which do not currently have assigned passwords.

   ☒ **C** is wrong because the `init S` command is used to bring down the system to run level S (single-user mode). **D** is wrong because the */var/adm/loginlog* file is used to log failed terminal session user login attempts.

5. ☑ **D.** All of the answers are correct. By issuing the `init (Run Level #)` command, you can switch between run levels and perform functions such as halting and rebooting the Solaris operating system. Additionally, you can shut down the system with this command:

   ```
   shutdown -i init-level -g grace-period -y
   ```

   where *init-level* is 0, 1, 2, 5, 6 or S (which is the default) and *grace-period* is the time (in seconds) before the system is shut down (the default is 60 seconds). For example, to shut down the system to run level S and therefore disable all logins, you would use this command: `shutdown -y`

6. ☑ **D.** To display the extended user login status for a particular user, issue the `logins - x -l user` command.

☒ **A** is incorrect because the `logins` command will display general information concerning all login accounts organized in ascending order by user ID. **B** is incorrect because the `logins user` command will display only general information about a particular user account. **C** is wrong because the `logins -p` command will display user accounts that currently do not have assigned passwords.

7. ☑ **E.** By issuing `init 6` you will stop the operating system and reboot.

☒ **A** is incorrect because `init S` is used to enter single-user state for administrative functions. **B** is wrong because `init 0` is used to enter firmware maintenance mode. **C** is wrong because `init 2` is used to enter multi-user state where NFS is not running. **D** is wrong because `init 5` is used to shut down the operating system altogether.

8. ☑ **A.** By issuing `init S` you will enter single-user mode.

☒ **B** is wrong because `init 0` is used to enter firmware maintenance mode. **C** is wrong because `init 2` is used to enter multi-user state where NFS is not running. **D** is wrong because `init 5` is used to shut down the operating system altogether. **E** is incorrect because by issuing `init 6` you will stop the operating system and reboot.

9. ☑ **F.** All of the answers are correct. Disabling user logins can be accomplished by creating a /etc/nologin file, bringing the system down to single-user mode (by issuing the `init S` or `shutdown` command with the default `init` state), and disabling user accounts individually with the Solaris Management Console (SMC) interface.

Configure syslog, Customize the System Logging Facility, and Monitor and Control Superuser

10. ☑ **A.** True. The su program usage, by default, is already monitored through the /etc/default/su file as `SULOG=/var/adm/sulog`, and the syslog logging facility will determine whether or not to log all su attempts with the `SYSLOG=YES` entry.

11. ☑ **B.** To detect and display superuser access attempts actively on the console in real time, uncomment the `CONSOLE=/dev/console` entry in the /etc/default/su file.

☒ **C** is wrong because by uncommenting the `CONSOLE=/dev/console` entry in the /etc/default/login file, you will disable remote superuser login access. The rest of the answers don't make sense.

12. ☑ **B.** The syslog daemon that controls the logging facilities is located in the */etc/init.d* directory as *syslog*.

☒ **A** and **E** are wrong because device-specific files are stored in the */etc* and */devices* directories, which are common targets for attackers to attempt to gain access to the operating system, especially for creating backdoors to the system. **C** is wrong because */usr/local* is an example of a typical download directory used to store files and programs by the current user. **D** is wrong because */usr/asset* is the working directory for ASET.

13. ☑ **B** and **C.** Capturing unsuccessful terminal session login attempts is accomplished by creating a *var/adm/loginlog* file. To monitor all failed login attempts, edit the */etc/default/login file* and make sure that the SYSLOG=YES and SYSLOG_FAILED_LOGINS=0 entries are uncommented.

☒ **A** is incorrect because by uncommenting the RETRIES entry in the */etc/default/login* file and editing the SYSLOG_FAILED_LOGINS=*some number* you'll force the system to close the login connection after some predefined number of unsuccessful login attempts.

LAB ANSWER

The first task that ABCD Inc. hired you to perform is to set up syslog to monitor all failed user login attempts. To do so:

1. Log in to the server with an account that has root privileges, or use the su command to become superuser.

2. Edit the */etc/default/login* file by uncommenting the SYSLOG=YES and SYSLOG_FAILED_ LOGINS=0 entries.

3. Create the log file in the */var/adm* directory with the visual editor (vi) or by issuing the touch /var/adm/authlog command.

4. Assign the appropriate read/write permissions for root to the log file with this command: chmod 600 /var/adm/authlog

5. Change the *authlog* file group membership to *sys* with the command chgrp sys /var/ adm/authlog

6. Edit the *syslog.conf* file to send all failed login attempts to the authlog file with this entry: auth.notice   /var/adm/authlog

7. Stop and start the syslog daemon by issuing these commands: /etc/init.d/syslog stop and /etc/init.d/syslog start. Be sure to test that the system is logging failed login attempts by unsuccessfully logging in to the system and then viewing the */var/adm/authlog* file contents.

The second task that the client requires of you is to monitor uses of the switch user (su) program. The su program usage, by default, is already monitored through the *letc/default/su* file as SULOG=/var/adm/sulog, and the syslog logging facility will determine whether or not to log all su attempts with the SYSLOG=YES entry. Therefore, you must ensure that the SYSLOG=YES entry is uncommented in the *letc/default/login* file. At that point, monitoring the output in the *sulog* file is accomplished by viewing the file with a command such as more /var/adm/sulog from the terminal.

The su logging in the *lvar/adm/sulog* file entries displays useful information, including the date and time that the command was executed, whether or not the su attempt was successful, the port from which the su program was executed, and the user name that ran the program as well as the user name to which the user switched. This file should be monitored on a regular basis to pinpoint potential malicious access attempts.

5

Solaris Auditing, Planning, and Management

Regularly scheduled audits of network defense should occur, especially with regard to safeguarding assets against techniques used by intruders and analyzing post intrusion. An effective security implementation comprises several life-cycle components, including security policies, perimeter defenses, and disaster recovery plans, to name a few. Event auditing can be a valuable tool for security forensics, real-time event monitoring, and tracing potential attackers. In this chapter, we'll talk about the components involved in Solaris auditing, steps to take to configure the components, and how to analyze the data in an audit trail.

Before we begin, it's important to note that Solaris auditing, especially with the new Solaris 10 kernel, is such a complex subsystem that an entire book would be necessary to cover all of its features and customizations. In this chapter, we'll cover only the material required by the exam.

Configure Solaris Auditing and Customize Audit Events

Although auditing is not proactive in and of itself, it can be used proactively to monitor events as they occur and detect unauthorized and malicious activity. Some of the more important events that generate audit records include the following:

- System boot and shutdown
- User and superuser login and logout
- Process, thread, and object creation, destruction, and manipulation
- Permission modifications
- Software installations
- System administration

What's more, a new feature in Solaris 10 allows you to use the syslog system logging facility (discussed in Chapter 4) to monitor audit records. Logs can be stored locally, on multiple partitions, on an NFS-mounted file server, on remote networks, and directly to remote systems (using UDP for remote logging). In this section, we'll look at steps to plan, configure, and customize Solaris auditing, including the use of syslog for storing audit records.

Solaris Auditing

Auditing alone cannot provide intrusion prevention; however, it can help you determine how a system was compromised and what steps to take to secure the system. You can use a logical approach to install and configure Solaris auditing, and this section covers that, beginning with the planning stage.

Audit Planning

Auditing can be an overwhelming task, with several components that may require some preparation. Sun Microsystems has published guidelines that highlight the issues related to auditing as preinstallation points to consider. These issues range from determining who and what to audit and where to store audit records, to what to do with the audit files after they are generated.

What to Audit   Auditing can be a daunting undertaking when monitoring a large group of users and systems, or even for a small group of very active systems. Deciding who and what to audit should be carefully planned to allow for available storage space—whether it be local or on a remote storage system. Therefore, it's important that you plan efficiently. After deciding which systems require auditing, be sure to plan for primary and secondary audit directories for each audited system, and determine where to place them. Then create a visual diagram containing each audit directory and map them to their respective systems to get an overall picture, as illustrated in Figure 5-1.

Under normal conditions, the audit files for a system are placed in the primary audit directory; the audit files for a system are placed in the secondary audit directory if the primary audit directory is full or not available. You can also configure

FIGURE 5-1

Mapping audited
systems to
preconfigured
audit directories

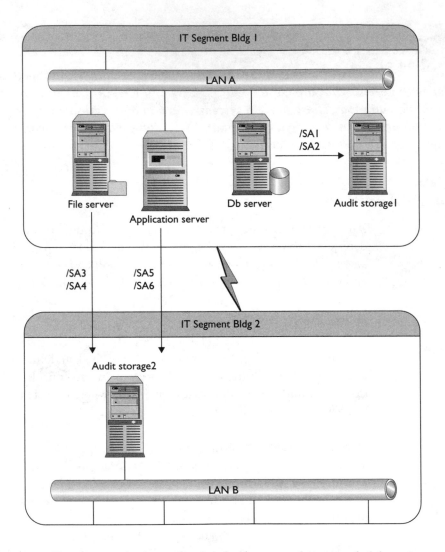

a *directory of last resort*, which is a local audit directory that is used if the primary and all secondary audit directories become unavailable. The directories are specified in the *audit_control* file, which we'll talk about later.

When planning for individual auditing selections, the audit classes and policies can be customized for each site. Depending on your current setup, before accessing the audit configuration files, you may have to assume the superuser or the Primary Administrator role and run the *bsmconv* script, located at */etc/security*, using the `./bsmconv` command. This script is used to enable the Basic Security Module (BSM), which provides additional security features defined as C2 in the Trusted Computer System Evaluation Criteria (TCSEC), and features that are not supplied in standard UNIX, such as the security auditing subsystem. However, Sun recommends first customizing your audit configuration before starting the audit service (be sure to run the script again to stop the audit service to customize the configuration files). All configuration files for auditing will be created as well in the */etc/security* folder. After running the script, you'll be prompted to restart the system (which you can do with the `init 6` command), and the following audit system and configuration files should be available:

```
# ls /etc/security
audit              audit_user       dev                lib
audit_class        audit_warn       device_allocate    policy.conf
audit_control      auth_attr        device_maps        priv_names
audit_event        bsmconv          device_policy      prof_attr
audit_record_attr  bsmunconv        exec_attr          spool
audit_startup      crypt.conf       extra_privs
```

ⓦatch *Many versions of the exam will ask you questions regarding how to preselect audit classes and customize audit procedures. Be sure to remember that you do so in the audit_control file.*

The *audit_control* file can be modified to preselect audit classes, and you can execute the `auditconfig -lspolicy` command to see the available policy options—the audit policy is established by the `auditconfig` command, which is automatically started in the *audit_startup* script. We'll talk more about customizing the auditing system in the "Audit Configuration" section later in this chapter.

Audit File Storage   After you determine where to store the primary and secondary audit directories and which audited systems will use them, you should determine the storage space alert threshold and establish a procedure to follow when audit directories run out of space. Since the degree of storage requirements depends on such variables as the number of users and systems as well as the levels of auditing and usage, no standard formula can be used to predetermine storage size requirements. However, you should determine the minimum free disk space available for audit files before warnings are sent, who should receive warnings, and what to do when an audit trail overflows.

First, you'll specify the location for audit data on a system. You need to modify the *letc/security/audit_control* file by adding the `dir` argument followed by the system primary, secondary, and optional last resort directory, one per line. It's important that you save a backup of the original file to avoid any potential corruption. For example, to specify the primary directory *lvar/audit/1/data*, the secondary directory *lvar/audit/2/ data*, and directory of last resort *lvar/audit*, you would add the following lines to the beginning of your *audit_control* file, in order:

```
# ident "@(#)audit_control.txt  1.4     00/07/17 SMI"
#
dir:/var/audit/1/data
dir:/var/audit/2/data
dir:/var/audit
```

Optionally, you can create partitions for audit files as required, especially if you add drives or have partitions on disks that are not currently mounted. See your device and file system administration guide for thorough instructions, or follow these simple steps:

1. Log in with an account that has root privileges, or use the `su` command to become superuser.

2. Create a partition using the `newfs` command as follows:

   ```
   newfs /dev/rdsk/name
   ```

   where *name* is the raw device name for the partition.

3. Create mount points for the partition using the `mkdir` command as follows:

   ```
   mkdir /var/audit/server-name.id-number
   ```

   where *server-name* is the name of the server and *id-number* is some unique number that will be used to identify the partition, which is useful if many audit partitions are in use.

4. Edit the *letc/vfstab* file by including an entry to mount the new partition automatically, such as the following:

```
/dev/dsk/name /dev/rdsk/name /var/audit/server-name.id-number   ufa   2    yes
```

   where *name* is the name of the partition, *server-name* is the name of the server, and *id-number* is the unique number that will be used to identify the partition.

5. Mount the new partition using the `mount` command:

   ```
   mount /var/audit/server-name.id-number
   ```

   where *server-name* is the name of the server and *id-number* is the unique partition identification number.

6. Create the audit directories on the new partition with the `mkdir` command:

   ```
   mkdir /var/audit/var/audit/server-name.id-number/audit-dir
   ```

   where *server-name* is the name of the server, *id-number* is the unique partition identification number, and *audit-dir* is the name of the new audit directory on the partition to which you wish to store audit files.

7. Modify the permissions on the mount point and new directory to allow for the auditing subsystem to store output:

   ```
   chmod - R 750 /var/audit/server-name.id-number/audit-dir
   ```

   where *server-name* is the name of the server, *id-number* is the unique partition identification number, and *audit-dir* is the name of the new audit directory.

After the partitions have been set, to set the minimum free disk space for an audit file before a warning is sent, you need to modify the */etc/security/audit_control* file by adding the `minfree` argument followed by a percentage. Again, it's important that you first save a backup of the original file before making changes. For example, to set the minimum free-space level for all audit file systems so that a warning is sent when 15 percent of the file system is available, edit the *audit_control* file and modify the line item `minfree:`*xx*, where *xx* is a percentage less than 100. The recommended percentage is 30%. When you are finished, be sure to save the changes before exiting the editor.

Next, we change the `minfree` argument/minimum free disk space to 15 percent, as shown in the following extract:

```
# ident "@(#)audit_control.txt  1.4    00/07/17 SMI"
#
dir:/var/audit/1/data
dir:/var/audit/2/data
dir:/var/audit
flags:
minfree:15
naflags:lo
```

A *warning alias* is the e-mail account that will receive warnings generated from the *audit_warn* script, such as when the minimum free space level is reached. You can set up a warning alias in two ways. The easiest method is to edit the *etc/security/ audit_warn* file by changing the e-mail alias in the script at entry ADDRESS=audit_ warn, like so:

```
#--------------------------------------------------------------------
send_msg() {
        MAILER=/usr/bin/mailx
        SED=/usr/bin/sed
        LOGCMD="$LOGGER -p daemon.alert"
        ADDRESS=audit_warn                 # standard alias for audit alerts
```

The second way is a little more complicated and requires that you redirect the *audit_warn* e-mail alias to the appropriate account. To do this, add the *audit_warn*

e-mail alias to the new alias file—in */etc/mail/ aliases* or the *mail_aliases* database in the name space—like so: audit_warn: alertadmin.

Finally, when audit files run out of free space altogether, you do have options regarding how the audit system should proceed. By default, the system will count audit records and continue to function despite the lack of free space, but audit records will not be recorded. However, if security is a higher priority than availability, you can configure the *audit_startup* file (which determines the audit policy) to halt the system when audit space is unavailable. To do so, simply disable the cnt policy (which allows the system to continue functioning) and enable the ahlt policy (which stops the system when audit partitions are full) with the following entries:

```
#!/bin/sh
/usr/bin/echo "Starting BSM services."
/usr/sbin/deallocate -Is
/usr/sbin/auditconfig -conf
/usr/sbin/auditconfig -aconf
/usr/sbin/auditconfig -setpolicy -cnt
/usr/sbin/auditconfig -setpolicy +ahlt
```

Note the minus (–) and plus (+) prior to policies that either disable or enable policies, respectively.

INSIDE THE EXAM

Manually Setting the Free Space Warning Threshold to 25 Percent

Following are the steps for manually changing the free space threshold before a warning is sent for all audit file systems:

1. Log in with an account that has root privileges, or use the su command to become superuser.

```
cp /etc/security/audit_control /etc/security/audit_control.bak
```

2. Save a backup copy of the original *audit_control* file, as shown:

3. Edit the *audit_control* file in your text editor by issuing this command:

```
vi /etc/security/audit_control
```

4. Modify the minfree entry (by pressing the I key on the keyboard

at the current percentage):

```
minfree:25
```

5. End insert mode by pressing the ESC key, and then save the file and exit the editor with the :wq command.

Optimal Auditing   Given the burden that auditing can impart on systems and available storage, you can ensure that you are auditing optimally in several ways. Sun recommends the following techniques for the most efficient auditing, while still adhering to security prioritizations:

- For large networks with limited storage capacity, try randomly auditing a percentage of users at one time.

- Perform routine audit file maintenance by reducing the disk-storage requirements by combining, removing, and compressing older log files. It's good practice to develop procedures for archiving the files, for transferring the files to removable media, and for storing the files offline.

- Monitor the audit data for unusual events in real time. Also set up procedures to monitor the audit trail for certain potentially malicious activities. Adhere to company policy and immediately execute mitigations with regard to substantiated malicious findings.

- Deploy a script to trigger an automatic increase in the auditing of certain users or certain systems in response to the detection of unusual or potentially malicious events.

w a t c h   *Remember that the most efficient audit methodology is accomplished by randomly auditing only a small percentage of users at any one time, compressing files, archiving older audit logs, monitoring in real time, and automatically increasing unusual event auditing.*

Audit Configuration

We've already covered some of the auditing preconfiguration and planning steps for Solaris, so let's continue in this section by choosing what classes of system events to audit, which user events to audit, and how to configure syslog audit logs.

Choosing What Classes of System Events to Audit   In the *audit_control* file, the `flags` and `naflags` arguments define which attributable and nonattributable events (the *na* preceding the second argument specifies nonattributable events) should be audited for the entire system—that is, all users on the system. Incidentally, you can specify events by using the `bsmrecord` command (see the bsmrecord man page for more information). Events can be added to the `flags` and `naflags` arguments separated by commas. Following is a sample extract:

```
# ident "@(#)audit_control.txt   1.4     00/07/17 SMI"
#
dir:/var/audit/1/data
dir:/var/audit/2/data
dir:/var/audit
flags:lo
minfree:25
naflags:lo,na
```

In this extract, the attributable `lo` class events and nonattributable `lo` and `na` class events will be audited for all users on the system.

On the other hand, to configure the auditing subsystem not to audit the system—say, for example, if you wish to audit only specific users (explained in the next section)—simply leave out the class selections after the `flags` and `naflags` arguments, as shown next:

w a t c h   *For the exam, remember that the `flags` and `naflags` arguments define which events should be audited for all users on the system. The arguments are defined in the audit_control file.*

```
# ident "@(#)audit_control.txt  1.4    00/07/17 SMI"
#
dir:/var/audit/1/data
dir:/var/audit/2/data
dir:/var/audit
flags:
minfree:25
naflags:
```

With regard to classes of events, *audit_event* is the event database that can be read to determine which events are part of classes you can audit. The event numbers include the following, with the exception of 0, which is reserved as an invalid event number:

- 1–2047   Solaris Kernel events
- 2048–32767   Solaris TCB programs (6144–32767 also used for SunOS 5.X user level audit events)
- 32768–65535   Third-party TCB applications

You can use the `more audit_event` command to view the entire database. The database file format is as follows: *event number:event name:event description:event classes*.

Make sure you understand the importance of the audit_event *file, and know which event numbers are reserved for which events. Event number 0 is reserved as an invalid event number; 1–2047 for Solaris Kernel events, 2048–32767 for Solaris programs (6144–32767 also includes SunOS 5.X user-level audit events), and 32768–65535 for third-party applications.*

Therefore, to audit events associated with user telnet sessions you would include the lo class, which is specified in the database as event number 6154, as shown here:

```
6154:AUE_telnet:login - telnet:lo
```

Choosing Specific Users and Events to Audit   The *audit_user* file is the user database that can be modified to include individual user-specified events as part of classes that should be audited. To add users to the user database—say, for example, if you disabled auditing for the entire system including all users (as explained in the previous section) and wish to audit specific users only—simply add the entries to the *audit_user* file in the following format: *username:always-audit:never-audit*; where *username* is the name of the user to be audited, *always-audit* is the list of classes of events that should be always audited, and *never-audit* is the list of classes of events that should never be audited. Keep in mind that adding user-specific classes in the *audit_user* file can also be included along with the auditing of the entire system if you wish to modify the system audit configuration to add or remove some classes for specific users.

On the other hand, as noted in the previous section, you can configure the auditing subsystem not to audit the system and audit only specific users by leaving out the class selections after the `flags` and `naflags` arguments in the *audit_control* file and adding users and classes to the *audit_user* file, as shown next.

For *audit_control* file configuration:

```
# ident "@(#)audit_control.txt  1.4     00/07/17 SMI"
#
dir:/var/audit/1/data
dir:/var/audit/2/data
dir:/var/audit
flags:
minfree:25
naflags:
```

INSIDE THE EXAM

Manually Selecting Users and Classes of Events to Audit

Following are steps for manually selecting users and classes of events to audit:

1. Log in with an account that has root privileges, or use the `su` command to become superuser.

```
cp /etc/security/audit_user /etc/security/audit_user.bak
```

2. Save a backup copy of the original *audit_user* file, as shown:

3. Edit the *audit_user* file in your text editor:

```
vi /etc/security/audit_user
```

4. Add user entries, one per line, in the following format: *username:classes-to-audit:classes-not-to-audit*. Separate multiple classes with commas. As a reference, the *audit_event* file defines which events are part of classes you can audit. You can use the `more /etc/security/audit_event` command in a terminal session to view the entire database.

5. End insert mode by pressing the ESC key, and then save the file and exit the editor with the `:wq` command.

For *audit_user* file configuration:

```
# ident "@(#)audit_user.txt      1.6      00/07/17 SMI"
#
root:lo:no
b_friedman:lo
j_public:lo,pf
```

Configuring Syslog Audit Logs   The auditing subsystem supports the collection of binary data, which is indicated in the previous sections, as well as binary data

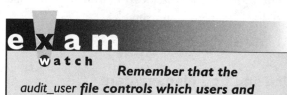

Remember that the *audit_user* file controls which users and event classes are to be audited.

and a subset of the binary as text audit data. The binary and text audit data collection combination can be accomplished with the syslog auditing plug-in. The binary collection of audit data is enabled by default; therefore, to add the syslog feature, you'll need to specify the plug-in in the *audit_control* file. A plug-in is configured using the following:

```
plugin:name=audit_syslog.so.1; p_flags=classes
```

where `classes` defines a subset of the audit classes of events that are indicated in the `flags` and `naflags` entries in the *audit_control* file (as explained in previous sections). Currently there is only one plugin available. Use the `more audit_event` command to view the entire database of classes to audit.

Following is a sample extract that includes the syslog plug-in:

```
# ident "@(#)audit_control.txt  1.4     00/07/17 SMI"
#
dir:/var/audit/1/data
dir:/var/audit/2/data
dir:/var/audit
flags:lo
minfree:25
naflags:lo,na
plugin:name=audit_syslog.so.1; p_flags=-lo,-na
```

In this configuration extract, the `flags` and `naflags` attributes direct the auditing subsystem to audit all login, logout, and nonattributable events in the default binary format (as classes `lo` and `na` defined in the *audit_event* database). However, the *plugin* entry takes auditing a step further by instructing syslog also to collect login and nonattributable event failures indicated with the p_flags classes -lo and -na.

The syslog text logs can generate massive log files, so be sure to monitor and archive them regularly. In addition, you should never store syslog audit files in the same location as binary data. Therefore, the next step is to edit the *etc/syslog.conf* file by adding an audit.notice entry followed by the location in which to place syslog files. Here's an example:

```
audit.notice          /var/audit/slogs
```

Enabling the Auditing Service and Log Management

After you plan for and customize your auditing solution, you must enable the auditing service. In this section, we'll look at the simple steps involved in enabling the service as well as disabling the service for times when auditing is not required or for offline forensics. In addition, we'll talk about how to update the service in case you make changes to the configuration files. Finally, we'll discuss ways to manage audit records by monitoring and displaying them and merging audit files into a single grouping, which is useful for analyzing a complete audit trail.

Enabling and Disabling the Auditing Service As mentioned, before accessing some of the audit configuration files, you may have to assume superuser or the Primary Administrator role and run the *bsmconv* script located in */etc/security* with the ./bsmconv command. This script is used to enable the Basic Security Module (BSM), which starts the auditing subsystem. All configuration files for auditing will be created as well in the */etc/security* folder. To enable the auditing service, follow these simple steps:

1. Log in with an account that has root privileges, or use the su command to become superuser.

2. Bring down the system to single-user mode using the init 1 command.

3. In the */etc/security* directory, run the *bsmconv* script to enable the auditing service, like so: ./bsmconv

4. Bring the system into multi-user mode using the init 6 command.

For the exam, remember that the *bsmconv* **script should be used to toggle the auditing service. The auditing configuration files are stored in the** */etc/ security* **folder.**

If the auditing service is not required—for example, to make configuration modifications before auditing a production environment or for offline forensics—you can disable the service by following the same steps you took to enable the service. That is, become superuser, bring the system down to single-user state, run the *bsmconv* script again—this time to disable the service—and then bring the system back into multi-user state.

Updating the Auditing Service After you start the auditing service in a production environment, you may find that you need to tweak the configuration to audit more classes or perhaps audit specific users more closely. After making changes, you'll need to update the auditing service. This simply restarts the auditd daemon, which in effect will apply the new configuration changes to the service. To do this, Sun recommends using the following steps:

1. Log in with an account that has root privileges, or use the su command to become superuser. Additionally, you can assume a role that includes the Audit Control.

2. Refresh the kernel with the audit -s command.

3. Refresh the auditing service with the auditconfig -conf command.

4. If users were added to the audit list, ensure that each user is being audited with the auditconfig -setmask *user-id classes* command; where *user-id* is the user's ID and *classes* are the preselected audit classes of events mentioned throughout this chapter.

Whenever you make changes to or update the auditing service you need to issue the audit -s **command. This renews the kernel, and the** auditconfig -conf **command, which refreshes the auditing service in order for your changes to apply properly.**

CERTIFICATION OBJECTIVE 5.02

Generate an Audit Trail and Analyze the Audit Data

After you preconfigure and start the auditing subsystem, you'll need to analyze log files regularly—whether you need to view audit records of a system program (that is, log in), an entire class of events (that is, `lo`), or create a complete audit trail. The topic of managing log files could literally take up an entire chapter; therefore, we'll address only some of the specifics required by the examination.

We'll start with the `bsmrecord` command and use it to create a particular record format as well as display formats of all audit records of a program and class. To display all audit record formats, you can issue the `bsmrecord -a` command. For convenience, you can also parse all record formats into an HTML file that you can open with any web browser for simple traversal. To do so, simply add the `-h` option followed by a filename, like so: `bsmrecord -a -h > audit.formats.html`. Finally, to display audit record formats of a particular program or class, use the `-p` *program* and `-c` *class* options, respectively, where *program* is the name of the program and *class* is the name of the class. For example, to display all audit record formats of the *login* program, issue the `bsmrecord -p login` command. On the other hand, to display all audit record formats of the `lo` class of events, you would execute the `bsmrecord -c lo` command.

e x a m

w a t c h

For the exam, remember that the bsmrecord command should be used to display record formats of a program and class. For example, issue the bsmrecord -a command to display all records.

Binary audit files can be merged to create an audit trail. This is especially useful during incident response or when tracing a suspected intruder. The `auditreduce` command is used to merge the files into a single output source, thus creating an audit trail. To do this, follow these steps:

1. Log in with an account that has root privileges, or use the `su` command to become superuser. Additionally, you can assume a role that includes the Audit Review profile.

2. Create an audit trail directory with limited access permissions:

```
mkdir audit-trail-1
chmod 700 audit-trail-1
```

3. From the audit trail directory, merge binary audit records into a single audit trail output source using `auditreduce -Uoption -O suffix`, where `Uoption` can be one of the following:

   ■ An uppercase `A` to select all files

   ■ `C` to select only complete files

   ■ `M` to select only files with a particular suffix

   ■ `O` to create the audit file with the suffix specified as *suffix* in the current directory (includes timestamp for start and end time)

Here's an example: `auditreduce -A -O all-files`

The `auditreduce` command also accepts lowercase filtering options in the following format: *auditreduce –loption argument optional-file*.

■ *optional-file* is the name of an audit file

■ *argument* is an attribute that an *loption* would require (that is, an audit class if specifying the `-c` option)

■ *loption* is a lowercase `d` to select all events on a specific date (*argument* must be in yyyymmdd format), `u` to select all events pertaining to a particular user (*argument* is the user name), `c` to select all events with regard to a specific class (*argument* is the class), and `m` to select the instances of an event (*argument* is the event).

exam
Watch

For the exam, you should know that to create an audit trail, the **auditreduce** *command is used to merge audit files into a single output source that you can specify.*

The `praudit` command is used to view binary audit files. What's more, for your convenience it can be combined with the `auditreduce` command, separated by the pipe character (|). The `praudit` command accepts the following options:

■ `-1` to display records one-per-line

■ `-s` to display records in short format (one token per line)

■ `-r` to display records in their raw format (one token per line)

■ `-x` to display records in XML format (one token per line)

For example, we could issue the following command to view a specific audit file:

`praudit audit-file | more`

where `audit-file` is the name of the file.

We could also issue the following command to display all `lo` class audit records in short format:

```
auditreduce -c lo | praudit -s
```

For more information on the complete usage of `bsmrecord`, `auditreduce`, and `praudit`, be sure to read their man pages.

TWO-MINUTE DRILL

Here are some of the key points from the certification objectives in Chapter 5.

Configure Solaris Auditing and Customize Audit Events

❑ Events that are capable of creating audit logs include system startup and shutdown, login and logout, identification and authentication, privileged rights usage, permission changes, process and thread creation and destruction, object creation and manipulation, application installation, and system administration.

❑ The *audit_control* file can be modified to preselect audit classes and customize audit procedures.

❑ The audit policy is automatically started in the *audit_startup* script.

❑ The *audit_warn* script generates e-mail to an alias called *audit_warn*. You can change the alias by editing the *etc/security/audit_warn* file and changing the e-mail alias in the script at entry ADDRESS=audit_warn, or by redirecting the *audit_warn* e-mail alias to a different account.

❑ When auditing is enabled, the contents of the *etc/security/audit_startup* file determine the audit policy.

❑ To audit efficiently, Sun recommends randomly auditing only a small percentage of users at any one time, compressing files, archiving older audit logs, monitoring in real time, and automatically increasing unusual event auditing.

❑ In the *audit_control* file, the flags and naflags arguments define which attributable and nonattributable events should be audited for all users on the system.

❑ You can manually issue the bsmrecord command to add events that should be audited.

❑ The *audit_event* file is the event database that defines which events are part of classes you can audit.

❑ The audit event numbers—with the exception of 0, which is reserved as an invalid event number—are 1–2047 for Solaris Kernel events, 2048–32767 for Solaris programs (6144–32767 also includes SunOS 5.X user-level audit events), and 32768–65535 for third-party applications.

❏ The *audit_user* file defines specific users and classes of events that should always or never be audited for each user.

❏ Syslog audit files should never be placed in the same locations as binary data.

❏ Syslog files should be monitored and archived regularly to accommodate potentially extensive outputs.

Generate an Audit Trail and Analyze the Audit Data

❏ Execute the *bsmconv* script to enable and disable the auditing service.

❏ Issue the `audit -s` command to refresh the kernel, and use the `auditconfig -conf` command to refresh the auditing service.

❏ To display audit records formats, use the `bsmrecord` command.

❏ To merge audit files into a single output source to create an audit trail, use the `auditreduce` command.

SELF TEST

The following questions will help you measure your understanding of the material presented in this chapter. Read all the choices carefully, because there might be more than one correct answer. Choose all correct answers for each question. Some questions are fill-in-the-blank and short-answer questions to ensure you have a good understanding of the material.

Configure Solaris Auditing and Customize Audit Events

1. Which configuration file specifies the primary and secondary audit directories?
   A. *audit_control*
   B. *audit_startup*
   C. *audit_warn*
   D. *audit_user*
   E. All of the above

2. How would you manually set the minimum free disk space for an audit file before a warning is sent?

3. When auditing is enabled, the contents of the *etc/security/audit_startup* file determine the _____.

4. In the *audit_control* file, which arguments define what attributable and nonattributable events should be audited for the entire system?
   A. `flags`
   B. `minfree`
   C. `dir:`
   D. `naflags`
   E. All of the above

5. You can specify events that should be audited by using the `bsmrecord` command.
   A. True
   B. False

6. Which configuration file specifies classes of events that should always or never be audited for each user?
   A. *audit_control*
   B. *audit_startup*
   C. *audit_warn*
   D. *audit_user*
   E. All of the above

7. Which of the following are events that are capable of creating audit logs?
   A. Privileged rights usage
   B. Object creation and destruction
   C. Permission changes
   D. Process creation and destruction
   E. Thread creation and destruction
   F. All of the above

8. Which of these techniques can be implemented for the most efficient auditing while still adhering to security prioritizations?
   A. Auditing only a small percentage of users at any one time
   B. Compressing files
   C. Archiving older audit logs
   D. Monitoring in real time
   E. Automatically increasing unusual event auditing
   F. All of the above

9. With regard to the Solaris auditing subsystem, what is the directory of last resort?

10. With regard to classes of events, the *audit_event* file is the event database that can be read to find out which events are part of classes you can audit. Which event numbers are available for third-party TCB applications?
    A. 1–2047
    B. 2048–32767
    C. 6144–32767
    D. 32768–65535
    E. All of the above

11. Which of these techniques can be used to set up a warning alias, which is the e-mail account that will receive warnings generated from the *audit_warn* script, such as when the minimum free-space level is reached?
    A. Redirecting the *audit_warn* e-mail alias to the appropriate account
    B. Edit the *etc/security/audit_warn* file by changing the e-mail alias in the script at entry `ADDRESS=audit_warn`
    C. Edit the *audit_control* file in your text editor and modify the `minfree` entry by specifying the *audit_warn* e-mail alias
    D. All of the above

12. With regard to classes of events, the *audit_event* file is the event database that can be read to find out which events are part of classes you can audit. Which event numbers are reserved for the Solaris kernel events?

A. 1–2047

B. 2048–32767

C. 6144–32767

D. 32768–65535

E. All of the above

13. Syslog audit files should be placed in the same locations as binary data.

A. True

B. False

14. Which of the following can be executed to refresh the auditing service?

A. `audit -s`

B. `auditconfig -conf`

C. `bsmconv`

D. `bsmrecord`

E. `auditreduce`

F. All of the above

15. Which of the following can be executed to disable the auditing service?

A. `audit -s`

B. `auditconfig -conf`

C. `bsmconv`

D. `bsmrecord`

E. `auditreduce`

F. All of the above

Generate an Audit Trail and Analyze the Audit Data

16. Which of the following can be used to display audit record formats?

A. `audit -s`

B. `auditconfig -conf`

C. `bsmconv`

D. `bsmrecord`

E. `auditreduce`

F. All of the above

17. Which of the following can be used to merge audit files into a single output source to create an audit trail?

A. `audit -s`

B. `auditconfig -conf`

C. `bsmconv`

D. `bsmrecord`

E. `auditreduce`

F. All of the above

LAB QUESTION

ABCD Inc. hired you to make the following Solaris auditing subsystem configurations:

- Preselect audit classes. In this case, the attributable `lo` class events and nonattributable `lo` class events should be audited for all users on the system.

- Specify the primary and secondary audit directories as well as the directory of last resort. The primary directory should be */var/audit/sysp/data*, the secondary directory should be */var/audit/syss/data*, and the directory of last resort should be */var/audit*.

- Set the minimum free disk space for an audit file to 30 percent before a warning is sent.

- Configure syslog audit logs for classes `lo` and `na`.

- Enable the auditing service.

- After a few days of baseline auditing, merge audit files into a single output source (`all-files`) to create a sample audit trail in an *audit-trail-sample* directory.

What steps would you perform to provide the requested services?

SELF TEST ANSWERS

Configure Solaris Auditing and Customize Audit Events

1. ☑ **A.** The primary and secondary audit directories are specified in the *audit_control* file.
   ☒ **B** is wrong because the audit policy is established by the `auditconfig` command, which is automatically started in the *audit_startup* script. **C** is incorrect because the *audit_warn* script generates e-mail to an e-mail alias called *audit_warn*. **D** is wrong because the *audit_user* file defines specific users and classes of events that should always or never be audited for each user.

2. ☑ To set the minimum free disk space for an audit file before a warning is sent, you need to modify the */etc/security/audit_control* file by adding the `minfree` argument followed by a percentage. It's important first to save a backup of the original file before making changes. For example, to set the minimum free space level for all audit file systems so that a warning is sent when 15 percent of the file system is available, edit the *audit_control* file and modify the line item `minfree:xx`, where *xx* is a percentage less than 100.

3. ☑ When auditing is enabled, the contents of the *etc/security/audit_startup* file determine the audit policy. Audit policy determines the characteristics of the audit records. When auditing is enabled, the contents of the *etc/security/audit_startup* file determine the audit policy.

4. ☑ **A and D.** In the *audit_control* file, the `flags` and `naflags` arguments define which attributable and nonattributable events (the *na* preceding the second `flags` argument specifies nonattributable events) should be audited for the entire system—that is, all users on the system.
   ☒ **B** is wrong because the `minfree` argument is used to set the free space warning threshold, and **C** is incorrect because the `dir:` attribute is used to specify primary and secondary audit directories.

5. ☑ **A.** True. In the *audit_control* file, the `flags` and `naflags` arguments define which attributable and nonattributable events (the *na* preceding the second `flags` argument specifies nonattributable events) should be audited for the entire system—that is, all users on the system. Incidentally, you can specify events by using the `bsmrecord` command.

6. ☑ **D.** The *audit_user* file defines specific users and classes of events that should always or never be audited for each user.
   ☒ **A** is wrong because general configuration specifications such as the primary and secondary audit directories are specified in the *audit_control* file. **B** is wrong because the audit policy is established by the `auditconfig` command, which is automatically started in the *audit_startup* script. **C** is incorrect because the *audit_warn* script generates mail to an e-mail alias called *audit_warn*.

7. ☑ **F.** All of the answers are correct. Events that are capable of creating audit logs include system startup and shutdown, login and logout, identification and authentication, privileged rights usage, permission changes, process and thread creation and destruction, object creation and manipulation, application installation, and system administration.

8. ☑ **F.** All of the answers are correct. Sun recommends the following techniques for the most efficient auditing while still adhering to security prioritizations: For large networks with limited storage capacity, try randomly auditing a percentage of users at any one time. Perform routine audit file maintenance by reducing the disk-storage requirements by combining, removing, and compressing older log files. It's good practice to develop procedures for archiving the files, for transferring the files to removable media, and for storing the files offline. Monitor the audit data for unusual events in real time. Also set up procedures to monitor the audit trail for certain potentially malicious activities. Adhere to company policy and immediately execute mitigations with regard to substantiated malicious findings. Deploy a script to trigger an automatic increase in the auditing of certain users or certain systems in response to the detection of unusual or potentially malicious events.

9. ☑ A directory of last resort is a local audit directory that is used if the primary and all secondary audit directories become unavailable.

10. ☑ **D.** The event numbers available for third-party TCP applications are 32768–65535.
☒ **A** is wrong because 1–2047 is reserved for the Solaris kernel events. **B** is wrong because 2048–32767 is reserved for the Solaris TCB programs. **C** is wrong because 6144–32767 is used for SunOS 5.X user-level audit events.

11. ☑ **A** and **B.** Setting up a warning alias can be accomplished in two ways. The easiest method is to edit the *etc/security/audit_warn* file by changing the e-mail alias in the script at entry ADDRESS=audit_warn, like so:

```
#-------------------------------------------------------------------------
send_msg() {
        MAILER=/usr/bin/mailx
        SED=/usr/bin/sed
        LOGCMD="$LOGGER -p daemon.alert"
        ADDRESS=audit_warn                      # standard alias for audit alerts
```

The second way is a little more complicated and requires redirecting the *audit_warn* e-mail alias to the appropriate account. To do so, add the *audit_warn* e-mail alias to the new alias file—in */etc/mail/aliases* or the *mail_aliases* database in the name space—such as audit_warn: alertadmin.
☒ **C** is wrong because that procedure is used to set the free-space warning threshold manually.

12. ☑ **A.** The event numbers 1–2047 are reserved for the Solaris Kernel events.
    ☒ **B** is incorrect because 2048–32767 is reserved for the Solaris TCB programs. **C** is incorrect because 6144–32767 is used for SunOS 5.X user-level audit events. **D** is incorrect because 32768–65535 is available for third-party TCB applications.

13. ☑ **B.** False. The syslog text logs can generate massive log files, so be sure to monitor and archive them regularly. In addition, you should never store syslog audit files in the same location as binary data.

14. ☑ **B.** After you start the auditing service in a production environment, at times you may need to tweak the configuration to audit more classes or perhaps audit specific users more closely. After making changes, you'll need to update the auditing service. This simply restarts the auditd daemon, which in effect will apply the new configuration changes to the service. To refresh the auditing service, issue the `auditconfig -conf` command.
    ☒ **A** is wrong because that command is used to refresh the kernel. **C** is wrong because you would run the *bsmconv* script to enable and disable the auditing service. **D** is wrong because the `bsmrecord` command can be used to display record formats. **E** is wrong because the `auditreduce` command can be used to merge audit files into a single output source to create an audit trail.

15. ☑ **C.** Run the *bsmconv* script to enable and disable the auditing service.
    ☒ **A** is wrong because that command is used to refresh the kernel. **B** is wrong because that command is used to refresh the auditing service. **D** is wrong because the `bsmrecord` command can be used to display record formats. **E** is wrong because the `auditreduce` command can be used to merge audit files into a single output source to create an audit trail.

Generate an Audit Trail and Analyze the Audit Data

16. ☑ **D.** The `bsmrecord` command can be used to display audit record formats.
    ☒ **A** is wrong because that command is used to refresh the kernel. **B** is wrong because that command is used to refresh the auditing service. **C** is wrong because you would run the *bsmconv* script to enable and disable the auditing service. **E** is wrong because the `auditreduce` command can be used to merge audit files into a single output source to create an audit trail.

17. ☑ **E.** The `auditreduce` command can be used to merge audit files into a single output source to create an audit trail.
    ☒ **A** is wrong because that command is used to refresh the kernel. **B** is wrong because that command is used to refresh the auditing service. **C** is wrong because you would run the *bsmconv* script to enable and disable the auditing service. **D** is wrong because the `bsmrecord` command can be used to display record formats.

LAB ANSWER

Assuming everything is in order and you have the appropriate privileges, the first task that ABCD Inc. hired you to perform is to preselect audit classes—the attributable `lo` class events and nonattributable `lo` class events—to be audited for all users on the system. In the *audit_control* file, the `flags` and `naflags` arguments define which attributable and nonattributable events should be audited. After making a backup of the original file, the following modifications should be made:

```
flags:lo
naflags:lo
```

The next task involves specifying the primary and secondary audit directories as well as the directory of last resort. The primary directory should be */var/audit/sysp/data*, the secondary directory should be */var/audit/syss/data*, and the directory of last resort should be */var/audit*. To do this, you need to modify the */etc/security/audit_control* file again by adding the `dir` argument followed by the system primary, secondary, and optional last resort directory, one per line:

```
dir:/var/audit/sysp/data
dir:/var/audit/syss/data
dir:/var/audit
```

The third required task is to set the minimum free disk space for an audit file to 30 percent before a warning is sent. To do so, you need to modify the */etc/security/audit_control* file by adding the `minfree` argument followed by a percentage:

```
minfree:30
```

The fourth task is to configure syslog audit logs for classes `lo` and `na`. The binary and text audit data collection combination is accomplished with the syslog auditing plug-in, which is specified in the *audit_control* file. The plug-in is configured with the following format:

```
plugin:name=audit_syslog.so.1; p_flags=classes
```

where `classes` defines a subset of the audit classes of events that are indicated in the `flags` and `naflags` entries in the *audit_control* file. Following is an extract that includes the syslog plug-in:

```
plugin:name=audit_syslog.so.1; p_flags=-lo,-na
```

In this configuration extract, the `flags` and `naflags` attributes direct the auditing susbsystem to audit all login, logout, and nonattributable events in the default binary format (as classes `lo` and `na` defined in the *audit_event* database). However, the `plugin` entry takes auditing a step further by instructing syslog to collect login and nonattributable event failures indicated with the `p_flags` classes `-lo` and `-na`.

Now that you've preconfigured the auditing subsystem and saved the configuration as well as valid backups, as per the customer's requirements, the next step is to enable the service. To do so, bring down the system to single-user mode using the `init 1` command. Next, in the *letc/security* directory, run the *bsmconv* script to enable the auditing service, like so: `./bsmconv`. Then bring the system back into multi-user mode using the `init 6` command.

Finally, after a few days of baseline auditing, the customer has requested that you merge audit files into a single output source to create a sample audit trail in an *audit-trail-sample* directory. To do so, assume the appropriate privileges on the system and create the audit trail directory with limited access permissions:

```
mkdir audit-trail-sample
chmod 700 audit-trail-sample
```

From within the audit trail directory, merge binary audit records into a single audit trail output source using the `auditreduce -A -O all-files` command.

6

Device, System, and File Security

By maintaining physical security and controlling access to device and machine resources, we can prevent unintentional misuse and malicious usage of the Solaris operating system. This chapter takes us further into the realm of system security and management by controlling access to devices using device policy and allocation and checking the integrity of files using the Basic Audit Reporting Tool (BART). Another mechanism is used to control access to files by protecting files with access control lists (ACLs), but this will be covered in detail in Chapter 10.

CERTIFICATION OBJECTIVE 6.01

Control Access to Devices by Configuring and Managing Device Policy and Device Allocation

Controlling access devices on a Solaris operating system is accomplished by two mechanisms: *device policy* and *device allocation*. In essence, device policy is a default kernel-level mechanism that restricts and prevents access to devices that are integral to the system by mandating that processes that open such a device—for example, a network interface—require certain privileges, such as reading and writing. Device allocation, which is not enabled by default, is enforced during user allocation to require user authorization in order to access a peripheral device such as a CD-ROM or printer.

This section contains discussions on using both device policy and device allocation to mitigate security risks associated with peripheral devices and devices integral to the system. Since some devices are integral to the system, they can pose serious security consequences if accessed inappropriately.

<table>
<tr><td>

e x a m

ⓦ **a t c h** *For the exam, you should remember that device policy is enabled by default and enforced in the kernel to restrict and prevent access to devices that are integral to the system. Device allocation is not enabled by default and is enforced during user allocation time to require user authorization to access peripheral devices.*

</td></tr>
</table>

Device Policy

The Solaris kernel enforces device policy to restrict or completely prevent access to devices that are integral to the system. We'll discuss several tasks that comply with the exam requirements with regard to configuring device policy. These tasks include listing device policies, adding and modifying device policies, removing device policies, and auditing device policies.

Listing Device Policies

Viewing the device policies for all devices or for a particular device that is integral to the system is easy using the `getdevpolicy` command. For example, to view the device policy for all integral devices on the system, issue the `getdevpolicy | more` command. Following is the typical output from a standard Solaris installation:

```
# getdevpolicy | more
DEFAULT
        read_priv_set=none
        write_priv_set=none
ip:*
        read_priv_set=net_rawaccess
        write_priv_set=net_rawaccess
icmp:*
        read_priv_set=net_icmpaccess
        write_priv_set=net_icmpaccess
hme:*
        read_priv_set=net_rawaccess
        write_priv_set=net_rawaccess
eri:*
        read_priv_set=net_rawaccess
        write_priv_set=net_rawaccess
sad:admin
        read_priv_set=sys_config
        write_priv_set=sys_config
mm:allkmem
        read_priv_set=all
        write_priv_set=all
mm:kmem
        read_priv_set=none
        write_priv_set=all
mm:mem
        read_priv_set=none
        write_priv_set=all
ce:*
        read_priv_set=net_rawaccess
        write_priv_set=net_rawaccess
fssnap:ctl
        read_priv_set=sys_config
        write_priv_set=sys_config
```

```
ge:*
        read_priv_set=net_rawaccess
        write_priv_set=net_rawaccess
qfe:*
        read_priv_set=net_rawaccess
        write_priv_set=net_rawaccess
md:admin
        read_priv_set=none
        write_priv_set=sys_config
envctrltwo:*
        read_priv_set=sys_config
        write_priv_set=sys_config
keysock:*
        read_priv_set=sys_net_config
        write_priv_set=sys_net_config
ipsecah:*
        read_priv_set=sys_net_config
        write_priv_set=sys_net_config
ipsecesp:*
        read_priv_set=sys_net_config
        write_priv_set=sys_net_config
ip6:*
        read_priv_set=net_rawaccess
        write_priv_set=net_rawaccess
icmp6:*
        read_priv_set=net_icmpaccess
        write_priv_set=net_icmpaccess
random:*
        read_priv_set=none
        write_priv_set=sys_devices
spdsock:*
        read_priv_set=sys_net_config
        write_priv_set=sys_net_config
bge:*
        read_priv_set=net_rawaccess
        write_priv_set=net_rawaccess
dmfe:*
        read_priv_set=net_rawaccess
        write_priv_set=net_rawaccess
```

Using the same command, but following a specific device or devices (separated by spaces), the system will list the device policy for each of them in procession, as shown next:

```
# getdevpolicy /dev/hme /dev/mem
/dev/hme
        read_priv_set=net_rawaccess
        write_priv_set=net_rawaccess
/dev/mem
        read_priv_set=none
        write_priv_set=all
```

<table>
<tr><td>e x a m
ⓦ a t c h</td><td>**Remember for the exam that the** `getdevpolicy` **command is used to view device policy for all integral devices on the system. Also know that device policy restricts and prevents access to devices.**</td></tr>
</table>

Adding and Modifying Device Policies

Device policy is enabled by default, and therefore, it contains a default configuration. When attempting to adhere to company policy or to deal with other specific cases, you may find that you need to modify an existing device policy. Doing so can be accomplished in two steps:

1. Log in with an account that has root or Device Security privileges, or use the su command to become superuser.

2. Issue the update_drv -a -p *policy device-driver* command; where *policy* is the device policy or policies (separated by a space) for *device-driver*, which is the device driver whose device policy you wish to modify.

If you need to add a new device driver to the system altogether, you can issue this command:

```
add_drv -b basedir -c class_name -i identify_name -m permission
-n -f -v device_driver
```

where

- ■ -b *basedir* installs the driver on the system with a root directory of *basedir*
- ■ -c *class_name* refers to the driver being added to the system to export the class *class_name*
- ■ -i *identify_name* is a white space–separated list of aliases for the driver *device_driver*

- -m *permission* specifies the file system permissions for device nodes created by the system on behalf of *device_driver*
- -n means to not try to load and attach *device_driver* but instead just modify the system configuration files for the *device_driver*
- -f forces add_drv to add the driver even if a reconfiguration boot is required
- -v causes add_drv to provide additional information regarding the success or failure of a driver's configuration into the system
- *device_driver* is the new device driver being added

Removing Device Policies   To remove a device policy for a specific device, you simply modify the device policy by specifying only the policy you wish to enable. For example, if you need to remove the read set of privileges from the ipnat device, you would assume the appropriate user privileges and issue this command:

```
update_drv -a -p write_priv_set=net_rawaccess ipnat
```

In this example, the read set of privileges would be removed from the ipnat device policy.

Additionally, you can issue the rem_drv *device_driver* command to remove a device or device driver. You should also always confirm any changes you make to device policies by issuing the getdevpolicy /dev/ipnat command.

e x a m

w a t c h   *For the exam, you'll need to know the command to modify or remove device policies for a specific device. As indicated in the text, you should use the* update_drv -a -p policy device-driver *command; where* policy *is the device policy or policies (separated by a space) for* device-driver, *which is the device driver whose device policy you wish to modify or remove.*

Auditing Device Policies

The Solaris auditing subsystem can be used to audit changes in device policy. The audit event AUE_MODDEVPLCY is included in the as audit class, which can be used to audit device policies. (See Chapter 5 for details on how to configure and manage the auditing subsystem.)

To audit device policies, you'll need to add the *as* class to the *audit_control* file flags argument. This defines which attributable events should be audited for the entire system, and it includes all users on the system. Events can be added to the flags argument separated by commas. Following is a sample extract:

```
# ident "@(#)audit_control.txt  1.4     00/07/17 SMI"
#
dir:/var/audit/1/data
dir:/var/audit/2/data
dir:/var/audit
flags:lo,as
minfree:25
naflags:lo,na
```

ⓦatch ***To audit device policies you'll need to add the as class to the*** *audit_control* ***file*** `flags` ***argument which defines auditing attributes for the entire system and all of the system's users.***

In this extract, the attributable `lo` and `as` class events will be audited for all users on the system. On the other hand, to configure the auditing subsystem not to audit the class that includes the device policy audit event (the `as` class), simply edit out the class selection and save the file.

Device Allocation

The Solaris auditing kernel enforces device allocation, which is used to prevent or restrict access to peripheral devices. Users will require the appropriate authorization to access allocatable devices. We'll discuss several tasks in this section to comply with the exam requirements regarding device allocation. These tasks include making devices allocatable, viewing device allocation information, auditing device allocation, allocating and mounting a device, and deallocating a device.

Making Devices Allocatable

After starting the auditing subsystem, device allocation will be enabled on the system. To do this, you assume superuser or the Primary Administrator role and run the *bsmconv* script, located in */etc/security*, with the `./bsmconv` command. This script is used to enable the Basic Security Module (BSM), which starts the auditing subsystem.

To enable the auditing services, follow these steps:

1. Log in with an account that has root privileges, or use the `su` command to become superuser.

2. Bring down the system to single-user mode using the `init 1` command.

3. In the */etc/security* directory, run the *bsmconv* script to enable the auditing service: `./bsmconv`

4. Bring the system into multi-user mode using the `init 6` command.

Viewing Device Allocation Information

To view allocation information about a device, you must assume superuser or a role that has Device Security rights. At that point, simply display information about allocatable devices by issuing the `list_devices device-name` command; where `device-name` is `audio` (for microphone and speakers), `fd(n)` (for diskette drive), `sr(n)` (for CD-ROM drive), and `st(n)` (for tape drive). The `(n)` specifies the number of the device. See the `list_devices` command man page for more details and examples.

Auditing Device Allocation

The Solaris auditing subsystem can also be used to audit device allocation. The audit class OTHER (`ot`) is used to audit allocatable devices. (Be sure to review Chapter 5 for details on how to configure the auditing subsystem properly.)

To audit device allocation, you'll need to add the `ot` class to the *audit_control* file `flags` argument, which defines which attributable class events should be audited for the entire system. Events added to the `flags` argument are separated by commas. Following is an example:

```
# ident "@(#)audit_control.txt  1.4    00/07/17 SMI"
#
dir:/var/audit/1/data
dir:/var/audit/2/data
dir:/var/audit
flags:lo,as,ot
minfree:25
naflags:lo,na
```

In this extract, the attributable lo, as, and ot class events will be audited for all users on the system. On the other hand, to configure the auditing subsystem not to audit the class that includes device allocation (again, the ot class), simply edit out that class selection and save the file.

Allocating and Mounting a Device

Before a user can allocate a device, he or she needs to be authorized to do so. Sun provides the following four steps for granting authorization:

1. Assume the Primary Administrator role, or become superuser.

2. Create a rights profile that contains the appropriate authorization and commands. Typically, you would create a rights profile that includes the `solaris.device.allocate` authorization. (See Chapter 9 for security implications when creating or changing a rights profile.) Give the rights profile appropriate properties, such as the following:

   ■ Rights profile name: `Device Allocation`

   ■ Granted authorizations: `solaris.device.allocate`

   ■ Commands with security attributes: mount with the `sys_mount` privilege, and umount with the `sys_mount` privilege

3. Create a role for the rights profile, and use the following role properties as a guide:

   ■ Role name: `devicealloc`

   ■ Role full name: `Device Allocator`

   ■ Role description: `Allocates and mounts allocated devices`

   ■ Rights profile: `Device Allocation` (This rights profile must be at the top of the list of profiles that are included in the role.)

4. Assign the role to every user who is permitted to allocate a device.

At this point, a user with the appropriate rights and authorization can allocate a device simply by issuing the `allocate` command. For example, to allocate tape drive 0, the user would issue `allocate st0`. As another example, if the user wishes to allocate a microphone, he or she would issue the `allocate audio` command. Finally, let's say the user wishes to allocate sales-printer-1. To do so, the following command would be executed: `allocate /dev/lp/sales-printer-1`.

Forcing Allocation   Unfortunately, if a device is allocated by another user, it will not be available for allocation to a new user. To remedy that quickly, you can forcibly deallocate a device, which we'll talk more about later, or forcibly allocate (which is to reallocate) a device. To verify that you have the appropriate rights (such as `solaris.device.revoke`) to do this, you can issue the `auths` command:

```
$ auths
Solaris.device.allocate solaris.device.revoke
```

Users need the appropriate rights and authorization to allocate and deallocate devices. The authorization required to allocate a device is `solaris.device.allocate`. The authorization required to allocate or deallocate a device forcibly is `solaris.device.revoke`.

After confirming that you have authorization, to allocate a device forcibly, you must issue the `allocate -U` *user-name* command, where *user-name* is the name of the user to which you will forcibly allocate the device.

Mounting an Allocated Device   Though this is not typically covered by the exam, it's important to note that after a device is allocated, you must mount it to the system before you can use it. Following are Sun's recommended steps for doing so:

1. Assume a role that can allocate and mount a device.
2. Create and protect a mount point in the role's home directory. You need to do this step only the first time you need a mount point:

   ```
   mkdir mount-point ; chmod 700 mount-point
   ```

3. List the allocatable devices:

   ```
   list_devices -l
   ```

4. Allocate the device:

   ```
   allocate device-name
   ```

5. Mount the device:

   ```
   mount -o ro -F filesystem-type device-path mount-point
   ```

   ■   `-o ro` indicates that the device is to be mounted read-only. Use `-o rw` to indicate that you should be able to write to the device.

- ■ `-F filesystem-type` indicates the file system format of the device. Typically, a CD-ROM is formatted with an HSFS file system. A diskette is typically formatted with a PCFS file system.
- ■ `device-path` indicates the path to the device. The output of the `list_devices -l` command includes the device-path.
- ■ `mount-point` indicates the mount point that you created in step 2.

watch　　　*Users with the appropriate rights and authorization can allocate a device by issuing the* `allocate` device-name *command and deallocate a device by issuing the* `deallocate` device-name *command.*

Deallocating a Device

If a device is allocated and mounted, to deallocate it safely you must first unmount it and then deallocate it by issuing all of the following commands:

```
cd $HOME

unmount mount-point

deallocate device-name
```

As mentioned earlier, you can forcibly deallocate a device by issuing the `deallocate -F device` command. For example, to force the deallocation of the printer (also mentioned earlier) you would issue this command: `deallocate/dev/lp/sales-printer-1`

INSIDE THE EXAM

Checking Device Allocation Authorization and Allocating a Device

Following are steps for checking whether or not you have the appropriate allocation authorization; if you do, you can then allocate CD-ROM(0):

1. Log in with your user account.

2. From a terminal session, issue the `auths` command and verify that you have `solaris.device.allocate` device allocation authorization rights.

3. Allocate the CD-ROM by issuing the `allocate sr0` command.

CERTIFICATION OBJECTIVE 6.02

Use the Basic Audit Reporting Tool to Create a Manifest and Check System Integrity

After you have installed and configured a Solaris system, you can create a baseline (control) manifest of it and use the BART to check the integrity of the system from that control manifest. BART will report file-level changes that have occurred on the system.

BART includes several components—enough to warrant discussion in an entire chapter—and in this section, we'll cover only those you should know for the exam. The components you need to understand for certification are *creating a manifest* and *comparing manifests*.

Creating a Manifest

With BART, you can create a file-level image of the system in a catalog of files that contain information such as attributes and checksum of files for which you have permission to access. In other words, any user can run BART to catalog and monitor files as long as the user has permission to access them. Also, when running BART as superuser, the output will be available to everyone on the system, unless you specify permission restrictions.

Creating a manifest with BART is accomplished by issuing this command:

```
bart create options > control-manifest
```

where *options* can be the following:

- -R specifies the root directory for the manifest. All paths specified by the rules will be interpreted relative to this directory. All paths reported in the manifest will be relative to this directory.

- -I accepts a list of individual files to be cataloged, either on the command line or read from standard input.

- ■ -r is the name of the rules file for this manifest. Note that -, when used with the -r option, will be read the rules file from standard input.
- ■ -n turns off content signatures for all regular files in the file list. This option can be used to improve performance, or you can use this option if the contents of the file list are expected to change, as in the case of system log files.
- ■ *control manifest* is an optional control filename.

Alternatively, to create a manifest of every file installed on the system, you can issue the bart create command without any options. Here's an example:

```
# bart create
! Version 1.0
! Monday, July 12, 2004 (08:45:40)
# Format:
#fname D size mode acl dirmtime uid gid
#fname P size mode acl mtime uid gid
#fname S size mode acl mtime uid gid
#fname F size mode acl mtime uid gid contents
#fname L size mode acl lnmtime uid gid dest
#fname B size mode acl mtime uid gid devnode
#fname C size mode acl mtime uid gid devnode
.
.

snipped for brevity

.
.
/var/tmp/.solaris_shellsap F 0 100600 user::rw-,group::---,mask:---,other:--- 40
eb072e 0 0 d41d8cd98f00b204e9800998ecf8427e
/var/tmp/.solaris_userhomedirectory F 0 100600 user::rw-,group::---,mask:---,oth
er:--- 40eb072b 0 0 d41d8cd98f00b204e9800998ecf8427e
/var/tmp/dict_cache45461.tmp F 12288 100644 user::rw-,group::r--,mask:r--,other:
r-- 40a3a5c5 0 1 9357c0d4c7d0763b6f3d17d5a779972d
.
.

snipped for brevity

.
.
/var/yp/Makefile F 18686 100555 user::r-x,group::r-x,mask:r-x,other:r-x 40a11aa5
 0 2 b86f622e26dfb736a97476f7ffbae670
/var/yp/aliases F 153 100555 user::r-x,group::r-x,mask:r-x,other:r-x 40a11406 0
2 1c1060af6f4c66ccadc8fd77134f2fd7
/var/yp/nicknames F 226 100644 user::rw-,group::r--,mask:r--,other:r-- 40a114060 2
034820835249426d8982612207ed5539
/var/yp/updaters F 870 100500 user::r-x,group::---,mask:---,other:--- 403eb163 0
 2 4430ce4a2aaf0fe668df60e0b615bce4
```

Every line in the manifest is a file entry. Lines that start with an exclamation (!) indicate metadata, and those with a pound sign (#) indicate comments and are ignored during comparisons. Following are the manifest file types you should know for the exam:

- Type F for file.
- Type D for directory.

Also, each line in the manifest contains the following types of information:

- Size
- Content
- User ID
- Group ID
- Permissions

Another common BART manifest example that you should know for the exam is how to create a manifest about specific files only. To do so, let's say for the */etc/ passwd* file, simply issue the `bart create -I /etc/passwd` command, as shown here:

```
# bart create -I /etc/passwd
! Version 1.0
! Monday, July 12, 2004 (08:54:27)
# Format:
#fname D size mode acl dirmtime uid gid
#fname P size mode acl mtime uid gid
#fname S size mode acl mtime uid gid
#fname F size mode acl mtime uid gid contents
#fname L size mode acl lnmtime uid gid dest
#fname B size mode acl mtime uid gid devnode
#fname C size mode acl mtime uid gid devnode
/etc/passwd F 730 100644 user::rw-,group::r--,mask:r--,other:r-- 40eb074e 0 3 10
b15c4f69b25fce6f3b4f4aa9116a07
```

Note that you can create a manifest of more than one file simply by separating the file names with a space—the following is an example:

```
bart create -I /etc/passwd /etc/shadow
```

Comparing Manifests

Perhaps the most useful feature of BART is to compare manifests over time to monitor file-level changes. By doing so, you can verify the integrity of files and detect corrupt files and security breaches, all of which help troubleshoot the system. Following are Sun's recommended steps for comparing manifests:

1. Assume the Primary Administrator role, or become superuser.
2. Create a control manifest of all files or specific files you wish to monitor.
3. Create a test manifest that is prepared identically to the control manifest whenever you want to monitor changes to the system:

   ```
   bart create -R /etc > test-manifest
   ```

INSIDE THE EXAM

Creating and Comparing BART Manifests

Following are steps for creating and then comparing BART manifests to check file-level changes:

1. Log in as superuser or assume the Primary Administrator role.
2. Create a BART control manifest of, for example, the password files:

   ```
   bart create -I /etc/passwd /etc/shadow > passwd.control.071204.
   ```

   The filename can be anything you want to use. In this case, we are specifying a manifest of the password files (`passwd.`), specifying that it's a control manifest (`control.`), and the date is `071204`.

3. After some period of time, create a manifest to compare with the control manifest to detect any file-level changes:

   ```
   bart create -I /etc/passwd /etc/shadow > passwd.compare.071904
   ```

4. Compare the control and compare manifests:

   ```
   bart compare passwd.control.071204 passwd.compare.071904
   ```

   Or parse the information into a report file with this:

   ```
   bart compare passwd.control.071204 passwd.compare.071904 > bart-report
   ```

The output will display any changes since the control manifest was created.

4. Compare the control manifest with the new comparison manifest:

```
bart compare options control-manifest compare-manifest > bart-report
```

where

- **-r** is the name of the rules file for this comparison. Using the -r option with the - means that the directives will be read from standard input.

- **-i** allows the user to set global IGNORE directives from the command line.

- **-p** is the programmatic mode that generates standard nonlocalized output for programmatic parsing.

- *control-manifest* is the output from the `bart create` command for the control system or control manifest on the same system.

- *compare-manifest* is the output from the `bart create` command of the new system or the comparison manifest on the same system.

5. Examine the BART report for file-level changes and oddities.

TWO-MINUTE DRILL

Here are some of the key points from the certification objectives in Chapter 6.

Control Access to Devices by Configuring and Managing Device Policy and Allocation

❑ Device policy is enabled by default and enforced in the kernel to restrict and prevent access to devices that are integral to the system. Device allocation is not enabled by default and is enforced during user allocation time to require user authorization to access peripheral devices.

❑ To view device policies for all devices or specific ones, use the `getdevpolicy` command.

❑ To modify or remove device policies for a specific device, use the `update_ drv -a -p` *policy device-driver* command; where *policy* is the device policy or policies (separated by a space) for *device-driver*, which is the device driver whose device policy you wish to modify or remove.

❑ The `AUE_MODDEVPLCY` audit event is part of the `as` audit class by default, which is used to audit changes in device policy. To audit device policies, you'll need to add the `as` class to the *audit_control* file `flags` argument.

❑ Run the *bsmconv* script to enable the auditing service, which also enables device allocation.

❑ The `ot` audit class is used to audit device allocation. To audit allocatable devices, you'll need to add the `ot` class to the *audit_control* file `flags` argument.

❑ Users with the appropriate rights and authorization can allocate and deallocate devices. The authorization required to allocate a device is `solaris.device .allocate`. The authorization required to allocate or deallocate a device forcibly is `solaris.device.revoke`.

❑ Users with the appropriate rights and authorization can allocate a device by issuing the `allocate` *device-name* command and deallocate a device by issuing the `deallocate` *device-name* command.

Use the Basic Audit Reporting Tool to Create a Manifest and Check System Integrity

❑ The Basic Audit Reporting Tool (BART) can report file-level changes that have occurred on the system.

❑ To compare a control manifest with a new comparison manifest issue this command:

```
bart compare options control-manifest compare-manifest > bart-report
```

SELF TEST

The following questions will help you measure your understanding of the material presented in this chapter. Read all the choices carefully, because there might be more than one correct answer. Choose all correct answers for each question.

Control Access to Devices by Configuring and Managing Device Policy and Allocation

1. Which of the following commands would you issue to view device policies for all devices or just for specific devices?
   A. `list_devices`
   B. `getdevpolicy`
   C. `allocate` *device-name*
   D. All of the above

2. Which of the following can be used to restrict and prevent access to devices integral to the system?
   A. AUE_MODDEVPLCY event
   B. Device policy
   C. Running the *bsmconv* script
   D. Device allocation
   E. Issuing the `update_drv -a -p policy` *device-driver* command
   F. All of the above

3. Which of the following can be used to report file-level changes that have occurred on the system?
   A. Access control lists (ACLs)
   B. Device policy
   C. Device allocation
   D. Basic Audit Reporting Tool (BART)
   E. All of the above

4. Which of the following can be used to control access to devices on a Solaris system?
   A. Access control lists (ACLs)
   B. Device policy
   C. Device allocation
   D. Basic Audit Reporting Tool (BART)
   E. All of the above

5. What command would you execute to verify that you have the appropriate rights to deallocate a device forcibly?
   A. `auths`
   B. `verify -rights`
   C. `allocate`
   D. All of the above

6. Which of the following can be used to control access to files on a Solaris system?
   A. Access control lists (ACLs)
   B. Device policy
   C. Device allocation
   D. Basic Audit Reporting Tool (BART)
   E. All of the above

7. Users with the appropriate rights and authorization can allocate and deallocate devices. Which of these authorizations is required to allocate a device forcibly?
   A. `solaris.device.allocate`
   B. `solaris.device.revoke`
   C. Both `solaris.device.allocate` and `solaris.device.revoke`
   D. All of the above

8. Which of the following can be used to restrict and prevent access to peripheral devices?
   A. `AUE_MODDEVPLCY` event
   B. Device policy
   C. Running the *bsmconv* script
   D. Device allocation
   E. Issuing the `update_drv -a -p policy` *device-driver* command
   F. All of the above

Use the Basic Audit Reporting Tool to Create a Manifest and Check the System Integrity

9. By comparing BART manifests over time, which of these can you accomplish?
   A. Detect corrupt files.
   B. Verify the integrity of files.
   C. Detect security breaches.
   D. Troubleshoot the system.
   E. All of the above

10. Which of the following can be used to check the integrity of the system's files?

    A. Access control lists (ACLs)

    B. Device policy

    C. Device allocation

    D. Basic Audit Reporting Tool (BART)

    E. All of the above

11. You can create a manifest of more than one file by separating the filenames with a comma.

    A. True

    B. False

12. Which of these types of information are commonly found in a BART manifest?

    A. Group ID

    B. Content

    C. User ID

    D. Permissions

    E. Size

    F. All of the above

LAB QUESTION

Your favorite customer, ABCD Inc., called you in to enable device allocation, report the device allocation for tape drive(1) and the CD-ROM, and use BART to create a control manifest of every file installed on the system. What steps would you perform to provide the requested services?

SELF TEST ANSWERS

Control Access to Devices by Configuring and Managing Device Policy and Allocation

1. ☑ **B.** To view device policies for all devices or specific ones, you would use the `getdevpolicy` command.
    ☒ **A** is wrong because `list_devices` is used to display information about allocatable devices. **C** is wrong because a user with the appropriate rights and authorization can allocate a device by issuing the `allocate device-name` command.

2. ☑ **B and E.** Device policy is a default kernel-level mechanism that restricts and prevents access to devices integral to the system by mandating that processes that open such a device require certain privileges such as reading and writing. To modify or update a device policy for a specific device to restrict or prevent access, you would use the `update_drv -a -p policy device-driver` command.
    ☒ **A** is wrong because the AUE_MODDEVPLCY audit event is part of the as audit class by default and is used to audit changes in device policy. **C** is incorrect because the *bsmconv* script is used to enable the auditing service, which also enables device allocation. **D** is wrong because device allocation is enforced during user allocation to require user authorization in order to access a peripheral device such as a CD-ROM or printer.

3. ☑ **D.** The Basic Audit Reporting Tool (BART) is used to check the integrity of files by reporting file-level changes that have occurred on the system.
    ☒ **A** is wrong because access control lists (ACLs) are used to control access to files. **B and C** are wrong because device policy and device allocation are used to control access to devices.

4. ☑ **B and C.** Controlling access to devices on a Solaris operating system is accomplished by two mechanisms: *device policy* and *device allocation*. Device policy is a default kernel-level mechanism that restricts and prevents access to devices integral to the system by mandating that processes that open such a device require certain privileges such as reading and writing. Device allocation, which is not enabled by default, is enforced during user allocation to require user authorization in order to access a peripheral device.
    ☒ **A** is wrong because access control lists (ACLs) are used to control access to files. **D** is incorrect because the Basic Audit Reporting Tool (BART) is used to check the integrity of files.

5. ☑ **A.** To verify that you have the appropriate rights to forcibly deallocate a device (for example, `solaris.device.revoke`), you can issue the `auths` command.
    ☒ The remaining choices are irrelevant.

6. ☑ **A.** Access control lists (ACLs) are used to control access to files.

☒ **B** and **C** are wrong because device policy and device allocation are used to control access to devices. **D** is incorrect because the Basic Audit Reporting Tool (BART) is used to check the integrity of files.

7. ☑ **B.** The authorization required to allocate or deallocate a device forcibly is `solaris.device.revoke`.

☒ **A** is wrong because `solaris.device.allocate` is the authorization required to allocate a device.

8. ☑ **C** and **D**. The *bsmconv* script is used to enable the auditing service, which also enables device allocation. Device allocation is enforced during user allocation to require user authorization to access a peripheral device such as a CD-ROM or printer.

☒ **A** is wrong because the `AUE_MODDEVPLCY` audit event is part of the `as` audit class by default and is used to audit changes in device policy. **B** is incorrect because device policy is a default kernel-level mechanism that restricts and prevents access to devices integral to the system. **E** is wrong because to modify or update a device policy for a specific device to restrict or prevent access, you would use the `update_drv -a -p` *policy device-driver* command.

Use the Basic Audit Reporting Tool to Create a Manifest and Check System Integrity

9. ☑ **E.** The most useful feature of BART is its ability to compare manifests over time to monitor file-level changes. By doing this, you can verify the integrity of files and detect corrupt files and security breaches, all of which help troubleshoot the system.

10. ☑ **D.** The Basic Audit Reporting Tool (BART) is used to check the integrity of files.

☒ **A** is wrong because access control lists (ACLs) are used to control access to files. **B** and **C** are wrong because device policy and device allocation are used to control access to devices.

11. ☑ **B.** False. You can create a manifest of more than one file by separating the filenames with a space.

12. ☑ **F.** Each line in a BART manifest contains the following types of file information: size, content, user ID, group ID, and permissions.

LAB ANSWER

The first task that ABCD Inc. hired you to perform is to enable device allocation. To do so, you must assume superuser or the Primary Administrator role and run the *bsmconv* script located in */etc/security* with the `./bsmconv` command. This script is used to enable the Basic Security Module (BSM), which starts the auditing subsystem:

1. Log in with an account that has root privileges, or use the `su` command to become superuser.
2. Bring down the system to single-user mode using the `init 1` command.
3. In the */etc/security* directory, run the *bsmconv* script to enable the auditing service: `./bsmconv`
4. Bring the system into multi-user mode using the `init 6` command.

The next task is to report the device allocation for tape drive(1) and the CD-ROM. To view allocation information about a device, you must assume superuser or a role that has Device Security rights. At that point, to display information about allocatable devices use the `list_devices` *device-name* command; therefore, you would issue these commands to report the device allocation for tape drive(1) and the CD-ROM:

```
list_devices st1 and list_devices sr0
```

Remember that *device-name* can be `audio` (for microphone and speakers), `fd(n)` (for diskette drive), `sr(n)` (for CD-ROM drive), and `st(n)` (for tape drive). The `(n)` specifies the number of the device.

The final task you need to perform is to use BART to create a control manifest of every file installed on the system. Creating a manifest with BART is accomplished by issuing this command:

```
bart create options > control-manifest
```

where *options* can be as follows:

- `-R` specifies the root directory for the manifest. All paths specified by the rules will be interpreted relative to this directory. All paths reported in the manifest will be relative to this directory.
- `-I` accepts a list of individual files to be cataloged, either on the command line or read from standard input.
- `-r` is the name of the rules file for this manifest. Note that -, when used with the `-r` option, will be read the rules file from standard input.

■ -n turns off content signatures for all regular files in the file list. This option can be used to improve performance. Or you can use this option if the contents of the file list are expected to change, as in the case of system log files.

■ `control manifest` is an optional control filename.

Therefore, to create a manifest of every file installed on the system, you would issue the `bart create` command without any options.

Part III

Security Attacks

7

Denial of Service Attacks

S ecurity attacks on computer infrastructures are becoming an increasingly serious problem and, among others, the Solaris operating system has become a regular target. In this chapter, we'll examine different types of attacks and discuss ways to alleviate some of the most common forms while mitigating ensuing risks. Specifically, this chapter deals with distinguishing between several common types of Denial of Service (DoS) attacks, understanding how and why DoS attacks are executed, and establishing courses of action to help prevent DoS attacks. All of these topics are covered on the exam.

In this chapter, when we edit a system file, we'll be using the operating system's visual editor (vi). (For more information on vi, see Chapter 4.)

CERTIFICATION OBJECTIVE 7.01

Differentiate Between the Types of Host-Based Denial of Service Attacks and Understand How Attacks Are Executed

For purposes of the exam, DoS can be defined simply as malicious resource or service overuse, interruption, or annexation. In other words, the attack exhausts system resources so authorized users cannot log in or access resources on the target server, which directly affects availability. DoS attacks are constantly evolving and targeted as network-based or host-based assaults. We'll talk about several DoS attack types in this chapter as well as the many ways to mitigate DoS risks and countermeasure the inherent system vulnerabilities.

The most common forms of DoS attacks we should be concerned with include program buffer overflow; malformed packets such as overlapping IP fragments, Teardrop, Ping of Death, Smurf, Bonk, Boink, NewTear, WinNuke, Land, and LaTierra; as well as other general types of attacks such as SYN flooding. It is important that you understand that regardless of the particular type of DoS attack, all affect system availability.

Denial of Service (DoS) attacks are the most common threats on the Internet. DoS attacks may target a user or an entire organization and can affect the availability of target systems and networks.

Program Buffer Overflow

When executable stacks with permissions set to read, write, and execute are allowed by default, programs may be inherently vulnerable to buffer overflow attacks. A *buffer* is commonly defined as a temporary storage space that allows a CPU time to store data before processing it. Generally, a buffer overflow occurs when a program process or task receives unwarranted and/or an abundance of data (sometimes referred to as "smashing the stack") that it is not properly programmed to deal with. As a result, the program typically operates in such an unexpected way that an intruder can abuse or misuse it, usually by inserting executable code into the stack with a payload that causes service denial or worse, giving the intruder access—many times with root privileges—to the system. More often than not, an intruder can gain root access to the system during a buffer overflow attack. Once inside, and after performing some damage or data theft, the intruder would typically delete traces of illegal access by removing activity logs when possible.

Here's a good example: An intruder sends a vulnerable program more data than it was programmed to handle. As a result, the program overruns the memory that was allotted for it and writes the extra data into system memory. At that point, the extra data, which usually contains a remote access Trojan (which we'll talk about in the next chapter), can be executed, thus allowing the intruder remote access to the system later on at the intruder's leisure. Technically speaking, these types of attacks contain instructions that patch the kernel to execute another program.

Sun recommends that you always monitor programs that are executed with privileges as well as the users who have rights to execute them. To do so, you can search your system for unauthorized use of the setuid (set user ID) and setgid (set group ID) permissions on programs to gain superuser privileges. Although we'll cover this in more detail in Chapters 9 and 10, the rest of this section provides a synopsis of how to find files with setuid permissions.

In a terminal session with superuser privileges, search for files with setuid permissions by using the `find` command:

```
find directory -user root -perm -4000 -exec ls -ldb {} \; >/tmp/filename
```

where

- `find directory` checks all mounted paths starting at the specified directory, which can be root (/), sys, bin, or mail.
- `-user root` displays files owned only by root.
- `-perm -4000` displays files only with permissions set to 4000.
- `-exec ls -ldb` displays the output of the find command in `ls -ldb` format.
- `>/tmp/filename` writes results to this file.

e✗**a m**
ⓦ**a t c h**

On the exam, be prepared for questions regarding how intruders cover their tracks. After penetrating a target system, an attacker would erase traces of the incident by deleting activity logs and leaving backdoors in place to allow later clandestine access to the system.

Following is sample output of what you can expect to see while finding files with setuid permissions:

```
-r-sr-xr-x 1 root bin 38836 Aug 10 16:16 /usr/bin/at-r-sr-xr-x 1 root bin 19812
Aug 10 16:16 /usr/bin/crontab
---s--x--x 1 root sys 46040 Aug 10 15:18 /usr/bin/ct
-r-sr-xr-x 1 root sys 12092 Aug 11 01:29 /usr/lib/mv_dir
-r-sr-sr-x 1 root bin 33208 Aug 10 15:55 /usr/lib/lpadmin
-r-sr-sr-x 1 root bin 38696 Aug 10 15:55 /usr/lib/lpsched
---s--x--- 1 root rar 45376 Aug 18 15:11 /usr/rar/bin/sh
-r-sr-xr-x 1 root bin 12524 Aug 11 01:27 /usr/bin/df
-rwsr-xr-x 1 root sys 21780 Aug 11 01:27 /usr/bin/newgrp
-r-sr-sr-x 1 root sys 23000 Aug 11 01:27 /usr/bin/passwd
-r-sr-xr-x 1 root sys 23824 Aug 11 01:27 /usr/bin/su
```

EXERCISE 7-1

Find Files with setuid Permissions

In this exercise, we'll use the `find` command to locate files with setuid permissions and then view the results with the `more` command.

Using the find Command to Locate Files with setuid Permissions

1. Log in with an account that has root privileges or use the switch user (`su`) command to become superuser. As superuser you'll have full privileges, which may be required to search all files. For example, to switch to root, simply open a terminal session and type **su root,** press ENTER, and then enter root's password at the prompt.

2. Search for files with setuid permissions with this command:

```
find directory -user root -perm -4000 -exec ls -ldb {} \; >/tmp/findresults.
```

Viewing the Results

3. View the results in */tmp/findresults* using the `more` command, like so:

```
more /tmp/findresults
```

where `findresults` is the filename to which you wrote your find results in the */tmp* directory.

Malformed Packet Attacks and Flooding

Malformed packet attacks come in several flavors and have been around for many years. To carry out this type of attack successfully, maliciously formatted Internet Protocol (IP) packets that include the Transmission Control Protocol (TCP) or User Datagram Protocol (UDP) are sent to a program that was not properly developed to handle unexpected packets. As a result, the target program would typically crash or at least function at a snail's pace, denying services of the software and/or system to authorized users. The most popular types of malformed packet attacks that you've likely heard about include overlapping IP fragments, Teardrop, Ping of Death, Smurf, Bonk, Boink, NewTear, WinNuke, Land, and LaTierra.

Since many of the attack types mentioned are common variations, we'll talk a little bit about the more conventional methods, including Teardrop, Ping of Death, and Smurf attacks. In Teardrop, the attacker modifies the length and fragmentation offset fields in IP packets, which causes the target to crash. Ping of Death, on the other hand, is an example of a malformed ICMP packet attack. The attacker sends an oversized ping packet (or ICMP datagrams) in an attempt to overflow the system's buffer to crash, freeze, or in some cases restart the system. In other words, an oversized packet would crash the server when the system tries to reconstruct it. In a Smurf attack, a normal-sized ping request is broadcast to every system on the target's trusted network. The sending address, however, is spoofed to be the same as the target victim system. As a result, the target would receive all of the replies from the broadcast, which would overload it and cause service denial.

The most common form of flooding we need to be aware of is in the form of a *SYN attack*. A SYN attack takes place during the TCP handshake. Before we talk more about how a SYN attack occurs, we should review the fundamentals of the TCP handshake process. But, first, let's define ports with regard to TCP and UDP. In network communications with TCP/IP and UDP, a *port* is an endpoint to a logical connection. In other words, the port number identifies a type of service and traffic. For example, port 80 is a well-known port typically used for HTTP traffic, and port 443 is used for HTTPS. A TCP handshake process is used to establish TCP connections between two IP nodes (for example, a web server and web browser). In other words, a server is listening on a particular port, waiting for a connection attempt to that port for a particular service. The process is simple: the client sends a connection request, the server acknowledges the request, the client then acknowledges the acknowledgement, and finally the connection is established. This is called a *three-way handshake*.

An excellent, detailed explanation of the TCP handshake was published by our friends at Microsoft in Knowledge Base article Q172983. As a technical review, we'll examine a summary of the article.

TCP implies a *connection-oriented* connection, which means that a reliable, ordered, guaranteed transfer of data must be obtained and acknowledged between a sender and receiver. At the TCP level, connection establishment, sending data, and connection termination maintain specific control parameters that govern the handshake process and ensure its completion. The control bits are listed here:

- **URG**   Urgent Pointer field significant
- **ACK**   Acknowledgement field significant
- **PSH**   Push function
- **RST**   Reset the connection
- **SYN**   Synchronize sequence numbers
- **FIN**   No more data from sender

A three-way handshake will take place in two scenarios: when establishing a connection (an active open) and when terminating a connection (an active close). To further explain the TCP handshake process, the next few sections review a sample capture.

Establishing a Connection

The following sequence shows the process of a TCP connection being established. As you see in the first frame, the client, *NTW3*, sends a SYN packet (TCP . . . . S.). This is a request to the server to synchronize the sequence numbers. It specifies its initial sequence number (ISN), which is incremented by 1, (8221821 + 1 = 8221822), and that is sent to the server. For security purposes, it is important that ISNs be unpredictable by third parties. To initialize a connection, the client and server must synchronize each other's sequence numbers. The Acknowledgement field (ack: 0) is set to zero because this is the first part of the three-way handshake. Following is the extract from packet 1:

```
1    2.0785 NTW3 --> BDC3 TCP ....S., len: 4, seq: 8221822-8221825, ack: 0,
win: 8192, src: 1037  dst:  139 (NBT Session) NTW3 --> BDC3 IP

TCP: ....S., len: 4, seq: 8221822-8221825, ack: 0, win: 8192, src: 1037
dst:  139 (NBT Session)

  TCP: Source Port = 0x040D
   TCP: Destination Port = NETBIOS Session Service
   TCP: Sequence Number = 8221822 (0x7D747E)
   TCP: Acknowledgement Number = 0 (0x0)
   TCP: Data Offset = 24 (0x18)
   TCP: Reserved = 0 (0x0000)
   TCP: Flags = 0x02 : ....S.

      TCP: ..0..... = No urgent data
       TCP: ...0.... = Acknowledgement field not significant
       TCP: ....0... = No Push function
       TCP: .....0.. = No Reset
       TCP: ......1. = Synchronize sequence numbers
       TCP: .......0 = No Fin

  TCP: Window = 8192 (0x2000)
   TCP: Checksum = 0xF213
   TCP: Urgent Pointer = 0 (0x0)
   TCP: Options

        TCP: Option Kind (Maximum Segment Size) = 2 (0x2)
         TCP: Option Length = 4 (0x4)
         TCP: Option Value = 1460 (0x5B4)

  TCP: Frame Padding

00000:   02 60 8C 9E 18 8B 02 60 8C 3B 85 C1 08 00 45 00    .`.....`.;....E.
00010:   00 2C 0D 01 40 00 80 06 E1 4B 83 6B 02 D6 83 6B    .,..@....K.k...k
00020:   02 D3 04 0D 00 8B 00 7D 74 7E 00 00 00 00 60 02    .......}t~....`.
00030:   20 00 F2 13 00 00 02 04 05 B4 20 20                .........
```

Request Acknowledgement   In the second packet, the server, *BDC3*, sends an ACK and a SYN on this segment (TCP .A..S.). In this segment, the server is acknowledging the request of the client for synchronization. At the same time, the server is also sending its request to the client for synchronization of its sequence numbers. However, you'll see one noticeable difference in this segment—the server transmits an acknowledgement number (8221823) to the client. The acknowledgement is just proof to the client that the ACK is specific to the SYN that the client initiated. The process of acknowledging the client's request allows the server to increment the client's sequence number by 1 and uses it as its acknowledgement number. Following is the extract from packet 2:

```
2    2.0786 BDC3 --> NTW3   TCP .A..S., len: 4, seq: 1109645-1109648, ack:
8221823, win: 8760, src: 139 (NBT Session)  dst: 1037 BDC3 --> NTW3   IP

TCP: .A..S., len:    4, seq:   1109645-1109648, ack:    8221823, win: 8760,
src:  139 (NBT Session)  dst: 1037

  TCP: Source Port = NETBIOS Session Service
   TCP: Destination Port = 0x040D
   TCP: Sequence Number = 1109645 (0x10EE8D)
   TCP: Acknowledgement Number = 8221823 (0x7D747F)
   TCP: Data Offset = 24 (0x18)
   TCP: Reserved = 0 (0x0000)
   TCP: Flags = 0x12 : .A..S.

      TCP: ..0..... = No urgent data
       TCP: ...1.... = Acknowledgement field significant
       TCP: ....0... = No Push function
       TCP: .....0.. = No Reset
       TCP: ......1. = Synchronize sequence numbers
       TCP: .......0 = No Fin

   TCP: Window = 8760 (0x2238)
    TCP: Checksum = 0x012D
    TCP: Urgent Pointer = 0 (0x0)
    TCP: Options

          TCP: Option Kind (Maximum Segment Size) = 2 (0x2)
           TCP: Option Length = 4 (0x4)
           TCP: Option Value = 1460 (0x5B4)

   TCP: Frame Padding

00000:   02 60 8C 3B 85 C1 02 60 8C 9E 18 8B 08 00 45 00    .`.;...`......E.
00010:   00 2C 5B 00 40 00 80 06 93 4C 83 6B 02 D3 83 6B    .,[.@....L.k...k
00020:   02 D6 00 8B 04 0D 00 10 EE 8D 00 7D 74 7F 60 12    ...........}t `.
00030:   22 38 01 2D 00 00 02 04 05 B4 20 20                "8.-......
```

Acknowledging the Request In the third packet, the client sends an ACK on this segment (TCP .A....). In this segment, the client is acknowledging the request from the server for synchronization. The client uses the same algorithm the server implemented in providing an acknowledgement number. The client's acknowledgment of the server's request for synchronization completes the process of establishing a reliable connection, and as a result a three-way handshake takes place. Following is the extract from packet 3:

```
3   2.787 NTW3 --> BDC3  TCP .A...., len: 0, seq: 8221823-8221823, ack:
1109646, win: 8760, src: 1037  dst:  139 (NBT Session)  NTW3 --> BDC3   IP


TCP: .A...., len:    0, seq:   8221823-8221823, ack:    1109646, win: 8760,
src: 1037  dst:  139 (NBT Session)

  TCP: Source Port = 0x040D
   TCP: Destination Port = NETBIOS Session Service
   TCP: Sequence Number = 8221823 (0x7D747F)
   TCP: Acknowledgement Number = 1109646 (0x10EE8E)
   TCP: Data Offset = 20 (0x14)
   TCP: Reserved = 0 (0x0000)
   TCP: Flags = 0x10 : .A....

     TCP: ..0..... = No urgent data
      TCP: ...1.... = Acknowledgement field significant
      TCP: ....0... = No Push function
      TCP: .....0.. = No Reset
      TCP: ......0. = No Synchronize
      TCP: .......0 = No Fin

  TCP: Window = 8760 (0x2238)
   TCP: Checksum = 0x18EA
   TCP: Urgent Pointer = 0 (0x0)
   TCP: Frame Padding

00000:  02 60 8C 9E 18 8B 02 60 8C 3B 85 C1 08 00 45 00    .`.....`.;....E.
00010:  00 28 0E 01 40 00 80 06 E0 4F 83 6B 02 D6 83 6B    .(..@....O.k...k
00020:  02 D3 04 0D 00 8B 00 7D 74 7F 00 10 EE 8E 50 10    .......}t ....P.
00030:  22 38 18 EA 00 00 20 20 20 20 20 20               "8....
```

Terminating a Connection

Although the three-way handshake requires only three packets to be transmitted over the network, the termination of this reliable connection will necessitate the transmission of four packets. Because a TCP connection is *full duplex* (that is, data can be flowing in each direction independent of the other), each direction must be terminated independently.

In the next session of packets, we see the client sending a FIN that is accompanied by an ACK (TCP .A...F). This segment has two basic functions: first, when the FIN parameter is set, it will inform the server that it has no more data to send. Second, the ACK is essential in identifying the specific connection they have established. Following is the extract from packet 4:

```
4   16.0279 NTW3 --> BDC3 TCP .A...F, len: 0, seq: 8221823-8221823,
ack:3462835714, win: 8760, src: 2337  dst: 139 (NBT Session)  NTW3 --> BDC3
IP

TCP: .A...F, len:   0, seq: 8221823-8221823, ack:  1109646, win: 8760, src:
1037  dst:  139 (NBT Session)

  TCP: Source Port = 0x040D
   TCP: Destination Port = NETBIOS Session Service
   TCP: Sequence Number = 8221823 (0x7D747F)
   TCP: Acknowledgement Number = 1109646 (0x10EE8E)
   TCP: Data Offset = 20 (0x14)
   TCP: Reserved = 0 (0x0000)
   TCP: Flags = 0x11 : .A...F

      TCP: ..0..... = No urgent data
       TCP: ...1.... = Acknowledgement field significant
       TCP: ....0... = No Push function
       TCP: .....0.. = No Reset
       TCP: ......0. = No Synchronize
       TCP: .......1 = No more data from sender

  TCP: Window = 8760 (0x2238)
   TCP: Checksum = 0x236C
   TCP: Urgent Pointer = 0 (0x0)

00000:  00 20 AF 47 93 58 00 A0 C9 22 F5 39 08 00 45 00    . .G.X...".9..E.
00010:  00 28 9B F5 40 00 80 06 21 4A C0 5E DE 7B C0 5E    .(..@...!J.^.{.^
00020:  DE 57 09 21 05 48 0B 20 96 AC CE 66 AE 02 50 11    .W.!.H. ...f..P.
00030:  22 38 23 6C 00 00                                  "8#l..
```

Acknowledging the FIN In packet 5, you do not see anything special, except for the server acknowledging the FIN that was transmitted from the client. Following is the extract from packet 5:

```
5   16.0281 BDC3 --> NTW3 TCP .A...., len:   0, seq: 1109646-1109646,
ack: 8221824, win:28672, src: 139  dst: 2337 (NBT Session) BDC3 -->   NTW3
IP
```

```
TCP: .A...., len:    0, seq: 1109646-1109646, ack: 8221824, win:28672, src:
139  dst: 2337 (NBT Session)

  TCP: Source Port = 0x040D
   TCP: Destination Port = NETBIOS Session Service
   TCP: Sequence Number = 1109646 (0x10EE8E)
   TCP: Acknowledgement Number = 8221824 (0x7D7480)
   TCP: Data Offset = 20 (0x14)
   TCP: Reserved = 0 (0x0000)
   TCP: Flags = 0x10 : .A....

     TCP: ..0..... = No urgent data
      TCP: ...1.... = Acknowledgement field significant
      TCP: ....0... = No Push function
      TCP: .....0.. = No Reset
      TCP: ......0. = No Synchronize
      TCP: .......0 = No Fin

  TCP: Window = 28672 (0x7000)
   TCP: Checksum = 0xD5A3
   TCP: Urgent Pointer = 0 (0x0)
   TCP: Frame Padding

00000:    00 A0 C9 22 F5 39 08 00 02 03 BA 84 08 00 45 00    ...".9........E.
00010:    00 28 D2 82 00 00 3F 06 6B BD C0 5E DE 57 C0 5E    .(....?.k..^.W.^
00020:    DE 7B 05 48 09 21 CE 66 AE 02 0B 20 96 AD 50 10    .{.H.!.f... ..P.
00030:    70 00 D5 A3 00 00 90 00 01 00 86 00              p..........
```

After receiving the FIN from the client computer, the server will ACK, as shown in packet 6. Even though TCP has established connections between the two computers, the connections are still independent of one another. Therefore, the server must also transmit a FIN (TCP .A...F) to the client. Following is the extract from packet 6:

```
6   17.0085 BDC3 --> NTW3 TCP .A...F, len: 0, seq: 1109646-1109646, ack:
8221824, win:28672, src: 139 dst: 2337 (NBT Session) BDC3 -->  NTW3    IP

TCP: .A...F, len:  0, seq: 1109646-1109646, ack: 8221824, win:28672, src:
139  dst: 2337 (NBT Session)

  TCP: Source Port = 0x0548
   TCP: Destination Port = 0x0921
   TCP: Sequence Number = 1109646 (0x10EE8E)
   TCP: Acknowledgement Number = 8221824 (0x7D7480)
   TCP: Data Offset = 20 (0x14)
   TCP: Reserved = 0 (0x0000)
   TCP: Flags = 0x11 : .A...F
```

```
TCP: ..0..... = No urgent data
 TCP: ...1.... = Acknowledgement field significant
 TCP: ....0... = No Push function
 TCP: .....0.. = No Reset
 TCP: ......0. = No Synchronize
 TCP: .......1 = No more data from sender

TCP: Window = 28672 (0x7000)
 TCP: Checksum = 0xD5A2
 TCP: Urgent Pointer = 0 (0x0)
 TCP: Frame Padding


00000:  00 A0 C9 22 F5 39 08 00 02 03 BA 84 08 00 45 00   ...".9........E.
00010:  00 28 D2 94 00 00 3F 06 6B AB C0 5E DE 57 C0 5E   .(....?.k..^.W.^
00020:  DE 7B 05 48 09 21 CE 66 AE 02 0B 20 96 AD 50 11   .{.H.!.f... ..P.
00030:  70 00 D5 A2 00 00 02 04 05 B4 86 00               p...........
```

Acknowledging the Close of a TCP Connection   Finally, in packet 7, the
client responds in the same format as the server by ACKing the server's FIN and
incrementing the sequence number by 1. The client ACKing the FIN notification
from the server identifies the close of a TCP connection. Following is the extract
from packet 7:

```
7   17.0085 NTW3 --> BDC3 TCP .A...., len: 0, seq: 8221824-8221824, ack:
1109647, win: 8760, src: 2337  dst: 139 (NBT Session) NTW3 --> BDC3 IP

TCP: .A...., len:    0, seq: 8221824-8221824, ack: 1109647, win: 8760, src:
2337  dst: 139   (NBT Session)

 TCP: Source Port = 0x0921
  TCP: Destination Port = 0x0548
  TCP: Sequence Number = 8221824 (0x7D7480)
  TCP: Acknowledgement Number = 1109647 (0x10EE8F)
  TCP: Data Offset = 20 (0x14)
  TCP: Reserved = 0 (0x0000)
  TCP: Flags = 0x10 : .A....

    TCP: ..0..... = No urgent data
     TCP: ...1.... = Acknowledgement field significant
     TCP: ....0... = No Push function
     TCP: .....0.. = No Reset
     TCP: ......0. = No Synchronize
     TCP: .......0 = No Fin
```

```
TCP: Window = 8760 (0x2238)
 TCP: Checksum = 0x236B
 TCP: Urgent Pointer = 0 (0x0)

00000:  00 20 AF 47 93 58 00 A0 C9 22 F5 39 08 00 45 00    . .G.X...".9..E.
00010:  00 28 BA F5 40 00 80 06 02 4A C0 5E DE 7B C0 5E    .(..@....J.^.{.^
00020:  DE 57 09 21 05 48 0B 20 96 AD CE 66 AE 03 50 10    .W.!.H. ...f..P.
00030:  22 38 23 6B 00 00                                  "8#k..
```

Understanding SYN Attacks

Making a connection-oriented communication link between a client and a server is a delicate process. Now that you have a general understanding of the SYN-ACK procedure, let's discuss SYN attacks. During a SYN attack, by exploiting the TCP handshake process, the attacker sends a flood of connection requests but does not respond to any of the replies. This is referred to as a *half-open* connection, because during a normal connection between a client and a server, the connection is considered to be *open* after the handshake process. At that point, data can be exchanged between the client and the server. Therefore, when the server has not received an ACK from the client, the connection is perceptibly only *half-open*.

Half-open connections are typically achieved using *IP spoofing*. IP spoofing during a SYN attack happens when the attacker sends SYN messages to a target server that appear to originate from some other host. Unfortunately, the spoofed host address does not reply to SYN-ACK messages, thus keeping half-open connections with the target. The SYN messages will usually flood the server, and as a result the target system will basically fill up with requests until it is unable to accommodate new requests. In some cases, the system could consume available memory, crash, or be rendered inoperative. In other words, the target system will inevitably time-out each request after waiting for a response, thus causing the system to use up resources and potentially become unavailable. Because the source address is spoofed, it is difficult to determine the true origin of these packets.

To verify that this type of attack is occurring on Solaris systems, you can check the state of the server system's network traffic. To do so, you can manually use the `netstat` command in a terminal session. The `netstat` command displays network status and protocol statistics. You can display the status of TCP and UDP endpoints in table format and various types of network data, depending on the command-line option that is selected. The syntax options for this command are listed in Table 7-1.

| TABLE 7-1 | Netstat Parameters |

Option	Description
`-a`	Shows the state of all sockets, all routing table entries, or all interfaces, both physical and logical.
`-f address_family`	Limit all displays to those of the specified `address_family`. The value of `address_family` can be one of the following: `inet` For the AF_INET address family showing IPv4 information `inet6` For the AF_INET6 address family showing IPv6 information `unix` For the AF_UNIX address family
`-f filter`	With `-r` only, limits the display of routes to those matching the specified filter. A filter rule consists of a *keyword:value* pair. The known keywords and the value syntax are as follows: `af:{inet|inet6|unix|number.}` Selects an address family. This is identical to `-f address_family` and both syntaxes are supported. `{inif|outif}:{name|ifIndex|any|none}` Selects an input or output interface. You can specify the interface by name (such as `hme0`) or by `ifIndex` number (for example, 2). If any is used, the filter matches all routes having a specified interface (anything other than null). If none is used, the filter matches all routes having a null interface. Note that you can view the index number (`ifIndex`) for an interface with the `-a` option of `ifconfig(1M)`. `{src|dst}:{ip-address[/mask]|any|none}` Selects a source or destination IP address. If specified with a mask length, any routes with matching or longer (more specific) masks are selected. If any is used, all but addresses 0 are selected. If none is used, address 0 is selected. `flags:[+ -]?[ABDGHLU]+` Selects routes tagged with the specified flags. By default, the flags as specified must be set in order to match. With a leading +, the flags specified must be set but others are ignored. With a leading -, the flags specified must not be set and others are permitted.
`-g`	Shows the multicast group memberships for all interfaces.
`-i`	Shows the state of the interfaces that are used for IP traffic. Normally this shows statistics for the physical interfaces. When combined with the `-a` option, this will also report information for the logical interfaces.
`-m`	Shows the STREAMS memory statistics.
`-n`	Shows network addresses as numbers. Netstat normally displays addresses as symbols. This option may be used with any of the display formats.
`-p`	Shows the net to media tables.
`-r`	Shows the routing tables. Normally, only interface, host, network, and default routes are shown, but when this option is combined with the `-a` option, all routes will be displayed, including cache.

| TABLE 7-1 | Netstat Parameters (*cont.*) |

Option	Description
-s	Shows per-protocol statistics. When used with the -M option, shows multicast routing statistics instead. When used with the -a option, per-interface statistics will be displayed, when available, in addition to statistics global to the system.
-v	Verbose. Shows additional information for the sockets, STREAMS memory statistics, and the routing table.
-I interface	Shows the state of a particular interface, which can be any valid interface such as hme0 or le0. When combined with the -a option, information for the logical interfaces is also reported.
-M	Shows the multicast routing tables. When used with the -s option, shows multicast routing statistics instead.
-P protocol	Limits display of statistics or state of all sockets to those applicable to protocol. The protocol can be either ip, ipv6, icmp, icmpv6, igmp, udp, tcp, or rawip. rawip can also be specified as raw. The command accepts protocol options only as all lowercase.
-D	Shows the status of DHCP configured interfaces.

on the
Job *The netstat command with -a and -f inet switches can be used to show the state of all sockets and all routing table entries for the AF_INET address family showing IPv4 information only.*

As an example we'll issue the netstat -a -f inet command. The following is an extract from the sample output during an attack:

```
172.16.43.11.22    172.16.43.100.21834    0    0  9112    0  SYN_RECEIVED
172.16.43.11.22    172.16.43.100.22090    0    0  9112    0  SYN_RECEIVED
172.16.43.11.22    172.16.43.100.22346    0    0  9112    0  SYN_RECEIVED
172.16.43.11.22    172.16.43.100.22602    0    0  9112    0  SYN_RECEIVED
172.16.43.11.22    172.16.43.100.22858    0    0  9112    0  SYN_RECEIVED
172.16.43.11.22    172.16.43.100.23114    0    0  9112    0  SYN_RECEIVED
172.16.43.11.22    172.16.43.100.24854    0    0  9112    0  SYN_RECEIVED
172.16.43.11.22    172.16.43.100.25080    0    0  9112    0  SYN_RECEIVED
172.16.43.11.22    172.16.43.100.26386    0    0  9112    0  SYN_RECEIVED
172.16.43.11.22    172.16.43.100.27609    0    0  9112    0  SYN_RECEIVED
172.16.43.11.22    172.16.43.100.28853    0    0  9112    0  SYN_RECEIVED
172.16.43.11.22    172.16.43.100.29134    0    0  9112    0  SYN_RECEIVED
localhost.32801    localhost.32799    73620  0 73620    0  ESTABLISHED
localhost.32799    localhost.32801    73620  0 73620    0  ESTABLISHED
```

```
localhost.32803   localhost.32799      73620  0 73620   0 ESTABLISHED
localhost.32799   localhost.32803       3620  0 73620   0 ESTABLISHED
localhost.32805   localhost.32771      73620  0 73620   0 ESTABLISHED
localhost.32771   localhost.32805      73620  0 73620   0 ESTABLISHED
localhost.32810   localhost.32809      36810  0 73620   0 ESTABLISHED
localhost.32809   localhost.32810      73620  0 73620   0 ESTABLISHED
localhost.32813   localhost.32812      73620  0 73620   0 ESTABLISHED
localhost.32812   localhost.32813      73620  0 73620   0 ESTABLISHED
localhost.32816   localhost.32799      73620  0 73620   0 ESTABLISHED
localhost.32799   localhost.32816      73620  0 73620   0 ESTABLISHED
localhost.32819   localhost.32818      36810  0 73620   0 ESTABLISHED
localhost.32818   localhost.32819      73620  0 73620   0 ESTABLISHED
localhost.32822   localhost.32799      73620  0 73620   0 ESTABLISHED
localhost.32799   localhost.32822      73620  0 73620   0 ESTABLISHED
localhost.32825   localhost.32824      73620  0 73620   0 ESTABLISHED
localhost.32824   localhost.32825      73620  0 73620   0 ESTABLISHED
```

The interesting part of this example accommodates only the first 12 lines. In them, we see SYN packets from a trusted but spoofed host using contact port 22 (which is Secure Shell, or SSH). Notice the change in source port numbers. In addition, too many connections in the SYN_RECEIVED state would typically indicate that the system is being attacked here.

CERTIFICATION OBJECTIVE 7.02

Establish Courses of Action to Prevent Denial of Service Attacks

This section offers a discussion on various techniques you can deploy to help prevent some of the DoS attack variations mentioned in this chapter. Although you can't be completely safe from evolving DoS attacks, you can mitigate risks to an acceptable level.

Before we start, let's review only the common Solaris Run Levels you should know. By issuing the init (Run Level #) command, you can switch between run levels and perform functions such as halting and rebooting the Solaris operating system. In essence, init is the process *spawner*, while a run level is a software configuration for a selected group of processes. As an example, to shut down the operating system and reboot the computer, you'd open a terminal session with the appropriate administrative privileges and type **init 6**.

Table 7-2 lists a summary of the run levels with which you should be concerned.

TABLE 7-2	Level	Description
	S	Single-user state for administrative functions
Common Run Levels	0	Goes into firmware maintenance mode
	2	Multi-user state where NFS is not running
	5	Shuts down
	6	Stops the operating system and reboots

Preventing Stack-Based Buffer Overflow Attacks

If you do not have access to program source code and you don't have the programming savvy to test code thoroughly by validating input from users to verify that data is being allocated properly, you can still defend yourself against stack-based buffer overflow attacks.

First of all, be sure to keep up-to-date patch implementations, which we'll talk more about in the next section. Second, always monitor programs that are executed with privileges as well as the users who have rights to execute them. User and file permissions should be regularly audited to ensure the principle of least privilege is enforced. To put it briefly, this principle states that any process in the system should be allocated only the absolute minimal set of privileges needed to successfully perform a desired task. Any additional privilege possessed by a process increases the damage incurred if a vulnerability in the program is exploited. The same model can be applied to user access rights and many other situations in computer security. We'll talk more about deploying this principle with user and file permissions in Chapters 9 and 10.

Another defense mechanism against stack smashing is configuring attributes so that code cannot be executed from the stack. In the Solaris operating system, the `noexec_user_stack` variable gives you the option of allowing or disallowing executable stack mappings. In other words, by executing a simple command, you can mitigate your risk to program stack buffer overflows with extra data that can be executed. If the `noexec_user_stack` variable is set to non-zero (by default, the variable is set to zero), the operating system will apply *non-executable* but *readable* and *writable* attributes to every process stack.

When you disallow executable stacks, programs that attempt to execute code on their stack will abort with a core dump. At that time, a warning message will be displayed with the name of the program, its process ID, and the UID of the user who ran the program. In addition, the message can be logged by syslog when the syslog kern facility is set to notice level (refer to Chapter 4 for more information on logging). But because of hardware limitations, monitoring and reporting executable stacks is available only on microSPARC (sun4m) and UltraSPARC (sun4u) platforms.

Additionally, you can disable or enable executable stack message logging. If enabled, when a program attempts to execute stack code, the attempt will be logged by syslog. To enable message logging, follow these steps:

1. Assume the role of superuser.

2. Edit the */etc/system* file and add `set noexec_user_stack_log=1`.

3. Reboot the system.

Conversely, to disable executable stack message logging, add `set noexec_user_stack_log=0` to the */etc/system* file and reboot the system.

INSIDE THE EXAM

Disabling Executable Stacks

Although most programs will run smoothly without running code from the stack, it's important to note that some software may require executable stacks. Therefore, if you disable executable stacks, programs that require the contrary will be aborted; that's why it's crucial to first test this procedure on a nonproduction system.

Following are steps for manually disabling programs from using executable stacks:

1. Assume the role of superuser.

2. Change the directory to the */etc* folder and edit the system file (*/etc/system*)

by adding `set noexec_user_stack=1`. To do so type **cd /etc**, press ENTER, and then type **vi system** and press ENTER again.

3. In the visual editor, press the I key (to switch to edit mode and insert text). Type **set noexec_user_stack=1** and then press ENTER.

4. Next, press the ESC key (to enter into command mode), and type **:wq**. Then press ENTER to save and exit.

5. At the terminal prompt, reboot the system by typing the command **init 6** and then pressing ENTER.

EXERCISE 7-2

Disable Executable Stacks and Enable Stack Message Logging

In this exercise, we are going to disable executable stacks and enable stack message logging in the */etc/system* file; then we'll reboot the operating system to initiate the changes.

Disabling Executable Stacks

1. Log in with an account that has root privileges, or use the `su` command to become superuser.

2. Change the directory to the */etc* folder and edit the system file (*/etc/system*) by adding **`set noexec_user_stack=1`**.

Enabling Stack Message Logging

3. While editing the */etc/system* file, add **`set noexec_user_stack_log=1`**.

4. Save the changes and exit the editor.

Rebooting the Operating System

5. Issue the `init 6` command to restart the server.

Preventing General DoS Attacks, Malformed Packet Attacks, and Flooding

To prevent and defend against DoS attacks, including malformed packet attacks and flooding, Sun Microsystems recommends using egress filtering, TCP wrappers, firewalling, disabling unnecessary service ports, monitoring networks, and implementing a patch program. To reduce IP-spoofed SYN attacks, Sun recommends using filtering. Using firewalls and network monitoring is helpful for detecting Ping of Death and Smurf attacks. In this section, we'll talk about disabling IP ports and services and using Sunsolve—Sun's patch portal.

Disabling Ports and Services

Ports are used in UDP and TCP to name the ends of logical connections with regard to conversations between two systems. When a host contacts another host that is providing a service, a service contact port is defined. The following list is an extract from the */etc/services* file in the Solaris operating system that specifies the ports used by the server processes as contact ports (also known as *well-known ports*):

```
Tcpmux       1/tcp
echo         7/tcp
echo         7/udp
discard      9/tcp       sink null
discard      9/udp       sink null
systat       11/tcp      users
daytime      13/tcp
daytime      13/udp
netstat      15/tcp
chargen      19/tcp      ttytst source
chargen      19/udp      ttytst source
ftp-data     20/tcp
ftp          21/tcp
ssh          22/tcptelnet      23/tcp
smtp         25/tcp      mail
time         37/tcp      timserver
time         37/udp      timserver
name         42/udp      nameserver
whois        43/tcp      nicname
domain       53/udp
domain       53/tcp
bootps       67/udpbootpc      68/udp
kerberos     88/udp      kdckerberos      88/tcp      kdchostnames   101/tcp
hostnamepop2      109/tcp      pop3      110/tcpsunrpc   111/udp      rpcbind
sunrpc       111/tcp     rpcbind
imap         143/tcp     imap2ldap      389/tcp
ldap         389/udp
submission   587/tcp
submission   587/udp
ldaps        636/tcp
ldaps        636/udp
```

For a complete list of ports, their associated services, and descriptions, visit www .iana.org/assignments/port-numbers on the Web.

By disabling access to extraneous ports, the operating system will in effect disable the service (and vice versa) from being available and potentially vulnerable to an attack. We'll do so by commenting out services in the */etc/inetd.conf* file. This file controls the startup of services and defines how the inetd daemon handles common Internet service requests. Following is an extract from the *inetd.conf* file:

```
time        stream      tcp6  nowait      root      internal
time        dgram       udp6  wait        root    internal
echo        stream      tcp6  nowait      root    internal
echo        dgram       udp6  wait        root    internal
discard     stream      tcp6  nowait      root    internal
discard     dgram       udp6  wait        root    internal
daytime     stream      tcp6  nowait      root    internal
daytime     dgram       udp6  wait        root    internal
chargen     stream      tcp6  nowait      root    internal
chargen     dgram       udp6  wait        root    internal
name        dgram       udp   wait        root    /usr/sbin/in.tnamed      in.tnamed
telnet      stream      tcp6  nowait      root    /usr/sbin/in.telnetd
ftp         stream      tcp6  nowait      root    /usr/sbin/in.ftpd
```

   As shown in the extract, the time, echo, discard, daytime, chargen name, telnet, and ftp services are enabled. As an example, let's say that we do not require the use of the echo, chargen, name, and file transfer protocol (ftp) services in the list. By inserting a hash character (#) in front of these services, we'll prevent access to them by disabling the services, as shown here:

```
time        stream      tcp6  nowait      root    internal
time        dgram       udp6  wait        root    internal
# echo      stream      tcp6  nowait      root    internal
# echo      dgram       udp6  wait        root    internal
discard     stream      tcp6  nowait      root    internal
discard     dgram       udp6  wait        root    internal
daytime     stream      tcp6  nowait      root    internal
daytime     dgram       udp6  wait        root    internal
# chargen   stream      tcp6  nowait      root    internal
# chargen   dgram       udp6  wait        rootinternal
# name      dgram       udp   wait        root    /usr/sbin/in.tnamed      in.tnamed
telnet      stream      tcp6  nowait      root    /usr/sbin/in.telnetd
# ftp       stream      tcp6  nowait      root    /usr/sbin/in.ftpd
```

   After commenting out the unnecessary services, we need to save the modified *inetd.conf* file and then register the change with inetd by restarting its process or rebooting the server.

on the Job

Incidentally, it's important to note that attackers tend to target the /etc and /devices directories to manipulate device- and service-specific files to gain illicit access to the system. We'll talk more about those types of techniques throughout the rest of the chapters in this book.

exam
watch

To disable an unneeded port and prevent unauthorized access to the associated service, comment out the service in the /etc/inetd.conf file and then restart the inetd process or reboot the server if the service started through the inetd daemon.

INSIDE THE EXAM

Disabling Services

To disable a service (for example, ftp) that is defined in inetd, we simply comment it out in the /etc/inetd.conf file by inserting a hash character in the very first character position before the service. Next, we need to identify the process ID (PID) for inetd, and then restart the process by following these steps:

1. Log in with an account that has root privileges or use the switch user (su) command to become superuser.

2. Traverse to the /etc folder and edit the inetd.conf file (/etc/inetd.conf), or open a terminal session and use vi.

3. Disable the ftp service by inserting a hash character before the service, as shown here:

```
# ftp   stream   tcp6   nowait   root   /usr/sbin/in.ftpd
```

Then save the change to the modified inetd.conf file, and exit.

4. From a terminal session, identify the PID for inetd with the following command: ps -eaf | grep inetd.

```
root 181   1   0  08:46:02 ?
```

5. Restart the inetd process with the kill -1 (PID) command—for example, kill -1 181; where 181 is the PID for inetd, as shown

For example, the following output with the process for inetd could be shown as:

```
0:00 /usr/bin/inetd -s
```

in the example output in step 4. Otherwise, simply reboot the server (although this may not be always appropriate).

EXERCISE 7-3

Disable the Post Office and Internet Mail Access Protocols

In this exercise, we are going to disable the POP3 and IMAP services in the */etc/ inetd.conf* file, and then restart the inetd process to initiate the changes.

Disabling Services

1. Log in with an account that has root privileges, or use the `su` command to become superuser.

2. Disable the POP3 and IMAP services by editing the *inetd.conf* file (*/etc/inetd. conf*) and inserting a hash character before the POP3 and IMAP services, like so: `# pop3` and `# imap`. Then save the change to the modified *inetd.conf* file and exit.

Identifying and Restarting the inetd Process

3. Identify the PID for inetd with the `ps -eaf | grep inetd` command.

4. Restart the inetd process with the `kill -1 177` command, where `177` is the PID for inetd.

Implementing a Patch Update Program

Not only does Sun recommend that you deploy a patch program, but good security practice mandates that you regularly check for and install new updates and security patches to help keep your operating system software current. You should be able to categorize patches and updates within two groups:

- **Critical updates** Security fixes and other important updates that must be installed to keep your software current and your network secure.

- **Recommended updates** Includes patches, third-party software updates, and other important updates that are not critical with regard to the security of your system and can be installed if or when appropriate.

Any update that is critical to the functionality and security of your operating system is considered a *critical update*. These updates are provided to help resolve known issues and to protect your system from known security vulnerabilities. A critical update applies to your operating system, software programs, or hardware, and should be listed in the critical updates category. You should make a regular schedule to install critical updates. Recommended updates, on the other hand, can be evaluated and possibly condensed and then added to your patch schedule as necessary to ensure your software remains current and stable. SunSolve.sun.com (see Figure 7-1) is Sun's online community, where you'll find the latest patches and updates for Solaris. By clicking the Patch Portal link, you can use Sun's patch manager to automate your patch management, locate and download a particular patch using the PatchFinder search engine, and view Solaris OS Patch Reports from a simple drop-down menu system.

Table 7-3 lists security patches available as of this writing from Sun's Patch Portal; the list was extracted directly from the current lengthy report for Solaris 9. The patches are listed with a patch number followed by its version. For example, *115754* is Sun's zlib security patch and the *02* indicates that it's in the second revision. Also in the report (not included here, for brevity) you'll find new patches, updates, recommended patches, obsolete patches, and a complete listing of released patches.

Viewing, Installing, Verifying, and Removing Patches   Viewing your system's current patches is almost effortless: you issue the `showrev -p` command from a terminal session. The output, which is too long to show here, will display a patch number, whether a patch makes a previous patch obsolete, whether any prerequisite patches for a current patch are available, whether a patch is incompatible with other patches, and what packages are directly affected by a patch.

FIGURE 7-1

Sun's online Patch Portal

TABLE 7-3	Number	Patch
Current Solaris 9 Security Patches	112233-12	SunOS 5.9: Kernel patch
	112601-09	SunOS 5.9: PGX32 Graphics
	112617-02	CDE 1.5: rpc.cmsd patch
	112661-06	SunOS 5.9: IIIM and X Input & Output Method patch
	112807-14	CDE 1.5: dtlogin patch
	112808-06	CDE1.5: Tooltalk patch
	112810-06	CDE 1.5: dtmail patch
	112817-23	SunOS 5.9: Sun GigaSwift Ethernet 1.0 driver patch
	112874-31	SunOS 5.9: lgroup API libc patch
	112875-01	SunOS 5.9: patch /usr/lib/netsvc/rwall/rpc.rwalld
	112907-04	SunOS 5.9: libgss patch
	112908-17	SunOS 5.9: krb5 shared object patch
	112911-14	SunOS 5.9: ifconfig patch
	112921-06	SunOS 5.9: libkadm5 patch
	112922-02	SunOS 5.9: krb5 lib patch
	112923-03	SunOS 5.9: krb5 usr/lib patch
	112925-05	SunOS 5.9: ktutil kdb5_util kadmin kadmin.local kadmind patch
	112926-06	SunOS 5.9: smartcard patch
	112945-33	SunOS 5.9: wbem patch
	112960-24	SunOS 5.9: patch libsldap ldap_cachemgr libldap
	112963-19	SunOS 5.9: linker patch
	112970-07	SunOS 5.9: patch libresolv
	112998-03	SunOS 5.9: patch /usr/sbin/syslogd
	113073-14	SunOS 5.9: ufs and fsck patch
	113146-06	SunOS 5.9: Apache Security patch
	113240-11	CDE 1.5: dtsession patch
	113273-10	SunOS 5.9: /usr/lib/ssh/sshd patch
	113278-09	SunOS 5.9: NFS Daemon, rpcmod patch
	113279-01	SunOS 5.9: klmmod patch
	113280-06	SunOS 5.9: patch /usr/bin/cpio
	113319-21	SunOS 5.9: libnsl nispasswdd patch
	113322-02	SunOS 5.9: patch uucp

TABLE 7-3	Number	Patch
Current Solaris 9 Security Patches (*cont.*)	113329-12	SunOS 5.9: lp patch
	113451-09	SunOS 5.9: IKE patch
	113575-05	SunOS 5.9: sendmail patch
	113579-08	SunOS 5.9: ypserv/ypxfrd patch
	113713-18	SunOS 5.9: pkginstall patch
	113718-02	SunOS 5.9: usr/lib/utmp_update patch
	113798-02	CDE 1.5: libDtSvc patch
	114008-01	SunOS 5.9: cachefsd patch
	114014-09	SunOS 5.9: libxml, libxslt and Freeware man pages patch
	114016-01	tomcat security patch
	114049-12	SunOS 5.9: NSPR 4.1.6 / NSS 3.3.4.5
	114125-01	SunOS 5.9: IKE config.sample patch
	114133-02	SunOS 5.9: mail patch
	114135-03	SunOS 5.9: at utility patch
	114219-11	CDE 1.5: sdtimage patch
	114332-19	SunOS 5.9: c2audit & *libbsm.so.1 patch
	114344-09	SunOS 5.9: arp, dlcosmk, ip, and ipgpc patch
	114361-01	SunOS 5.9: /kernel/drv/lofi patch
	114495-01	CDE 1.5: dtprintinfo patch
	114503-12	SunOS 5.9: usr/sadm/lib/usermgr/VUserMgr.jar patch
	114564-04	SunOS 5.9: /usr/sbin/in.ftpd patch
	114569-02	SunOS 5.9: libdbm.so.1 patch
	114571-02	SunOS 5.9: libc.so.*.9/bcp patch
	114636-03	SunOS 5.9: KCMS security fix
	114684-03	SunOS 5.9: samba patch
	114713-02	SunOS 5.9: newtask patch
	114729-01	SunOS 5.9: usr/sbin/in.telnetd patch
	114861-01	SunOS 5.9: /usr/sbin/wall
	114875-01	SunOS 5.9: XML library source patch
	114971-02	SunOS 5.9: usr/kernel/fs/namefs patch
	115172-01	SunOS 5.9: kernel/drv/le patch
	115553-15	SunOS 5.9: USB Drivers and Framework patch

TABLE 7-3	Number	Patch
Current Solaris 9 Security Patches (*cont.*)	115754-02	SunOS 5.9: zlib security patch
	116237-01	SunOS 5.9: pfexec patch
	116243-01	SunOS 5.9: umountall patch
	116247-01	SunOS 5.9: audit_warn patch
	116308-01	CDE 1.5: libDtHelp patch
	116340-03	SunOS 5.9: gzip and Freeware info files patch
	116453-02	SunOS 5.9: sadmind patch
	116489-01	SunOS 5.9: ttymux patch
	116494-01	SunOS 5.9: libdevice patch
	116559-01	SunOS 5.9: powerd pmconfig patch
	116774-03	SunOS 5.9: ping patch
	116807-01	SunOS 5.9: patch usr/sadm/lib/smc/lib/preload/jsdk21.jar
	117071-01	SunOS 5.9: memory leak in llc1_ioctl()
	117162-01	SunOS 5.9: patch usr/src/uts/common/sys/cpc_impl.h
	117427-03	SunOS 5.9: ufs patch
	117445-01	SunOS 5.9: newgrp patch
	117455-01	SunOS 5.9: in.rwhod patch
	118305-02	SunOS 5.9: TCP patch
	119433-01	SunOS 5.9: telnet

Sun recommends installing every patch that is part of the critical (Sun recommended) list on SunSolve. Other patches should be evaluated individually for relevance. If you do not have a nonproduction experimental system available on which to install and test patches, be sure that you at least have a full current system backup of your production Solaris system before installing any patches.

To install a patch, follow these steps:

1. Download a patch to any folder (such as */tmp/patch*).

2. Assume the role of superuser.

3. If necessary, uncompress the patch file using the following commands: `uncompress` (if the patch ends with .Z); `gunzip` (if the patch ends with .gz); or `unzip` (if the patch ends with .zip).

INSIDE THE EXAM

Installing, Verifying, and Removing Patches

To install a patch, simply use the `patchadd` command `patchadd /dir/filename`; where *dir* is the folder that contains the patch and *filename* is the name of the patch. To install a group of patches in succession, simply add the additional filenames to your command sequence separated by a space:

```
patchadd /dir/filename1 filename2 filename3 filename4
```

To verify that a patch was successfully installed, issue the `showrev` command, like so: `showrev -p`. Or, to verify a specific individual patch, use this command: `showrev -p | grep filename`; where *filename* is the name of the patch.

Once a patch is installed, if necessary, you can remove it using the `patchrm` command, like so: `patchrm filename`; where *filename* is the name of the patch or patch cluster.

4. If necessary, unwrap the patch using the `tar` command, like so: `tar xvf filename.tar`; where *filename*`.tar` is the name of the file and extension.

5. Open a terminal session and invoke the `patchadd` command, as shown here: `patchadd /tmp/patch/112233-11`; where `/tmp/patch` is the folder where you filed your patch and `112233-11` is the name of the patch.

Some patches will accompany installation requirements that must be followed to install them safely. Be sure to refer to the patch report for each patch you intend to implement for installation instructions.

✓ TWO-MINUTE DRILL

Here are some of the key points from the certification objectives in Chapter 7.

Differentiate Between the Types of Host-Based Denial of Service Attacks and Understand How Attacks Are Executed

❏ The most common forms of DoS attacks include program buffer overflow, malformed packets (that is, overlapping IP fragments), Teardrop, Ping of Death, Smurf, Bonk, Boink, NewTear, WinNuke, Land, LaTierra, and SYN attacks.

❏ After penetrating a target system, an attacker would typically attempt to erase any traces of the incident by deleting activity logs and leaving backdoors in place to allow later clandestine access to the system.

❏ When default executable stacks with permissions set to read/write/execute are allowed, programs may be targets for buffer overflow attacks. A buffer overflow occurs when a program process or task receives extraneous data that is not properly programmed. As a result, the program typically operates in such a way that an intruder can abuse or misuse it.

❏ During a SYN attack, the attacker abuses the TCP three-way handshake by sending a flood of connection requests (SYN packets) while not responding to any of the replies. To verify that this type of attack is occurring, you can check the state of the system's network traffic with the `netstat` command.

❏ In a Teardrop attack, the attacker modifies the length and fragmentation offset fields in IP packets, which causes the target to crash.

❏ Ping of Death is a malformed ICMP packet attack whereby an attacker sends an oversized ping packet in an attempt to overflow the system's buffer.

❏ A Smurf attack involves a broadcasted ping request to every system on the target's network with a spoofed return address of the target.

Establish Courses of Action to Prevent Denial of Service Attacks

❏ To help prevent DoS attacks against the Solaris operating system, Sun advocates disabling executable stacks, disabling extraneous IP services/ports, using egress filtering, using firewalls, monitoring networks, and implementing a patch update program.

❑ Sun recommends that you always monitor programs that are executed with privileges as well as the users that have rights to execute them. You can search your system for unauthorized use of the setuid and setgid permissions on programs to gain superuser privileges using the `find` command:

```
find directory -user root -perm -4000 -exec ls -ldb {} \; >/tmp/filename
```

where `find directory` checks all mounted paths starting at the specified directory, which can be root (/), sys, bin, or mail; `-user root` displays files owned only by root; `-perm -4000` displays files only with permissions set to 4000; `-exec ls -ldb` displays the output of the `find` command in `ls -ldb` format; and `>/tmp/filename` writes results to this file.

❑ To defend against stack smashing, you can configure attributes so that code cannot be executed from the stack by setting the `noexec_user_stack=1` variable in the */etc/system* file. If you disable executable stacks, programs that require the contrary will be aborted, so it's crucial that you first test this procedure on a nonproduction system.

❑ The *inetd.conf* defines how the inetd daemon handles common Internet service requests. To disable an unneeded port and prevent unauthorized access to the associated service, comment out the service in the */etc/inetd.conf* file with the hash character and then restart the inetd process or reboot the server if the service started through the inetd daemon.

❑ Use the `showrev -p` command from a terminal session to view your system's current patches.

❑ To install a patch, use the `patchadd` command:

```
patchadd /dir/filename
```

where `dir` is the folder that contains the patch, and `filename` is the name of the patch.

SELF TEST

The following questions will help you measure your understanding of the material presented in this chapter. Read all the choices carefully, because there might be more than one correct answer. Choose all correct answers for each question.

Differentiate Between the Types of Host-Based Denial of Service Attacks and Understand How Attacks Are Executed

1. When executable stacks with permissions set to read/write/execute are allowed, programs by default will be vulnerable to buffer overflow attacks.
   A. True
   B. False

2. Half-open connections are commonly initiated by an attacker in which of the following types of attacks?
   A. Program buffer overflow
   B. Ping of Death
   C. Executable stacks
   D. SYN flooding
   E. Smurf attacks
   F. All of the above

3. Which of the following are common forms of DoS attacks against Solaris operating systems?
   A. Program buffer overflow
   B. Extraneous IP ports
   C. Teardrop
   D. Executable stacks
   E. SYN flooding
   F. All of the above

4. Which type of attack occurs when a program process or task receives extraneous data that is not properly programmed?
   A. Program buffer overflow
   B. Ping of Death
   C. Executable stacks

    D. SYN flooding

    E. Smurf attacks

    F. All of the above

5. Which type of attack occurs when an attacker sends an oversized ICMP packet in an attempt to overflow the target system's buffer?

    A. Program buffer overflow

    B. Ping of Death

    C. Executable stacks

    D. SYN flooding

    E. Smurf attacks

    F. All of the above

6. Which type of attack occurs when a broadcasted ping request is sent to every system on the target's network?

    A. Program buffer overflow

    B. Ping of Death

    C. Executable stacks

    D. SYN flooding

    E. Smurf attacks

    F. All of the above

Establish Courses of Action to Prevent Denial of Service Attacks

7. By commenting out extraneous inetd services, the operating system will disable the service from being available and potentially vulnerable to an attack.

    A. True

    B. False

8. To prevent and defend against DoS attacks, Sun recommends which of the following mechanisms?

    A. Using egress filtering

    B. Installing recommended patches from SunSolve

    C. Disabling unnecessary service ports

    D. Using TCP wrappers

E. Network monitoring and deploying a firewall

F. All of the above

9. From within a terminal session, which command would you execute to view the system's current installed patches?

A. grep *filename*

B. showpatch -p

C. showrev -p

D. vi system

E. All of the above

10. In which of these files would you find the list that specifies the ports used by the server processes as contact ports (also known as *well-known ports*)?

A. /usr/sbin/in.telnetd

B. /tmp/patch

C. /etc/services

D. /etc/inetd.conf

E. All of the above

11. When viewing your system's current patches from a terminal session, the output will display what useful information?

A. A list of current installed patches

B. Whether a patch obsoletes a previous patch

C. Whether a patch is incompatible with other patches

D. Which packages are directly affected by a patch

E. If any prerequisite patches exist for a current patch

F. All of the above

12. Which of the following should be added to the /etc/system file manually to disable programs from using executable stacks?

A. set noexec_user_stack=1

B. set noexec_user_stack_log=1

C. set noexec_program_stack=0

D. set noexec_user_stack_log=0

E. All of the above

13. Which command would display the following output in a terminal session that could indicate that the system is being attacked?

```
10.16.3.11.22       10.16.3.100.21834       0       0   9112       0 SYN_RECEIVED
10.16.3.11.22       10.16.3.100.22090       0       0   9112       0 SYN_RECEIVED
10.16.3.11.22       10.16.3.100.22346       0       0   9112       0 SYN_RECEIVED
10.16.3.11.22       10.16.3.100.22602       0       0   9112       0 SYN_RECEIVED
10.16.3.11.22       10.16.3.100.22858       0       0   9112       0 SYN_RECEIVED
```

    A. find directory -user root

    B. netstat -a -f inet

    C. showrev -p

    D. grep inetd.conf

    E. All of the above

14. To disable an extraneous service and associated IP port, which file would you edit?

    A. /usr/sbin/in.telnetd

    B. /tmp/patch

    C. /etc/services

    D. /etc/inetd.conf

    E. All of the above

15. Assuming the syslog kern facility is set to notice level, when you disallow executable stacks, programs that attempt to execute code on their stack will likely do which of these?

    A. Execute the program with privileges.

    B. Display a warning message with the name of the program, its process ID, and the UID of the user who ran the program.

    C. Monitor executable stacks.

    D. Log a message by syslog.

LAB QUESTION

ABCD Inc. hired you as a consultant with regard to two production Solaris servers. To mitigate the risk of any potential DoS attacks against extraneous services, management informed you that FTP and Name services are not required on their first server; however, they do not want you to bring down the system completely. What steps would you perform to disable the unneeded services?

In addition, management informed you that based on a recent audit of the second server, to alleviate new buffer overflow vulnerabilities, they are required to install and verify the latest SunOS 5.9 kernel patch (112233-11). Assuming the patch was already downloaded into the /tmp directory, what steps would you perform to install and verify the required patch?

SELF TEST ANSWERS

Differentiate Between the Types of Host-Based Denial of Service Attacks and Understand How Attacks Are Executed

1. ☑ **B.** False. When default executable stacks with permissions set to read, write, and execute are allowed, programs may be inherently vulnerable to buffer overflow attacks.

   ☒ **A** is incorrect because, by default, programs are not inherently vulnerable to stack smashing. This is especially true when the latest patches have been applied.

2. ☑ **D.** During a SYN attack, the attacker sends a flood of connection requests but does not respond to any of the replies. This is referred to as a *half-open connection* because during a normal connection between a client and a server, the connection is considered to be open after the handshake process. When the server has not received an ACK from the client, the connection is considered to be half-open.

   ☒ **A** is incorrect because a program buffer overflow occurs when a program process or task receives unwarranted and/or an abundance of data that is not properly programmed. **B** is incorrect because Ping of Death is a malformed ICMP packet attack, whereby an attacker sends an oversized ping packet in an attempt to overflow the system's buffer. **C** is incorrect because executable stacks involve program buffer overflows. **E** is incorrect because a Smurf attack involves a broadcasted ping request to every system on the target's network with a spoofed return address of the target.

3. ☑ **A, C,** and **E.** A buffer overflow occurs when a program process or task receives extraneous data that is not properly programmed. As a result, the program typically operates in such a way that an intruder can abuse or misuse it. In a Teardrop attack, the attacker modifies the length and fragmentation offset fields in IP packets, which causes the target to crash. During a SYN attack, the attacker sends a flood of connection requests but does not respond to any of the replies, thus leaving the connection half-open. The SYN messages will usually flood the server, and as a result the target system will fill up with requests until it is unable to accommodate any new requests. In some cases, the system could consume available memory, crash, or be rendered inoperative.

   ☒ **B** is incorrect because although extraneous IP ports and services could be potential targets for DoS attacks, they're not forms of attacks in and of themselves. **D** is incorrect because when default executable stacks with permissions set to read/write/execute are allowed, programs may be targets for buffer overflow attacks; executable stacks alone are not an attack. It's also important to note that some software may require executable stacks. Therefore, if you disable executable stacks, programs that require them will be aborted.

4. ☑ **A.** A program buffer overflow occurs when a program process or task receives unwarranted data and/or an abundance of data that is not properly programmed.

   ☒ **B** is incorrect because Ping of Death is a malformed ICMP packet attack whereby an attacker sends an oversized ping packet in an attempt to overflow the system's buffer. **C** is incorrect because executable stacks involve program buffer overflows. **D** is incorrect because, during a SYN attack, the attacker sends a flood of connection requests but does not respond to any of the replies. **E** is incorrect because a Smurf attack involves a broadcasted ping request to every system on the target's network with a spoofed return address of the target.

5. ☑ **B.** Ping of Death is a malformed ICMP packet attack, whereby an attacker sends an oversized ping packet in an attempt to overflow the system's buffer.

   ☒ **A** is incorrect because a program buffer overflow occurs when a program process or task receives unwarranted data and/or an abundance of data that is not properly programmed. **C** is incorrect because executable stacks involve program buffer overflows. **D** is incorrect because during a SYN attack, the attacker sends a flood of connection requests but does not respond to any of the replies. **E** is incorrect because a Smurf attack involves a broadcasted ping request to every system on the target's network with a spoofed return address of the target.

6. ☑ **E.** A Smurf attack involves a broadcasted ping request to every system on the target's network with a spoofed return address of the target.

   ☒ **A** is incorrect because a program buffer overflow occurs when a program process or task receives unwarranted data and/or an abundance of data that is not properly programmed. **B** is incorrect because Ping of Death is a malformed ICMP packet attack whereby an attacker sends an oversized ping packet in an attempt to overflow the system's buffer. **C** is incorrect because executable stacks involve program buffer overflows. **D** is incorrect because during a SYN attack, the attacker sends a flood of connection requests but does not respond to any of the replies.

Establish Courses of Action to Prevent Denial of Service Attacks

7. ☑ **A.** True. To disable a service that is defined in inetd, you comment it out in the */etc/inetd.conf* file by inserting a hash character in the first character position before the service. To activate the change, restart the process or reboot the operating system.

   ☒ **B** is incorrect, because unless the service is enabled in inetd the port and service will not be listening for connection attempts.

8. ☑ **F.** All of the answers are correct. To prevent DoS attacks against the Solaris operating system, Sun advocates disabling executable stacks, disabling extraneous IP ports, using egress filtering, monitoring networks, using firewalls, and implementing a patch update program.

9. ☑ **C.** To verify that a patch was successfully installed, issue the `showrev -p` command, or to verify a specific individual patch, use `showrev -p | grep filename`; where *filename* is the name of the patch.

☒ **A** is incorrect because grep filename is an option to the `showrev` command when verifying that a specific patch was successfully installed. **B** is incorrect because the command `showpatch -p` does not exist. **D** is incorrect because vi is the system's visual editor that is used to create and modify text within files. Depending on where you executed the command `vi system`, the editor would either create a new file entitled *system* or open the current *system* file for editing.

10. ☑ **C.** The *etc/services* file specifies the ports used by the server processes as contact ports, which are also known as well-known ports.

☒ **A** is incorrect because that file is used with the telnet service. **B** is incorrect because the file does not typically exist. **D** is incorrect because the *inetd.conf* defines how the inetd daemon handles common Internet service requests.

11. ☑ **F.** All of the answers are correct. Viewing your system's current patches using the `showrev -p` command will display installed patches, patch numbers, whether a patch obsoletes a previous patch, if any prerequisite patches are required for a current patch, whether a patch is incompatible with other patches, and what packages are directly affected by a patch.

12. ☑ **A.** If the `noexec_user_stack` variable is set to non-zero, the operating system will apply nonexecutable but readable and writable attributes to every process stack.

☒ **B** and **D** are incorrect because these settings are used to disable or enable executable stack message logging. **C** is incorrect because that option does not exist.

13. ☑ **B.** The `netstat` command with `-a` and `-f inet` switches can be used to show the state of all sockets and all routing table entries for the `AF_INET` address family showing IPv4 information only.

☒ **A** is incorrect because `find directory -user root` is used to check all mounted paths starting at the specified directory and to display files owned by root. **C** is incorrect because the command `showrev -p` is used for viewing the system's current installed patches. **D** is incorrect because `grep inetd.conf` as it stands will produce nothing.

14. ☑ **D.** The *inetd.conf* defines how the inetd daemon handles common Internet service requests.

☒ **A** is incorrect because that file is used with the telnet service. **B** is incorrect because the file does not typically exist. **C** is incorrect because the *etc/services* file specifies the ports used by the server processes as contact ports, which are also known as well-known ports.

15. ☑ **B and D.** When you disallow executable stacks, programs that attempt to execute code on their stack will abort with a core dump. At that time, a warning message will be displayed with the name of the program, its process ID, and the UID of the user who ran the program. In addition, the message can be logged by syslog when the syslog kern facility is set to notice level.
☒ **A** is incorrect because when a program attempts to execute code on its stack when you disallow executable stacks, the program will abort. **C** is incorrect because whether or not you are monitoring executable stacks has nothing to do with the results of a program that attempts to execute code on its stack.

LAB ANSWER

The first task that ABCD Inc. hired you to perform is to disable the FTP and Name services on one of its servers without completely bringing down the system. To disable these services, you simply comment them out with a hash character in the */etc/inetd.conf* file, in the very first character position on each line of the service. After saving the modified file, you would identify the PID for inetd using the `ps -eaf | grep inetd` command, and then restart the process with the `kill -1` (`PID`) command, where *PID* is the process number for inetd on that system.

The second task that management requires you to perform is to install and verify the latest SunOS 5.9 kernel patch (filename: *112233-11*) on the other server. The patch was downloaded into the */tmp* directory. If ABCD Inc. does not have a nonproduction pilot system available on which you can install and test the patch in advance, be sure you are provided a full current system backup of the production system before installing the patch. Next, be sure to refer to the patch report for this patch on Sunsolve.Sun.com for any specific installation instructions. Upon doing so, you'll know that you need to install this patch in single-user state and then restart the system. Therefore, you start by issuing the `init S` command to enter single-user mode. Next, to install the patch, you simply execute the `patchadd` command as follows: `patchadd /tmp/112233-11`. At that point, you restart the system with the `init 6` command. Finally, to verify that the patch was successfully installed, you issue the `showrev` command as follows: `showrev -p | grep 112233-11`.

8

Remote Access Attacks

I n accordance with the exam requirements, this chapter focuses primarily on identifying and detecting Trojan horse programs and clarifying the differences between backdoors, rootkits, and malicious loadable kernel modules. We'll also look at several techniques and automated tools you can employ to help defend against Trojan horse, backdoor, and rootkit attacks. In addition, we'll briefly explore a digest from a real-world attack that was detected and monitored using some of the same tools we'll cover later in Parts V and VI of this book.

CERTIFICATION OBJECTIVE 8.01

Identify, Detect, and Protect Against Trojan Horse Programs and Backdoors

Before we delve into specifics about remote access attacks, let's define some of the terms this chapter exemplifies. A *Trojan horse program* (Trojan) is basically a malicious program that is disguised as some useful software. Upon execution, Trojans typically install some form of *backdoor* program on the system that will allow a remote attacker unfettered access at a later time. However, in some cases, successfully implemented Trojans that are disguised as legitimate programs will actually perform the anticipated functions while also secretly executing the intended malicious actions. The most popular examples provided by Sun Microsystems are a malicious substitute switch user (su) program placed in a public directory that is waiting to be accidentally executed and a shell script that spoofs the login program. On the flipside, a popular form of permissible backdoor that can potentially be exploitable is a program set up by a programmer to provide remote access to the system to perform debugging and troubleshooting tasks.

A *worm* is not the same thing as a Trojan; a worm is a self-replicating program that copies itself from system-to-system, sometimes using up all available resources on infected systems. Of late, worms have been receiving a lot of press, given their quick replication by rapidly spreading to thousands of computers all over the Internet and affecting their availability. In addition, some worms include payloads that open up backdoors on systems similar to that of Trojans. For example, upon execution, the latest Bagel.U variant has a backdoor that listens at TCP port 4751. At that point, the worm will attempt to connect to a web page hosting a PHP script, which is how the worm notifies the attacker that the system on which it currently resides can be remotely accessed through TCP port 4751.

A *logic bomb* is malicious source code that is inserted into legitimate programming code and is designed to execute under specific circumstances, such as upon someone opening a particular file, when the system is rebooted, or on a specific date. Be sure not to confuse a logic bomb with a *fork bomb*. The latter is a system process that replicates itself until it exceeds the maximum number of allowable processes; therefore, no new processes will be able to initiate. In essence, a fork bomb is a form of denial of service (DoS) attack. Refer back to Chapter 7 for information regarding DoS attacks and remediation.

One final bad boy that should be mentioned is a *virus*. A virus can be defined as a program or code that can self-replicate and that is typically loaded onto your computer without you being aware of its presence. Viruses have various payloads, such as using up available memory or halting your system. Refer to Figure 8-1 for an excellent virus-worm-Trojan comparison, courtesy of Brian and Mark at ThinkQuest.

Securing the System from Trojans and Backdoors

Several techniques can be exercised to help detect and protect against Trojans and backdoors on a system running Solaris. In this section, we'll focus on methods that Sun recommends and that are also covered by the exam. These include tasks that can be performed to harden your system, such as educating users, installing anti-virus software, removing unnecessary compilers, securing file and directory permissions, monitoring path variables, and using file digests, checksums, and the Solaris Fingerprint Database. Let's start by examining ways to harden the Solaris operating system with regard to Trojans and backdoors.

FIGURE 8-1 Virus, worm, and Trojan comparison

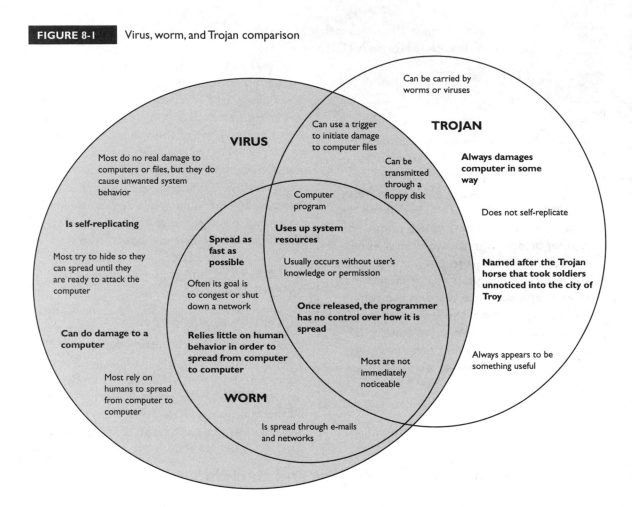

Taking Protective Measures

Probably the most important key to protecting against Trojans and backdoors is user awareness. Executing unknown programs from unknown sources is a risk that users should understand completely. User awareness training and frequent security policy memorandums are critical to help mitigate risks associated with Trojans and backdoors. Anti-virus software should be installed and kept up-to-date on every desktop and server in the infrastructure. In addition, e-mail filters should be deployed and configured to block dangerous attachments.

Some of the most popular anti-virus solutions for Solaris are the following:

- F-Prot Antivirus (www.f-prot.com/products/corporate_users/solaris)
- Sophos Anti-Virus (www.sophos.com/products/sav)
- Trend Micro (www.trendmicro.com)
- Symantec AntiVirus Command Line Scanner (http://enterprisesecurity .symantec.com/products/products.cfm?productID=65&pageID=940&EID=0)
- McAfee System Protection VirusScan (www.nai.com/us/products/mcafee/ antivirus/desktop/vs_unix.htm)
- RAV AntiVirus (www.ravantivirus.com)

watch

Remember Sun's recommendations for hardening Solaris against Trojan horse programs by educating users, installing and updating anti-virus software, removing unnecessary compilers, securing file and directory permissions, and monitoring path variables.

In addition to user awareness and maintaining anti-virus definition updates, Sun recommends a few Solaris-specific tasks to harden operating systems and protect against Trojans:

- Removing unnecessary compilers
- Securing file and directory permissions
- Monitoring path variables

We'll cover in detail user, file, and directory permissions in Chapters 9 and 10; in this section, we'll talk about removing compilers and monitoring path variables.

Removing Unnecessary Compilers A *compiler* is a program that processes code written in a programming language and builds the machine code (also known as *compiling*) that the system can understand. One method used to harden Solaris systems so that a user or attacker cannot compile malicious code on it is to remove compilers that are not needed for normal operation. Some administrators go so far as to remove all compilers, and then reinstall them only as needed. Among the most popular development suites for Solaris that contain compilers is the Sun ONE Studio. As an example, we'll remove the Sun ONE Studio 8 compilers with the command-line uninstaller that was built during the standard installation. The uninstaller for the Sun ONE Studio 8 compilers is *uninstall_Compilers.class*.

To remove the Sun ONE Studio 8 compilers with the command-line uninstaller, follow these steps:

1. Log in with an account that has root privileges, or use the su command to become superuser. As superuser, you'll have full privileges; for example, to switch to root, simply open a terminal session and type **su root**, press ENTER, and then enter root's password at the prompt.

2. In a terminal session, go to the product directory using the following command:

   ```
   cd /var/sadm/prod/com.sun.s1s8_compiler_collection_fcs
   ```

3. To determine the uninstaller .class filename for the software you want to uninstall, type **ls –l** to see the list of uninstaller .class filenames or use the standard uninstaller filename for the Sun ONE Studio 8 compilers, which is *uninstall_Compilers.class*.

4. Type the following command to run the command-line uninstaller:

   ```
   /usr/bin/java uninstall_Compilers -nodisplay
   ```

   Or to uninstall the entire product without any additional prompts (in silent mode), use this:

   ```
   /usr/bin/java uninstall_uninstaller-class-file-name -nodisplay –noconsole
   ```

   where *uninstaller-class-file-name* is the name of the class file.

5. Press ENTER to continue.

6. If you want to uninstall all components of the product, type **1** and skip to step 9.

7. If you want to uninstall only certain components of the product, type **2**. The uninstaller displays a list of the components of the product with checked boxes indicating which components will be uninstalled.

8. If you do not want a component uninstalled, type its number to deselect it. Otherwise, type **0**. The uninstaller displays an updated list showing which components of the product will be uninstalled. Select another component that you want uninstalled and type its number, or type **0** to proceed with uninstallation.

9. The uninstaller lists the components that will be uninstalled and asks you what you would like to do. Type **1** if you want to uninstall the product components now, and proceed to step 10. Type **2** if you want to start over with the uninstallation process, and go back to step 3. Type **3** if you want to exit the uninstaller, and proceed to step 11.

10. When uninstallation is complete, you have the option of viewing the product's log file by typing its corresponding number. When finished, type the number that corresponds to Done. The installer exits.

11. (Optional) If you performed the uninstallation using a remote display, on the display computer, disable client access by typing % **xhost - *source-computer-name*.**

12. Exit from superuser privileges on the source computer by typing **exit.**

Monitoring Paths   The next step with regard to hardening your Solaris operating system, specifically to help protect against Trojans, is more of an ongoing task. Monitoring paths, in particular the PATH and LD_LIBRARY_PATH environment variables, is an important preventative measure, especially for that of privileged users (that is, root). Directories that are referenced should have the appropriate permissions as well as the files that reside in those directories, which we'll talk more about in Chapters 9 and 10.

As an example of this predicament, take a look at root's path. This path—or any path, for that matter—is set at login (through the startup files *.login*, *.profile*, or *.cshrc*, depending on users' default shell) and should never contain a parameter indicated with a dot (.). This parameter would cause the system to search for executables or libraries within that path. If a user placed a Trojan unknowingly or an attacker maliciously planted one in a directory in that path with which privileges were set, at some point root could come by and execute the program by accident.

In addition, you should not allow a search path for root to contain the current directory such as in the following path statement: PATH=./:/usr/bin. In other words, the previously mentioned PATH variables that include the period would permit a condition where root could potentially run the wrong program and execute a Trojan. Other good examples of this concern include these PATH variables: PATH=/usr/bin:/usr/sbin:.:/usr/tools/bin and PATH=/usr/bin:/usr/sbin:. If you find a dot parameter in your PATH variables, you should consider removing it at once, unless otherwise temporarily implemented by administration. You should set up the user search path so that the current directory (.) comes last. The path variable for superuser should *never* include the current directory.

Using the Automated Security Enhancement Tool

To help ensure that path variables are correct, among other things, Sun recommends using the Automated Security Enhancement Tool (ASET). ASET enables you to monitor and restrict access to system files and directories with automated administration governed by a preset security level—low, medium, or high. At the low level, ASET does not take action or affect system services, it ensures that attributes of system files are set to standard release values, and it performs several checks while reporting any potential security weaknesses. At the medium level, ASET does not affect system services; it modifies settings of system files and parameters, restricts system access, and reports security weaknesses and modifications that were previously made to restrict access. Finally, at the high level setting, ASET adjusts system files and parameter settings to minimum access permissions. At this level, most system applications and commands continue to function normally; however, security considerations take precedence over other system behaviors.

Sun recommends running regularly scheduled ASET tasks during off-peak hours or when system activities as well as the user load are low. These tasks include system files permissions tuning, system files checks, user and group checks, system configuration files check, environment variables check, EEPROM (electrically erasable programmable read-only memory) check, and firewall setup. In the remaining sections we'll take a closer look at each of these tasks.

Table 8-1 contains a list of the ASET report filenames for each of the tasks that ASET performs. You should note that messages in each report are enclosed with a beginning and an ending banner. Be sure to examine these files closely every time ASET is run to monitor and solve security problems. The reports are stored in the */usr/aset/reports* directory, within subdirectories that are named in accordance with the time and date the reports are created.

TABLE 8-1	Task	Report File
ASET Tasks and Associated Report Files	System files permissions tuning	*tune.rpt*
	System files checks	*cklist.rpt*
	User and group checks	*usrgrp.rpt*
	System configuration files check	*sysconf.rpt*
	Environment variables check	*env.rpt*
	EEPROM check	*eeprom.rpt*
	Firewall setup	*firewall.rpt*

System Files Permissions Tuning   Tuning system files permissions automatically sets system file permissions according to the security level you choose. At the high level, setting permissions are assigned to restrict access; at the medium level, permissions are tightened just enough for most normal operating environments; and at the low level setting, permissions are set for open sharing. For example, if a system is placed in a demilitarized zone (DMZ) or configured as a perimeter firewall, many administrators tend to set a high level to secure system file permissions further. On the other hand, if a system is placed in a local area network (LAN) that is behind a perimeter, security administrators tend to use the medium level setting. Finally, when a system is placed in an offline network or for a system that is unconditionally trusted—maybe even a development subnet or for testing—administrators can use the low setting for an open information-sharing environment.

When the system is installed, the system files permissions tuning task will run by default; however, after making security-level adjustments, it should be run again to modify system file permissions accordingly. Any changes made using this task will be logged in the *tune.rpt* file.

System Files Checks   Fundamentally, system files checks is a file comparison check from a master file that is created when the task is first executed. For each security level, a list of directories that contains files to check is automatically defined; however, this list can be modified. Upon running this task, the following criteria are checked for each file in each directory in the list:

- Owner and group
- Permission bits
- Size and checksum
- Number of links
- Last modification time

It's common to come across questions about preventing backdoor attacks on the exam. Be sure to know what checksum is and how it can help prevent backdoor attacks.

Probably one of the most useful criteria checks in system files checks is the checksum. Traditionally, a checksum is a special count of bits in a particular transmission, which is included with the transmission, so that the receiver can verify that the same bits arrived during the transmission. If the counts match, it's assumed that the transmission was successfully received intact. Similarly, the system files checks checksum uses a sum command to produce a Cyclic Redundancy Check (CRC) and block count for files that exist in specified directories. Upon running the task, the checksum component can help prevent backdoor attacks by verifying the integrity of files. When the system files checks task finds inconsistencies between the criteria in the master file and the file being checked, they are reported in the *cklist.rpt* file.

User and Group Checks   The user and group checks task is used to verify the integrity of user accounts, their passwords, and their groups. The primary check is made from the *passwd* and *group* files, and the passwords in *local*, *NIS*, and *NIS+* files. Upon running this task, the following criteria are checked for violations and are reported in the *usrgrp.rpt* file:

- Duplicate names or IDs
- Entries in incorrect format
- Accounts without a password
- Invalid login directories
- The nobody account
- Null group password
- A plus sign (+) in the */etc/passwd* file on an NIS server or an NIS+ server

System Configuration Files Check   During the system configuration files check, ASET checks the integrity of, inspects, and makes modifications to system configuration files mostly found in the */etc* directory, and reports problems in the *sysconf.rpt* file. The files that this task checks are of great importance:

- */etc/default/login*
- */etc/hosts.equiv*
- */etc/inetd.conf*
- */etc/aliases*
- */var/adm/utmpx*
- */.rhosts*
- */etc/vfstab*
- */etc/dfs/dfstab*
- */etc/ftpd/ftpusers*

Environment Variables Check   The environment variables check task inspects the PATH and UMASK environment variables. These are found in the */.profile, /.login,* and */.cshrc* files. As you may recall from earlier in this chapter, the path should never contain a parameter indicated with a dot (.). This parameter would cause the system to search for executables or libraries within that path (the current directory). If a user placed a Trojan unknowingly or an attacker maliciously planted one in a directory in that path with which privileges were set, at some point root could execute the program by accident. This potential problem is one of the primary concerns of the environment variables check. Environment security results are reported in the *env.rpt* file.

EEPROM Check   In short, the EEPROM check inspects the EEPROM security parameter to ensure that it is set to the appropriate security level and has not been tampered with. The EEPROM security level options can be set either to none, command, or full. If set to command or full, the system will prompt for the PROM security password; however, the default is none. During the EEPROM check, ASET will not modify this setting but will report recommendations in the *eeprom.rpt* report file.

Firewall Setup   The firewall setup task simply ensures that the system can be safely used as a perimeter gateway—or as Sun calls it, a secure "network relay." This task can help secure a system by setting up a firewall daemon that can be used not only to separate a trusted network from an untrusted network, but to disable Internet Protocol (IP) packet forwarding and conceal routing information from the untrusted or external network, among other things. Of course, you do have the option of eliminating the firewall setup task by editing the *asetenv* file if you choose not to use the system as a network relay. This task reports findings in the *firewall.rpt* report file.

Configuring and Running ASET   To configure ASET, and although you can simply run the suite using its predefined default parameters, you can adjust settings in the configuration files that can be found in */usr/aset/asetenv, /usr/aset/masters/tune.low,*

/usr/aset/masters/tune.med, and */usr/aset/masters/tune.high*. To begin, let's take a look
at the */usr/aset/asetenv* file:

```
#############################################
#                                           #
#       User Configurable Parameters        #
#                                           #
#############################################
CKLISTPATH_LOW=${ASETDIR}/tasks:${ASETDIR}/util:${ASETDIR}/masters:/etc
CKLISTPATH_MED=${CKLISTPATH_LOW}:/usr/bin:/usr/ucb
CKLISTPATH_HIGH=${CKLISTPATH_MED}:/usr/lib:/sbin:/usr/sbin:/usr/ucblib
YPCHECK=false
UID_ALIASES=${ASETDIR}/masters/uid_aliases
PERIODIC_SCHEDULE="0 0 * * *"
TASKS="firewall env sysconf usrgrp tune cklist eeprom"
```

The *asetenv* file has two sections—the user configurable parameters section and
the internal environment variables section—but only the user configurable parameters
part is shown in the extract, and for good reason. To avoid corrupting the program,
you should not make any changes to the internal environment variables section.
However, user configurable parameters can be modified by specifying the directories
for the system files checks task, extending checks to NIS+ tables, specifying a UID
aliases file, scheduling ASET execution, and choosing which tasks to run:

- Specifying the directories for the system files checks task is accomplished
  by defining which directories to check for each security level; the
  CKLISTPATH_LOW variable defines the directories to be checked at the
  low security level, the CKLISTPATH_MED for the medium security level,
  and CKLISTPATH_HIGH for the high level. As shown in the extract, the
  lower level directories need to be specified in the higher level path; for
  example, in CKLISTPATH_MED=${CKLISTPATH_LOW}:/usr/bin:/usr/
  ucb, the CKLISTPATH_LOW directories are automatically included.

- To extend checks to NIS_ tables, the YPCHECK environment variable would
  have to be enabled with a true parameter. This is particularly useful if it is
  required to check the NIS+ *passwd* table; otherwise only the local *passwd* file
  is checked. We'll talk more about that in the sections that follow.

- The UID_ALIASES variable specifies an aliases file that lists shared UIDs.

- The PERIODIC_SCHEDULE parameter is used by ASET to determine when
  to execute tasks. The format of PERIODIC_SCHEDULE follows that of
  crontab entries.

■ In the remaining parts of this section, we'll take a closer look at each individual task that ASET runs. Choosing which tasks to run in the user configurable parameters section of the */usr/aset/asetenv* file is relatively easy. By default, it contains all seven ASET tasks shown in this extract:

```
TASKS="firewall env sysconf usrgrp tune cklist eeprom"
```

To exclude tasks, simply remove them from the list.

By editing the */usr/aset/masters/tune.low, /usr/aset/masters/tune.med,* and */usr/aset/ masters/tune.high* files, you can restrict permissions to values that are appropriate for default system settings. The higher the security level tune file (that is, *tune.high*), the more restrictive permissions can be. According to Sun, each entry in a tune file occupies one line. The fields in an entry appear in the following order:

1. *pathname*   The full path name of the file
2. *mode*   A five-digit number that represents the permission setting
3. *owner*   The owner of the file
4. *group*   The group owner of the file
5. *type*   The type of file

In addition, you must follow these nine rules when making modifications to the tune files:

1. You can use regular shell wildcard characters (that is, asterisks and question marks) in the path name.
2. *mode* represents the least restrictive value. If the current setting is already more restrictive than the specified value, ASET does not loosen the permission settings.
3. You must use names for owners and groups instead of numeric IDs.
4. You can use a question mark (?) in place of owner, group, and type.
5. *type* can be a symlink, directory, or file.
6. Higher security level tune files set file permissions to be at least as restrictive as file permissions at lower levels.
7. A file can match more than one tune file entry.

8. File permission is set to the most restrictive value despite entries with different permissions.

9. The last entry has priority when two entries have different owner or group designations.

When you're ready to run ASET, you can manually execute ASET tasks or simply schedule ASET to run periodically. To run ASET manually at any given time, simply log in as root or become superuser and then issue this command:

```
/usr/aset/aset -l level -d pathname
```

where *level* is security level value (low, medium, or high), and *pathname* is the working directory for ASET (the default is */usr/aset*).

On the other hand, to run ASET automatically at a predefined time, simply edit the PERIODIC_SCHEDULE variable in the */usr/aset/asetenv* file to the desired start time and then add ASET to the crontab file (which is a list of tasks that are run on regular schedules). For more information on the crontab utility, visit http://docs .sun.com/db/doc/817-0689/6mgfkpclp?q=crontab&a=view on the Web or use the command man crontab.

INSIDE THE EXAM

Scheduling ASET to Run Automatically

Following are steps for scheduling ASET to run tasks automatically:

1. Log in with an account that has root privileges, or use the switch user (su) command to become superuser. For example, to switch to root, simply open a terminal session and type **su root**, press ENTER, and then enter root's password at the prompt.

2. Edit the PERIODIC_SCHEDULE variable in the */usr/aset/asetenv* file to

an appropriate start time (by default, it's set to run every day at midnight: PERIODIC_SCHEDULE="0 0 * * *").

3. Insert a line in the crontab file to start ASET at the time determined by the PERIODIC_SCHEDULE environment variable, using /usr/ aset/aset -p

4. Alternatively, to stop ASET from running periodically, simply edit the crontab file and remove the entry for ASET.

File/Message Digests

One popular method that Sun supports for verifying whether files were maliciously altered is to use *message digest algorithms*. A message digest is a one-way function for a stream of binary data as verification that the data was not altered since the message digest was first generated. For example, many times when downloading a patch, update, or program, you'll see output such as the following along with your download link:

```
Filename: 200404-patch.zip
 Creation Date: April 12, 2004
 Release Date: April 12, 2004
 File Size: 4.63 MB
MD5: B12A24F23E37B0EFC4B9C42B1247B8B9
```

This information was published with a message digest signature (that is, an MD5 hash) when the file was created. In this example, after downloading the file, you would run the MD5 utility on it to verify that you get the same MD5 hash output that was posted with the download link. If the signature or hash is different from that posted, you can assume that the file was either corrupted during transfer or possibly maliciously altered since the hash was first published.

The MD5 and the Secure Hashing Algorithm (SHA1) are among the most popular message digest algorithms. MD5 was developed by Ron Rivest in 1991 at the MIT Laboratory for Computer Science and RSA Data Security, Inc. The MD5 algorithm takes a message of arbitrary length and produces a 128-bit message digest. SHA1—a revision to the original SHA that was published in 1994—is similar to the MD4 family of hash functions developed by Rivest. The algorithm takes a message and produces a 160-bit message digest. Although MD5 and SHA1 were developed to help detect corrupt or maliciously altered files, Sun recommends using a more comprehensive package called Tripwire. In addition to Tripwire, to help prevent unauthorized changes from being made to system files, Sun also recommends using ASET (discussed in the previous section) and the Basic Security Module (BSM), which is discussed in Chapter 5. Finally, the Solaris cryptographic framework supports a command that can also be used to check the integrity of files. For example, using the `digest` command, you can compute a message digest for one or more files.

We'll talk more about the cryptographic framework, including creating symmetric keys and encrypting files, in Chapter 11; here, we'll take a succinct look at how to create digests of files using the MD5 and SHA1 algorithms.

Computing a Digest of a File   By comparing digests of a file, you are checking the file's integrity to ensure that it has not been corrupted or altered. In the Solaris cryptographic framework environment, we can perform digest computations using the following syntax:

```
digest -v -a algorithm input-file > digest-listing
```

Where -v displays the output with file information, -a *algorithm* is the algorithm used to compute a digest (that is, MD5 or SHA1), *input-file* is the input file for the digest to be computed, and *digest-listing* is the output file for the digest command.

INSIDE THE EXAM

Creating and Viewing File Digests

Following are steps for manually creating file digests with the digest command using both MD5 and SHA1 mechanisms within the cryptographic framework:

1. To compute an MD5 digest for file *solpatch* into output file *solpatchmd5*, issue this command:

```
digest -v -a md5 solpatch >> $HOME/solpatchmd5
```

2. You can then concatenate or display the resulting file with the cat command, cat ~/solpatchmd5, to view the following output:

```
md5 (solpatch) = 83c0e53d1a5cc71ea42d9ac8b1b25b01
```

3. To compute an SHA1 digest for file *solpatch* into output file *solpatchsha1*, issue this command:

```
digest -v -a sha1 solpatch >> $HOME/solpatchsha1
```

4. You can then issue the cat command, cat ~/solpatchsha1, to view the following output:

```
sha1 (solpatch) = 1ef50e5ad219e34f0b911a097b7b588e31f9b438
```

The Solaris Fingerprint Database

The Solaris Fingerprint Database (sfpDB) is a free tool from Sun that allows you to check the integrity of system files through cryptographic checksums. By doing this, you can determine whether system binaries and patches are safe in accordance with their original checksums stored at Sun. This includes files distributed with Solaris OE media kits, unbundled software, and patches.

MD5 software binaries that can be used with sfpDB for Intel and SPARC architectures can be freely downloaded from Sun at http://SunSolve.Sun.com/md5/md5.tar.Z. Currently, foreign language versions are not supported, but suggestions and requests can be sent to fingerprints@sun.com.

The MD5 software is compressed in the tar file format; therefore, after downloading to a directory (such as */usr/local*), unpack the archive with the following command:

```
zcat md5.tar.Z | tar xvf -
```

The software will be unpacked into a MD5 subdirectory.

Installing MD5 Software   After downloading and unpacking the MD5 archive, the file permissions must be modified before they can be executed. To permit only root, for example, to read, write, and execute the MD5 programs, issue the `chmod 700 /usr/local/md5/*` command (`chmod` is a command used to change file access permissions). Additionally, the owner and group of the MD5 files must be modified to belong to a system user and associated group. Given the particular functionality, traditionally they should be owned by root; therefore, you should also issue the command `chown root:root /usr/local/md5/*` (`chown` is a command used to change file owners; see Chapter 10 for more on this command).

Using MD5 Software   Creating hexadecimal MD5 digital fingerprints is simple. For example, based on the installation mentioned previously, to create an MD5 fingerprint for the *su* program on a SPARC system, you would enter this command:

```
/usr/local/md5/md5-sparc /usr/bin/su
```

The output should look something like this:

```
MD5 (/usr/bin/su) = cb2b71c32f4eb00469cbe4fd529e690c
```

Furthermore, by placing a space between target files, you can create MD5 fingerprints for more than one file at a time, such as for the *su* and *ls* programs, by issuing this command:

```
/usr/local/md5/md5-sparc /usr/bin/su /usr/bin/ls
```

The output should look something like this:

```
MD5 (/usr/bin/su) = cb2b71c32f4eb00469cbe4fd529e690c
MD5 (/usr/bin/ls) = 351f5eab0baa6eddae391f84d0a6c192
```

Finally, to create MD5 fingerprints for all files in the */usr/bin* directory, you could issue the MD5 command along with the `find` command, such as in the following:

```
find /usr/bin -type f -print \
| xargs -n100 /usr/local/md5/md5-sparc > /tmp/md5output.txt
```

As indicated, the output will be printed to the */tmp* directory in file *md5output.txt*. The contents of the file can easily be copied into the online fingerprint database for integrity checks.

You can check the integrity of your files against the sfpDB portal database at http://SunSolve.sun.com (see Figure 8-2).

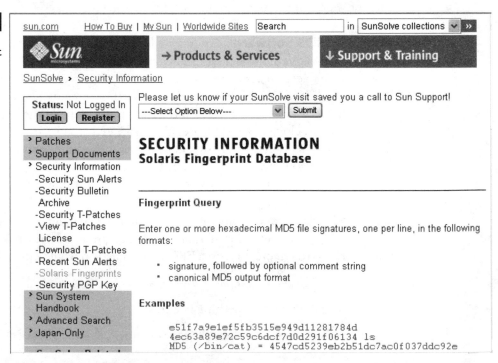

The online front-end interface to the database is easy to use—no assembly required. Simply scroll down to the query form (shown in Figure 8-3) and copy and paste one or more hexadecimal MD5 file signatures (one per line for a maximum of 256 possible entries) in signature format, followed by an optional comment string or in canonical MD5 output format. Currently, the database includes 2,717,303 fingerprints, 22,702 package names, and 23,658 patches. In other words, if your Sun binary, patch, or file is legitimate, it's likely listed in the database.

Upon submitting your query, the database search results will contain information regarding a signature match or mismatch, as depicted in Figure 8-4. File-specific information with regard to signature matches includes the following:

- Canonical-path
- Package
- Version
- Architecture
- Source

FIGURE 8-3

Solaris Fingerprint Database query form

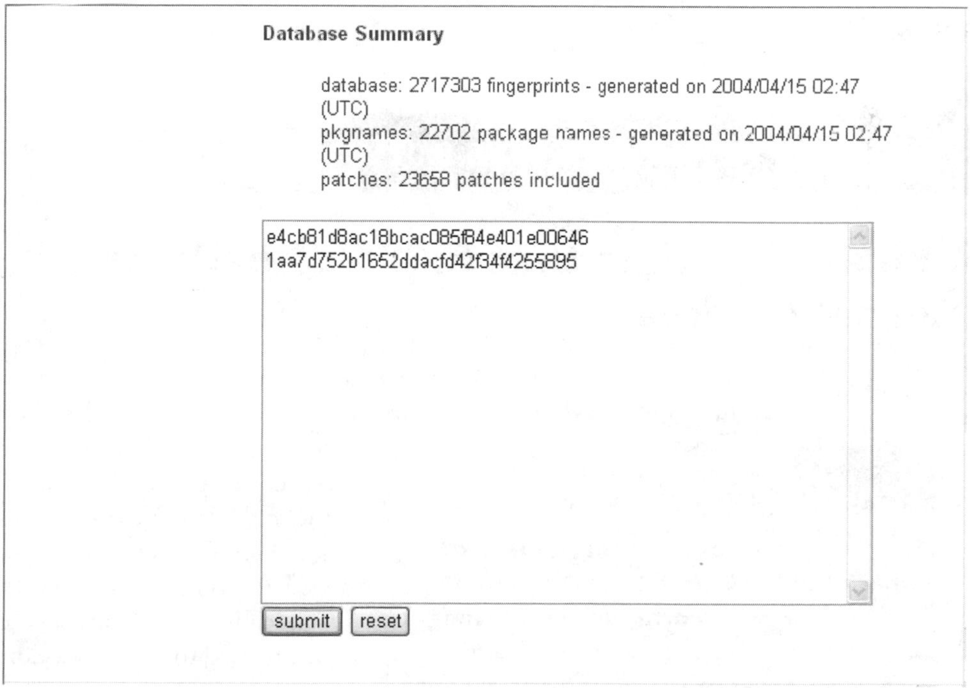

Database Summary

database: 2717303 fingerprints - generated on 2004/04/15 02:47 (UTC)
pkgnames: 22702 package names - generated on 2004/04/15 02:47 (UTC)
patches: 23658 patches included

e4cb81d8ac18bcac085f84e401e00646
1aa7d752b1652ddacfd42f34f4255895

submit reset

> Patches
> Support Documents
> Security Information
  -Security Sun Alerts
  -Security Bulletin
   Archive
  -Security T-Patches
  -View T-Patches
   License
  -Download T-Patches
  -Recent Sun Alerts
  -Solaris Fingerprints
  -Security PGP Key
> Sun System
  Handbook
> Advanced Search
> Japan-Only

SunSolve Related:
- SunSolve WorldWide
- SupportForum
- About SunSolve
- Feedback
- Site Map
- Features/etc.
- SunSolve Home
- Help

SECURITY INFORMATION
Solaris Fingerprint Database

Results of Last Search

```
e4cb81d8ac18bcac085f84e401e00646 - - 1 match(es)
```
   * canonical-path: /usr/sbin/md5
   * package: SUNWkeymg
   * version: 1.5
   * architecture: sparc
   * source: SunScreen EFS 3.0 rev A

```
1aa7d752b1652ddacfd42f34f4255895 - - 1 match(es)
```
   * canonical-path: /usr/sbin/md5
   * package: SUNWkeymg
   * version: 1.5
   * architecture: i386
   * source: SunScreen EFS 3.0 rev A

Fingerprint Query

Enter one or more hexadecimal MD5 file signatures, one per line, in the following
formats:

CERTIFICATION OBJECTIVE 8.02

Explain Rootkits that Exploit Loadable Kernel Modules

A *rootkit* is sometimes referred to as an *advanced Trojan horse program*. A rootkit utility can be used not only to provide remote backdoor access to attackers, but it typically also attempts to hide the attacker's presence on the system. Finally, a loadable kernel module (LKM) is actually part of the system kernel. Therefore, LKMs are usually considered kernel extensions that contain dynamically loadable kernel components, typically used to load device drivers. In this

---

e x a m

ⓦatch

For the exam, know that a rootkit utility is used to provide remote backdoor access to attackers and to hide the attacker's presence on the system. Also, some types of rootkit utilities exploit the use of loadable kernel modules.

section, we'll discuss rootkit utilities that exploit the use of LKMs to modify the running kernel for malicious purposes.

Rootkits and Loadable Kernel Modules

To understand rootkits and LKMs better, let's take a look at an actual "black-hat" hacking example that was detected and monitored using two different intrusion detection systems' (IDS) sensors, as well as a popular sniffer (EtherPeek NX by WildPackets). The target company name will be concealed for privacy, so therefore we'll refer to them in this example as *TargetABC*.

Real-World Attack Synopsis

TargetABC headquarters is located in the United States Midwest region. Despite critical warnings from two separate third-party security auditors, TargetABC proceeded to ignore or nonprioritize alleviation recommendations with regard to a vulnerable Solaris system on a branch office network that connects to the headquarters via a virtual private network (VPN) over a broadband connection. The attack began with a series of port scans against the Solaris system, which, like so many secondhand or backburner systems, was not properly patched or updated. As you know by now, port scanning is among the first steps in the discovery process used to fingerprint potentially vulnerable systems.

After detecting this particular system, it appeared that various vulnerability scanners were also employed, potentially to map out any known weaknesses in the system. At that point, we believe the attacker effortlessly located a Remote Procedure Call (RPC) weakness in *rpc.ttdbserverd* (ToolTalk), *rpc.cmsd* (Calendar Manager), and *rpc.statd* that could allow immediate root compromise to the operating system. After gaining root access and accessing a shell, the attacker created a few backdoor user accounts, one with root privileges.

The next time the attacker logged in and switched to the backdoor root account, he downloaded, unpacked, and installed a few rootkits, all from his remote location. Among other things, the rootkits replaced the *ps* program, which can be used to list any processes running on the system (apparently to hide his presence by concealing processes used by the rootkit). In addition, device-specific files were

exam
🅦atch   *Device-specific files in the* /etc *and* /devices *directories are common targets for attackers to attempt to gain access to the operating system, especially for creating backdoors to the system.*

also targeted for deploying backdoors on the system. Unfortunately for TargetABC, the attack didn't end there. A kernel-level rootkit was also employed to patch the kernel, likely in place of simply replacing other commands as with the *ps* program, to remap system functions to execute code without having to do any legwork on system programs themselves. This way, when a legitimate user logged in and ran an ordinarily normal program, the Trojaned kernel would instead execute malicious code.

Defending Against Rootkits and Trojaned Loadable Kernel Modules

In this section, we'll discuss ways that Sun advocates to defend against general rootkits and kernel-level rootkits.

As discussed previously in this chapter, frequently using integrity checking mechanisms such as checksums and the sfpDB can help detect maliciously altered programs. If a rootkit is detected, Sun recommends restoring the operating system from trusted sources, followed by reinstalling applications, and finally restoring data from secured backups. Unfortunately, however, kernel-level rootkits are not as easily detectable using integrity-checking mechanisms given that the kernel itself is involved in the process. Building a kernel that does not support loadable kernel modules, or a *monolithic* kernel, is not feasible with regard to the Solaris operating system. For this reason, Sun recommends building a kernel that monitors and controls the system's treatment of its loadable kernel modules, especially for perimeter security or outside systems operating as gateways, web, and mail agents. On the other hand, if restricting loadable kernel modules is not practical, Sun recommends taking advantage of the Solaris Cryptographic services. We'll revisit these techniques later in Parts V and VI of this book.

One final point about the Solaris system file should be considered here. The system kernel configuration file (*/etc/system*) contains commands that are read when the kernel is initialized. These commands can be used in particular to modify the system's operation concerning how to handle loadable kernel modules. Commands that modify the handling of LKMs require you to specify the module type by listing the module's namespace, thus giving you the ability to load a loadable kernel module or exclude one from being loaded.

Following is Sun's sample system file:

```
* Force the ELF exec kernel module to be loaded during kernel
* initialization. Execution type modules are in the exec namespace.
forceload: exec/elfexec
* Change the root device to /sbus@1,f8000000/esp@0,800000/sd@3,0:a.
* You can derive root device names from /devices.
* Root device names must be the fully expanded Open Boot Prom
* device name. This command is platform and configuration specific.
* This example uses the first partition (a) of the SCSI disk at
* SCSI target 3 on the esp host adapter in slot 0 (on board)
* of the SBus of the machine.
* Adapter unit-address 3,0 at sbus unit-address 0,800000.
rootdev: /sbus@1,f8000000/esp@0,800000/sd@3,0:a
* Set the filesystem type of the root to ufs. Note that
* the equal sign can be used instead of the colon.
rootfs:ufs
* Set the search path for kernel modules to look first in
* /usr/phil/mod_test for modules, then in /kernel/modules (the
* default) if not found. Useful for testing new modules.
* Note that you can delimit your module pathnames using
* colons instead of spaces: moddir:/newmodules:/kernel/modules
moddir:/usr/phil/mod_test /kernel/modules.
* Set the configuration option {_POSIX_CHOWN_RESTRICTED} :
* This configuration option is enabled by default.
set rstchown = 1
* Disable the configuration option {_POSIX_CHOWN_RESTRICTED} :
set rstchown = 0
* Turn on debugging messages in the modules mydriver. This is useful
* during driver development.
set mydriver:debug = 1
* Bitwise AND the kernel variable "moddebug" with the
* one's complement of the hex value 0x880, and set
* "moddebug" to this new value.
set moddebug & ~0x880
* Demonstrate the cumulative effect of the SET
* bitwise AND/OR operations by further modifying "moddebug"
* by ORing it with 0x40.
set moddebug | 0x40
```

Refer to the system—system configuration information file—man page in your Solaris Reference Manual Collection or online at http://docs.sun.com for supported namespaces and syntax. Although monolithic kernels are not feasible in the Solaris operating environment, you can at least control which LKMs should be loaded.

TWO-MINUTE DRILL

Here are some of the key points from the certification objectives in Chapter 8.

Identify, Detect, and Protect Against Trojan Horse Programs and Backdoors

❑ A Trojan horse program is a malicious program that is disguised as some useful software. Trojan examples include a shell script that spoofs the login program and a malicious substitute switch user (su) program.

❑ Device-specific files in the */etc* and */devices* directories are common targets for attackers to attempt to gain access to the operating system, especially for creating backdoors to the system.

❑ A worm is a self-replicating program that will copy itself from system to system, sometimes using up all available resources on infected systems or installing a backdoor on the system.

❑ A logic bomb is code that is inserted into programming code and is designed to execute under specific circumstances.

❑ A fork bomb is a process that replicates itself until it consumes the maximum number of allowable processes.

❑ A rootkit utility can be used not only to provide remote backdoor access to attackers but also to hide the attacker's presence on the system. Some types of rootkit utilities exploit the use of loadable kernel modules to modify the running kernel for malicious intent.

Explain Rootkits that Exploit Loadable Kernel Modules

❑ To harden your system and help protect against Trojan horse programs, Sun recommends user awareness education, installing and updating anti-virus software, removing unnecessary compilers, securing file and directory permissions, and monitoring path variables.

❑ Path variables should not contain a parameter indicated with a dot (.) that could cause the system to search for executables or libraries within that path, as well as a search path for root that contains the current directory.

❑ To monitor and help prevent unauthorized changes from being made to system files, Sun recommends using the Automated Security Enhancement

Tool (ASET), the Basic Security Module (BSM), Tripwire, and the Solaris cryptographic framework.

❑ ASET enables you to monitor and restrict access to system files and directories with automated administration governed by a preset security level (low, medium, or high). The seven tasks that ASET can regularly perform include system files permissions tuning, system files checks, user and group checks, system configuration files check, environment variables check, EEPROM check, and firewall setup.

❑ To run ASET at any given time, simply log in as root or become superuser, and then issue the /usr/aset/aset -l *level* -d *pathname* command; where *level* is the security level value (low, medium, or high), and *pathname* is the working directory for ASET (the default is */usr/asset*).

❑ To avoid resource encumbrance, ASET tasks should be run during off-peak hours or when system activities are low.

❑ Verify whether files were maliciously altered by using message digest algorithms. A message digest is a digital signature for a stream of binary data as verification that the data was not altered since the signature was first generated. The MD5 and the Secure Hashing Algorithm (SHA1) are among the most popular message digest algorithms.

❑ Using the digest command, you can compute a message digest for one or more files. In the Solaris cryptographic framework environment, you can perform digest computations using the syntax digest -v -a *algorithm input-file > digest-listing*; where -v displays the output with file information, -a *algorithm* is the algorithm used to compute a digest (that is, MD5 or SHA1), *input-file* is the input file for the digest to be computed, and *digest-listing* is the output file for the digest command.

❑ The Solaris Fingerprint Database (sfpDB) is a free tool from Sun that allows you to check the integrity of system files through cryptographic checksums online. By doing so, you can determine whether system binaries and patches are safe in accordance with their original checksums stored at Sun, which includes files distributed with Solaris OE media kits, unbundled software, and patches.

❑ Frequently using integrity checking mechanisms such as checksums and the sfpDB can help detect maliciously altered programs.

❑ If a rootkit is detected, Sun recommends restoring the operating system from trusted sources, followed by the reinstallation of applications, and finally data restoration from secured backups.

❑ Kernel-level rootkits are not as easily detectable using integrity checking mechanisms given that the kernel itself is involved in the process. Sun recommends building a kernel that monitors and controls the system's treatment of its loadable kernel modules, especially for perimeter security or outside systems operating as gateways, web, and mail agents. If restricting loadable kernel modules is not practical, Sun recommends taking advantage of the Solaris Cryptographic services.

❑ The system file (*/etc/system*) contains commands that are read when the kernel is initialized. These commands can be used to modify the system's operation concerning how to handle loadable kernel modules. Commands that modify the handling of LKMs require you to specify the module type by listing the module's namespace, thus giving you the ability to load a loadable kernel module or exclude one from being loaded.

SELF TEST

The following questions will help you measure your understanding of the material presented in this chapter. Read all the choices carefully because there might be more than one correct answer. Choose all correct answers for each question.

Identify, Detect, and Protect Against Trojan Horse Programs and Backdoors

1. Which of the following is a self-replicating program that will copy itself from system-to-system?
   A. Trojan horse
   B. Worm
   C. Logic bomb
   D. Fork bomb
   E. Rootkit
   F. All of the above

2. Which of the following is a form of denial of service acting as a system process that replicates itself until it exceeds the maximum number of allowable processes?
   A. Trojan horse
   B. Worm
   C. Logic bomb
   D. Fork bomb
   E. Rootkit
   F. All of the above

3. Which of these is code that is inserted into programming code that is designed to execute under specific circumstances?
   A. Trojan horse
   B. Worm
   C. Logic bomb
   D. Fork bomb
   E. Rootkit
   F. All of the above

4. A backdoor can be a legitimate remote access portal to perform debugging and troubleshooting tasks.
   A. True
   B. False

5. Which of the following does Sun recommend for hardening your system and helping to protect against Trojan horse programs?

    A. Removing unnecessary compilers

    B. Securing file and directory permissions

    C. Installing anti-virus software

    D. Monitoring path variables

    E. Educating users

    F. All of the above

6. To harden your system and help protect against Trojan horse programs, Sun recommends that path variables do *not* contain which of these?

    A. A parameter indicated with a dot (.)

    B. A search path for root that contains the current directory

    C. A parameter indicated with a forward slash (/)

    D. A search path for superuser that contains the current directory

    E. All of the above

7. Which of the following directories are the most common targets for attackers to attempt to gain access to the operating system, especially for creating backdoors to the system?

    A. /etc

    B. /usr/aset

    C. /usr/local

    D. /devices

    E. All of the above

Explain Rootkits that Exploit Loadable Kernel Modules

8. Which of these can be deployed to monitor and help prevent unauthorized changes from being made to system files?

    A. Tripwire

    B. BSM

    C. Solaris cryptographic framework

    D. ASET

    E. All of the above

9. Which of these is an ASET task that checks the integrity of, inspects, and makes modifications to system files mostly found in the /etc directory?

    A. System files permissions tuning

    B. System files checks

    C. User and group checks

    D. System configuration files check

    E. Environment variables check

    F. EEPROM check

    G. Firewall setup

    H. All of the above

10. Which of these is used to produce a Cyclic Redundancy Check (CRC) and block count for files that can help prevent backdoor attacks?

    A. ASET

    B. Message digest

    C. Checksum

    D. EEPROM check

    E. All of the above

11. Which of these is an ASET task that performs a file comparison check from a master file that is created when the task is first executed?

    A. System files permissions tuning

    B. System files checks

    C. User and group checks

    D. System configuration files check

    E. Environment variables check

    F. EEPROM check

    G. Firewall setup

    H. All of the above

12. Which of these is an ASET task that automatically sets system file permissions according to the security level you choose?

    A. System files permissions tuning

    B. System files checks

    C. User and group checks

    D. System configuration files check

    E. Environment variables check

    F. EEPROM check

    G. Firewall setup

    H. All of the above

13. Which of these is an ASET task that is used to verify the integrity of user accounts, their passwords, and their groups?

    A. System files permissions tuning

    B. System files checks

    C. User and group checks

    D. System configuration files check

    E. Environment variables check

    F. EEPROM check

    G. Firewall setup

    H. All of the above

14. Which of these tools can be used to check the integrity of system files?

    A. MD5

    B. The Solaris Fingerprint Database

    C. sfpDB

    D. SHA1

    E. System files checks

    F. All of the above

15. Which of these can be used not only to provide remote backdoor access to attackers but also to hide the attacker's presence on the system?

    A. Trojan horse

    B. Loadable Kernel Module

    C. Logic bomb

    D. Fork bomb

    E. Rootkit

    F. All of the above

LAB QUESTION

ABCD Inc. hired you to come in and manually run the Automated Security Enhancement Tool (ASET) at the high security level using the current parameters on a perimeter Solaris system. During your meeting with the customer, you were told that off-peak system utilization hours were from 9 P.M. to 4 A.M. The company also required that ASET be run periodically (every day at midnight). Finally, the server administrator at ABCD Inc. wanted help with manually creating an SHA1 file digest for the file *solsoft* using the Solaris cryptographic framework. What steps would you perform to provide the requested services?

SELF TEST ANSWERS

Identify, Detect, and Protect Against Trojan Horse Programs and Backdoors

1. ☑ **B.** A worm is a self-replicating program that will copy itself from system-to-system, sometimes using up all available resources on a target or installing a backdoor on the system.

☒ **A** is incorrect because a Trojan horse program is a malicious program that is disguised as some useful software. **C** is wrong because a logic bomb is code that is inserted into programming code designed to execute under specific circumstances. **D** is incorrect because a fork bomb is a system process that replicates itself until it exceeds the maximum number of allowable processes. **E** is incorrect because a rootkit is used not only to provide remote backdoor access to attackers but also to hide the attacker's presence on the system. Some types of rootkit utilities exploit the use of loadable kernel modules to modify the running kernel for malicious intent.

2. ☑ **D.** A fork bomb is a system process that replicates itself until it exceeds the maximum number of allowable processes.

☒ **A** is wrong because a Trojan horse program is a malicious program that is disguised as some useful software. **B** is incorrect because a worm is a self-replicating program that will copy itself from system-to-system. **C** is wrong because a logic bomb is code that is inserted into programming code designed to execute under specific circumstances. **E** is incorrect because a rootkit is used not only to provide remote backdoor access to attackers but also to hide the attacker's presence on the system.

3. ☑ **C.** A logic bomb is code that is inserted into programming code designed to execute under specific circumstances.

☒ **A** is wrong because a Trojan horse program is a malicious program that is disguised as some useful software. **B** is incorrect because a worm is a self-replicating program that will copy itself from system to system. **D** is wrong because a fork bomb is a system process that replicates itself until it exceeds the maximum number of allowable processes. **E** is incorrect because a rootkit is used not only to provide remote backdoor access to attackers but also to hide the attacker's presence on the system.

4. ☑ **A.** True. A popular form of permissible backdoor that can potentially be exploitable is a program set up by a programmer to provide remote access to the system to perform debugging and troubleshooting tasks.

5. ☑ **F.** All of the answers are correct. To harden your system and help protect against Trojans, Sun recommends educating users, installing and updating anti-virus software, removing unnecessary compilers, securing file and directory permissions, and monitoring path variables.

6. ☑ **A, B,** and **D.** To harden your system and help protect against Trojan horse programs, Sun recommends that path variables do not contain a parameter indicated with a dot (.) that could cause the system to search for executables or libraries within that path, as well as a search path for root or superuser that contains the current directory.

   ☒ **C** is wrong because a forward slash is legitimately used in the search path to indicate root and subdirectories.

7. ☑ **A** and **D.** Device-specific files in the */etc* and */devices* directories are common targets for attackers to attempt to gain access to the operating system, especially for creating backdoors to the system.

   ☒ **B** is incorrect because */usr/asset* is the working directory for ASET, and **C** is incorrect because */usr/local* is simply an example of a typical download directory used to store files and programs by the current user.

Explain Rootkits that Exploit Loadable Kernel Modules

8. ☑ **E.** All answers are correct. To monitor and help prevent unauthorized changes from being made to system files, Sun recommends using Tripwire, the Basic Security Module (BSM), the Solaris cryptographic framework, and the Automated Security Enhancement Tool (ASET).

9. ☑ **D.** During the system configuration files check, ASET checks the integrity of, inspects, and makes modifications to system files mostly found in the */etc* directory, and reports problems in the *sysconf.rpt* file.

   ☒ **A** is incorrect because the system files permissions tuning task automatically sets system file permissions according to the security level you choose. **B** is incorrect because system files checks is a file comparison check from a master file that is created when the task is first executed. **C** is incorrect because the user and group checks task is used to verify the integrity of user accounts, their passwords, and their groups. **E** is incorrect because the environment variables check task inspects the PATH and UMASK environment variables. These are found in the */.profile, /.login,* and */.cshrc* files. **F** is incorrect because the EEPROM check inspects the EEPROM security parameter to ensure that it is set to the appropriate security level and has not been tampered with. **G** is incorrect because the firewall setup task simply ensures that the system can be safely used as a perimeter gateway or secure network relay.

10. ☑ **C.** Checksum uses the sum command to produce a CRC and block count for files that can help prevent backdoor attacks.

    ☒ **A** is incorrect because ASET enables you to monitor and restrict access to system files and directories with automated administration governed by a preset security level (low, medium, or high). **B** is wrong because a message digest is a digital signature for a stream of binary data as verification that the data was not altered since the signature was first generated. **D** is incorrect because the EEPROM check is an ASET task that inspects the EEPROM security parameter to ensure that it is set to the appropriate security level and has not been tampered with.

11. ☑ **B.** System files checks is a file comparison check from a master file that is created when the task is first executed. For each security level, a list of directories that contains files to check is automatically defined; however, this list can be modified.

☒ **A** is incorrect because the system files permissions tuning task automatically sets system file permissions according to the security level you choose. **C** is incorrect because the user and group checks task is used to verify the integrity of user accounts, their passwords, and their groups. **D** is incorrect because, during the system configuration files check, ASET checks the integrity of, inspects, and makes modifications to system files mostly found in the /etc directory, and reports problems in the *sysconf.rpt* file. **E** is incorrect because the environment variables check task inspects the PATH and UMASK environment variables. These are found in the /*.profile*, /*.login*, and /*.cshrc* files. **F** is incorrect because the EEPROM check inspects the EEPROM security parameter to ensure that it is set to the appropriate security level and has not been tampered with. **G** is incorrect because the firewall setup task ensures that the system can be safely used as a perimeter gateway or secure network relay.

12. ☑ **A.** The system files permissions tuning task automatically sets system file permissions according to the security level you choose. At the high level setting, permissions are assigned to restrict access; at the medium level, permissions are tightened just enough for most normal operating environments; and at the low level setting, permissions are set for open sharing.

☒ **B** is incorrect because system files checks is a file comparison check from a master file that is created when the task is first executed. For each security level, a list of directories that contains files to check is automatically defined; however, this list can be modified. **C** is incorrect because the user and group checks task is used to verify the integrity of user accounts, their passwords, and their groups. **D** is incorrect because during the system configuration files check, ASET checks the integrity of, inspects, and makes modifications to system files mostly found in the /etc directory, and reports problems in the *sysconf.rpt* file. **E** is incorrect because the environment variables check task inspects the PATH and UMASK environment variables. These are found in the /*.profile*, /*.login*, and /*.cshrc* files. **F** is incorrect because the EEPROM check inspects the EEPROM security parameter to ensure that it is set to the appropriate security level and has not been tampered with. **G** is incorrect because the firewall setup task simply ensures that the system can be safely used as a perimeter gateway or secure network relay.

13. ☑ **C.** The user and group checks task is used to verify the integrity of user accounts, their passwords, and their groups. The primary check is made from the *passwd* and *group* files, and the passwords in *local,* and the *NIS* and *NIS+* files.

☒ **A** is wrong because the system files permissions tuning task automatically sets system file permissions according to the security level you choose. **B** is incorrect because system files checks is a file comparison check from a master file that is created when the task is first executed. For each security level, a list of directories that contains files to check is automatically defined; however, this list can be modified. **D** is incorrect because during the system configuration files check ASET checks the integrity of, inspects, and makes modifications to system files mostly found in the /*etc* directory, and reports problems in the *sysconf.rpt* file. **E** is incorrect because the environment variables check task inspects the PATH and UMASK environment variables. These are found in the /*.profile*, /*.login*, and /*.cshrc* files. **F** is incorrect because the EEPROM check inspects the EEPROM security parameter to ensure that it is set to the appropriate security level and has not been tampered with. **G** is incorrect because the firewall setup task simply ensures that the system can be safely used as a perimeter gateway or secure network relay.

14. ☑ **F.** All answers are correct. A message digest is a digital signature for a stream of binary data as verification that the data was not altered since the signature was first generated. The MD5 (for shorter message digests) and SHA1 (for larger message digests) are among the most popular message digest algorithms. The Solaris Fingerprint Database (sfpDB) is a free tool from Sun that allows you to check the integrity of system files online through cryptographic checksums stored in the database. System files checks is an ASET task used as a file comparison check from a master file that is created when the task is first executed.

15. ☑ **B** and **E.** A rootkit is used not only to provide remote backdoor access to attackers but also to hide the attacker's presence on the system. Some types of rootkit utilities exploit the use of loadable kernel modules to modify the running kernel for malicious intent.
     ☒ **A** is wrong because a Trojan horse program is a malicious program that is disguised as some useful software. **C** is wrong because a logic bomb is code that is inserted into programming code designed to execute under specific circumstances. **D** is wrong because a fork bomb is a system process that replicates itself until it exceeds the maximum number of allowable processes.

LAB ANSWER

The first task that ABCD Inc. hired you to perform is to run ASET manually at the high security level. To avoid resource encumbrance, and knowing that ASET tasks should be run during off-peak hours or when system activities as well as the user load are low, you'll execute ASET promptly at 9 P.M. To do so, log in as root or become superuser and then issue the /usr/aset/aset -l high -d /usr/asset command. At that time, you should notify the customer that you'll be gathering the report files to monitor and solve security problems. The reports are stored in the /*usr/aset/reports* directory.

The second task that the client requires you to perform is to have ASET run every day at midnight. To do so, log in with an account that has root privileges and verify that the `PERIODIC_SCHEDULE` variable in the *lusrlasetlasetenv* file is correctly set by default to run every day at midnight as shown here:

```
PERIODIC_SCHEDULE="0 0 * * *"
```

Next, insert a line in the crontab file to start ASET at the time determined by the `PERIODIC_SCHEDULE` environment variable with this command:

```
/usr/aset/aset -p
```

The third and final task that ABCD Inc. requires is to use the Solaris cryptographic framework to create an SHA1 file digest manually for the file *solsoft*. To compute the digest for file *solsoft* into an output file named *solsoftsha1*, simply issue this command:

```
digest -v -a sha1 solsoft >> $HOME/solsoftsha1
```

At that point, you can view the file digest with this command,

```
cat ~/solsoftsha1
```

with resulting output similar to the following extract:

```
sha1 (solpatch) = 1ef50e5ad219e34f0b911a097b7b588e31f9b438
```

Part IV

File and System Resources Protection

9

User and Domain
Account Management
with RBAC

B y assigning user accounts specific roles, Solaris 10 boosts security with Role-Based Access Control (RBAC) that relies on the *principle of least privilege*. In this chapter, we'll examine this principle, which states that a user should be given only enough privilege or permissions necessary for performing a job. We'll also look in detail at configuring profiles and using RBAC roles.

---

e x a m

ⓦ a t c h
For the exam, be sure to understand the principle of least privilege. It is an important concept in computer *security and encourages minimal user privileges on systems based on users' job necessities.*

CERTIFICATION OBJECTIVE 9.01

Describe the Benefits and Capabilities of Role-Based Access Control (RBAC)

With RBAC, when a user logs in and assumes a role, the associated rights profile grants specific authorizations and/or privileged commands to the user. In other words, system administrators can delegate privileged commands to non-root users without giving them full superuser access. It's important to note that privileged commands execute with administrative capabilities usually reserved for administrators.

For the exam, you should know the following components included in the RBAC model:

- **Authorization** An authorization is a permission to perform an action or class of actions. Can be assigned to a role or user but typically included in a rights profile.

- **Privilege** Privilege gives a process the ability to perform an operation and therefore enforces security policy in the kernel. Can be granted to a command, user, role, or system.

exam

w a t c h

RBAC or role-based security reduces the complexity and cost of security administration. For example, by using RBAC, system administrators can delegate privileged commands to non-root users without having to give them full superuser or root access to the system. This can save a lot of time by facilitating the administration process. Be sure to understand RBAC with regard to Solaris rights profiles for the exam. With a rights profile, administrators can assign specific authorizations to a user's role. A role is a type of user account that can run privileged applications and commands included in its rights profiles. Also know that Sun's best practices dictate that you do not assign rights profiles, privileges, and authorizations directly to users, or privileges and authorizations directly to roles. You should assign authorizations to rights profiles, assign rights profiles to user roles, and assign roles to user accounts.

- **Privileged application** Privileged application gives an application or program the ability to check for user IDs (UIDs), group IDs (GIDs), privileges, or authorizations.
- **Rights profile** Rights profiles can contain authorizations, privilege commands, or other rights profiles. Can be assigned to a role or user as a collection of administrative functions.
- **Role** A role is a predefined identity that can run privileged applications. Can be granted to users.

For all practical purposes, an authorization is included in a rights profile, the rights profile in turn is included in a role, and the role is assigned to a user. If you're not yet clear on these terms, we'll cover them in more detail later in this chapter.

To avoid having users override security policy, Sun recommends that you do not assign rights profiles, privileges, and authorizations directly to users. In addition, Sun advises against assigning privileges and authorizations directly to roles. Instead, you should assign authorizations to rights profiles. Rights profiles should then be included in roles. Finally, roles—conforming to the principle of least privilege—should be assigned to users.

Authorization

An *authorization* is a right that can be assigned to a role or a user; however, as stated previously, Sun advises against assigning authorizations directly to a user. Applications that comply with RBAC can check a user's authorizations before giving the user access. These applications include the following:

- Audit administration commands (`auditconfig` and `auditreduce`)
- Batch job commands (`at`, `atq`, `batch`, and `crontab`)
- Device commands (`allocate`, `deallocate`, `list_devices`, and `cdrw`)
- Printer administration commands (`lpadmin` and `lpfilter`)
- Solaris Management Console (includes all tools)

Privilege

A *privilege* is the right a process needs to perform an operation; therefore, it inherently protects kernel processes. Furthermore, with privileges, programs will not be required to make calls to `setuid`. In other words, programs do not need to run as root because privileges can mandate that programs run only with the privileges required for the program to operate. This is another example of the principle of least privilege.

So what's the bottom line here with regard to security? If you haven't already deduced the answer, privileges that have been removed from a program or process cannot be exploited. As a result, you can speculate that the privilege model is much more secure than the old superuser model. Under the privilege model, if a program or process was compromised, the attacker will have only the same privileges that the program or process had. Other unrelated programs and processes would theoretically not be compromised. Roles, on the other hand, get access to privileged commands through rights profiles that contain the commands. This is a secure way to allow users privileged access to specific commands—by assigning them certain roles.

Applications and commands that check for privileges include the following:

- Commands that control processes (`kill`, `pcred`, and `rcapadm`)
- File and file system commands (`chmod`, `chgrp`, and `mount`)
- Kerberos commands (`kadmin`, `kprop`, and `kdb5_util`)
- Network commands (`ifconfig`, `route`, and `snoop`)

Privileges fall into several areas, including the following:

- **FILE**   These privileges begin with the string *file* and pertain to system objects.
- **IPC**   These privileges begin with the string *ipc* and pertain to IPC object access controls.
- **NET**   These privileges begin with the string *net* and pertain to network functionality.
- **PROC**   These privileges begin with the string *proc* and pertain to giving processes the ability to modify restrictions.
- **SYS**   These privileges begin with the string *sys* and pertain to giving processes root access to a variety of system properties.

Processes obtain privileges either from inheritance (that is, via user login) or assignment (via rights profile). Every process has four sets of privileges:

- **Effective privilege set (E)**   Privileges currently in use (note that processes can add permitted privileges to the set)
- **Inheritable privilege set (I)**   Privileges a process can inherit
- **Permitted privilege set (P)**   Privileges available for use now
- **Limit privilege set (L)**   Outside privilege limits of which processes can shrink but never extend

To check the privileges available to your current shell's process, use the `ppriv -v pid $$` command; where *pid* is the process number, `$$` passes the process number of the parent shell to the command, and `-v` provides more detail/verbose listing.

Privileged Application

As you know, privileged applications can check for user IDs (UIDs), group IDs (GIDs), privileges, or authorizations via application or command. However, with RBAC, you can specify the UID or GID, say, for example, for commands. In other words, with RBAC, a user role whose rights profile contains permission to execute specific commands can do so without having to become superuser and can thus have full privileged access to all system commands and applications. Again, this falls right in line with the principle of least privilege.

Rights Profile

A *rights profile* can be assigned to a role or user and can contain authorizations, privilege commands, or other rights profiles. The rights profile name and authorizations can be found in the *prof_attr* database, whereas the rights profile name and commands with specific security attributes are stored in the *exec_attr* database. The *user_attr* database contains user and role information that supplements the *passwd* and *shadow* databases. This database also contains extended user attributes such as authorizations, rights profiles, and assigned roles.

Role

A *role* is a predefined identity—created by an administrator and assigned to users— that can run privileged applications. Just like a typical user account, roles have an assigned home directory, a password, a group, and other similar attributes. Any authorizations included in a rights profile that is included in a role and assigned to a user give that user limited administrative capabilities. Furthermore, a specific role can be assigned to more than one user.

It's important to note that a user must first log in and can then assume a role. In other words, roles cannot log in. What's more, users must first exit a role before assuming another role type. Role information can be found in the *passwd*, *shadow*, and *user_attr* databases.

CERTIFICATION OBJECTIVE 9.02

Explain How to Configure and Audit Role-Based Access Control (RBAC)

Creating profiles and assigning roles are not excessively difficult using the Solaris Management Console (see Figure 9-1). In this section, we'll talk about the tasks involved with configuring RBAC. However, before we begin, let's examine some important planning functions that should take place before implementing RBAC:

1. *Check company policy.* Your company's security policy should outline threats, risks, and remediation. Be sure to plan profiles and roles that adhere to your policy.

2. *Determine RBAC roles.* Decide what levels of RBAC and which rights profiles and roles your company needs.

3. *Determine which users should be assigned to roles.* Follow the principle of least privilege and assign roles to users with the level of permissions required to do their jobs.

FIGURE 9-1

The Solaris Management Console Users interface

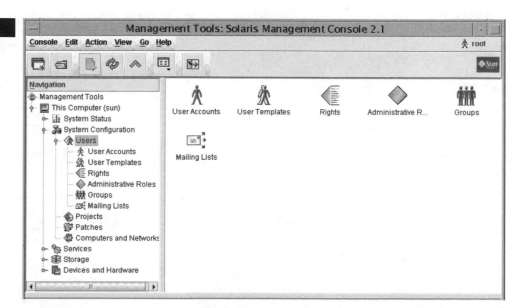

Managing Rights and Roles

Although you can manage rights and roles directly from the command line, we'll focus on using the console. Creating custom rights and editing current rights is easy with the Solaris Management Console. To start the console, simply type the following command at a terminal prompt

```
/usr/sbin/smc &
```

or right-click the desktop and choose Tools/Solaris Management Console from the drop-down Workspace menu. Then click the current system from the Navigation menu, and click System Configuration. Next, click Users and then log in with an appropriate administrative or root account.

Creating Rights

From the console, click Rights to enter the Solaris Management Console Users Rights interface, shown in Figure 9-2. This tool is used for managing rights. A *right* is a named collection consisting of commands, authorizations to use specific applications (or to perform specific functions within an application), and other previously created rights, whose use can be granted or denied to an administrator.

In the Uses Rights interface, you should see a collection of default rights created during the installation or upgrade of Solaris. You can click to select a particular right

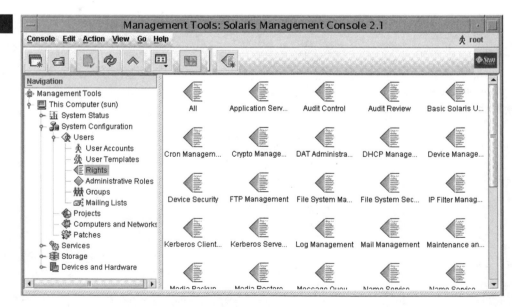

FIGURE 9-2

The Solaris Management Console Users Rights interface

FIGURE 9-3

The Solaris
Management
Console Add
Right interface

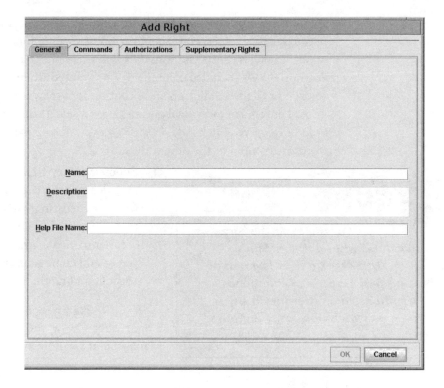

FIGURE 9-3

The Solaris Management Console Add Right interface

for modification. Otherwise, to create a right, select Add Right from the Action menu. This will invoke the Add Right interface shown in Figure 9-3.

A few configurable tabs appear in the Add Right interface:

- **General tab**   Add or view the right's name and description.
- **Commands tab**   Add commands to this right (by placing them in the Commands Permitted column), or remove them. When a user or role enters a command in an administrator's shell, the command can be executed only if it is included in a right assigned to the user or role. (The user must have been given an administrator's shell—through the User Properties dialog box—or must type pfsh, pfcsh, or pfksh on the command line of one of the normal user shells.) To add or remove individual commands or directories of commands, select the command or directory and click Add or Remove. Click Add All or Remove All to move all commands from one column to the other.

■ **Authorizations tab** Used to view or modify authorizations. An authorization permits the use of a specific application or specific functions within an application. The authorizations added to this right (by being placed in the Authorizations Included column) will be granted when this right is granted to users or to roles. Click an authorization to display information about it. To add or remove individual authorizations, select the authorization and click Add or Remove. Click Add All or Remove All to move all authorizations from one column to the other.

■ **Supplementary Rights tab** Used to include or exclude supplementary rights, which are existing, previously created rights that you can add to this right—they make it easier to create a new right by allowing you to add commands and authorizations without adding the individual items.

When you're through creating or modifying a right, click OK on the bottom of the Solaris Management Console Add Right interface.

Creating Roles

Creating roles using the console GUI is just as easy as creating rights. By default, no roles should be on the system. Assuming you've already created users that will assume any roles you create, and you have administrator access, you can start the console and click the Administrative Roles icon. Select Add Administrative Role from the Action menu option shown in Figure 9-4. (Incidentally, the `roleadd` command can be used to create roles and associates a role with an authorization or a profile as well.)

Sun's official definition of a *role* is a special user account used to grant rights. Users can assume only those roles they have been granted permission to assume. Once a user takes on a role, the user relinquishes his or her own user identity and takes on the properties, including the rights, of that role.

You'll see a few dialog boxes with which to create a new role in the new role wizard. Follow these steps from Sun to create a new role:

Step 1. Enter a role name. The role name is the name an administrator uses to log in to a specific role. Each role name must

■ Be unique within a domain
■ Contain 2 to 32 letters, numerals, underscores (_), hyphens (-), and periods (.)

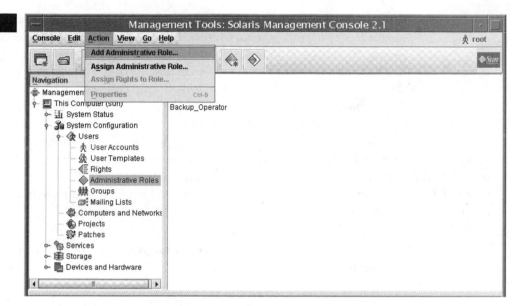

FIGURE 9-4

Adding an
Administrative
Role from
the Solaris
Management
Console

- Begin with a letter
- Have at least one lowercase letter
- Not contain spaces

If you later change a role name in a Role Properties dialog box, the name of the mailing list associated with this role is automatically changed as well.

Step 2. Enter the role password.   Enter the password for this role. A password must consist of a combination of 6 to 15 case-sensitive letters, numbers, and special characters (only the first 8 characters are used, but 15 are available for users who want longer passwords). Within the first 6 characters, at least 2 must be alphabetic and at least 1 must be a number or special character. Inform each user entitled to assume this role of this password and of the need to use it when assuming the role. Click Next to continue.

Step 3. Assign role rights.   Assign rights to this role by choosing from the list of Available Rights and adding them to the list of Granted Rights. Click each right for additional information about that right. Click Next to continue.

Step 4. Enter the home directory.   Enter the home directory server where this role's private files will be stored. Click Next to continue.

Step 5. Assign users. Add the user names of users who will be permitted to assume this role. After you have finished adding this role, you can always assign additional users. The most direct method is to choose Action | Assign Administrative Role (in the Administrative Roles tool), and use the dialog box that opens. Or use a Role Properties dialog box or a User Properties dialog box. Incidentally, the usermod command associates a user's login with a role, profile, and authorization in the /etc/user_attr database, which can also be used to grant a user access to a role. Click Next to continue.

Step 6. Click Finish and verify role assignment. When you're through with the five steps in the new role wizard, click Finish. To verify a role assignment, go to the User Accounts interface within the console and click to open any user name to which you assigned a role. From the User Properties window, click the Roles tab to verify assigned roles (see Figure 9-5).

Sun-Defined Roles

Following are three examples that Sun provides as templates for creating roles for administrator, operator, and security-related rights profiles:

Creating a Role for the System Administrator Rights Profile   In this example, the new role can perform system administration tasks that are not connected to security. The role is created by performing the preceding procedure with the following parameters:

- Role name: sysadmin
- Role full name: System Administrator
- Role description: Performs nonsecurity administration tasks
- Rights profile: System Administrator

This rights profile is at the top of the list of profiles that are included in the role.

FIGURE 9-5

Verifying user
role assignment

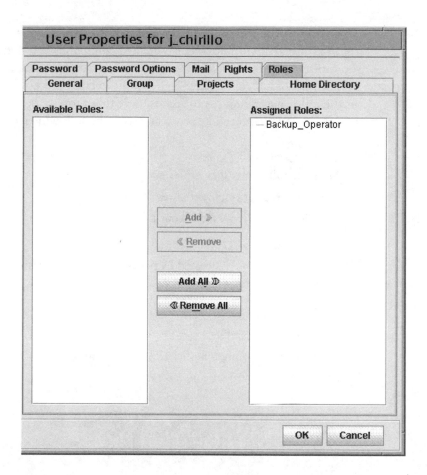

Creating a Role for the Operator Rights Profile   The Operator rights profile
can manage printers and back up the system to offline media. You might want to
assign the role to one user on each shift. To do so, you would select the role mailing
list option in Step 1. The Operator role would have the following definition:

- Role name: operad
- Role full name: Operator
- Role description: Backup operator
- Rights profile: Operator

This rights profile must be at the top of the list of profiles that are included in
the role.

Creating a Role for a Security-Related Rights Profile   By default, the only rights profile that contains security-related commands and rights is the Primary Administrator profile. If you want to create a role that is not as powerful as Primary Administrator but can handle some security-related tasks, you must create the role. In the following example, you create a role that protects devices. The role is created by performing the preceding procedure with the following parameters:

- Role name: devicesec \
- Role full name: Device Security
- Role description: Configures devices
- Rights profile: Device Security

In the following example, you create a role that secures systems and hosts on the network. The role is created by performing the preceding procedure with the following parameters:

- Role name: netsec
- Role full name: Network Security
- Role description: Handles IPSEC, IKE, and SSH
- Rights profile: Network Security

INSIDE THE EXAM

Create a Role for the System Administrator Rights Profile

Following are steps for creating a role for the System Administrator rights profile:

1. Log in as superuser.
2. Start the management console and click the Administrative Roles icon.
3. Enter the role name: **sysadmin**.
4. Enter the role full name: **System Administrator**.
5. Enter the role description: **Performs nonsecurity administrative tasks**.
6. Enter the role password.
7. Assign the role rights: **System Administrator**.
8. Enter the home directory or accept the default.
9. Add the user names of users who will be permitted to assume this role.

Assuming Roles

Once a role is assigned to a user, that role can be assumed at any time from a terminal window. To do so

1. Log in as a user and open a terminal session.
2. Type **roles** to verify which roles are available to you.
3. Issue the su command followed by the role name to assume that role:

   su backup_operator

4. Enter the associated password.
5. To verify that the role has been assumed, issue the /usr/ucb/whoami command.

Auditing Roles

You should recall that recurring security-relevant event assessments are part of problem identification and auditing for network defense testing against techniques used by intruders and for post-intrusion analysis. In other words, regularly scheduled auditing should be practiced. This applies not only to components with regard to outside intrusions but is applicable to internal intrusions as well.

As you should recall from Chapter 5, the */etc/security/audit_control* file can be modified to preselect audit classes. In the *audit_control* file, the flags and naflags arguments define which attributable and nonattributable events (the na preceding the second flags argument specifies nonattributable events) should be audited for the entire system—that is, all users on the system. To audit a role, you should add the ua or the as event to the flags line, as shown in the following extract:

```
# ident "@(#)audit_control.txt  1.4    00/07/17 SMI"
#
flags:as
```

Be sure to configure the remaining auditing components as specified in Chapter 5, and then start the auditing service using these steps:

1. Log in with an account that has root privileges, or use the su command to become superuser.
2. Bring down the system to single-user mode using the init command: init 1
3. In the */etc/security* directory, run the *bsmconv* script to enable the auditing service: ./bsmconv
4. Bring the system into multi-user mode using the init command: init 6

Finally, see Objective 5.02 in Chapter 5 for details on analyzing log files.

✓ TWO-MINUTE DRILL

Here are some of the key points from the certification objectives in Chapter 9.

Describe the Benefits and Capabilities of Role-Based Access Control (RBAC)

❑ With RBAC, system administrators can delegate privileged commands to non-root users without giving them full superuser access.

❑ The principle of least privilege states that a user should not be given any more privilege or permissions necessary for performing a job.

❑ A rights profile grants specific authorizations and/or privilege commands to a user's role. Privilege commands execute with administrative capabilities usually reserved for administrators.

❑ Sun's best practices dictate that you do not assign rights profiles, privileges, and authorizations directly to users, or privileges and authorizations directly to roles. It's best to assign authorizations to rights profiles, rights profiles to roles, and roles to users.

❑ Applications that check authorizations include audit administration commands, batch job commands, device commands, printer administration commands, and the Solaris Management Console tool suite.

❑ Privileges that have been removed from a program or process cannot be exploited. If a program or process was compromised, the attacker will have only those privileges that the program or process had. Other unrelated programs and processes would not be compromised.

❑ Roles get access to privileged commands through rights profiles that contain the commands.

❑ Commands that check for privileges include commands that control processes, file and file system commands, Kerberos commands, and network commands.

❑ The four sets of process privileges are the effective privilege set (E), which are privileges currently in use; the inheritable privilege set (I), which are privileges a process can inherit; the permitted privilege set (P), which are privileges available for use now; and the limit privilege set (L), which is outside privilege limits of which processes can shrink but never extend.

❑ With RBAC, a user role whose rights profile contains permission to execute specific commands can do so without having to become superuser.

❑ A rights profile can be assigned to a role or user and can contain authorizations, privilege commands, or other rights profiles.

❑ The rights profile name and authorizations can be found in the *prof_attr* database, the profile name and commands with specific security attributes are stored in the *exec_attr* database, and the *user_attr* database contains user and role information that supplements the *passwd* and *shadow* databases.

❑ A role is a type of user account that can run privileged applications and commands included in its rights profiles.

Explain How to Configure and Audit Role-Based Access Control (RBAC)

❑ Before implementing RBAC, you should properly plan by creating profiles and roles that adhere to company policy and abide by the principle of least privilege when assigning permissions.

❑ A right is a named collection consisting of commands, authorizations to use specific applications (or to perform specific functions within an application), and other previously created rights whose use can be granted or denied to an administrator.

❑ The `roleadd` command can be used to create roles and associates a role with an authorization or a profile from the command line.

❑ From the command line, the `usermod` command associates a user's login with a role, profile, and authorization in the */etc/user_attr* database, which can also be used to grant a user access to a role.

❑ A role is a special user account used to grant rights.

❑ Users can assume only those roles they have been granted permission to assume. Once a user takes on a role, the user relinquishes his or her own user identity and takes on the properties, including the rights, of that role.

❑ To audit a role, you should add the `ua` or the `as` event to the flags line in the *audit_control* file, and then start the auditing service.

SELF TEST

The following questions will help you measure your understanding of the material presented in this chapter. Read all the choices carefully, because there might be more than one correct answer. Choose all correct answers for each question. Some questions are short-answer questions to ensure you have a good understanding of the material.

Describe the Benefits and Capabilities of Role-Based Access Control (RBAC)

1. Which of the following are benefits of Role-Based Access Control (RBAC)?
   A. Privilege commands can execute with administrative capabilities usually reserved for administrators.
   B. System administrators can delegate privileged commands to non-root users without giving them full superuser access.
   C. Rights profiles, privileges, and authorizations can be assigned directly to users.
   D. Users can be assigned only the exact privileges and permissions necessary for performing a job.
   E. All of the above

2. Which of the following can be assigned to a role or user as a collection of administrative functions and can contain authorizations and privilege commands or rights profiles?
   A. Authorization
   B. Privilege
   C. Privileged application
   D. Rights profile
   E. Role
   F. All of the above

3. What is the principle of least privilege?

4. It is advisable not to assign rights profiles, privileges, and authorizations directly to users.
   A. True
   B. False

5. Which of the following is an example of the principle of least privilege?
   A. Programs—using privileges—that do not require making calls to `setuid`.
   B. System administrators can delegate privileged commands to non-root users without giving them full superuser access.

C. A user should be given privileges or permissions only as necessary for performing a job.

D. Privilege commands execute with administrative capabilities usually reserved for administrators.

E. All of the above

6. Which of these are privileges in common with every process?

A. E

B. I

C. D

D. P

E. G

F. All of the above

7. Which of the following can check for user IDs (UIDs), group IDs (GIDs), privileges, or authorizations via application or command?

A. Authorization

B. Privilege

C. Privileged application

D. Rights profile

E. Role

F. All of the above

8. Which of the following are applications or commands that check for privileges?

A. *prof_attr*

B. Commands that control processes

C. File commands

D. *ifconfig*

E. *user_attr*

F. All of the above

9. Which of the following can be granted to a command, user, role, or system and gives a process the ability to perform an operation and therefore enforces security policy in the kernel?

A. Authorization

B. Privilege

C. Privileged application

D. Rights profile

E. Role

F. All of the above

10. It is advisable to assign privileges and authorizations directly to roles.

    A. True

    B. False

11. Which rights profile database contains user and role information that supplements the *passwd* and *shadow* databases?

    A. *prof_attr*

    B. *exec_attr*

    C. *user_attr*

    D. *passwd*

    E. *shadow*

    F. All of the above

12. Which of the following types of applications comply with RBAC and therefore can check a user's authorizations before giving the user access?

    A. Audit administration commands

    B. The Solaris Management Console tool suite

    C. Printer administration commands

    D. Batch job commands

    E. Device commands

    F. All of the above

13. Which rights profile database contains the profile name and commands with specific security attributes?

    A. *prof_attr*

    B. *exec_attr*

    C. *user_attr*

    D. *passwd*

    E. *shadow*

    F. All of the above

14. Which of these databases contains role information?

    A. *prof_attr*

    B. *exec_attr*

    C. *user_attr*

    D. *passwd*

    E. *shadow*

    F. All of the above

15. Explain the meaning of a *role* as it pertains to Role-Based Access Control (RBAC).

Explain How to Configure and Audit Role-Based Access Control (RBAC)

16. Which command associates a user's login with a role, profile, and authorization in the */etc/ user_attr* database, which can also be used to grant a user access to a role?

    A. `ppriv`

    B. `smc &`

    C. `usermod`

    D. `roleadd`

    E. All of the above

17. To audit a role, which event(s) should be added to the flags line in the *audit_control* file?

18. Which command can be used to check the privileges available to your current shell's process?

    A. `ppriv`

    B. `smc &`

    C. `usermod`

    D. `roleadd`

    E. All of the above

19. Which command can be used to create roles and associates a role with an authorization or a profile from the command line?

    A. `ppriv`

    B. `smc &`

    C. `usermod`

    D. `roleadd`

    E. All of the above

20. Explain the meaning of a *right* as it pertains to Role-Based Access Control (RBAC).

LAB QUESTION

Your customer, ABCD Inc., called you in to create a role for backup using the Operator rights profile in its Role-Based Access Control (RBAC) system. What steps would you perform to provide the requested service?

SELF TEST ANSWERS

Describe the Benefits and Capabilities of Role-Based Access Control (RBAC)

1. ☑ **B** and **D**. Role-Based Access Control (RBAC) allows system administrators to delegate privileged commands to non-root users without giving them full superuser access to the system. Similarly, users can be assigned only the exact privileges and permissions necessary for performing a job.

   ☒ **A** is wrong, because although it's true that privilege commands execute with administrative capabilities usually reserved for administrators, that statement does not describe a benefit to RBAC. **C** is wrong because Sun's best practices dictate that you do not assign rights profiles, privileges, and authorizations directly to users or privileges and authorizations directly to roles. It's best to assign authorizations to rights profiles, rights profiles to roles, and roles to users.

2. ☑ **D**. A rights profile can be assigned to a role or user as a collection of administrative functions. Rights profiles can contain authorizations, privilege commands, or other rights profiles.

   ☒ **A** is wrong because authorization can be assigned to a role or user. **B** is wrong because a privilege can be granted to a command, user, role, or system. Privilege gives a process the ability to perform an operation and therefore enforces security policy in the kernel. **C** is wrong because a privileged application can check for user IDs (UIDs), group IDs (GIDs), privileges, or authorizations via an application or command. **E** is wrong because a role is a predefined identity that can run privileged applications.

3. ☑ The principle of least privilege states that a user should not be granted any more privileges or permissions than those necessary for performing a specific job.

4. ☑ **A**. True. Sun's best practices dictate that you do not assign rights profiles, privileges, and authorizations directly to users, or privileges and authorizations directly to roles. It's best to assign authorizations to rights profiles, rights profiles to roles, and roles to users.

5. ☑ **A, B,** and **C**. Examples of the principle of least privilege include programs—using privileges—that do not require making calls to `setuid`, when system administrators delegate privileged commands to non-root users without giving them full superuser access, and users that are only given privilege or permission necessary for performing their jobs.

   ☒ **D** is wrong because it's simply a true statement concerning privileged commands.

6. ☑ **A, B,** and **D**. Every process has four sets of privileges: the effective privilege set (E), which are privileges currently in use (note that processes can be used to add permitted privileges to the set); inheritable privilege set (I), which are privileges a process can inherit; permitted privilege set (P), which are privileges available for use now; and limited privilege set (L), which are outside privilege limits of which processes can shrink but never extend.

   ☒ **C** and **E** are wrong because they don't exist.

7. ☑ **C.** A privileged application can check for user IDs (UIDs), group IDs (GIDs), privileges, or authorizations via an application or command.

    ☒ **A** is wrong because authorization can be assigned to a role or user. **B** is wrong because a privilege can be granted to a command, user, role, or system. Privilege gives a process the ability to perform an operation and therefore enforces security policy in the kernel. **D** is wrong because a rights profile can be assigned to a role or user as a collection of administrative functions. **E** is wrong because a role is a predefined identity that can run privileged applications.

8. ☑ **B, C,** and **D.** Applications and commands that check for privileges include commands that control processes (such as `kill`, `pcred`, and `rcapadm`), file and file system commands (such as `chmod`, `chgrp`, and `mount`), Kerberos commands (such as `kadmin`, `kprop`, and `kdb5_util`), and network commands (such as `ifconfig`, `route`, and `snoop`).

    ☒ **A** and **E** are wrong because they are databases.

9. ☑ **B.** A privilege can be granted to a command, user, role, or system. Privilege gives a process the ability to perform an operation and therefore enforces security policy in the kernel.

    ☒ **A** is wrong because authorization can be assigned to a role or user. **C** is wrong because a privileged application can check for user IDs (UIDs), group IDs (GIDs), privileges, or authorizations via an application or command. **D** is wrong because a rights profile can be assigned to a role or user as a collection of administrative functions. **E** is wrong because a role is a predefined identity that can run privileged applications.

10. ☑ **B.** False. Sun's best practices dictate that you do not assign rights profiles, privileges, and authorizations directly to users, or privileges and authorizations directly to roles. It's best to assign authorizations to rights profiles, rights profiles to roles, and roles to users.

11. ☑ **C.** The *user_attr* database contains user and role information that supplements the *passwd* and *shadow* databases. This database also contains extended user attributes such as authorizations, rights profiles, and assigned roles.

    ☒ **A** is incorrect because the rights profile name and authorizations are found in the *prof_attr* database. **B** is wrong because the rights profile name and commands with specific security attributes are stored in the *exec_attr* database. **D** and **E** are wrong because the *passwd* and *shadow* databases do not contain user and role information that supplements themselves.

12. ☑ **F.** All answers are correct. Applications that comply with RBAC can check a user's authorizations before giving the user access. These applications include the following audit administration commands (`auditconfig` and `auditreduce`), batch job commands (`at`, `atq`, `batch`, and `crontab`), device commands (`allocate`, `deallocate`, `list_devices`, and `cdrw`), printer administration commands (`lpadmin` and `lpfilter`), and the Solaris Management Console (includes all tools).

13. ☑ **B.** The rights profile name and commands with specific security attributes are stored in the *exec_attr* database.

    ☒ **A** is wrong because the rights profile name and authorizations are in the *prof_attr* database. **C** is wrong because the *user_attr* database contains user and role information that supplements the *passwd* and *shadow* databases. **D** and **E** are wrong because those databases don't apply here.

14. ☑ **C, D,** and **E.** Role information can be found in the *user_attr*, *passwd*, and *shadow* databases. The *user_attr* database contains user and role information that supplements the *passwd* and *shadow* databases.

    ☒ **A** is wrong because the rights profile name and authorizations can be found in the *prof_attr* database. **B** is wrong because the rights profile name and commands with specific security attributes are stored in the *exec_attr* database.

15. ☑ A role is a special user account used to grant rights. Users can assume only those roles they have been granted permission to assume. Once a user takes on a role, the user relinquishes his or her own user identity and takes on the properties, including the rights, of that role.

Explain How to Configure and Audit Role-Based Access Control (RBAC)

16. ☑ **C.** The `usermod` command associates a user's login with a role, profile, and authorization in the */etc/user_attr* database, which can also be used to grant a user access to a role.

    ☒ **A** is wrong because to check the privileges available to your current shell's process, you would use the `ppriv -v pid $$` command. **B** is wrong because in order to start the management console, you would issue the `/usr/sbin/smc &` command. **D** is wrong because the `roleadd` command is used to create roles and associates a role with an authorization or a profile from the command line.

17. ☑ To audit a role, you should add the `ua` or the `as` event to the flags line in the *audit_control* file, and then start the auditing service.

18. ☑ **A.** To check the privileges available to your current shell's process, you would use the `ppriv -v pid $$` command.

    ☒ **B** is wrong because in order to start the management console you would issue the `/usr/sbin/smc &` command. **C** is wrong because the `usermod` command associates a user's login with a role, profile, and authorization in the */etc/user_attr* database, which can also be used to grant a user access to a role. **D** is wrong because the `roleadd` command is used to create roles and associates a role with an authorization or a profile from the command line.

19. ☑ **D.** The `roleadd` command can be used to create roles and associates a role with an authorization or a profile from the command line.

 ☒ **A** is wrong because to check the privileges available to your current shell's process, you would use the `ppriv -v pid $$` command. **B** is wrong because in order to start the management console you would issue the `/usr/sbin/smc &` command. **C** is wrong because the `usermod` command associates a user's login with a role, profile, and authorization in the */etc/user_attr* database, which can also be used to grant a user access to a role.

20. ☑ A *right* is a named collection, consisting of commands, authorizations to use specific applications (or to perform specific functions within an application), and other previously created rights, whose use can be granted or denied to an administrator.

LAB ANSWER

The Operator rights profile can manage printers and back up the system to offline media. ABCD Inc. hired you to create a role for backup using the Operator rights profile in their Role-Based Access Control (RBAC) system. To do so, you should follow these steps:

1. Log in as superuser.

2. Start the Management Console and click the Administrative Roles icon.

3. Enter the role name: **operadm**.

4. Enter the role full name: **Operator**.

5. Enter the role description: **Backup operator**.

6. Enter the role password.

7. Assign the role rights: **Operator**.

8. Enter the home directory or accept the default.

9. Add the user names of users who will be permitted to assume this role.

10

Fundamentals of
Access Control

F iles can generally be secured by using two methods: standard UNIX file permissions and access control lists (ACLs). UNIX file permissions provide read, write, and execute permissions for three user classes (file owner, group, and other users), whereas ACLs take security a step further by enabling you to define file permissions for each user class. For example, let's say you want the sales user group to read a particular file; however, you want only the sales manager—part of the sales group—to have additional permission to make changes to, or write to, that file. With UNIX file permissions, you're limited to making the file either read-only or read-write for the sales group. On the other hand, by using ACLs, you can make the file read-only for the sales group, with the exception of read-write for the sales manager.

e x a m

ⓦatch *For the exam, be sure to know that access control lists (ACLs) allow you to define file permissions for each user class. This provides for file security at the user level, and can be unique to each user or class of users.*

In this chapter, we'll talk about access control with regard to file security. We'll look at protecting files with UNIX permissions and also enhancing file security with ACLs.

CERTIFICATION OBJECTIVE 10.01

Use UNIX Permissions to Protect Files

When we refer to *files* in this chapter, we're including all types, as shown in Table 10-1.

TABLE 10-1	File Type	Symbol
File Types	Text or program	-
	Block special file	b
	Character special file	c
	Directory	d
	Door	D
	Symbolic link	i
	Socket	s
	Named pipe	P

By using UNIX file permissions, you can set file ownership to the user, group, and other user classes:

- **User class**   File or directory owner
- **Group class**   All users in a group
- **Other user class**   All other users not in the group and not the file owner

Following are the permissions you can assign to each class:

- **Read** (r)   This permission allows users to open and read a file and list files in a directory.
- **Write** (w)   This permission allows users to open, read, delete, and modify the contents of a file, and list and add files and links in a directory or remove them.
- **Execute** (x)   This permission allows users to execute a file (program or shell script) in a directory.
- **Deny** (-)   This permission denies read, write, and execute access.

Listing and Securing Files and Directories

We'll be concerned with four commands used for listing and securing files and directories from the command line:

- ls   List files and some information about the files contained within a directory.
- chown   Change user ownership of a file.
- chgrp   Change group ownership of a file.
- chmod   Change permissions on a file.

The ls command supports several options—for a complete list, see its man page. Perhaps the most commonly used option is -l for long listing, which is used to see file permissions and other information. Here's an example using the command:

```
$ ls -l
total 5722
-rwxrwxrwx+  1 b_jones   dev       10876   Sep  8  9:00 sample
-rw-r--r--   1 root      other     549722  Sep  9 10:49 1
-rw-r--r--   1 root      other     255246  Sep 13 15:14 10-1
```

```
-rw-r--r--    1 root      other       549722 Sep  9 10:49 2
-rw-r--r--    1 root      other       533622 Sep  9 10:49 3
-rw-r--r--    1 root      other       549722 Sep  9 13:54 9-4
-rw-r--r--    1 root      other       400472 Sep  9 13:55 9-5
-rw-r--r--    1 j_chirillo root         1772 Sep  9 10:47 cdkeydl
drwxr-xr-x    2 j_chirillo root          512 Sep 13 15:43 dioc
drwxr-xr-x    2 j_chirillo root          512 Sep 13 15:43 docs
```

Take a look at this output from right to left. You see that the current directory holds several files. Let's focus on the first file, *sample*. We see the last time that file's contents were modified was 9:00 A.M. on September 8. The file contains 10,876 characters, or bytes. The owner of the file, or the user, belongs to the group *dev* (the development group), and his or her login name is *b_jones*. The number, in this case 1, indicates the number of links to the file *sample*. The plus sign indicates that an ACL is associated with the file. Finally, the dash and letters at the front of the line tell you that user, group, and others have permissions to read, write, and execute *sample*. The execute (x) symbol here occupies the third position of the three-character sequence. A - in the third position would have indicated a denial of execution permissions. Following are definitions of the permissions:

- **r**   The file is readable.
- **w**   The file is writable.
- **x**   The file is executable.
- **-**   The indicated permission is not granted.
- **s**   The set-user-ID or set-group-ID bit is on, and the corresponding user or group execution bit is also on.
- **S**   The undefined bit state (the set-user-ID bit) is on and the user execution bit is off.
- **t**   The 1000 (octal) bit, or sticky bit, is on—see chmod(1)—and execution is on.
- **T**   The 1000 bit is turned on, and execution is off (undefined bit state).

The chown command is used to change file ownership. It will set the user ID of the file named by each file to the user ID specified by owner and, optionally, will set the group ID to that specified by group. If chown is invoked by other than the superuser, the set-user-ID bit is cleared. Only the owner of a file (or the superuser) may change the owner of that file. The syntax of chown is chown [-fhR] *owner* [*:group*] *file*. Following are the options you can use with the chown command:

- -f   Do not report errors.
- -h   If the file is a symbolic link, change the owner of the symbolic link. Without this option, the owner of the file referenced by the symbolic link is changed.
- -R   Recursive. The chown command descends through the directory and any subdirectories, setting the ownership ID as it proceeds. When a symbolic link is encountered, the owner of the target file is changed (unless the -h option is specified), but no recursion takes place.

Let's look at an example of the chown command. We'll change the owner of our *sample* file to *j_chirillo*:

```
chown j_chirillo sample
```

If we list the directory contents in long format, here's what we'll get:

```
$ ls -l
total 5722
-rwxrwxrwx+   1 j_chirillo dev         10876  Sep  8 9:00 sample
-rw-r--r--    1 root       other      549722 Sep   9 10:49 1
-rw-r--r--    1 root       other      255246 Sep 13 15:14 10-1
-rw-r--r--    1 root       other      549722 Sep   9 10:49 2
-rw-r--r--    1 root       other      533622 Sep   9 10:49 3
-rw-r--r--    1 root       other      549722 Sep   9 13:54 9-4
-rw-r--r--    1 root       other      400472 Sep   9 13:55 9-5
-rw-r--r--    1 j_chirillo root         1772 Sep   9 10:47 cdkeydl
drwxr-xr-x    2 j_chirillo root          512 Sep 13 15:43 dioc
drwxr-xr-x    2 j_chirillo root          512 Sep 13 15:43 docs
```

The chgrp command is used to change group ownership of a file and has the same options as the chown command. This command will set the group ID of the file named by each file operand to the group ID specified by the group operand. For each file operand, chgrp will perform actions equivalent to the chown function, called with the following arguments:

- The file operand will be used as the path argument.
- The user ID of the file will be used as the owner argument.
- The specified group ID will be used as the group argument.

Unless `chgrp` is invoked by a process with appropriate privileges, the set-user-ID and set-group-ID bits of a regular file will be cleared upon successful completion; the set-user-ID and set-group-ID bits of other file types may be cleared.

The most powerful command—with regard to this chapter—of the group we mentioned in this section is the `chmod` command. The command changes or assigns the mode of a file (permissions and other attributes), which may be absolute or symbolic. An absolute mode is specified using octal numbers, in this format: `chmod nnnn file`; where *n* is a number from 0 to 7. The octal numbers used are listed here:

- **4000** Set user ID on execution.
- **20#0** Set group ID on execution if # is 7, 5, 3, or 1. Enable mandatory locking if # is 6, 4, 2, or 0.
- **1000** Turn on sticky bit. The sticky bit protects files within a directory in that a file can be deleted only by the owner or privileged user.
- **0400** Allow read by owner.
- **0200** Allow write by owner.
- **0100** Allow execute (search in directory) by owner.
- **0700** Allow read, write, and execute (search) by owner.
- **0040** Allow read by group.
- **0020** Allow write by group.
- **0010** Allow execute (search in directory) by group.
- **0070** Allow read, write, and execute (search) by group.
- **0004** Allow read by others.
- **0002** Allow write by others.
- **0001** Allow execute (search in directory) by others.
- **0007** Allow read, write, and execute (search) by others.

A `chmod` symbolic mode uses the following format: `chmod <symbolic-mode-list> file`; where `<symbolic-mode-list>` is a comma-separated list (with no intervening white space) of symbolic mode expressions of the form `[who] operator [permissions]`. Here, `who` can be u, g, o, and a, specifying whose permissions are to be changed or assigned:

- u   User's permissions
- g   Group's permissions

- o   Others' permissions
- a   All permissions (user, group, and other)

The *operator* is either +, -, or = signifying how permissions are to be changed:

- +   Add permissions.
- -   Take away permissions.
- =   Assign permissions absolutely.

The *permissions* are any compatible combination of the following letters:

- r   Read permission.
- w   Write permission.
- x   Execute permission.
- l   Mandatory locking.
- s   User- or group-set-ID.
- t   Sticky bit.
- u, g, o   Permission is to be taken from the current user, group, or other mode, respectively.

You can use the chmod command to set permissions in *absolute mode*, which uses numbers to represent file permissions, or *symbolic mode*, which uses combinations of letters and symbols to add permissions or remove permissions.

Set-Group-ID and Set-User-ID

On occasion, a user who is not the owner of a file may need permission to execute the file. For example, to grant a user the ability to change passwords, that user will require permission to use the passwd command. Executable files and public directories can be assigned special permissions that, upon execution, will allow the user to assume the ID of the owner or group. These are the setuid (set-user-ID) and setgid (set-group-ID) permissions.

When setuid permission is set on an executable file, a process that runs this file is granted access on the basis of the owner of the file. In other words, since it is not based on the user, the setuid permission allows a user to access files and directories that are normally available only to the owner. This permission presents a security risk, as attackers can find a way to maintain the permissions that are granted to them by the setuid process, even after the process has finished executing.

For the exam, you'll need to know the values in the following list, which better explains the values for setting file permissions in absolute mode:

- *Value = 0, permission set = - - - for no permissions*
- *Value = 1, permission set = - -x for execute permission only*
- *Value = 2, permission set = -w- for write permission only*
- *Value = 3, permission set = -wx for write and execute permissions*
- *Value = 4, permission set = r- - for read permission only*
- *Value = 5, permission set = r-x for read and execute permissions*
- *Value = 6, permission set = rw- for read and write permissions*
- *Value = 7, permission set = rwx for read, write, and execute permissions*

You use these numbers in sets of three, which set permissions for owner, group, and other, in that order only. Let's look at some examples of the chmod command:

- *To deny the execute permission of our sample file to everyone, use chmod a-x sample.*
- *To allow only read permission of our sample file to everyone, use chmod 444 sample.*
- *To allow everyone to read, write, and execute the sample file and turn on the set group-ID, use chmod a=rwx,g+s sample and then chmod 2777 sample.*
- *The value 644 sets read and write permissions for owner, and read-only permissions for group and other.*

The setgid permission is similar to the setuid permission in that the process's effective group ID (GID) is changed to the group that owns the file, and a user is granted access based on the permissions that are granted to that group. When the permission is applied to a directory, files that were created in this directory belong to the group to which the directory belongs.

You should monitor your system for any unauthorized use of the setgid and setuid permissions. According to Sun, a suspicious permission grants program access to an unusual group rather than to root or bin. Sun recommends that you always monitor programs that are executed with privileges as well as the users that have rights to execute them. To do so, you can search your system for unauthorized use of the setuid and setgid permissions on programs to gain superuser privileges. In a terminal session with superuser privileges, search for files with setuid permissions by using the find command, like so:

```
find directory -user root -perm -4000 -exec ls -ldb {} \; >/tmp/filename
```

where find directory checks all mounted paths starting at the specified directory, which can be root (/), sys, bin, or mail; -user root displays files owned only by root; -perm -4000 displays files only with permissions set to 4000; -exec ls -ldb displays the output of the find command in ls -ldb format; and >/tmp/filename writes results to this file.

Following is a sample of output you can expect to see while finding files with setuid permissions:

```
-r-sr-xr-x 1 root bin 38836 Aug 10 16:16 /usr/bin/at
-r-sr-xr-x 1 root bin 19812 Aug 10 16:16 /usr/bin/crontab
---s--x--x 1 root sys 46040 Aug 10 15:18 /usr/bin/ct
-r-sr-xr-x 1 root sys 12092 Aug 11 01:29 /usr/lib/mv_dir
-r-sr-sr-x 1 root bin 33208 Aug 10 15:55 /usr/lib/lpadmin
-r-sr-sr-x 1 root bin 38696 Aug 10 15:55 /usr/lib/lpsched
---s--x--- 1 root rar 45376 Aug 18 15:11 /usr/rar/bin/sh
-r-sr-xr-x 1 root bin 12524 Aug 11 01:27 /usr/bin/df
-rwsr-xr-x 1 root sys 21780 Aug 11 01:27 /usr/bin/newgrp
-r-sr-sr-x 1 root sys 23000 Aug 11 01:27 /usr/bin/passwd
-r-sr-xr-x 1 root sys 23824 Aug 11 01:27 /usr/bin/su
```

EXERCISE 10-1

Find Files with setuid Permissions

In this exercise, we use the `find` command to locate files with `setuid` permissions and then view the results with the `more` command.

Using the find Command to Locate Files with setuid Permissions

1. Log in with an account that has root privileges so you'll have full privileges that may be required to search all files.

2. Search for files with `setuid` permissions with the `find` command:

```
find directory -user root -perm -4000 -exec ls -ldb {} \; >/dump/results
```

Viewing the Results

3. View the results in /dump/results using the `more` command:

```
more /dump/results
```

where `results` is the name of the file in the /dump directory to which you wrote your `find` results.

For added security—by preventing executable files from compromising the system—you can disable programs from using executable stacks. In the Solaris operating system, the `noexec_user_stack` variable gives you the option of allowing or disallowing executable stack mappings. In other words, by executing a simple command, you can mitigate your risk to program stack buffer overflows with extra data that can be executed. If the `noexec_user_stack` variable is set to non-zero (the variable is set to zero by default), the operating system will apply nonexecutable but readable and writable attributes to every process stack.

When you disallow executable stacks, programs that attempt to execute code on their stack will abort with a core dump. At that time, a warning message will be displayed with the name of the program, its process ID, and the UID of the user who ran the program. In addition, the message can be logged by syslog when the syslog kern facility is set to notice level (refer to Chapter 4 for more information on logging and using syslog). But because of hardware limitations, monitoring and reporting

INSIDE THE EXAM

Disabling Executable Stacks

Although most programs will run smoothly without running code from the stack, it's important to note that some software may require executable stacks. Therefore, if you disable executable stacks, programs that require an executable stack will be aborted; it's crucial to test this procedure first on a non-production system.

Following are steps for manually disabling programs from using executable stacks:

1. Assume the role of superuser.

2. Change the directory to the /etc folder and begin to edit the system file (/etc/system).

3. Type **cd /etc**, press ENTER, and then type **vi system** and press ENTER again.

4. In the visual editor, press the I key (to switch to edit mode and insert text) and type **set noexec_user_stack=1**, and then press ENTER.

5. Press the ESC key (to enter into command mode) and type **:wq**; then press ENTER to save and exit.

6. At the terminal prompt, reboot the system by typing the command **init 6** and then pressing ENTER.

executable stacks is available only on microSPARC (sun4m) and UltraSPARC (sun4u) platforms.

You can disable or enable executable stack message logging. If enabled, when a program attempts to execute stack code, the attempt will be logged by syslog. To enable message logging, follow these steps:

1. Assume the role of superuser.

2. Edit the /etc/system file and add `set noexec_user_stack_log=1`.

3. Reboot the system.

atch *You should always monitor the system for unauthorized* `setuid` *and* `setgid` *permissions to gain superuser privileges.*

Conversely, to disable executable stack message logging, add `set noexec_user_stack_log=0` to the *etc/system* file and reboot the system.

EXERCISE 10-2

Disable Executable Stacks and Enable Stack Message Logging

In this exercise, we disable executable stacks and enable stack message logging in the /etc/system file; then we reboot the operating system to initiate the changes.

Disabling Executable Stacks

1. Log in with an account that has root privileges or become superuser.

2. Change the directory to the /etc folder and edit the system file in your favorite editor.

3. Type **set noexec_user_stack=1**.

Enabling Stack Message Logging

4. While editing the /etc/system file, add **set noexec_user_stack_log=1**.

5. Save the changes and exit the editor.

Rebooting the Operating System

6. Restart the server.

Using the Desktop Environment to Change Standard File Permissions

You can use the Solaris desktop environment to view and modify file permissions. Perhaps the easiest way to do so is by opening the File Manager, right-clicking a file for which you are the owner, and selecting Properties from the File menu. This should open a file properties interface similar to that shown in Figure 10-1. You probably noticed the Show Access Control List button on the file properties interface. You can view and modify ACLs graphically as well, which we'll cover in the next section.

In particular, notice the Basic Permissions section of the file properties interface. You can set permissions on a file or folder, including Read Permission, which allows access to retrieve, copy, or view the contents of the object; Write Permission, which allows access to change the contents of the file and to create or delete objects from the folder; and Execute Permission, which allows access to run the file (for executable

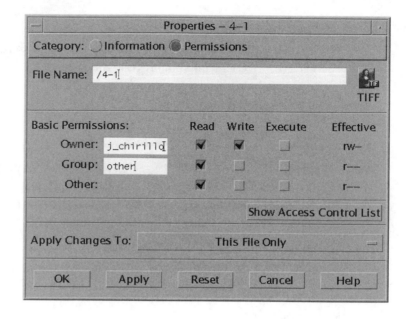

FIGURE 10-1

Managing file permissions from the file properties interface

files, scripts, and actions) and search and lists the folder's contents. For example, to grant permissions on a file for everyone to use, but to protect it so it cannot be overwritten, click to change the file's properties, giving read and execute permission to Owner, Group, and Other, but giving no one write permission.

CERTIFICATION OBJECTIVE 10.02

Use Access Control Lists to Set File Permissions

Remember that ACLs provide greater security by enabling you to define file permissions for each user class. With UNIX file permissions, you're limited to making a file either read-only or read-write; however, by using ACLs, you can make files read-only for a certain group, and also read-write for a specific user in that group. In this section, we'll determine whether a file has an ACL, how to add an ACL to a file, and finally how to tweak ACLs.

Working with ACLs

The first step is to determine whether a file or files already has an ACL. This is easy to do with the ls command. Simply issue the command ls -l *filename*, where *filename* is the name of a specific file or directory. Take a look at the following example:

```
ls - l memo.txt
-rwxr-----+   1 john        memos              167 Dec 01 9:30 memo.txt
```

You know the file has an ACL because the plus sign (+) is listed after the mode field in this output. Unless you have added ACL entries that extend UNIX file permissions, the plus sign does not display to the right of the mode field.

Adding ACLs to a File and Modifying ACLs

To set an ACL on a file, we use the setfacl command:

```
setfacl -s user::perms,group::perms,other:perms,mask:perms,acl-entry-list filename ...
```

where

- ■ -s sets an ACL on the file. If a file already has an ACL, it is replaced. This option requires at least the user::, group::, and other:: entries.
- ■ user::*perms* specifies the file owner permissions.
- ■ group::*perms* specifies the group ownership permissions.
- ■ other:*perms* specifies the permissions for users other than the file owner or members of the group.
- ■ mask:*perms* specifies the permissions for the ACL mask. The mask indicates the maximum permissions that are allowed for users (other than the owner) and for groups.
- ■ *acl-entry-list* specifies the list of one or more ACL entries to set for specific users and groups on the file or directory. You can also set default ACL entries on a directory.
- ■ *filename* ... specifies one or more files or directories on which to set the ACL. Multiple filenames are separated by spaces.

Let's consider the following example:

```
setfacl - s user::rw-,group::r--,other:---,mask:rw-,user:joe:rw- memo.txt
```

Here, the owner permissions are set to read and write (user::rw-); group permissions are set to read only (group::r--); other permissions are set to none (other:---); the ACL mask permissions are set to read and write (mask:rw-, which means that no user or group can have execute permissions); and user joe is granted read and write permissions (user:joe:rw-) on file *memo.txt*. Note that if an ACL already exists on a file, the -s option replaces the entire ACL with the new one. To verify the file has your ACL, issue the getfacl *filename* command.

If you should need to copy an ACL of one file to another file, you can do so by issuing this command:

```
getfacl filename1 | setfacl -f -filename2
```

where, *filename1* is the file whose ACL you wish to apply to *filename2*.

If you should need to modify or delete ACL entries, use the command

```
setfacl (-d or -m) acl-entry-list filename ...
```

where

- ■ -d deletes the specified ACL entries.
- ■ -m modifies the existing ACL entry.
- ■ *acl-entry-list* specifies the list of one or more ACL entries to modify on the file or directory. You can also modify default ACL entries on a directory.
- ■ *filename* ... specifies one or more files or directories, separated by a space.

✓ TWO-MINUTE DRILL

Here are some of the key points from the certification objectives in Chapter 10.

Use UNIX Permissions to Protect Files

❑ Access control lists (ACLs) provide better file security by enabling you to define file permissions for each user class.

❑ The ls command is used to list files and some information about the files contained within a directory.

❑ The chown command is used to change file ownership.

❑ The chgrp command is used to change group ownership of a file.

❑ The chmod command is used to change permissions on a file. The command changes or assigns the mode of a file (permissions and other attributes), which may be absolute or symbolic.

❑ When setuid permission is set on an executable file, a process that runs this file is granted access on the basis of the owner of the file. This permission presents a security risk, as attackers can find a way to maintain the permissions that are granted to them by the setuid process even after the process has finished executing.

❑ You should always monitor the system for unauthorized setuid and setgid permissions to gain superuser privileges.

Use Access Control Lists to Set File Permissions

❑ Unless you have added ACL entries that extend UNIX file permissions, the plus sign (+) does not display to the right of the mode field.

❑ To set an ACL on a file, use the setfacl command. Note that if an ACL already exists on a file, the -s option replaces the entire ACL with the new one. To verify the file has your ACL, issue the getfacl *filename* command.

SELF TEST

The following questions will help you measure your understanding of the material presented in this chapter. Read all the choices carefully, because there might be more than one correct answer. Choose all correct answers for each question, and in some cases explain your answer. Some questions are short-answer questions to ensure you have a good understanding of the material.

Use UNIX Permissions to Protect Files

1. With regard to general UNIX file permissions, which permissions can be applied?

2. Explain the difference between UNIX file permissions and ACLs.

3. You can set general UNIX file permissions to which user classes?

4. What are the attributes of the Read permission?

5. What are the attributes of the Write permission?

6. What are the attributes of the Execute permission?

7. What are the attributes of the permission indicated with the - symbol?

8. Which of the following commands is used to change user ownership of a file?
   A. ls
   B. chown
   C. chgrp
   D. chmod
   E. All of the above

9. Which of the following commands is used to change permissions on a file?
   A. ls
   B. chown
   C. chgrp
   D. chmod
   E. All of the above

10. Which of the following commands is used to list files and some information about the files contained within a directory?
    A. ls
    B. chown
    C. chgrp

     D. chmod

     E. All of the above

11. Which of the following commands is used to change group ownership of a file?

     A. ls

     B. chown

     C. chgrp

     D. chmod

     E. All of the above

12. Explain why the setuid permission set on an executable file poses a security risk.

13. Explain how to locate files with setuid permissions using the find command.

14. What steps should you take to disable executable stacks and enable stack message logging?

Use Access Control Lists to Set File Permissions

15. What command(s) would you use to set an ACL on a file?

16. What command(s) would you use to verify an ACL was set?

17. What command(s) would you use to modify or delete ACL entries?

LAB QUESTION

You are called to ABCD Inc.'s site to prevent executable files from compromising the system by disabling programs from using executable stacks. The customer has already confirmed that its software does not require running code from the stack. Additionally, ABCD would like to have the system log any time a program attempts to execute stack code. What steps would you perform onsite?

SELF TEST ANSWERS

Use UNIX Permissions to Protect Files

1. ☑ UNIX file permissions provide read, write, and execute permissions.

2. ☑ Using standard UNIX file permissions, you can provide read, write, and execute permissions for three user classes (file owner, group, and other users), whereas ACLs take security a step further by enabling you to define file permissions for each user class. For example, let's say you want the sales user group to read a particular file; however, you want only the sales manager— part of the sales group—also to have permission to make changes to that file. With UNIX file permissions, you're limited to making the file either read-only or read-write for the sales group. On the other hand, by using ACLs, you can make the file read-only for the sales group, with the exception of read-write for the sales manager.

3. ☑ UNIX file permissions provide permissions for three user classes (file owner, group, and other users).

4. ☑ The Read permission is indicated with the symbol r. This permission allows users to open and read a file and list files in a directory.

5. ☑ The Write permission is indicated with the symbol w. This permission allows users to open, read, delete, and modify the contents of a file, and list and add files and links in a directory or remove them.

6. ☑ The Execute permission is indicated with the symbol x. This permission allows users to execute a file (program or shell script) in a directory.

7. ☑ The Deny permission is the one indicated with the symbol $-$. This permission denies read, write, and execute access.

8. ☑ **B.** The chown command is used to change user ownership of a file.
   ☒ **A** is wrong because ls is used to list files and some information about the files contained within a directory. **C** is wrong because chgrp is used to change group ownership of a file. **D** is wrong because chmod is used to change permissions on a file.

9. ☑ **D.** The chmod command is used to change permissions on a file.
   ☒ **A** is wrong because ls is used to list files and some information about the files contained within a directory. **B** is wrong because chown is used to change user ownership of a file. **C** is wrong because chgrp is used to change group ownership of a file.

10. ☑ **A.** The `ls` command is used to list files and some information about the files contained within a directory.

    ☒ **B** is wrong because `chown` is used to change user ownership of a file. **C** is wrong because `chgrp` is used to change group ownership of a file. **D** is wrong because `chmod` is used to change permissions on a file.

11. ☑ **C.** The `chgrp` command is used to change group ownership of a file.

    ☒ **A** is wrong because `ls` is used to list files and some information about the files contained within a directory. **B** is wrong because `chown` is used to change user ownership of a file. **D** is wrong because `chmod` is used to change permissions on a file.

12. ☑ When `setuid` permission is set on an executable file, a process that runs this file is granted access on the basis of the owner of the file. This permission presents a security risk, as attackers can find a way to maintain the permissions that are granted to them by the `setuid` process, even after the process has finished executing.

13. ☑ Use the `find` command to locate files with `setuid` permissions and then view the results with the `more` command. First, log in with an account that has root privileges, or use the switch user (`su`) command to become superuser. As superuser, you'll have full privileges, which may be required to search all files. Next, search for files with `setuid` permissions with the `find` command:

    ```
    find directory -user root -perm -4000 -exec ls -ldb {} \; >/tmp/findresults
    ```

    View the results in */tmp/findresults* using the `more` command, like so:

    ```
    more /tmp/findresults
    ```

    where *findresults* is the name of the file to which you wrote your find results to in the */tmp* directory.

14. ☑ To disable executable stacks and enable stack message logging, you need to make changes in the */etc/system* file, and then reboot the operating system to initiate the changes.

    1. Log in with an account that has root privileges, or use the `su` command to become superuser.
    2. Change directory to the */etc* folder and edit the system file (*/etc/system*) by adding `set noexec_user_stack=1`.
    3. While editing the */etc/system* file, add `set noexec_user_stack_log=1`.
    4. Save the changes and exit the editor.
    5. Issue the command `init 6` to restart the server.

Use Access Control Lists to Set File Permissions

15. ☑ To set an ACL on a file, use the `setfacl` command.

16. ☑ To verify the file has your ACL, issue the `getfacl filename` command. Use the `setfacl` command with the following syntax:

```
setfacl -s user::perms,group::perms,other:perms,mask:perms,acl-entry-list filename ...;
```

where:

- -s sets an ACL on the file. If a file already has an ACL, it is replaced. This option requires at least the user::, group::, and other:: entries.
- user::*perms* specifies the file owner permissions.
- group::*perms* specifies the group ownership permissions.
- other:*perms* specifies the permissions for users other than the file owner or members of the group.
- mask:*perms* specifies the permissions for the ACL mask. The mask indicates the maximum permissions that are allowed for users (other than the owner) and for groups.
- *acl-entry-list* specifies the list of one or more ACL entries to set for specific users and groups on the file or directory. You can also set default ACL entries on a directory.
- *filename* ... specifies one or more files or directories on which to set the ACL. Multiple filenames are separated by spaces.

17. ☑ If you should need to modify or delete ACL entries, use the setfacl (-d or -m) acl-entry-list filename... command; where:

- -d deletes the specified ACL entries.
- -m modifies the existing ACL entry.
- *acl-entry-list* specifies the list of one or more ACL entries to modify on the file or directory. You can also modify default ACL entries on a directory.
- *filename* ... specifies one or more files or directories, separated by a space.

LAB ANSWER

Most programs will run smoothly without running code from the stack; however, the customer has confirmed that its software does not require executable stacks. Therefore, if you can, you should disable executable stacks. To do so, follow these steps:

1. Assume the role of superuser.
2. Change directory to the */etc* folder and edit the system file (*/etc/system*) by adding set noexec_user_stack=1. To do so, type **cd /etc**, press ENTER, and then type **vi system** and press ENTER again.
3. In the visual editor, press the I key (to switch to edit mode and insert text), type **set noexec_user_stack=1**, and then press ENTER.

4. Press the ESC key (to enter into command mode) and type **:wq**. Then press ENTER to save and exit.

5. At the terminal prompt, reboot the system by typing the command **init 6** and then pressing ENTER.

To enable executable stack message logging, follow these steps:

1. Assume the role of superuser.

2. Edit the */etc/system* file and add `set noexec_user_stack_log=1`.

3. Reboot the system.

Part V

Solaris Cryptographic Framework

11
Using Cryptographic Services

Cryptography provides for the integrity, confidentiality, and authenticity of information. Technically speaking, *cryptography* is the art of encrypting readable plain text into an unreadable format call *cipher text*. Without a secret key, the cipher text cannot be decrypted. (Well, that may be true in a perfect world, because cryptanalysts have devised ways of cracking many older encryption techniques.) In Solaris, the cryptographic framework provides a repository of algorithms that can be used for cryptographic services. *Algorithms* are *symmetric* (secret key) or *asymmetric* (public key) computational procedures that encrypt or hash whatever you apply them to, such as text or files. In symmetric algorithms, the same key is used for both encryption and decryption—anyone knowing the key can both encrypt and decrypt messages. With asymmetric algorithms, two keys are used: one to encrypt a message and another to decrypt it.

e x **a m**

w a t c h
For the exam, be sure you know the difference between symmetric "secret key" or asymmetric "public key" algorithms. Remember that in symmetric algorithms, the same key is used for both encryption and decryption, and in asymmetric algorithms, two keys are used—one to encrypt and another to decrypt a message.

e x **a m**

w a t c h
It's important to remember that the Solaris cryptographic framework allows only three types of plug-ins: user-level plug-ins, kernel-level plug-ins, and hardware plug-ins. This framework helps protect the integrity of files against eavesdropping.

Although cryptography encompasses a whole spectrum of material—enough to accommodate an entire book—in this chapter, we'll examine only what is required by the exam: the Solaris framework for cryptographic services, specifically how to ensure the integrity of files, protect files from eavesdropping, administer the cryptographic framework, and enable a provider to be added to the Solaris cryptographic framework. *Providers* are cryptographic plug-ins that consumers use. *Consumers* can be applications, end users, or kernel operations. According to Sun, the framework allows only three types of plug-ins: user-level plug-ins, which are shared objects that provide services by using PKCS #11 libraries; kernel-level plug-ins, which provide for implementations of algorithms in software; and hardware plug-ins, which are device drivers and their associated hardware accelerators.

Given the importance of the material in this chapter with regard to the exam, some of the sections are a brief reiteration and elaboration of topics we've touched upon earlier in the book.

CERTIFICATION OBJECTIVE 11.01

Explain How to Protect Files Using the Solaris Cryptographic Framework

Protecting files is a core component in Sun's Solaris security strategy. Although MD5 and SHA1 were developed to help detect corrupt or maliciously altered files, Sun also recommends using a more comprehensive package as well, called Tripwire (www.tripwire.com). In addition to Tripwire, Sun recommends that you use the Automated Security Enhancement Tool (ASET, discussed in Chapter 8) and the Basic Security Module (BSM, discussed in Chapter 5) to help prevent unauthorized changes from being made to system files.

In this section, we'll look in detail at using the Solaris Cryptographic Framework to protect the integrity of files. We'll learn how to generate a random key for use with the encrypt and mac commands, provide a checksum that ensures the integrity of a file, protect a file with a message authentication code (MAC) and verify to the receiver of your message that you were the sender, and protect the content of files with encryption.

ω a t c h   *For the exam, remember the four methods Sun recommends to monitor and help prevent unauthorized changes from being made to system files, specifically ASET, which is discussed in Chapter 8, and BSM, which is covered in Chapter 5.*

Generating Symmetric Keys

Symmetric keys, or secret keys, are computational procedures used for encryption, where the same key is used for both encryption and decryption. The first step in creating a symmetric key is to determine the length (in bytes) required by your encryption algorithm. To do so, simply list the *bit range* of all supported algorithms with the encrypt -l and mac -l commands, as shown here:

```
encrypt -l
Algorithm        Keysize:   Min   Max (bits)
------------------------------------------------
aes                         128   128
arcfour                     8     128
des                         64    64
```

```
3des                                    192    192
mac -l
Algorithm              Keysize:    Min    Max (bits)
--------------------------------------------------
des_mac                             64     64
sha1_hmac                            8    512
md5_hmac                             8    512
```

The next step is to determine the key length *in bytes* by dividing the minimum and maximum key sizes by 8. Note that when the minimum and maximum key sizes are different, intermediate key sizes are possible. At that point, you can generate the symmetric key with the dd command:

```
dd if=/dev/urandom of=keyfile bs=n count=n
```

where if=/dev/urandom is the input file (for a random key, use the */dev/urandom* file), of=keyfile is the output file that holds the generated key, bs=n is the key size in bytes (for the length in bytes divide the key length in bits by 8), and count=n is the count of the input blocks.

For example, to create a key for the MD5 algorithm in a file for later decryption, you can issue this command:

```
dd if=/dev/urandom of=$HOME/md5key/md5key64 bs=64 count=1
```

Notice that the minimum and maximum bit key sizes for MD5 are different, so we used 64, which is the maximum byte size (that is, 512/8). The same rules apply for creating an AES key (note that AES uses a mandatory 128-bit key, or 16 bytes). Here's an example:

```
dd if=/dev/urandom of=$HOME/aeskey/aeskey16 bs=16 count=1
```

Ensuring the Integrity of Files Using Checksum

You can ensure that files weren't altered using the Solaris cryptographic framework by using message digest algorithms. As you know, a *message digest* is a one-way function for a stream of binary data that serves as verification that the data was not altered since the message digest was first generated—such as from when a file was compiled or modified. An example of a message digest is as follows:

```
Filename: tgpids.tar.Z
 Creation Date: October 05, 2004
 File Size: 500 KB
MD5: A12A24F23E36B0EFC4A9C42C3747B8B8
```

In this example, the message digest was created using an MD5 checksum utility. This particular utility was developed by Fourmilab (www.fourmilab.ch/md5/md5 .tar.gz). John Walker of Fourmilab submitted an excellent man page for the utility, in which he describes the message digest as a compact digital signature for an arbitrarily long stream of binary data. An ideal message digest algorithm would never generate the same signature for two different sets of input, but achieving such theoretical perfection would require a message digest as long as the input file. Message digest algorithms have much in common with techniques used in encryption, but the means provide a different end: verification that data has not been altered since the signature was published.

Many older programs requiring digital signatures employed 16- or 32-bit cyclical redundancy codes (CRCs) that were originally developed to verify correct transmission in data communication protocols; but these short codes, while adequate to detect the kind of transmission errors for which they were intended, are insufficiently secure for applications such as electronic commerce and verification of security-related software distributions.

The most commonly used present-day message digest algorithm is the 128-bit MD5 algorithm, developed by Ron Rivest of the MIT Laboratory for Computer Science and RSA Data Security, Inc. The algorithm, with a reference implementation, was published as Internet RFC 1321 in April 1992 and was placed into the public domain at that time. Message digest algorithms such as MD5 are not deemed "encryption technology" and are not subject to the export controls some governments impose on other data security products. For example, Sun states that export law in the United States requires that the use of open cryptographic interfaces be restricted. The Solaris cryptographic framework satisfies the current law by requiring that kernel cryptographic providers and PKCS#11 cryptographic providers be signed.

Again, referring to the example, after downloading the file, you would run the command-line MD5 utility on it to ensure that you get the same MD5 hash output posted with the download link from when the file was originally created or modified. If the signature or hash is different, you can assume that the file was either corrupted during transfer or possibly maliciously altered.

The MD5 and the Secure Hashing Algorithm (SHA1) are among the most popular message digest algorithms. The MD5 algorithm takes a message of arbitrary length and produces a 128-bit message digest. SHA1—a revision to the original SHA that was published in 1994—is similar to the MD4 family of hash functions developed by Rivest. The algorithm takes a message and produces a 160-bit message digest. Finally, the Solaris cryptographic framework supports a command that can be used to check the integrity of files in this fashion. You can issue the `digest` command to compute a message digest for one or more files.

Computing a Digest of a File

By comparing digests of a file, you are checking its integrity to ensure that the file has not been corrupted or altered. In the Solaris cryptographic framework environment, you can perform digest computations using the following syntax:

```
digest -v -a algorithm input-file > digest-listing
```

where `-v` displays the output with file information, `-a algorithm` is the algorithm used to compute a digest (that is, MD5 or SHA1), `input-file` is the input file for the digest to be computed, and `digest-listing` is the output file for the `digest` command.

With regard to checking the integrity of files, be sure to take advantage of the Solaris Fingerprint Database (sfpDB). As you should know by now, sfpDB is a free tool from Sun that allows you to check the integrity of system files through online cryptographic checksums. By doing so, you can determine whether system binaries and patches are safe in accordance with their original checksums among a huge database stored at Sun. MD5 software binaries that can be used with sfpDB for Intel and SPARC architectures can be freely downloaded from Sun at http://SunSolve.Sun.com/md5/md5.tar.Z.

The MD5 software is compressed in the tar file format; therefore, after downloading to a directory (such as */usr/local*), unpack the archive with the following command:

```
zcat md5.tar.Z | tar xvf -
```

INSIDE THE EXAM

Creating and Viewing File Digests

Following are steps for manually creating file digests with the `digest` command using both MD5 and SHA1 mechanisms within the cryptographic framework:

1. To compute an MD5 digest for file *tgpids.tar.Z* into output file *tgpidsmd5*, issue this command:

   ```
   digest -v -a md5 tgpids.tar.Z >> $HOME/tgpidsmd5
   ```

2. You can then concatenate or display the resulting file with the `cat` command, `cat ~/tgpidsmd5`, to view the following output:

   ```
   md5 (tgpids.tar.Z) = A12A24F23E36B0EFC4A9C42C3747B8B8
   ```

3. To compute an SHA1 digest for file *tgpids.tar.Z* into output file *tgpidssha1*, issue this command:

   ```
   digest -v -a sha1 tgpids.tar.Z >> $HOME/tgpidssha1
   ```

4. You can then issue the `cat` command, `cat ~/tgpidssha1`, to view the following output:

   ```
   sha1 (tgpids.tar.Z) = 1ef97e5ad217e34f0a911a097a7a588b31f9b411
   ```

The software will be unpacked into an MD5 subdirectory. After downloading and unpacking the MD5 archive, the file permissions must be modified before they can be executed. To permit only root, for example, to read, write, and execute the MD5 programs, issue the command `chmod 700 /usr/local/md5/*`. Additionally, the owner and group of the MD5 files must be modified to belong to a system user and associated group. Given the particular functionality, traditionally they should be owned by root; therefore, you should also issue the `chown root:root /usr/local/md5/*` command.

Using MD5 Software   Creating hexadecimal MD5 digital fingerprints is simple. For example, based on the installation mentioned previously, to create an MD5 fingerprint for the *su* program on a SPARC system, you would enter this command:

```
/usr/local/md5/md5-sparc /usr/bin/su
```

The output should look something like this:

```
MD5 (/usr/bin/su) = cb2b71c32f4eb00469cbe4fd529e690c
```

Furthermore, by placing a space between target files, you can create MD5 fingerprints for more than one file at a time, such as for the *su* and *ls* programs, by issuing this command:

```
/usr/local/md5/md5-sparc /usr/bin/su /usr/bin/ls
```

The output should look something like this:

```
MD5 (/usr/bin/su) = cb2b71c32f4eb00469cbe4fd529e690c
MD5 (/usr/bin/ls) = 351f5eab0baa6eddae391f84d0a6c192
```

Finally, to create MD5 fingerprints for all files in the */usr/bin* directory, you could issue the MD5 command, along with the `find` command, such as in the following:

```
find /usr/bin -type f -print \
| xargs -n100 /usr/local/md5/md5-sparc > /tmp/md5output.txt
```

The output will be printed to the */tmp* directory in file *md5output.txt*. The contents of the file can easily be copied into the online fingerprint database for integrity checks.

Protecting Files with a Message Authentication Code (MAC)

Without altering the original file, of course, and to protect a digest, you can compute a message authentication code (MAC) of a file. To do so, follow these steps:

1. List the available algorithms by issuing the `mac -l` command:

```
mac -l
Algorithm          Keysize:     Min    Max (bits)
--------------------------------------------------
des_mac                         64     64
sha1_hmac                       8      512
md5_hmac                        8      512
```

2. Generate a symmetric key using the `dd` command:

```
dd if=/dev/urandom of=keyfile bs=n count=n
```

For the exam, you should know how to create a MAC of a file. This algorithm creates a short message digest from a larger block of text by hashing it with a secret key.

where `if=/dev/urandom` is the input file (for a random key, use the */dev/urandom* file), `of=keyfile` is the output file that holds the generated key, `bs=n` is the key size in bytes (for the length in bytes divide the key length in bits by 8), and `count=n` is the count of the input blocks. For more detail and examples, see the "Generating Symmetric Keys" section earlier in this chapter.

3. Create a MAC using this command:

```
mac -v -a algorithm -k keyfile input-file
```

where `-v` displays the output in the following format: *algorithm (input-file) = mac*. Here, `-a algorithm` is the algorithm used to compute the MAC (type the algorithm as the algorithm appears in the output of the `mac -l` command), `-k keyfile` is the file that contains a key of algorithm-specified length, and *input-file* is the input file for the MAC.

INSIDE THE EXAM

Computing a MAC with the MD5_HMAC and SHA1_HMAC Mechanisms

Following is Sun's example of an e-mail attachment authenticated with the MD5_HMAC mechanism and your secret key, with the MAC listing saved to a file:

```
mac -v -a md5_hmac \ -k ~/keyf/03.09.mack64 email.attach
md5_hmac (email.attach) = 02df6eb6c123ff25d78877eb1d55710c
echo "md5_hmac (email.attach) = 02df6eb6c123ff25d78877eb1d55710c" \ >> ~/mac.daily.03.09
```

Following is Sun's example of the directory manifest authenticated with the SHA1_ HMAC mechanism and your secret key, with the results placed in a file:

```
mac -v -a sha1_hmac \ -k ~/keyf/03.09.mack64 docs/* > ~/mac.docs.legal.03.09

more ~/mac.docs.legal.03.09

sha1_hmac (docs/legal1) = 9b31536d3b3c0c6b25d653418db8e765e17fe07a
sha1_hmac (docs/legal2) = 865af61a3002f8a457462a428cdb1a88c1b51ff5
sha1_hmac (docs/legal3) = 076c944cb2528536c9aebd3b9fbe367e07b61dc7
sha1_hmac (docs/legal4) = 7aede27602ef6e4454748cbd3821e0152e45beb4
```

Encrypting and Decrypting Files

When you encrypt a file using the encrypt command, the original file is not modified in any way—unlike many other encryption utilities—but the output file is an encrypted form of the original file. To encrypt a file, simply create a symmetric key using the same method detailed throughout this chapter, and then issue the encrypt command:

```
encrypt -a algorithm -k keyfile -i input-file -o output-file
```

INSIDE THE EXAM

Encrypting and Decrypting Files with the AES, DES, and DES3 Algorithms

Following are Sun's examples of properly using the encrypt and decrypt commands.

In the following example, a file is encrypted with the AES algorithm. AES mechanisms use a key of 128 bits, or 16 bytes:

```
encrypt -a aes -k ~/keyf/03.09.aes16 \ -i ticket.to.ride -o ~/enc/e.ticket.to.ride
```

The input file, *ticket.to.ride*, still exists in its original form.

In the next example, a file is encrypted with the DES algorithm. The DES algorithm requires a key of 64 bits, or 8 bytes:

```
encrypt -a des -i personal.txt \ -k ~/keyf/03.09.des8 -o ~/enc/e.personal.txt
```

To decrypt the output file, use the same key and encryption mechanism that encrypted the file. Pass these parameters to the decrypt command:

```
decrypt -a des -i ~/enc/e.personal.txt \ -k ~/keyf/03.09.des8 -o ~/personal.txt
```

In this example, a file is encrypted with the DES3 algorithm. The DES3 algorithm requires a key of 192 bits, or 24 bytes:

```
encrypt -a des3 -k ~/keyf/03.09.des24 \ -i ~/personal2.txt -o
~/enc/e.personal2.txt
```

To decrypt the output file, pass the same key and the same encryption mechanism that encrypted the file to the decrypt command:

```
decrypt -a des3 -k ~/keyf/03.09.des24 \ -i ~/enc/e.personal2.txt -o
~/personal2.txt
```

e**x**a m
watch

On some versions of Sun's exam, you'll be required to know how to encrypt and decrypt a file by creating a symmetric key, and then issuing the encrypt command. To decrypt the output *file, you need to pass the same key and the same encryption mechanism that encrypted the file but use the* decrypt *command.*

where -a *algorithm* is the algorithm to use to encrypt the file (type the algorithm as the algorithm appears in the output of the encrypt -l command), -k *keyfile* is the file that contains a key of algorithm-specified length (the key length for each algorithm is listed, in bits, in the output of the encrypt -l command), -i *input-file* is the input file that you want to encrypt (this file is left unchanged), and -o *output-file* is the output file that is the encrypted form of the input file. To decrypt the output file, use the decrypt command and simply pass the same key and the same encryption mechanism that encrypted the file.

CERTIFICATION OBJECTIVE 11.02

Administer the Solaris Cryptographic Framework

In this section, we'll administer software and hardware providers in the Solaris cryptographic framework. As required by the exam, we'll look specifically at how to list the algorithms, libraries, and hardware devices available for use, and how to prevent the use of a user-level mechanism and disable mechanisms from a kernel module.

Listing Available Providers

Using the *cryptoadm* utility, we can display cryptographic provider information for a system. The framework supports three types of providers: a user-level provider (a PKCS11 shared library), a kernel software provider (a loadable kernel software module), and a kernel hardware provider (a cryptographic hardware device). Following are the command's usage pertaining to the exam requirements:

- `cryptoadm list` Displays the list of installed providers.
- `cryptoadm -m` Displays a list of mechanisms that can be used with the installed providers. If a provider is specified, the command will display the name of the specified provider and the mechanism list that can be used with that provider.
- `cryptoadm list -p` Displays the mechanism policy for the installed providers. Also displays the provider feature policy. If a provider is specified, the command will display the name of the provider with the mechanism policy enforced on it only.

Listing Providers and Their Mechanisms at the User Level

To list only mechanisms at the user level that are available for use by regular users, you should execute the `cryptoadm list` command shown here:

```
# cryptoadm list
user-level providers:
        /usr/lib/security/$ISA/pkcs11_kernel.so
        /usr/lib/security/$ISA/pkcs11_softtoken.so
kernel software providers:
        des
        aes
        arcfour
        blowfish
        sha1
        md5
        rsa
kernel hardware providers:
```

Listing All Providers and Their Mechanisms

Use the `cryptoadm list` command with the -m option to list all providers and their mechanisms:

```
# cryptoadm list -m
user-level providers:
=====================
/usr/lib/security/$ISA/pkcs11_kernel.so: no slots presented.
/usr/lib/security/$ISA/pkcs11_softtoken.so:
CKM_DES_CBC,CKM_DES_CBC_PAD,CKM_DES_ECB,CKM_DES_KEY_GEN,CKM_DES_MAC_GENERAL,CKM_D
ES_MAC,CKM_DES3_CBC,CKM_DES3_CBC_PAD,CKM_DES3_ECB,CKM_DES3_KEY_GEN,CKM_AES_CBC,CK
```

```
M_AES_CBC_PAD,CKM_AES_ECB,CKM_AES_KEY_GEN,CKM_SHA_1,CKM_SHA_1_HMAC,CKM_SHA_1_HMAC
_GENERAL,CKM_SSL3_SHA1_MAC,CKM_MD5,CKM_MD5_HMAC,CKM_MD5_HMAC_GENERAL,CKM_SSL3_MD5
_MAC,CKM_RC4,CKM_RC4_KEY_GEN,CKM_DSA,CKM_DSA_SHA1,CKM_DSA_KEY_PAIR_GEN,CKM_RSA_PK
CS,CKM_RSA_PKCS_KEY_PAIR_GEN,CKM_RSA_X_509,CKM_MD5_RSA_PKCS,CKM_SHA1_RSA_PKCS,CKM
_DH_PKCS_KEY_PAIR_GEN,CKM_DH_PKCS_DERIVE,CKM_MD5_KEY_DERIVATION,CKM_SHA1_KEY_DERI
VATION,CKM_PBE_SHA1_RC4_128,CKM_PKCS5_PBKD2

kernel software providers:
==========================
des: CKM_DES_ECB,CKM_DES_CBC,CKM_DES3_ECB,CKM_DES3_CBC
aes: CKM_AES_ECB,CKM_AES_CBC
arcfour: CKM_RC4
blowfish: CKM_BF_ECB,CKM_BF_CBC
sha1: CKM_SHA_1,CKM_SHA_1_HMAC,CKM_SHA_1_HMAC_GENERAL
md5: CKM_MD5,CKM_MD5_HMAC,CKM_MD5_HMAC_GENERAL
rsa: CKM_RSA_PKCS,CKM_RSA_X_509,CKM_MD5_RSA_PKCS,CKM_SHA1_RSA_PKCS

kernel hardware providers:
==========================
```

Listing All Providers and Their Mechanisms Permitted by Policy   By
issuing the -p option, you can display the list of providers and their mechanisms
that are permitted only by the administrator's policy. The administrator sets the
policy that determines which mechanisms are available for use.

```
# cryptoadm list -p

user-level providers:
=====================
/usr/lib/security/$ISA/pkcs11_kernel.so: all mechanisms are enabled.
/usr/lib/security/$ISA/pkcs11_softtoken.so: all mechanisms are enabled.

kernel software providers:
==========================
des: all mechanisms are enabled.
aes: all mechanisms are enabled.
arcfour: all mechanisms are enabled.
blowfish: all mechanisms are enabled.
sha1: all mechanisms are enabled.
md5: all mechanisms are enabled.
rsa: all mechanisms are enabled.

kernel hardware providers:
==========================
```

Preventing the Use of a User-Level Mechanism

While administrating the cryptographic framework on a Solaris system, you may have to remove mechanisms from a library provider that should not be used. To do so, you either need to become superuser or assume a role that includes the Crypto Management rights profile. From there, you can issue the `cryptoadm disable` command to disable the mechanisms that should not be used. For example, let's list only the mechanisms that are offered by a user-level software provider we extracted from the previous section:

```
# cryptoadm list -m /usr/lib/security/'$ISA'/pkcs11_softtoken.so
/usr/lib/security/$ISA/pkcs11_softtoken.so:
CKM_DES_CBC,CKM_DES_CBC_PAD,CKM_DES_ECB,CKM_DES_KEY_GEN,CKM_DES_MAC_GENERAL,CKM_D
ES_MAC,CKM_DES3_CBC,CKM_DES3_CBC_PAD,CKM_DES3_ECB,CKM_DES3_KEY_GEN,CKM_AES_CBC,CK
M_AES_CBC_PAD,CKM_AES_ECB,CKM_AES_KEY_GEN,CKM_SHA_1,CKM_SHA_1_HMAC,CKM_SHA_1_HMAC
_GENERAL,CKM_SSL3_SHA1_MAC,CKM_MD5,CKM_MD5_HMAC,CKM_MD5_HMAC_GENERAL,CKM_SSL3_MD5
_MAC,CKM_RC4,CKM_RC4_KEY_GEN,CKM_DSA,CKM_DSA_SHA1,CKM_DSA_KEY_PAIR_GEN,CKM_RSA_PK
CS,CKM_RSA_PKCS_KEY_PAIR_GEN,CKM_RSA_X_509,CKM_MD5_RSA_PKCS,CKM_SHA1_RSA_PKCS,CKM
_DH_PKCS_KEY_PAIR_GEN,CKM_DH_PKCS_DERIVE,CKM_MD5_KEY_DERIVATION,CKM_SHA1_KEY_DERI
VATION,CKM_PBE_SHA1_RC4_128,CKM_PKCS5_PBKD2
```

Next, let's find out which mechanisms are available for use. From our `cryptoadm list -p` command, covered in the previous section, we know that all mechanisms are enabled:

```
/usr/lib/security/$ISA/pkcs11_softtoken.so: all mechanisms are enabled.
```

Let's disable the CKM_DES_CBC CKM_DES_CBC_PAD CKM_DES_ECB mechanisms:

```
# cryptoadm disable /usr/lib/security/'$ISA'/pkcs11_softtoken.so \
CKM_DES_CBC CKM_DES_CBC_PAD CKM_DES_ECB>
```

To verify that the mechanisms were successfully disabled, issue the `cryptoadm list -p` command again, as shown here:

```
# cryptoadm list -p

user-level providers:
=====================
/usr/lib/security/$ISA/pkcs11_kernel.so: all mechanisms are enabled.
/usr/lib/security/$ISA/pkcs11_softtoken.so: all mechanisms are enabled, excep
t CKM_DES_CBC,CKM_SHA_1_HMAC_GENERAL,CKM_SHA_1_HMAC,CKM_DES_CBC_PAD,CKM_DES_E
CB
```

If you need to re-enable a mechanism—say, for example CKM_DES_CBC—simply issue the cryptoadm enable command:

```
# cryptoadm enable /usr/lib/security/'$ISA'/pkcs11_softtoken.so \
CKM_DES_CBC>
```

e x a m
w a t c h
To prevent the use of a user-level mechanism, issue the `cryptoadm disable provider \ mechanism(s)` *command.*

Disabling Kernel Software Providers

Using the same methodology in this section for preventing the use of user-level mechanisms, we can disable kernel software providers as well. After either becoming superuser or assuming a role that includes the Crypto Management rights profile, simply issue the cryptoadm disable command, as illustrated in these examples:

```
# cryptoadm disable aes CKM_AES_ECB

# cryptoadm list -p aes
aes: all mechanisms are enabled, except CKM_AES_ECB
```

If you need to remove the kernel software provider availability altogether, using aes in our example, simply issue the cryptoadm unload command:

```
# cryptoadm unload aes
```

To verify the removal, issue the cryptoadm list command again:

```
# cryptoadm list

user-level providers:
        /usr/lib/security/$ISA/pkcs11_kernel.so
        /usr/lib/security/$ISA/pkcs11_softtoken.so

kernel software providers:
        des
        aes (inactive)
        arcfour
        blowfish
        sha1
        md5
        rsa

kernel hardware providers:
```

To restore any inactive software providers, issue the `cryptoadm refresh` command:

```
# cryptoadm refresh
```

Alternatively, to remove a provider permanently, issue the `cryptoadm uninstall` command:

```
# cryptoadm uninstall aes
```

✓ TWO-MINUTE DRILL

Here are some of the key points from the certification objectives in Chapter 11.

Explain How to Protect Files Using the Solaris Cryptographic Framework

❏ Algorithms can be symmetric "secret key" or asymmetric "public key" computational procedures used for encryption. In symmetric algorithms, the same key is used for both encryption and decryption, and in asymmetric algorithms, two keys are used—one to encrypt and another to decrypt a message.

❏ Providers are cryptographic plug-ins that are used by applications, end users, or kernel operations—all termed *consumers*. The Solaris cryptographic framework allows only three types of plug-ins: user-level plug-ins, kernel-level plug-ins, and hardware plug-ins.

❏ To monitor and help prevent unauthorized changes from being made to system files, Sun recommends using the Automated Security Enhancement Tool (ASET), the Basic Security Module (BSM), Tripwire, and the Solaris cryptographic framework.

❏ Random keys can be generated using the `encrypt` and `mac` commands.

❏ To create a symmetric key, use the `dd` command:

`dd if=/dev/urandom of=keyfile bs=n count=n`

where `if=/dev/urandom` is the input file (for a random key, use the */dev/ urandom* file), `of=keyfile` is the output file that holds the generated key, `bs=n` is the key size in bytes (for the length in bytes divide the key length in bits by 8), and `count=n` is the count of the input blocks.

❏ To compute a message digest for one or more files, issue the `digest` command:

`digest -v -a algorithm input-file > digest-listing`

where `-v` displays the output with file information, `-a` `algorithm` is the algorithm used to compute a digest (that is, MD5 or SHA1), `input-file` is the input file for the digest to be computed, and `digest-listing` is the output file for the `digest` command.

❑ To create a MAC of a file, use the command

```
mac -v -a algorithm -k keyfile input-file
```

where -v displays the output in the following format: *algorithm* (*input-file*) = mac; -a *algorithm* is the algorithm to use to compute the MAC (type the algorithm as the algorithm appears in the output of the mac -l command); -k *keyfile* is the file that contains a key of algorithm-specified length; and *input-file* is the input file for the MAC.

❑ To encrypt and decrypt a file, simply create a symmetric key, and then issue the encrypt command:

```
encrypt -a algorithm -k keyfile -i input-file -o output-file
```

where -a *algorithm* is the algorithm to use to encrypt the file (type the algorithm as the algorithm appears in the output of the encrypt -l command), -k *keyfile* is the file that contains a key of algorithm-specified length (the key length for each algorithm is listed, in bits, in the output of the encrypt -l command), -i *input-file* is the input file that you want to encrypt (this file is left unchanged), and -o *output-file* is the output file that is the encrypted form of the input file. To decrypt the output file, you simply pass the same key and the same encryption mechanism that encrypted the file but to the decrypt command.

Administer the Solaris Cryptographic Framework

❑ To display the list of installed providers, issue the cryptoadm list command.

❑ To display a list of mechanisms that can be used with the installed providers, issue the cryptoadm list -m command.

❑ To display the mechanism policy for the installed providers and the provider feature policy, issue the cryptoadm list -p command.

❑ To prevent the use of a user-level mechanism, issue the cryptoadm disable *provider* \ *mechanism(s)* command.

❑ To disable a kernel software, issue the cryptoadm disable *provider* command; to restore an inactive software provider, issue the cryptoadm refresh command; to remove a provider permanently, issue the cryptoadm uninstall command.

SELF TEST

The following questions will help you measure your understanding of the material presented in this chapter. Read all the choices carefully, because there might be more than one correct answer. Choose, and in some cases explain, all correct answers for each question. Some questions are short-answer questions to ensure you have a good understanding of the material.

Explain How to Protect Files Using the Solaris Cryptographic Framework

1. In the Solaris cryptographic framework, which of the following best explains providers?
   A. Applications, end users, or kernel operations
   B. User-level plug-ins, kernel-level plug-ins, and hardware plug-ins
   C. Cryptographic plug-ins that consumers use
   D. All of the above

2. List and explain the providers supported by the Solaris cryptographic framework.

3. In the Solaris cryptographic framework, which of the following commands can be used to generate random keys?
   A. `dd`
   B. `digest`
   C. `encrypt`
   D. `mac`
   E. All of the above

4. Which of the following is inherently provided for by using cryptography?
   A. Authenticity
   B. Confidentiality
   C. Integrity
   D. RBAC
   E. Checksum
   F. All of the above

5. Explain the usage of a Message Authentication Code (MAC).

6. Explain the usage of message digest with regard to file integrity.

7. Which of the following provide for implementations of algorithms in software?
   A. Hardware plug-ins
   B. Kernel-level plug-ins

    C. User-level plug-ins

    D. All of the above

8. In which of the following is the same cryptographic key used for both encryption and decryption?

    A. Asymmetric algorithm

    B. Public key

    C. Secret key

    D. Symmetric algorithm

    E. All of the above

9. To monitor and help prevent unauthorized changes from being made to system files, which of the following does Sun recommend using?

    A. Automated Security Enhancement Tool (ASET)

    B. Basic Security Module (BSM)

    C. Solaris cryptographic framework

    D. Tripwire

    E. All of the above

10. In the Solaris cryptographic framework, which of the following best explains consumers?

    A. Applications, end users, or kernel operations

    B. User-level plug-ins, kernel-level plug-ins, and hardware plug-ins

    C. Cryptographic plug-ins that consumers use

    D. All of the above

Administer the Solaris Cryptographic Framework

11. What command would you issue to remove a kernel software provider permanently?

12. What command is used to prevent the use of a user-level mechanism?

13. In which of the following are two cryptographic keys used: one to encrypt a message and another to decrypt it?

    A. Asymmetric algorithm

    B. Public key

    C. Secret key

    D. Symmetric algorithm

    E. All of the above

14. What command displays the list of installed providers?

15. What commands would you issue to disable temporarily and then later restore the use of a kernel software provider?

16. What command displays the mechanism policy for the installed providers?

17. Which of the following are shared objects that provide services by using PKCS #11 libraries?
   A. Hardware plug-ins
   B. Kernel-level plug-ins
   C. User-level plug-ins
   D. All of the above

18. What command is used to display a list of mechanisms that can be used with the installed providers?

19. What command displays the provider feature policy? If a provider is specified, this command will display the name of the provider with the mechanism policy enforced on it only.

LAB QUESTION

Explain and demonstrate how to create a symmetric key, how to compute a digest of a file, and how to encrypt and decrypt a file using the AES algorithm.

SELF TEST ANSWERS

Explain How to Protect Files Using the Solaris Cryptographic Framework

1. ☑ **B** and **C.** Providers are cryptographic plug-ins that consumers use. According to Sun, the framework allows only three types of plug-ins: user-level plug-ins, which are shared objects that provide services by using PKCS #11 libraries; kernel-level plug-ins, which provide for implementations of algorithms in software; and hardware plug-ins, which are device drivers and their associated hardware accelerators.
☒ **A** is wrong because consumers, not providers, can be applications, end users, or kernel operations.

2. ☑ Providers are cryptographic plug-ins that applications, end users, or kernel operations—which are all termed *consumers*—use. The Solaris cryptographic framework allows only three types of plug-ins: user-level plug-ins, which are shared objects that provide services by using PKCS #11 libraries; kernel-level plug-ins, which provide for implementations of algorithms in software; and hardware plug-ins, which are device drivers and their associated hardware accelerators.

3. ☑ **C** and **D.** Random keys can be generated using the `encrypt` and `mac` commands.
☒ **A** is wrong because you generate the symmetric key with the `dd` command. **B** is wrong because you issue the `digest` command to compute a message digest for one or more files.

4. ☑ **A, B, C,** and **E.** Cryptography provides for the integrity, confidentiality, and authenticity of information. One of the features of the framework allows you to provide a checksum that ensures the integrity of a file.
☒ **D** is incorrect because Role-Based Access Control (RBAC) relies on the *principle of least privilege* which states that a user should be given only enough privileges or permissions necessary for performing a job.

5. ☑ This algorithm creates a short message digest from a larger block of text by hashing it with a secret key. Without altering the original file and to protect a digest, you can compute a MAC of a file.

6. ☑ A message digest is a one-way function for a stream of binary data that serves as verification that the data was not altered since the message digest was first generated, such as when a file was compiled or modified. With regard to checking the integrity of files, you can use the Solaris Fingerprint Database (sfpDB), a free tool from Sun that allows you to check the integrity of system files through online cryptographic checksums. By doing so, you can determine whether system binaries and patches are safe in accordance with their original checksums among a huge database stored at Sun.

7. ☑ **B.** Kernel-level plug-ins provide for implementations of algorithms in software.
   ☒ **A** is wrong because hardware plug-ins are device drivers and their associated hardware accelerators. **C** is wrong because user-level plug-ins are shared objects that provide services by using PKCS #11 libraries.

8. ☑ **C and D.** In symmetric (secret key) algorithms, the same key is used for both encryption and decryption—anyone knowing the key can both encrypt and decrypt messages.
   ☒ **A and B** are wrong because with asymmetric (public key) algorithms, two keys are used: one to encrypt a message and another to decrypt it.

9. ☑ **E.** All of the answers are correct. Protecting files is a core component in Sun's Solaris security strategy. Although MD5 and SHA1, part of the Solaris cryptographic framework, were developed to help detect corrupt or maliciously altered files, Sun also recommends using a more comprehensive package called Tripwire. In addition to Tripwire, to help prevent unauthorized changes from being made to system files, Sun also recommends using ASET (discussed in Chapter 8) and BSM (discussed in Chapter 5).

10. ☑ **A.** Consumers can be applications, end users, or kernel operations.
    ☒ **B and C** are wrong because providers are cryptographic plug-ins that consumers use. According to Sun, the framework allows only three types of plug-ins: user-level plug-ins, which are shared objects that provide services by using PKCS #11 libraries; kernel-level plug-ins, which provide for implementations of algorithms in software; and hardware plug-ins, which are device drivers and their associated hardware accelerators.

Administer the Solaris Cryptographic Framework

11. ☑ To remove a provider permanently, issue the `cryptoadm uninstall` command (for example: `cryptoadm uninstall des`).

12. ☑ To prevent the use of a user-level mechanism, issue the `cryptoadm disable` *provider* \ *mechanism(s)* command.

13. ☑ **A and B.** With asymmetric (public key) algorithms, two keys are used: one to encrypt a message and another to decrypt it.
    ☒ **C and D** are wrong because in symmetric (secret key) algorithms, the same key is used for both encryption and decryption—anyone knowing the key can both encrypt and decrypt messages.

14. ☑ The `cryptoadm list` command displays the list of installed providers.

15. ☑ To disable a kernel software provider, issue the `cryptoadm disable` *provider* command; to restore an inactive software provider, issue the `cryptoadm refresh` command.

16. ☑ The `cryptoadm list -p` command displays the mechanism policy for the installed providers. It also displays the provider feature policy. If a provider is specified, the command will display the name of the provider with the mechanism policy enforced on it only.

17. ☑ **C.** User-level plug-ins are shared objects that provide services by using PKCS #11 libraries.
☒ **A** is wrong because hardware plug-ins are device drivers and their associated hardware accelerators. **B** is wrong because kernel-level plug-ins provide for implementations of algorithms in software.

18. ☑ The `cryptoadm -m` command displays a list of mechanisms that can be used with the installed providers. If a provider is specified, the command will display the name of the specified provider and the mechanism list that can be used with that provider.

19. ☑ The `cryptoadm list -p` command displays the mechanism policy for the installed providers. It also displays the provider feature policy. If a provider is specified, the command will display the name of the provider with the mechanism policy enforced on it only.

LAB ANSWER

The first part of the lab requires you to explain and demonstrate how to create a symmetric key. To create a symmetric key use the `dd` command:

```
dd if=/dev/urandom of=keyfile bs=n count=n
```

where `if=/dev/urandom` is the input file (for a random key, use the */dev/urandom* file), `of=keyfile` is the output file that holds the generated key, `bs=n` is the key size in bytes (for the length in bytes divide the key length in bits by 8), and `count=n` is the count of the input blocks.

The first step in creating a symmetric key is to determine the length (in bytes) required by your encryption algorithm. To do so, simply list the bit range of all supported algorithms with the `encrypt -l` and `mac -l` commands, shown here:

```
encrypt -l
Algorithm          Keysize:    Min   Max (bits)
------------------------------------------------
aes                            128   128
arcfour                        8     128
des                            64    64
3des                           192   192
mac -l
Algorithm          Keysize:    Min   Max (bits)
------------------------------------------------
des_mac                        64    64
sha1_hmac                      8     512
md5_hmac                       8     512
```

The next step is to determine the key length in bytes by dividing the minimum and maximum key sizes by 8. Then you can generate the symmetric key with the dd command:

```
dd if=/dev/urandom of=keyfile bs=n count=n
```

where `if=/dev/urandom` is the input file (for a random key, use the */dev/urandom* file), `of=keyfile` is the output file that holds the generated key, `bs=n` is the key size in bytes (for the length in bytes divide the key length in bits by 8), and `count=n` is the count of the input blocks.

For example, to create a key for the AES algorithm in a file for later decryption, you can issue the command:

```
dd if=/dev/urandom of=$HOME/aeskey/aeskey16 bs=16 count=1
```

(Note that AES uses a mandatory 128-bit key or 16 bytes.)

The second part of the lab requires you to create a digest of a file. To compute a message digest for one or more files, issue the `digest` command:

```
digest -v -a algorithm input-file > digest-listing
```

where `-v` displays the output with file information, `-a algorithm` is the algorithm used to compute a digest (that is, MD5 or SHA1), `input-file` is the input file for the digest to be computed, and `digest-listing` is the output file for the `digest` command.

Following is an example of creating a file digest using the SHA1 mechanism within the cryptographic framework:

1. To compute an MD5 digest for file *testfile.tar.Z* into output file *testfilesha1*, issue this command:

   ```
   digest -v -a md5 testfile.tar.Z >> $HOME/testfilemd5
   ```

2. Then issue the `cat` command,

   ```
   cat ~/testfilemd5
   ```

   to view the following output:

   ```
   md5 (testfile.tar.Z) = 1ab89e5ad217e34f0a977a091a1b588b31f9b588
   ```

If *testfile.tar.z* was a system file, we could compare the output to that stored in the online sfpDB to determine whether system binaries and patches are safe in accordance with their original checksums. You can freely download MD5 software binaries that can be used with sfpDB for Intel and SPARC architectures at http://SunSolve.Sun.COM/md5/md5.tar.Z.

The third part of the lab requires you to encrypt and decrypt a file using the AES algorithm. To encrypt and decrypt a file, create a symmetric key, and then issue the `encrypt` command:

```
encrypt -a algorithm -k keyfile -i input-file -o output-file
```

where -a *algorithm* is the algorithm to use to encrypt the file (type the algorithm as the algorithm appears in the output of the encrypt -l command), -k *keyfile* is the file that contains a key of algorithm-specified length (the key length for each algorithm is listed, in bits, in the output of the encrypt -l command), -i *input-file* is the input file that you want to encrypt (this file is left unchanged), and -o *output-file* is the output file that is the encrypted form of the input file. To decrypt the output file, you pass the same key and the same encryption mechanism that encrypted the file, but use the decrypt command.

In the following example, a file is encrypted with the AES algorithm. Remember that AES mechanisms use a key of 128 bits, or 16 bytes:

```
encrypt -a aes -k ~/keyf/10.09.aes16 \ -i my.file -o ~/enc/e.my.file
```

The input file, *my.file*, will still exist in its original form. To decrypt the output file, pass the same key and the same encryption mechanism that encrypted the file to the decrypt command:

```
decrypt -a aes .-k ~/keyf/10.09.aes16 \ -i ~/enc/e.my.file -o ~/my.file
```

Part VI

Authentication Services and Secure Communication

12

Secure RPC Across NFS and PAM

This chapter was contributed by Sun security administrators as a discussion on how to use Secure Remote Procedure Calls (RPCs) to authenticate a host and a user across a Network File System (NFS) mount. Additionally, this chapter covers the Pluggable Authentication Module (PAM) framework, which provides a method to "plug in" authentication services and provides support for multiple authentication services. For brevity, the material presented in this chapter was condensed to contain only topics you should know for the exam.

CERTIFICATION OBJECTIVE 12.01

Explain and Configure Secure RPC to Authenticate a Host and a User Across an NFS Mount

The Network File System (NFS), originally designed by Sun, provides access to shared resources in client-server style, where users can log into a client system and access file systems by mounting the file systems from a server. As a result, files would appear to be local to the client. The Secure NFS service uses Secure RPC—which protects remote procedures with an authentication mechanism—to authenticate users who make requests to the service. The authentication mechanism (Diffie-Hellman) uses Data Encryption Standard (DES) encryption to encrypt the common key between client and server with a 56-bit key. Although more secure authentication services are available for use with Sun Solaris, in this section we'll be discussing Secure RPC across NFS. For more information on Solaris encryption services, refer to Chapter 11.

ⓦatch *For the exam, you should know that Secure RPC is a security protocol based on DES encryption. Clients that use programs using Secure RPC must have a public/secret key entry in a shared master public key file. In Solaris, the Secure NFS service uses Secure RPC to authenticate users who make requests to the service.*

Authentication is based on the ability of the sending system to use the common key to encrypt the current time. Then the receiving system can decrypt and check against its current time. The time on the client and the server must be synchronized. The public keys and private keys are stored in an NIS or NIS+ database. NIS stores the keys in the publickey map. NIS+ stores the keys in the cred table. These files

contain the public key and the private key for all potential users. The system administrator is responsible for setting up NIS maps or NIS+ tables, and for generating a public key and a private key for each user. The private key is stored in encrypted form with the user's password. This process makes the private key known only to the user.

Generating the Public and Secret Keys

Sometimes, prior to a transaction, the administrator runs either the `newkey` or the `nisaddcred` command to generate a public key and a secret key. Each user has a unique public key and secret key. The public key is stored in a public database, while the secret key is stored in encrypted form in the same database. The `chkey` command changes the key pair.

Running the keylogin Command

Normally, the login password is identical to the Secure RPC password. In this case, the `keylogin` command is not required. However, if the passwords are different, the users must log in and then run the `keylogin` command.

The `keylogin` command prompts the user for a Secure RPC password. The command then uses the password to decrypt the secret key. The command passes the decrypted secret key to the keyserver program, an RPC service with a local instance on every computer. The keyserver saves the decrypted secret key and waits for the user to initiate a Secure RPC transaction with a server.

If both the login password and the RPC password are the same, the login process passes the secret key to the keyserver. If the passwords are required to be different, the user must always run the `keylogin` command. When the command is included in the user's environment configuration file, such as the ~/.login, ~/.cshrc, or ~/.profile file, the command runs automatically whenever the user logs in.

Generating and Decrypting the Conversation Key

When the user initiates a transaction with a server, the following occurs:

- The keyserver randomly generates a conversation key.
- The kernel uses the conversation key, plus other material, to encrypt the client's timestamp.

- The keyserver looks up the server's public key in the public key database.
- The keyserver uses the client's secret key and the server's public key to create a common key.
- The keyserver encrypts the conversation key with the common key.

The transmission, which includes the encrypted timestamp and the encrypted conversation key, is then sent to the server. The transmission includes a credential and a verifier. The credential contains three components: the client's network name; the conversation key, which is encrypted with the common key; and a window, which is encrypted with the conversation key.

The *window* is the difference in time that the client says should be allowed between the server's clock and the client's timestamp. If the difference between the server's clock and the timestamp is greater than the window, the server rejects the client's request. Under normal circumstances, this rejection does not happen, because the client first synchronizes with the server before starting the RPC session.

The client's verifier contains the encrypted timestamp and an encrypted verifier of the specified window (which is decremented by 1). The window verifier is needed in case somebody wants to impersonate a user. The impersonator can write a program that, instead of filling in the encrypted fields of the credential and verifier, just inserts random bits. The server decrypts the conversation key into some random key. The server then uses the key to try to decrypt the window and the timestamp. The result is random numbers. After a few thousand trials, however, the random window/timestamp pair is likely to pass the authentication system. The window verifier lessens the chance that a fake credential could be authenticated.

exam ⓦatch *For the exam, you need to know the process of generating a conversation key when a user initiates a transaction with a server. Remember these steps: the keyserver randomly generates a conversation key, the kernel uses the conversation key among other attributes to encrypt the client's timestamp, the keyserver looks up the server's public key and then uses the client's secret key and the server's public key to create a common key, at which point the keyserver encrypts the conversation key with the common key.*

Decrypting the Conversation Key   When the server receives the transmission from the client, the following occurs:

- The keyserver that is local to the server looks up the client's public key in the public key database.
- The keyserver uses the client's public key and the server's secret key to deduce the common key. The common key is the same common key that is computed by the client. Only the server and the client can calculate the common key, because the calculation requires knowing one of the secret keys.
- The kernel uses the common key to decrypt the conversation key.
- The kernel calls the keyserver to decrypt the client's timestamp with the decrypted conversation key.

After the server decrypts the client's timestamp, the server stores four items of information in a credential table:

- The client's computer name
- The conversation key
- The window
- The client's timestamp

The server stores the first three items for future use, and it stores the client's timestamp to protect against replays. The server accepts only timestamps that are chronologically greater than the last timestamp seen. As a result, any replayed transactions are guaranteed to be rejected.

Returning the Verifier to the Client and Authenticating the Server   The server returns a verifier to the client, including the index ID, which the server records in its credential cache, and the client's timestamp minus 1, which is encrypted by the conversation key. The 1 is subtracted from the client's timestamp to ensure that the timestamp is out of date. An out-of-date timestamp cannot be reused as a client verifier.

The client receives the verifier and authenticates the server. The client knows that only the server could have sent the verifier, because only the server knows what timestamp the client sent.

With every transaction after the first transaction, the client returns the index ID to the server in its next transaction. The client also sends another encrypted timestamp. The server sends back the client's timestamp minus 1, which is encrypted by the conversation key.

Configuring Secure RPC for NIS, NIS+, and NFS

By requiring authentication for use of mounted NFS file systems, you increase the security of your network. In this section, we'll discuss procedures to configure Secure RPC for NIS, NIS+, and NFS.

How to Restart the Secure RPC Keyserver

To restart the secure RPC keyserver, you need to assume the Primary Administrator role or become superuser. The Primary Administrator role includes the Primary Administrator profile. Next, verify that the keyserv daemon is running with the command `ps -ef | grep keyserv` to get output such as this:

```
root 100 1 16 Apr 11 ? 0:00 /usr/sbin/keyserv
root 2215 2211 5 09:57:28 pts/0 0:00 grep keyserv
```

Next, if the daemon is not running, start the keyserver with this command: `/usr/sbin/keyserv`

How to Set Up a Diffie-Hellman Key for an NIS+ Host

This procedure should be done on every host in the NIS+ domain:

1. Assume the Primary Administrator role, or become superuser.
2. Enable the *publickey* table in the name service by adding the following line to the */etc/nsswitch.conf* file:

   `publickey: nisplus`
3. Initialize the NIS+ client with this command:

   `nisinit -cH hostname`

   where `hostname` is the name of a trusted NIS+ server that contains an entry in its tables for the client system.

4. Add the client to the cred table with the commands `nisaddcred local` and `nisaddcred des`.

5. Verify the setup by using the `keylogin` command. If you are prompted for a password, the procedure was successful.

How to Set Up a Diffie-Hellman Key for an NIS+ User

This procedure should be done on every user in the NIS+ domain:

1. Assume the Primary Administrator role, or become superuser.

2. Add the user to the cred table on the root master server with the following command:

   `nisaddcred -p unix.UID@domain-name -P username.domain-name. des`

   Note that, in this case, the *username.domain-name* must end with a dot (.).

3. Verify the setup by logging in as the client and typing the **keylogin** command.

How to Set Up a Diffie-Hellman Key for an NIS Host

This procedure should be done on every host in the NIS domain:

1. Assume the Primary Administrator role, or become superuser.

2. Enable the publickey map in the name service by adding the following line to the */etc/nsswitch.conf* file: `publickey: nis`

3. Create a new key pair by using the `newkey` command: `newkey -h` *hostname*; where *hostname* is the name of the client.

How to Set Up a Diffie-Hellman Key for an NIS User

This procedure should be done for every user in the NIS domain. Only system administrators, when logged in to the NIS master server, can generate a new key for a user.

1. Assume the Primary Administrator role, or become superuser.

2. Create a new key for a user:

   `newkey -u` *username*

   where *username* is the name of the user.

3. The system prompts for a password. You can type in a generic password. The private key is stored in an encrypted form by using the generic password.

4. Tell the user to log in and type the **chkey-p** command. This command allows users to re-encrypt their private keys with a password known only to the user.

Note: The chkey command can be used to create a new key pair for a user.

How to Share and Mount NFS Files with Diffie-Hellman Authentication

This procedure protects shared file systems on an NFS server by requiring authentication for access. Before you begin, Diffie-Hellman public key authentication must be enabled on the network.

1. Become superuser, or assume a role that includes the System Management profile.

2. Share a file system with Diffie-Hellman authentication:

    ```
    share -F nfs -o sec=dh /filesystem
    ```

    where `filesystem` is the file system that is being shared. The `-o sec=dh` option means that AUTH_DH authentication is now required to access the file system.

Following is how an NFS client mounts a file system that is protected with Diffie-Hellman authentication:

1. Become superuser, or assume a role that includes the System Management profile.

2. Mount a file system with Diffie-Hellman authentication:

    ```
    mount -F nfs -o sec=dh server:filesystem mount-point
    ```

    where

- *server* is the name of the system that is sharing file system.
- *filesystem* is the name of the file system that is being shared, such as *opt*.
- *mount-point* is the name of the mount point, such as */opt*.
- The `-o sec=dh` option mounts the file system with AUTH_DH authentication.

By requiring authentication for use of mounted NFS file systems, you increase the security of your network.

Use the PAM Framework to Configure the Use of System Entry Services for User Authentication

The Pluggable Authentication Module (PAM) framework lets you plug in new authentication technologies without changing system entry services, such as login, ftp, telnet, and so on. You can also use PAM to integrate the UNIX login with other security mechanisms, such as Kerberos. Mechanisms for account, credential, session, and password management can also be plugged in by using this framework.

The PAM framework allows you to configure the use of system entry services (ftp, login, telnet, or rsh, for example) for user authentication. Following are some benefits that PAM provides:

- Flexible configuration policy
  - Per-application authentication policy
  - The ability to choose a default authentication mechanism
  - Multiple passwords on high-security systems
- Ease of use for the end user
- No retyping of passwords if the passwords are the same for different mechanisms
- The ability to prompt the user for passwords for multiple authentication methods without having the user enter multiple commands
- The ability to pass optional parameters to the user authentication services
- The ability to implement a site-specific security policy without having to change the system entry services

The PAM software consists of a library, various service modules, and a configuration file. Solaris commands or daemons that take advantage of the PAM interfaces are also included.

Applications such as ftp, telnet, and login use the PAM library to call the configuration policy. The *pam.conf* file defines which modules to use and in what order the modules are to be used with each application. Results from the modules, which are based on the module responses and the configured control flags, are passed back through the library to the application. The PAM library provides the framework on which to load the appropriate modules and to manage the stacking process. The PAM library provides a generic structure to which all of the modules can plug in. The PAM framework provides a method for authenticating users with multiple services by using stacking. Depending on the configuration, the user can be prompted for passwords for each authentication method. The order in which the authentication services are used is determined through the PAM configuration file.

This section discusses some tasks that might be required to make the PAM framework use a particular security policy. You should be aware of some security issues that are associated with the PAM configuration file.

exam
ⓦatch
With the Pluggable Authentication Module (PAM) framework, we can provide the ability to plug-in technologies for system-entry services. For the exam, you should know that the PAM framework in Solaris lets you plug in new authentication technologies without changing system entry services and configure the use of system entry services for user authentication.

Planning for PAM Implementation

When you are deciding how best to use PAM in your environment, start by focusing on these issues:

- Determine your needs, especially regarding which modules you should select.
- Identify the services that need special attention.
- Decide on the order in which the modules should be run.
- Select the control flag for each module.
- Choose any options that are necessary for each module.

Here are some suggestions to consider before changing the PAM configuration file:

- Use other entries for each module type so that every application does not have to be included.
- Make sure to consider the security implications of the binding, sufficient, and optional control flags.
- Review the man pages that are associated with the modules. These man pages can help you understand how each module functions, what options are available, and the interactions between stacked modules.

Caution: If the PAM configuration file is misconfigured or the file becomes corrupted, all users might be unable to log in. Since the `sulogin` command does not use PAM, the root password would then be required to boot the machine into single-user mode and fix the problem.

After you change the /etc/pam.conf file, review the file as much as possible while you still have access to correct problems. Test all the commands that might have been affected by your changes. For example, suppose you add a new module to the telnet service. You use the `telnet` command and verify that your changes make the service behave as expected.

How to Add a PAM Module

To add a PAM module, you must first become superuser or assume an equivalent role. Next, you need to determine which control flags and other options should be used. Every PAM module implements a specific mechanism. When you set up PAM authentication, you need to specify both the module and the module type, which defines what the module does. More than one module type, such as auth, account, session, or password, can be associated with each module.

The following list describes the Solaris PAM modules, including the filename of the module as well as a description of the purpose of the module. The path of each module is determined by the instruction set that is available in the Solaris release that is installed. The default path to the modules is /usr/lib/security/$ISA. The value for $ISA is sparcv9 for 64-bit modules. For 32-bit modules, $ISA has no value, so the modules are in /usr/lib/security/.

- ■ *pam_authtok_check.so.1* Provides support for password management. This module performs password strength checks.
- ■ *pam_authtok_get.so.1* Provides password prompting for authentication.
- ■ *pam_authtok_store.so.1* Provides support for password management only. This module updates the authentication token for the user.
- ■ *pam_dhkeys.so.1* Provides support for Diffie-Hellman key management in authentication. This module supports Secure RPC authentication and Secure RPC authentication token management.
- ■ *pam_dial_auth.so.1* This module uses data that is stored in the /etc/dialups and /etc/d_passwd files for authentication.
- ■ *pam_krb5.so.1* Provides support for authentication, account management, session management, and password management. Kerberos credentials are used for authentication.

- ***pam_ldap.so.1*** Provides support for account and password management. It can also be configured for authentication with an LDAP bind. Data from an LDAP server are used for account management.

- ***pam_passwd_auth.so.1*** Provides support for authentication by the `passwd` command.

- ***pam_rhosts_auth.so.1*** Can be used only for authentication. This module uses data that is stored in the *~/.rhosts* and */etc/host.equiv* files through the `ruserok()` routine. This module is mainly used by the `rlogin` and `rsh` commands.

- ***pam_roles.so.1*** Provides support for account management only. The *user_attr* database determines which roles a user can assume.

- ***pam_sample.so.1*** Used for testing only. Provides support for authentication, account management, session management, and password management.

- ***pam_smartcard.so.1*** Provides support for authentication only.

- ***pam_unix_account.so.1*** Provides support for account management. This module retrieves password aging information from the repository that is specified in the *nsswitch.conf* file. Then the module verifies that the password and the user's account have not expired.

- ***pam_unix_auth.so.1*** Provides support for authentication management. The module verifies that the password is correct.

- ***pam_unix_cred.so.1*** Provides support for credential management. The module must be stacked with an authentication module.

- ***pam_unix_session.so.1*** Provides support for session management.

For security reasons, these module files must be owned by root and must not be writable through group or other permissions. If the file is not owned by root, PAM does not load the module. Ensure that the ownership and permissions are set so that the module file is owned by root and the permissions are 555. Then edit the PAM configuration file, */etc/pam.conf*, and add this module to the appropriate services.

For verification, you must test before the system is rebooted in case the configuration file is misconfigured. Run rlogin, su, and telnet before you reboot the system. The service might be a daemon that is spawned only once when the system is booted. Then you must reboot the system before you can verify that the module has been added.

How to Prevent Rhost-Style Access from Remote Systems with PAM

Remove all of the lines that include `rhosts_auth.so.1` from the PAM configuration file. This step prevents the reading of the ~/.*rhosts* files during an rlogin session. Therefore, this step prevents unauthenticated access to the local system from remote systems. All rlogin access requires a password, regardless of the presence or contents of any ~/.*rhosts* or /*etc*/*hosts.equiv* files.

To prevent other unauthenticated access to the ~/.*rhosts* files, remember to disable the rsh service. The best way to disable a service is to remove the service entry from the /*etc*/*inetd.conf* file. Changing the PAM configuration file does not prevent the service from being started.

How to Log PAM Error Reports

1. Become superuser or assume an equivalent role.

2. Edit the /*etc*/*syslog.conf* file to add any of the following entries to log PAM error reports:

   - `auth.alert` Messages about conditions that should be fixed immediately
   - `auth.crit` Critical messages
   - `auth.err` Error messages
   - `auth.info` Informational messages
   - `auth.debug` Debugging messages

3. Restart the syslog daemon, or send a SIGHUP signal to the daemon to activate the PAM error reporting.

In the following example, all alert messages are displayed on the console. Critical messages are mailed to root. Informational and debug messages are added to the /*var*/*log*/*pamlog* file:

```
auth.alert /dev/console
auth.crit 'root'
auth.info;auth.debug /var/log/pamlog
```

Each line in the log contains a timestamp, the name of the system that generated the message, and the message. The *pamlog* file is capable of logging a large amount of information.

✓ # TWO-MINUTE DRILL

Here are some of the key points from the certification objectives in Chapter 12.

Explain and Configure Secure RPC to Authenticate a Host and a User Across an NFS Mount

❑ The Secure NFS service uses Secure RPC to authenticate users who make requests to the service.

❑ The authentication mechanism (Diffie-Hellman) uses Data Encryption Standard (DES) encryption to encrypt the common key between client and server with a 56-bit key

❑ Normally a user login password is identical to the Secure RPC password, where the login process passes the secret key to the keyserver. If the passwords are different, the user must always run the `keylogin` command. When the command is included in the user's environment configuration file (such as ~/.login, ~/.cshrc, or ~/.profile), the command runs automatically whenever the user logs in.

❑ The process of generating a conversation key when a user initiates a transaction with a server begins with the keyserver randomly generating a conversation key. The kernel uses the conversation key, plus other material, to encrypt the client's timestamp. Next, the keyserver looks up the server's public key in the public key database and then uses the client's secret key and the server's public key to create a common key. At that point, the keyserver encrypts the conversation key with the common key.

❑ When decrypting a conversation key after the server receives the transmission from the client, the keyserver that is local to the server looks up the client's public key in the public key database. The keyserver then uses the client's public key and the server's secret key to deduce the common key. The kernel uses the common key to decrypt the conversation key, and then calls the keyserver to decrypt the client's timestamp with the decrypted conversation key.

❑ Returning the verifier to the client and authenticating the server starts when the server returns a verifier, including the index ID, which the server records in its credential cache, and the client's timestamp minus 1, which is encrypted by the conversation key. The client receives the verifier and authenticates the server. The client knows that only the server could have sent the verifier because only the server knows what timestamp the client sent. With every transaction after the first transaction, the client returns the index ID to the server in its next transaction. The client also sends another encrypted timestamp. The server sends back the client's timestamp minus 1, which is encrypted by the conversation key.

❑ By requiring authentication for use of mounted NFS file systems, you increase the security of your network.

Use the PAM Framework to Configure the Use of System Entry Services for User Authentication

❑ The Pluggable Authentication Module (PAM) framework lets you plug in new authentication technologies without changing system entry services and configure the use of system entry services (ftp, login, telnet, or rsh, for example) for user authentication.

❑ The PAM software consists of a library, various service modules, and a configuration file. The *pam.conf* file defines which modules to use and in what order the modules are to be used with each application. The PAM library provides the framework to load the appropriate modules and to manage the stacking process. The PAM library provides a generic structure to which all of the modules can plug in. The PAM framework provides a method for authenticating users with multiple services by using stacking. Depending on the configuration, the user can be prompted for passwords for each authentication method. The order in which the authentication services are used is determined through the PAM configuration file.

❑ If the PAM configuration file is misconfigured or the file becomes corrupted, all users might be unable to log in. Since the `sulogin` command does not use PAM, the root password would then be required to boot the machine into single-user mode and fix the problem.

❑ For security reasons, PAM module files must be owned by root and must not be writable through group or other permissions. If the file is not owned by root, PAM does not load the module. To load the module, ensure that the ownership and permissions are set so that the module file is owned by root and the permissions are 555. Then edit the PAM configuration file, */etc/pam .conf*, and add this module to the appropriate services. Then you must reboot the system before you can verify that the module has been added.

❑ To prevent rhost-style access from remote systems with PAM, remove all of the lines that include `rhosts_auth.so.1` from the PAM configuration file. This prevents unauthenticated access to the local system from remote systems. To prevent other unauthenticated access to the *~/.rhosts* files, remember to disable the rsh service by removing the service entry from the */etc/inetd.conf* file.

❑ Changing the PAM configuration file does not prevent the service from being started.

SELF TEST

The following questions will help you measure your understanding of the material presented in this chapter. Read all the choices carefully, because there might be more than one correct answer. Choose all correct answers for each question. Some questions are short-answer questions to ensure you have a good understanding of the material.

Explain and Configure Secure RPC to Authenticate a Host and a User Across an NFS Mount

1. With regard to Secure RPC to authenticate a host and a user across an NFS mount, where are the public and private keys stored?

   A. NIS database

   B. NIS+ database

   C. publickey map

   D. cred table

   E. All of the above

2. Normally, a user login password is identical to the Secure RPC password, where the login process passes the secret key to the keyserver. If the passwords are different, what must the user do?

3. Each user has a unique public key and secret key; the public key is stored in a public database and the secret key is stored in encrypted form in the same database.

   A. True

   B. False

4. Explain how the Secure NFS service authenticates users who make requests to the service.

5. What authentication mechanism uses DES encryption to encrypt the common key between client and server with a 56-bit key?

6. Explain the process of generating a conversation key when a user initiates a transaction with a server.

7. Which of the following commands is used to change an existing key pair?

   A. `newkey`

   B. `nisaddcred`

   C. `chkey`

   D. All of the above

8. Explain how the client knows that only the server could have sent the verifier?

9. Explain the process of decrypting the conversation key when a server receives the transmission from the client.

Use the PAM Framework to Configure the Use of System Entry Services for User Authentication

10. What does the PAM software consist of?

11. Which of the following are true regarding PAM module files?
    A. They must be owned by root.
    B. They must not be writable through group or other permissions.
    C. Permissions should be set to 555.
    D. All of the above

12. If the PAM configuration file is misconfigured or the file becomes corrupted, all users might be unable to log in. However, since the `sulogin` command does not use PAM, what should be done to fix the problem?

LAB QUESTION

Your favorite customer asked you to come in and, among other things, set up a Diffie-Hellman key for an NIS+ host and user. Assuming all setup and preconfiguration has been completed successfully, what steps would you perform onsite?

SELF TEST ANSWERS

Explain and Configure Secure RPC to Authenticate a Host and a User Across an NFS Mount

1. ☑ **E.** All of the answers are correct. Authentication is based on the capability of the sending system to use the common key to encrypt the current time. Then, the receiving system can decrypt and check against its current time. The time on the client and the server must be synchronized. The public keys and private keys are stored in an NIS or NIS+ database. NIS stores the keys in the publickey map. NIS+ stores the keys in the cred table.

2. ☑ Normally a user login password is identical to the Secure RPC password, where the login process passes the secret key to the keyserver. If the passwords are different, the user must always run the `keylogin` command. When the command is included in the user's environment configuration file (such as ~/.login, ~/.cshrc, or ~/.profile), the command runs automatically whenever the user logs in.

3. ☑ **A.** True. Sometimes prior to a transaction, the administrator generates a public key and a secret key. Each user has a unique public key and secret key. The public key is stored in a public database. The secret key is stored in encrypted form in the same database.

4. ☑ The Secure NFS service uses Secure RPC (Remote Procedure Call), which protects remote procedures with an authentication mechanism, to authenticate users who make requests to the service. The authentication mechanism (Diffie-Hellman) uses Data Encryption Standard (DES) encryption to encrypt the common key between client and server with a 56-bit key.

5. ☑ Diffie-Hellman uses Data Encryption Standard (DES) encryption to encrypt the common key between client and server with a 56-bit key.

6. ☑ The process of generating a conversation key when a user initiates a transaction with a server begins with the keyserver randomly generating a conversation key. The kernel uses the conversation key, plus other material, to encrypt the client's timestamp. Next the keyserver looks up the server's public key in the public key database and then uses the client's secret key and the server's public key to create a common key. At that point, the keyserver encrypts the conversation key with the common key.

7. ☑ **C.** The `chkey` command changes the key pair.
   ☒ **A** and **B** are wrong because sometime prior to a transaction, the administrator runs either the `newkey` or the `nisaddcred` command to generate a public key and a secret key.

8. ☑ Returning the verifier to the client and authenticating the server starts when the server returns a verifier that includes the index ID, which the server records in its credential cache, and the client's timestamp minus 1, which is encrypted by the conversation key. The client receives the verifier and authenticates the server. The client knows that only the server could have sent the verifier because only the server knows what timestamp the client sent. With every transaction after the first transaction, the client returns the index ID to the server in its next transaction. The client also sends another encrypted timestamp. The server sends back the client's timestamp minus 1, which is encrypted by the conversation key.

9. ☑ When decrypting a conversation key after the server receives the transmission from the client, the keyserver that is local to the server looks up the client's public key in the public key database. The keyserver then uses the client's public key and the server's secret key to deduce the common key. The kernel uses the common key to decrypt the conversation key, and then calls the keyserver to decrypt the client's timestamp with the decrypted conversation key.

Use the PAM Framework to Configure the Use of System Entry Services for User Authentication

10. ☑ The PAM software consists of a library, various service modules, and a configuration file. The *pam.conf* file defines which modules to use and in what order the modules are to be used with each application. The PAM library provides the framework to load the appropriate modules and to manage the stacking process. The PAM library provides a generic structure to which all of the modules can plug in. The PAM framework provides a method for authenticating users with multiple services by using stacking. Depending on the configuration, the user can be prompted for passwords for each authentication method. The order in which the authentication services are used is determined through the PAM configuration file.

11. ☑ **D.** All of the answers are correct. For security reasons, PAM module files must be owned by root and must not be writable through group or other permissions. To load the module, ensure that the ownership and permissions are set so that the module file is owned by root and the permissions are 555.

12. ☑ If the PAM configuration file is misconfigured or the file becomes corrupted, all users might be unable to log in. Since the `sulogin` command does not use PAM, the root password would then be required to boot the machine into single-user mode and fix the problem.

LAB ANSWER

To set up a Diffie-Hellman Key for an NIS+ host, which should be done on every host in the NIS+ domain anyway, assume the Primary Administrator role or become superuser. Next, enable the publickey table in the name service by adding the following line to the */etc/nsswitch.conf* file:

```
publickey: nisplus
```

At that point, initialize the NIS+ client with the command

```
nisinit -cH hostname
```

where *hostname* is the name of a trusted NIS+ server that contains an entry in its tables for the client system.

Then add the client to the cred table with the commands `nisaddcred local` and `nisaddcred des`. Be sure to verify the setup by using the `keylogin` command. If you are prompted for a password, the procedure has succeeded.

To set up a Diffie-Hellman key for an NIS+ user, which should also be done on every user in the NIS+ domain, after assuming superuser, add the user to the cred table on the root master server with the following command:

```
nisaddcred -p unix.UID@domain-name -P username.domain-name. des
```

Note that, in this case, the *username.domain-name* must end with a dot (.). Again, be sure to verify the setup by logging in as the client and typing the `keylogin` command.

13

SASL and
Secure Shell

A s required by the exam, this chapter was contributed by Sun security administrator Stephen Moore as a discussion on the Simple Authentication and Security Layer (SASL) and an introduction to the Solaris Secure Shell. It describes the steps necessary to access a remote host securely over an unsecured network. For brevity, the material has been condensed to contain only topics you should know for the exam.

CERTIFICATION OBJECTIVE 13.01

Explain the Simple Authentication and Security Layer (SASL) in Solaris

SASL provides authentication services and, optionally, integrity and confidentiality services to connection-based protocols. For the exam, be sure to know how SASL adds authentication support to network protocols.

In essence, the SASL adds authentication support to network protocols. Applications can utilize optional security services by calling the SASL library as a security layer inserted between the protocol and the connection. This section provides an overview of the SASL implementation as required by the exam.

SASL Overview and Introduction

For the exam, Sun refers to the official SASL RFC (no. 2222), shown in the following extract:

> To use the SASL specification, a protocol includes a command for identifying and authenticating a user to a server and for optionally negotiating a security layer for subsequent protocol interactions. The command has a required argument identifying an SASL mechanism. SASL mechanisms are named by strings, from 1 to 20 characters in length, consisting of uppercase letters, digits, hyphens, and/or underscores. SASL mechanism names must be registered with the IANA.
>
> If a server supports the requested mechanism, it initiates an authentication protocol exchange. This consists of a series of server challenges and client responses

that are specific to the requested mechanism. The challenges and responses are defined by the mechanisms as binary tokens of arbitrary length. The protocol's profile then specifies how these binary tokens are then encoded for transfer over the connection.

After receiving the authentication command or any client response, a server may issue a challenge, indicate failure, or indicate completion. The protocol's profile specifies how the server indicates which of the above it is doing. After receiving a challenge, a client may issue a response or abort the exchange. The protocol's profile specifies how the client indicates which of the above it is doing.

During the authentication protocol exchange, the mechanism performs authentication, transmits an authorization identity (frequently known as a userid) from the client to server, and negotiates the use of a mechanism-specific security layer. If the use of a security layer is agreed upon, then the mechanism must also define or negotiate the maximum cipher-text buffer size that each side is able to receive.

The transmitted authorization identity may be different than the identity in the client's authentication credentials. This permits agents such as proxy servers to authenticate using their own credentials, yet request the access privileges of the identity for which they are proxying. With any mechanism, transmitting an authorization identity of the empty string directs the server to derive an authorization identity from the client's authentication credentials.

If use of a security layer is negotiated, it is applied to all subsequent data sent over the connection. The security layer takes effect immediately following the last response of the authentication exchange for data sent by the client and the completion indication for data sent by the server. Once the security layer is in effect, the protocol stream is processed by the security layer into buffers of cipher-text. Each buffer is transferred over the connection as a stream of octets prepended with a four octet field in network byte order that represents the length of the following buffer. The length of the cipher-text buffer must be no larger than the maximum size that was defined or negotiated by the other side.

SASL Services and Options in Solaris

According to Sun, SASL can provide services that include the following:

- Loading plug-ins
- Determining the necessary security properties from the application to aid in the choice of a security mechanism
- A listing of available plug-ins to the application

- Choosing the best mechanism from a list of available mechanisms for a particular authentication attempt
- Routing the authentication data between the application and the chosen mechanism
- Providing information about the SASL negotiation back to the application

The SASL options that are supported in the Solaris 10 release are as follows:

ⓦatch *You should remember that SASL provides developers of applications and shared libraries with mechanisms for authentication, data integrity-checking, and encryption, and that SASL enables the developer to code to a generic API.*

- `auto_transition` Automatically transitions the user to other mechanisms when the user does a successful plain text authentication.
- `auxprop_login` Lists the name of auxiliary property plug-ins to use.
- `canon_user_plugin` Selects the canon_user plug-in to use.

- `mech_list` Lists the mechanisms that are allowed.
- `pwcheck_method` Lists the mechanisms used to verify passwords. Currently, `auxprop` is the only value allowed.
- `reauth_timeout` Sets the length of time, in minutes, that authentication information is cached for a fast reauthentication. This option is used by the DIGEST-MD5 plug-in. Setting this option to 0 disables the reauthentication.
- `use_authid` When creating the GSS client security context, the GSSAPI acquires the client credentials rather than using the default credentials.
- `log_level` Sets the desired level of logging for a server.

CERTIFICATION OBJECTIVE 13.02

Use Solaris Secure Shell to Access a Remote Host Securely Over an Unsecured Network

In Solaris Secure Shell, authentication is provided by the use of passwords, public keys, or both. All network traffic is encrypted. Thus, Solaris Secure Shell prevents a would-be intruder from being able to read an intercepted communication.

It also prevents an adversary from spoofing the system. Solaris Secure Shell can be used as an on-demand virtual private network (VPN), which can forward X Windows system traffic or can connect individual port numbers between the local machines and remote machines over an encrypted network link.

This section covers uses of the Solaris Secure Shell:

- Logging in to another host securely over an unsecured network
- Copying files securely between the two hosts
- Running commands securely on the remote host

e x a m

w a t c h   *Among the benefits of Solaris Secure Shell, you should remember for the exam that by using the protocol you can help prevent an intruder from being able to read an intercepted communication as well as from spoofing the system.*

Solaris Secure Shell supports two versions of the Secure Shell protocol: version 1 is the original version of the protocol, and version 2 is more secure—it amends some of the basic security design flaws of version 1. Version 1 is provided only to assist users who are migrating to version 2. Users are strongly discouraged from using version 1.

Solaris Secure Shell Authentication

The requirements for Solaris Secure Shell authentication are as follows:

- **User authentication**   A user can be authenticated through either of the following:
  - **Passwords**   The user supplies the account password as in the login process.
  - **Public keys**   The user can create a public/private key pair that is stored on the local host. The remote hosts are provided with the public key, which is required to complete the authentication. The source host maintains the private key. Target hosts are provided with the public key that is needed to complete authentication. Public key authentication is a stronger authentication mechanism than password authentication, because the private key never travels over the network. The public/private key pair is stored in the user's home directory under the *.ssh* subdirectory.
- **Host authentication**   Host authentication requires that the remote host have access to the local host's public key. A copy of the local host's public key is stored in the file *$HOME/.ssh/known_hosts* on the remote host.

Using Solaris Secure Shell—Key Generation

The standard procedure for generating a Solaris Secure Shell public/private key pair is as follows:

1. Start the key generation program:

```
ssh-keygen -t rsa
Generating public/private rsa key pair.
```

where -t is the type of algorithm, one of rsa, dsa, and rsa1.

2. Enter the path to the file that will hold the key. By default, the filename *id_rsa*, which represents an RSA v2 key, appears in parentheses. You can select this file by pressing the RETURN key. Or you can type an alternative filename.

```
Enter file in which to save the key (/home/jdoe/.ssh/id_rsa):
<Press Return>
```

The filename of the public key is created automatically by appending the string *.pub* to the name of the private key file.

3. Enter a passphrase for using your key. This passphrase is used for encrypting your private key. A good passphrase is 10 to 30 characters long, mixes alphabetic and numeric characters, and avoids simple prose and simple names. A null entry means no passphrase is used. A null entry is strongly discouraged for user accounts. Note that the passphrase is not displayed when you type it in.

```
Enter passphrase (empty for no passphrase): <Type passphrase>
```

4. Retype the passphrase to confirm it.

```
Enter same passphrase again: <Type passphrase>
Your identification has been saved in /home/jdoe/.ssh/id_rsa.
Your public key has been saved in /home/jdoe/.ssh/id_rsa.pub.
The key fingerprint is:
0e:fb:3d:57:71:73:bf:58:b8:eb:f3:a3:aa:df:e0:d1 jdoe@myLocalHost
```

5. Check the results. Check that the path to the key file is correct. In the example, the path is */home/jdoe/.ssh/id_rsa.pub*. At this point, you have created a public/private key pair.

6. Set up the *authorized_keys* file on the destination host.

   a. Copy the *id_rsa.pub* file to the destination host. Type the command on one line with no backslash:

```
cat $HOME/.ssh/id_rsa.pub | ssh myRemoteHost \
'cat >> .ssh/authorized_keys && echo "Key uploaded successfully"'
```

watch *The standard procedure for generating a Solaris Secure Shell public/private key pair is to start the key generation program using ssh-keygen -t rsa.*

b. When prompted, supply your login password. When the file is copied, the message "Key uploaded successfully" is displayed.

How to Change Your Passphrase for Solaris Secure Shell

The following procedure does not change the private key; the procedure changes the authentication mechanism for the private key—the passphrase.

To change your passphrase, enter the `ssh-keygen` command with the `-p` option (which requests changing the passphrase of a private key file) and answer the prompts:

```
ssh-keygen -p
Enter file which contains the private key (/home/jdoe/.ssh/id_rsa): <Press Return>
Enter passphrase (empty for no passphrase): <Type passphrase>
Enter same passphrase again: <Type passphrase>
```

How to Log in to Another Host with Solaris Secure Shell

1. Start a Solaris Secure Shell session. Type the **ssh** command and specify the name of the remote host:

   ```
   ssh myRemoteHost
   ```

   The first time that you run the **ssh** command, a prompt questions the authenticity of the remote host:

   ```
   The authenticity of host 'myRemoteHost' can't be established.
   RSA key fingerprint in md5 is: 04:9f:bd:fc:3d:3e:d2:e7:49:fd:6e:18:4f:9c:26
   Are you sure you want to continue connecting(yes/no)?
   ```

   This prompt is normal for initial connections to remote hosts. You should verify the authenticity of the remote host key, and then type **yes** and continue. Also, you should ensure that the global */etc/ssh/ssh_known_hosts* files are being distributed. Updated *ssh_known_hosts* files prevent this prompt from appearing.

2. Type the Solaris Secure Shell passphrase and the account password when you are prompted for them:

   ```
   Enter passphrase for key '/home/jdoe/.ssh/id_rsa': <Type passphrase>
   jdoe@myRemoteHost's password: <Type password>
   Last login: Fri Jul 20 14:24:10 2001 from myLocalHost
   myRemoteHost%
   ```

3. Conduct transactions on the remote host. The commands that you send are encrypted. Any responses that you receive are also encrypted.

4. Close the Solaris Secure Shell connection. When you are finished, type **exit** or use your usual method for exiting your shell.

```
myRemoteHost% exit
myRemoteHost% logout
Connection to myRemoteHost closed
myLocalHost%
```

How to Log in with No Password with the ssh-agent Command

If you do not want to type your passphrase and your password to use Solaris Secure Shell, you can use the agent daemon. Start the daemon at the beginning of the session. Then store your private keys with the agent daemon by using the `ssh-add` command. If you have different accounts on different hosts, add the keys that you need for the session.

You can start the agent daemon manually when needed, as described in the following procedure. Or you can set the agent daemon to run automatically at the start of every session.

1. Start the agent daemon:

```
ssh-agent
```

2. Verify that the agent daemon has been started:

```
eval 'ssh-agent'
Agent pid 9892
```

3. Add your private key to the agent daemon. Type the command

```
ssh-add
Enter passphrase for /home/jdoe/.ssh/id_rsa: <Type passphrase>
Identity added: /home/jdoe/.ssh/id_rsa(/home/jdoe/.ssh/id_rsa)
```

4. Start a Solaris Secure Shell session:

```
ssh myRemoteHost
```

You are not prompted for a passphrase.

How to Set up the ssh-agent Command to Run Automatically

You can avoid providing your passphrase and password whenever you use Solaris Secure Shell by automatically starting an agent daemon, ssh-agent. You can start the agent daemon from the *.dtprofile* script.

1. Start the agent daemon automatically in a user startup script. Add the following lines to the end of the *$HOME/.dtprofile* script:

```
if [ "$SSH_AUTH_SOCK" = "" -a -x /usr/bin/ssh-agent ]; then
eval '/usr/bin/ssh-agent'
fi
```

2. Terminate the agent daemon when you exit the CDE session. Add the following to the *$HOME/.dt/sessions/sessionexit* script:

```
if [ "$SSH_AGENT_PID" != "" -a -x /usr/bin/ssh-agent ]; then
/usr/bin/ssh-agent -k
fi
```

This entry ensures that no one can use the Solaris Secure Shell agent after a CDE session is terminated.

How to Use Port Forwarding in Solaris Secure Shell

You can specify that a local port be forwarded to a remote host. Effectively, a socket is allocated to listen to the port on the local side. The connection from this port is made over a secure channel to the remote host. For example, you might specify port 143 to obtain e-mail remotely with IMAP4. Similarly, a port can be specified on the remote side.

To use port forwarding, you must first enable port forwarding on the target Solaris Secure Shell server.

1. Assume the Primary Administrator role, or become superuser.

2. Configure the target Solaris Secure Shell server to allow port forwarding. Change the value of `AllowTcpForwarding` to `yes` in the file */etc/ssh/ sshd_config*:

```
# Port forwarding
AllowTcpForwarding yes
```

3. Stop and start the Solaris Secure Shell daemon. The daemon puts your configuration changes into effect.

```
targetHost# /etc/init.d/sshd stop
targetHost# /etc/init.d/sshd start
targetHost# /usr/bin/pgrep -lf sshd
1296 ssh -L 2001:targetHost:23 targetHost
```

4. To set up secure port forwarding, do one of the following:

■ To set a local port to receive secure communication from a remote port, specify two ports: the local port that listens for remote communication, and the remote host and the remote port that forward the communication:

```
myLocalHost% ssh -L localPort:remoteHost:remotePort
```

■ To set a remote port to receive a secure connection from a local port, specify two ports: the remote port that listens for remote communication, and the local host and the local port that forward the communication:

```
myLocalHost% ssh -R remotePort:localhost:localPort
```

How to Copy Files with Solaris Secure Shell

Use the scp command to copy encrypted files between hosts. You can copy encrypted files either between a local host and a remote host or between two remote hosts. The command operates similarly to the rcp command, except that the scp command prompts for passwords.

1. Start the secure copy program. Specify the source file, the user name at the remote destination, and the destination directory:

```
scp myfile.1 jdoe@myRemoteHost:~
```

2. Type the Solaris Secure Shell passphrase when prompted.

```
Enter passphrase for key '/home/jdoe/.ssh/id_rsa': <Type passphrase>
myfile.1 25% |******* | 640 KB 0:20 ETA
myfile.1
```

After you type the passphrase, a progress meter is displayed—see the second line in the preceding output. The progress meter displays

■ The filename

■ The percentage of the file that has been transferred

■ A series of asterisks that indicate the percentage of the file that has been transferred

■ The quantity of data transferred

■ The estimated time of arrival, or ETA, of the complete file (that is, the remaining amount of time)

How to Set up Default Connections to Hosts Outside a Firewall

You can use Solaris Secure Shell to make a connection from a host inside a firewall to a host on the other side of the firewall. This task is accomplished by specifying a proxy command for `ssh` either in a configuration file or as an option on the command line.

In general, you can customize your `ssh` interactions through a configuration file. You can customize either your own personal file in *$HOME/.ssh/config* or you can customize an administrative configuration file in */etc/ssh/ssh_config*.

The files can be customized with two types of proxy commands: one command is for HTTP connections, and the other command is for SOCKS5 connections.

1. Specify the proxy commands and hosts in a configuration file. Use the following syntax to add as many lines as you need:

```
[Host outside-host]
ProxyCommand proxy-command [-h proxy-server] \
[-p proxy-port] outside-host|%h outside-port|%p
```

■ *Host outside-host*   Limits the proxy command specification to instances when a remote host name is specified on the command line. If you use a wildcard for *outside-host*, you apply the proxy command specification to a set of hosts.

■ *proxy-command*   Specifies the proxy command. The command can be either of the following:

`/usr/lib/ssh/ssh-http-proxy-connect` for HTTP connections
`/usr/lib/ssh/ssh-socks5-proxy-connect` for SOCKS5 connections

■ *-h proxy-server* and *-p proxy-port*   These options specify a proxy server and a proxy port, respectively. If present, the proxies override any environment variables that specify proxy servers and proxy ports, such as HTTPPROXY, HTTPPROXYPORT, SOCKS5_PORT, SOCKS5_SERVER, and `http_proxy`. The `http_proxy` variable specifies a URL. If the options are not used, the relevant environment variables must be set. For more information, see the ssh-socks5-proxy-connect(1) and ssh-http-proxy-connect(1) man pages.

■ *outside-host*   Designates a specific host to connect to. Use the %h substitution argument to specify the host on the command line.

■ *outside_port*   Designates a specific port to connect to. Use the %p substitution argument to specify the port on the command line. By specifying %h and %p without using the Host *outside_host* option, the proxy command is applied to the host argument whenever the `ssh` command is invoked.

2. Run Solaris Secure Shell, specifying the outside host. For example, type the following:

```
myLocalHost% ssh myOutsideHost
```

This command looks for a proxy command specification for *myOutsideHost* in your personal configuration file. If the specification is not found, the command looks in the system-wide configuration file, */etc/ssh/ssh_config*. The proxy command is substituted for the `ssh` command.

exam

ⓦatch

For the exam, you'll be expected to know how you can use Solaris Secure Shell to make a connection from a host inside a firewall to a host on the other side of the firewall. Be sure to know how this task is done by specifying a proxy command for `ssh` *either in a configuration file or as an option on the command line.*

TWO-MINUTE DRILL

Here are some of the key points from the certification objectives in Chapter 13.

Explain the Simple Authentication and Security Layer (SASL) in Solaris

❑ SASL adds authentication support to network protocols, where applications can utilize optional security services by calling the SASL library as a security layer inserted between the protocol and the connection.

❑ SASL mechanisms are named by strings, from 1 to 20 characters in length, consisting of uppercase letters, digits, hyphens, and/or underscores.

❑ During the authentication protocol exchange, the mechanism performs authentication, transmits an authorization identity (that is, userid) from the client to server, and negotiates the use of a mechanism-specific security layer.

❑ The security layer takes effect immediately following the last response of the authentication exchange for data sent by the client and the completion indication for data sent by the server. Once the security layer is in effect, the protocol stream is processed by the security layer into buffers of cipher text.

❑ SASL provide services including plug-in support, determining the necessary security properties from the application to aid in the choice of a security mechanism, listing available plug-ins to the application, choosing the best mechanism for a particular authentication attempt, routing the authentication data between the application and the chosen mechanism, and providing information about the SASL negotiation back to the application.

Use Solaris Secure Shell to Access a Remote Host Securely Over an Unsecured Network

❑ In Solaris Secure Shell, authentication is provided by the use of passwords, public keys, or both, where all network traffic is encrypted. Some of the benefits of Solaris Secure Shell is the prevention of an intruder from being able to read an intercepted communication as well as from spoofing the system.

❑ The standard procedure for generating a Solaris Secure Shell public/private key pair is by using the key generation program, like so: `ssh-keygen -t rsa`

❑ To change your passphrase, type the `ssh-keygen` command with the `-p` option, and answer the prompts.

❑ To start a Solaris Secure Shell session, type the `ssh` command and specify the name of the remote host.

❑ You can avoid providing your passphrase and password whenever you use Solaris Secure Shell by automatically starting an agent daemon, ssh-agent. You can start the agent daemon from the *.dtprofile* script.

❑ You can specify that a local port be forwarded to a remote host. The connection from this port is made over a secure channel to the remote host. Similarly, a port can be specified on the remote side.

❑ Use the `scp` command to copy encrypted files between hosts. You can copy encrypted files either between a local host and a remote host or between two remote hosts. The command operates similarly to the `rcp` command, except that the `scp` command prompts for passwords.

❑ You can use Solaris Secure Shell to make a connection from a host inside a firewall to a host on the other side of the firewall. This task is done by specifying a proxy command for `ssh` either in a configuration file or as an option on the command line. In general, you can customize your `ssh` interactions through a configuration file. You can customize either your own personal file in *$HOME/.ssh/config* or you can customize an administrative configuration file in */etc/ssh/ssh_config*. The files can be customized with two types of proxy commands. One proxy command is for HTTP connections. The other proxy command is for SOCKS5 connections.

SELF TEST

The following questions will help you measure your understanding of the material presented in this chapter. Read all the choices carefully, because there might be more than one correct answer. Choose, and in some cases explain, all correct answers for each question. Some questions are short-answer questions to ensure you have a good understanding of the material.

Explain the Simple Authentication and Security Layer (SASL) in Solaris

1. Explain how SASL adds authentication support to network protocols.

2. Name at least three services provided for by SASL.

3. Which of the following are true regarding the SASL specification?
   A. SASL mechanisms are named by strings, from 1 to 20 characters in length, consisting of uppercase letters, digits, hyphens, and/or underscores.
   B. A protocol includes a command for identifying and authenticating a user to a server and for optionally negotiating a security layer for subsequent protocol interactions.
   C. The command has a required argument identifying an SASL mechanism.
   D. SASL mechanism names must be registered with the IANA.
   E. All of the above

Use Solaris Secure Shell to Access a Remote Host Securely Over an Unsecured Network

4. To change your passphrase, type the `ssh-keygen` command with the `-c` option.
   A. True
   B. False

5. How would you start a Solaris Secure Shell session?

6. Can you use Solaris Secure Shell to make a connection from a host inside a firewall to a host on the other side of the firewall? If yes, explain how.

7. What is the command used to copy files with Solaris Secure Shell?

8. Explain how to set up the `ssh-agent` command to run automatically.

9. Explain in detail the steps needed to generate keys for Solaris Secure Shell.

10. Which of the following are benefits of Solaris Secure Shell?
    A. Prevents Trojan horse programs from running
    B. Prevents an intruder from being able to read an intercepted communication
    C. Prevents an intruder from spoofing the system
    D. Encrypts all network traffic
    E. All of the above

11. By default, which file contains configuration information for the Solaris Secure Shell sshd daemon?
    A. /etc/ssh/sshd_config
    B. /etc/sshd_config
    C. /usr/local/etc/sshd_config
    D. /etc/ssh/sshd_config
    E. All of the above

12. Which application layer protocol provides data encryption, host authentication, and data integrity in the Solaris OE?
    A. Secure shell
    B. Restricted shell
    C. Kerberos
    D. PAM
    E. All of the above

13. Which Secure Shell program processes requests from the secure ftp program?
    A. sftp
    B. sftp-server
    C. ftpd
    D. sftpd
    E. All of the above

LAB QUESTION

After performing some general administration onsite at your client's locale, the IT manager asks you to show him how to use Solaris Secure Shell to make a connection from a host inside the firewall to a host on the other side of the firewall. Explain the steps in detail.

SELF TEST ANSWERS

Explain the Simple Authentication and Security Layer (SASL) in Solaris

1. ☑ The Simple Authentication and Security Layer (SASL) adds authentication support to network protocols. Basically, applications can utilize optional security services by calling the SASL library as a security layer inserted between the protocol and the connection.

2. ☑ SASL provides services including plug-in support, determining the necessary security properties from the application to aid in the choice of a security mechanism, listing available plug-ins to the application, choosing the best mechanism for a particular authentication attempt, routing the authentication data between the application and the chosen mechanism, and providing information about the SASL negotiation back to the application.

3. ☑ **E.** All of the answers are correct. To use the SASL specification, a protocol includes a command for identifying and authenticating a user to a server and for optionally negotiating a security layer for subsequent protocol interactions. The command has a required argument identifying an SASL mechanism. SASL mechanisms are named by strings, from 1 to 20 characters in length, consisting of uppercase letters, digits, hyphens, and/or underscores. SASL mechanism names must be registered with the IANA.

Use Solaris Secure Shell to Access a Remote Host Securely Over an Unsecured Network

4. ☑ **B.** False. The `ssh-keygen` command with the `-c` option does not change the passphrase. Instead, the `ssh-keygen` command with the `-p` option is used, like so:

```
ssh-keygen -p
Enter file which contains the private key (/home/jdoe/.ssh/id_rsa): <Press Return>
Enter passphrase (empty for no passphrase): <Type passphrase>
Enter same passphrase again: <Type passphrase>
```

5. ☑ To start a Solaris Secure Shell session, type the `ssh` command and specify the name of the remote host.

6. ☑ You can use Solaris Secure Shell to make a connection from a host inside a firewall to a host on the other side of the firewall. This task is done by specifying a proxy command for `ssh` either in a configuration file or as an option on the command line. In general, you can customize your `ssh` interactions through a configuration file. You can customize either your own personal file in *$HOME/.ssh/config* or you can customize an administrative configuration file in */etc/ssh/ssh_config*. The files can be customized with two types of proxy commands: one for HTTP connections, and another for SOCKS5 connections.

7. ☑ Use the `scp` command to copy encrypted files between hosts. You can copy encrypted files either between a local host and a remote host, or between two remote hosts. The command operates similarly to the `rcp` command, except that the `scp` command prompts for passwords.

8. ☑ You can avoid providing your passphrase and password whenever you use Solaris Secure Shell by automatically starting an agent daemon, ssh-agent. You can start the agent daemon from the *.dtprofile* script. Start the agent daemon automatically in a user startup script. Add the following lines to the end of the $HOME/.dtprofile script:

```
if [ "$SSH_AUTH_SOCK" = "" -a -x /usr/bin/ssh-agent ]; then
eval '/usr/bin/ssh-agent'
fi
```

Terminate the agent daemon when you exit the CDE session. Add the following to the $HOME/.dt/sessions/sessionexit script:

```
if [ "$SSH_AGENT_PID" != "" -a -x /usr/bin/ssh-agent ]; then
/usr/bin/ssh-agent -k
fi
```

This entry ensures that no one can use the Solaris Secure Shell agent after a CDE session is terminated.

9. ☑ The standard procedure for generating a Solaris Secure Shell public/private key pair is as follows:

1. Start the key generation program.

```
ssh-keygen -t rsa
Generating public/private rsa key pair.
```

where -t is the type of algorithm (rsa, dsa, or rsa1).

2. Enter the path to the file that will hold the key. By default, the filename *id_rsa*, which represents an RSA v2 key, appears in parentheses. You can select this file by pressing the RETURN key. Or you can type an alternative filename.

```
Enter file in which to save the key (/home/jdoe/.ssh/id_rsa): <Press Return>
```

The filename of the public key is created automatically by appending the string *.pub* to the name of the private key file.

3. Enter a passphrase for using your key. This passphrase is used for encrypting your private key. A good passphrase is 10 to 30 characters long, mixes alphabetic and numeric characters, and avoids simple prose and simple names. A null entry means no passphrase is used. A null entry is strongly discouraged for user accounts. Note that the passphrase is not displayed when you type it in.

```
Enter passphrase (empty for no passphrase): <Type passphrase>
```

4. Retype the passphrase to confirm it.

```
Enter same passphrase again: <Type passphrase>
Your identification has been saved in /home/jdoe/.ssh/id_rsa. Your public
key has been saved in /home/jdoe/.ssh/id_rsa.pub. The key fingerprint is:
0e:fb:3d:57:71:73:bf:58:b8:eb:f3:a3:aa:df:e0:d1 jdoe@myLocalHost
```

5. Check the results. Check that the path to the key file is correct. In the example, the path is */home/jdoe/.ssh/id_rsa.pub*. At this point, you have created a public/private key pair.

6. Set up the *authorized_keys* file on the destination host.

   a. Copy the *id_rsa.pub* file to the destination host. Type the command on one line with no backslash:

   ```
   cat $HOME/.ssh/id_rsa.pub | ssh myRemoteHost \
   'cat >> .ssh/authorized_keys && echo "Key uploaded successfully"'
   ```

   b. When you are prompted, supply your login password. When the file is copied, the message "Key uploaded successfully" is displayed.

10. ☑ **B, C,** and **D.** In Solaris Secure Shell, authentication is provided by the use of passwords, public keys, or both, where all network traffic is encrypted. Some of the benefits of Solaris Secure Shell is the prevention of an intruder from being able to read an intercepted communication as well as from spoofing the system.

    ☒ **A** is wrong because a Trojan horse program is a malicious program that is disguised as some useful software. Trojan examples include a shell script that spoofs the login program and a malicious substitute switch user (su) program. To harden your system and help protect against Trojan horse programs, Sun recommends user awareness education, installing and updating anti-virus software, removing unnecessary compilers, securing file and directory permissions, and monitoring path variables.

11. ☑ **A.** The */etc/ssh/sshd_config* file contains configuration information for the Solaris Secure Shell sshd daemon.

    ☒ **B, C,** and **D** are wrong because Solaris Secure Shell software stores the configuration file in the */etc/ssh/sshd_config* file by default.

12. ☑ **A.** The Secure shell application layer protocol provides data encryption, host authentication, and data integrity in the Solaris OE.

    ☒ **B** is wrong because a restricted shell is used to set up an environment more controlled than the standard shell. The user is restricted from using many of the normal shell functions, such as setting the PATH variable and specifying the full path name to a command. **C** is wrong because Kerberos is a security system developed at MIT that authenticates users. Kerberos supports network-based client-server authentication and integrates with PAM. **D** is wrong because the PAM framework uses runtime pluggable modules to provide authentication for local and remote system entry services. This authentication framework can be "plugged into" login, ftp, telnet, and other unsecured commands.

13. ☑ **B.** The Secure Shell program sftp-server processes requests from the secure ftp program.

    ☒ **A** is wrong because sftp is an interactive file transfer program that performs all operations over an encrypted connection and can be used to interactively browse files and directories. **C** is wrong because ftpdis the server process that supports FTP and processes all FTP requests. **D** is wrong because the server process that supports sftp is named sftp-server and not sftpd.

LAB ANSWER

The task of using Solaris Secure Shell to make a connection from a host inside the firewall to a host on the other side of the firewall is accomplished by specifying a proxy command for `ssh` either in a configuration file or as an option on the command line. You can customize your `ssh` interactions through a configuration file. You can customize either your own personal file in *$HOME/.ssh/config* or you can customize an administrative configuration file in */etc/ssh/ssh_config*.

The files can be customized with two types of proxy commands: one for HTTP connections and another for SOCKS5 connections. Specify the proxy commands and hosts in a configuration file. Use the following syntax to add as many lines as you need:

```
[Host outside-host]
ProxyCommand proxy-command [-h proxy-server] \
[-p proxy-port] outside-host|%h outside-port|%p
```

- *Host outside-host* Limits the proxy command specification to instances when a remote host name is specified on the command line. If you use a wildcard for *outside-host*, you apply the proxy command specification to a set of hosts.

- *proxy-command* Specifies the proxy command. The command can be either of the following:

  /usr/lib/ssh/ssh-http-proxy-connect for HTTP connections
  /usr/lib/ssh/ssh-socks5-proxy-connect for SOCKS5 connections

- *-h proxy-server* and *-p proxy-port* These options specify a proxy server and a proxy port, respectively. If present, the proxies override any environment variables that specify proxy servers and proxy ports, such as HTTPPROXY, HTTPPROXYPORT, SOCKS5_PORT, SOCKS5_SERVER, and http_proxy. The http_proxy variable specifies a URL. If the options are not used, the relevant environment variables must be set. For more information, see the ssh-socks5-proxy-connect(1) and ssh-http-proxy-connect(1) man pages.

- *outside-host* Designates a specific host to connect to. Use the %h substitution argument to specify the host on the command line.

- *outside_port* Designates a specific port to connect to. Use the %p substitution argument to specify the port on the command line. By specifying %h and %p without using the *Host outside_host* option, the proxy command is applied to the host argument whenever the `ssh` command is invoked.

Run Solaris Secure Shell, specifying the outside host. For example, type the following:

```
myLocalHost% ssh myOutsideHost
```

This command looks for a proxy command specification for *myOutsideHost* in your personal configuration file. If the specification is not found, the command looks in the system-wide configuration file, */etc/ssh/ssh_config*. The proxy command is substituted for the `ssh` command.

14

Sun Enterprise
Authentication
Mechanism

This chapter provides a discussion on the Sun Enterprise Authentication Mechanism (SEAM), as required by the exam. We'll go through a brief SEAM overview, detail some configuration issues that should be resolved before configuring SEAM, and then move on to SEAM configuration and administration using the SEAM GUI Administration Tool. As with much of the material in this book, this information has been condensed to include only the important topics you should know when preparing for the exam.

CERTIFICATION OBJECTIVE 14.01

Define the Sun Enterprise Authentication Mechanism and Configuration Issues

SEAM is a client/server architecture based on the Kerberos V5 network authentication protocol that provides secure transactions over networks via strong user authentication, data integrity, and privacy. SEAM uses strong authentication to verify the identities of both the sender and the recipient, verify the validity of data to provide data integrity, and encrypt the data during transmission to guarantee privacy. This section offers a discussion on how SEAM works and things to consider before configuring SEAM in your environment.

ⓦatch *For the exam, remember that SEAM verifies the identities of both the sender and the recipient. SEAM also provides data integrity and guaranteed privacy by performing data verification and encryption.*

How SEAM Works

Since SEAM is based on Kerberos, the whole system is ticket-based and therefore, when a transaction is initiated, a ticket is requested from a Key Distribution Center (KDC) that identifies the user and the user's access privileges. In most cases, before a SEAM session can begin, a user logs in and provides a Kerberos password. What's nice about SEAM is that you need to authenticate yourself to SEAM only once per session; therefore, all transactions during the session are automatically secured.

SEAM Authentication Process

According to Sun, the initial SEAM authentication occurs in three steps (refer to Figure 14-1):

1. A user or service begins a SEAM session by requesting a ticket-granting ticket (TGT) from the KDC. This request often occurs automatically at login. A TGT is needed to obtain other tickets for specific services. The TGT identifies you and allows you to obtain numerous tickets for remote machines or network services. TGTs have limited lifetimes.

2. The KDC creates a TGT and sends it back in encrypted form to the user or service, which then decrypts the TGT by using the appropriate password.

3. Now in possession of a valid TGT, the user or service can request tickets for all sorts of network operations, for as long as the TGT lasts (usually for a few hours). Each time the user or service performs a unique network operation, it requests a ticket for that operation from the KDC.

FIGURE 14-1

Initial SEAM
authentication
process

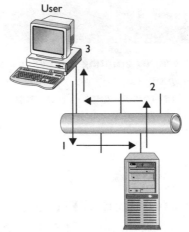

From that point onward, all subsequent SEAM authentications occur in the
following four steps (refer to Figure 14-2):

1. The user or service requests a ticket for a particular service (say, to `rlogin`
   into another machine) from the KDC by sending the KDC its TGT as proof
   of identity.

FIGURE 14-2

Process for all
subsequent SEAM
authentications

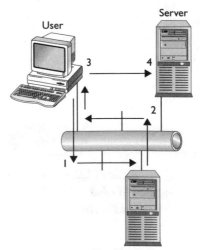

2. The KDC sends the ticket for the specific service to the user or service. Suppose, for example, that user *joe* wants to access an NFS that has been shared with krb5 authentication required. Since the user is already authenticated (that is, he already has a TGT), as he attempts to access the files, the NFS client system automatically and transparently obtains a ticket from the KDC for the NFS service. Therefore, if user *joe* uses `rlogin` on the server boston, since he is already authenticated (that is, he already has a TGT), he automatically and transparently obtains a ticket as part of the `rlogin` command. This ticket allows him to `rlogin` into boston as often as he wants until it expires. If *joe* wants to `rlogin` into the machine denver, he obtains another ticket, as in step 1.

3. The user or service sends the ticket to the server. When using the NFS service, the NFS client automatically and transparently sends the ticket for the NFS service to the NFS server.

4. The server allows the user or service access. These steps make it appear that the server doesn't even communicate with the KDC. The server does communicate, however; it registers itself with the KDC, just as the first user or service does.

e x a m

ⓦ a t c h

Subsequent SEAM authentication continues when a user or service requests a ticket for a particular service. The KDC sends the ticket for the specific service to the requesting user or service. The user or service sends the ticket to the server that hosts the requested service. The server then allows the user or service access.

SEAM Preconfiguration Planning

Before you install SEAM, you must resolve several configuration issues and consider your long-term goals. It's important to know that after the initial install, you cannot change the configuration. Be that as it may, managing SEAM gets more complicated as users are added to the system, and in some cases, you may need to perform a reinstallation altogether. Following are some of the issues you should consider in your preplanning.

SEAM Realms

A *realm* is a logical network that encompasses a group of systems that fall under the same master KDC. Before you configure SEAM, you should consider the realm name, the number and size of each realm, and the relationship of a realm to other realms for cross-realm authentication.

Realm Names   Although realm names can be any ASCII string, the realm name more commonly uses the same name as your DNS domain—in uppercase text. Not only does this convention help differentiate and facilitate problems with SEAM, as opposed to problems with the DNS namespace, but you'll be using a recognizable name. On the flipside, if you opt not to use DNS or wish to choose a different string, then, as mentioned previously, you can use any ASCII string. Keep in mind, though, that the configuration process will require more work upon doing so. Therefore, the use of realm names that follow the standard Internet naming structure is recommended.

According to Sun, the number of realms that your installation requires depends on the following factors:

- *The number of clients to be supported.* Too many clients in one realm make administration more difficult and eventually require that you split the realm. The primary factors that determine the number of clients that can be supported are as follows:
    - The amount of SEAM traffic that each client generates
    - The bandwidth of the physical network
    - The speed of the hosts

    Since each installation will have different limitations, there is no rule for determining the maximum number of clients.
- *How far apart the clients are.* It might make sense to set up several small realms if the clients are in different geographic regions.
- *The number of hosts that are available to be installed as KDCs.* Each realm should have at least two KDC servers (master and slave).

Realm Hierarchy   Realm hierarchy is important when you configure multiple realms for cross-realm authentication. How should you tie the realms together? You can establish a hierarchical relationship between the realms that provides automatic

e x a m

ⓦatch

For the exam, you should note that the number of realms required depends on the number of clients to be supported, the amount of SEAM traffic that each client generates, how far apart *the clients are, and the number of hosts that are available to be installed as KDCs. Remember that each realm should have at least two KDC servers—a master and a slave.*

paths to the associated domains. Be warned, though, that if many levels of domains are in use, you might not want to use the default path because of the amount of transactions it requires.

Another option is to establish the connection directly. This can be especially helpful when too many levels exist between two hierarchical domains or when no hierarchical relationship exists at all. In this case, the connection must be defined in the */etc/krb5/krb5.conf* file on all hosts that use the connection; therefore, additional work is required.

Mapping Host Names onto Realms

For mapping host names onto realm names, refer to the domain_realm section of the *krb5.conf* file. According to Sun, these mappings can be defined for a whole domain and for individual hosts, depending on the requirements. DNS can also be used to look up information about the KDCs. With that said, using DNS makes it much easier to change the information since you won't have to edit the *krb5.conf* file on each client every time you make a change.

Client and Service Principal Names

Again, Sun highly recommends that DNS services be configured and running on all hosts prior to SEAM implementation. DNS would have to be configured on all systems; otherwise, you should not configure it on any of them. When using DNS, the principal should contain the Fully Qualified Domain Name (FQDN) of each host. In other words, if the host name is *host1*, the DNS domain name is *company .com*, and the realm name is COMPANY.COM, then the principal name for the host should be *host/host1.company.com*@COMPANY.COM. Let's look at another example: if the host name is *chicago*, the DNS domain name is *mcgrawhill.com*, and

e x a m

Ⓦatch
For the principal names that include the FQDN of a host, it is important to match the string that describes the DNS domain name in /etc/ resolv.conf. SEAM requires that the DNS domain name be in lowercase letters when you are entering the FQDN for a principal. The DNS domain name can include uppercase and lowercase letters, but use only lowercase letters when you are creating a host principal.

the realm name is MCGRAWHILL.COM, then the principal name for the host should be *host/chicago.mcgrawhill.com@MCGRAWHILL.COM*.

e x a m

Ⓦatch
When you are using SEAM, it is strongly recommended that DNS services already be configured and running on all hosts. If DNS is used, it must be enabled on all systems or on none of them. If DNS is available, the principal should contain the Fully Qualified Domain Name (FQDN) of each host.

As indicated earlier in this section, SEAM can run without DNS services, and it should if DNS is not configured on all systems. However, key abilities—for example, the ability to communicate with other realms—will not work. If you opt not to configure DNS, then a simple host name can be used as the instance name. For example, referring to the previous example, the principal would be *host/ chicago@MCGRAWHILL.COM*. Also note that if DNS were to be enabled at a later time, then all host principals would have to be removed and replaced in the KDC database.

Ports for the KDC and Admin Services

The ports used for KDC are defined in the */etc/services* and */etc/krb5/krb5.conf* files on every client, and in the */etc/krb5/kdc.conf* file on each KDC. By default, they are the following:

- port 88 and 750 for the KDC
- port 749 for the KDC administration daemon

Note that different port numbers can be specified and therefore would have to be changed on every client and KDC.

Slave KDCs

Slave KDCs should be implemented as backup in case the master KDC becomes unavailable. You should implement one slave KDC for each realm; however, additional slave KDCs should be implemented based on the following factors:

- *Number of physical segments in the realm.* The network should be set up so that each segment can function without the rest of the realm; therefore, a KDC must be accessible from each segment whether it be a master or a slave.
- *Number of clients in the realm.* You can take the load off current servers by adding more servers.

It's important to note that you *can* have too many slave KDCs. Not only does each slave retain a copy of the KDC database, which increases the risk of a security breach, but the KDC database must be propagated to each server, which can cause latency or delay in getting the data updated throughout the realm.

Finally, consider cold-swap slave KDCs that can easily be configured to be swapped with the master KDC if it should fail.

Database Propagation   To synchronize KDCs properly, the master database—stored on the master KDC—must be regularly propagated to keep all KDCs current. Of course, you can configure only partial updates, rather than sending the entire database each time. Additionally, in large environments, you can configure more than one slave KDC to propagate data in parallel to reduce the time that it takes for the update process.

Clock Synchronization   Similar to the synchronization of the database, *all* hosts must have their internal clocks synchronized, as a default Kerberos authentication requirement, within a specified maximum amount of time. This process is known as *clock skew* and is actually a security feature, where requests are rejected if the clock is amiss. The most common clock synchronization method uses the Network Time Protocol (NTP) software.

A Note on Client Installation

According to Sun, a new feature in the Solaris 10 release is the *kclient* installation utility. The utility can be run in an interactive mode or a noninteractive mode. In the interactive mode, the user is prompted for Kerberos-specific parameter values, which allows the user to make changes to the existing installation when installing the client. In the noninteractive mode, a file with previously set parameter values is used. Also, command-line options can be used in the noninteractive mode. Both the interactive and noninteractive modes require less steps than the manual process, which should make the process quicker and less prone to error.

e x a m

ⓦatch *An encryption type is an identifier that specifies the encryption algorithm, encryption mode, and hash algorithms used in SEAM.*

A Note on Encryption Types

In SEAM, an *encryption type* is an identifier that encompasses the algorithm, encryption mode, and hash algorithms. The encryption type of the keys in SEAM identifies the cryptographic algorithm and mode to be used. Following are the supported encryption types:

- des-cbc-md5
- des-cbc-crc
- des3-cbc-sha1
- arcfour-hmac

If you should need to change the encryption type, do so when creating a new principal database.

CERTIFICATION OBJECTIVE 14.02

Configure and Administer the Sun Enterprise Authentication Mechanism

Parts of the configuration process depend on other parts and therefore must occur in a specific order. These procedures often establish services that are required to use SEAM. Other procedures are not dependent on any order and can occur whenever appropriate. Following are the tasks we'll cover in this section:

- Configuring KDC servers
- Configuring cross-realm authentication
- Configuring SEAM network application servers
- Configuring SEAM NFS servers
- Configuring SEAM clients
- Synchronizing clocks between KDCs and SEAM clients
- Administering the Kerberos database
- Increasing security

Configuring KDC Servers

After you install the SEAM software, you must configure the KDC servers. Configuring a master KDC and at least one slave KDC provides the service that issues credentials. These credentials are the basis for SEAM, so the KDCs must be installed before you attempt other tasks.

The most significant difference between a master KDC and a slave KDC is that only the master KDC can handle database administration requests. For instance, changing a password or adding a new principal must be done on the master KDC. These changes can then be propagated to the slave KDCs. Both the slave KDC and master KDC generate credentials. This feature provides redundancy in case the master KDC cannot respond.

How to Configure a Master KDC

1. Complete the prerequisites for configuring a master KDC. This procedure requires that DNS be running.

2. Become superuser on the master KDC.

3. Edit the Kerberos configuration file (*krb5.conf*). You need to change the realm names and the names of the servers.

```
kdc1 # cat /etc/krb5/krb5.conf
[libdefaults]
default_realm = EXAMPLE.COM
[realms]
EXAMPLE.COM = {
kdc = kdc1.example.com
kdc = kdc2.example.com
admin_server = kdc1.example.com
```

```
sunw_dbprop_enable = Y
sunw_dbprop_master_ulogsize = 2500
}
[domain_realm]
.example.com = EXAMPLE.COM
#
# if the domain name and realm name are equivalent,
# this entry is not needed
#
[logging]
default = FILE:/var/krb5/kdc.log
kdc = FILE:/var/krb5/kdc.log
[appdefaults]
gkadmin = {
help_url = http://denver:8888/ab2/coll.384.1/SEAM/@AB2PageView/6956
}
```

In this example, the lines for `default_realm`, `kdc`, `admin_server`, and all `domain_realm` entries were changed. Also, in the realms section, lines to enable incremental propagation and to select the number of updates the KDC master keeps in the log were added. In addition, the line that defines the help_url was edited.

4. Edit the KDC configuration file (*kdc.conf*). You need to change the realm name.

```
kdc1 # cat /etc/krb5/kdc.conf
[kdcdefaults]
kdc_ports = 88,750
[realms]
EXAMPLE.COM= {
profile = /etc/krb5/krb5.conf
database_name = /var/krb5/principal
admin_keytab = /etc/krb5/kadm5.keytab
acl_file = /etc/krb5/kadm5.acl
kadmind_port = 749
max_life = 8h 0m 0s
max_renewable_life = 7d 0h 0m 0s
}
```

In this example, the realm name definition in the realms section was changed.

5. Create the KDC database by using the `kdb5_util` command, which creates the KDC database. Also, when used with the `-s` option, this command creates a stash file that is used to authenticate the KDC to itself before the kadmind and krb5kdc daemons are started.

```
kdc1 # /usr/sbin/kdb5_util create -r EXAMPLE.COM -s
Initializing database '/var/krb5/principal' for realm 'EXAMPLE.COM'
master key name 'K/M@EXAMPLE.COM'
You will be prompted for the database Master Password.
It is important that you NOT FORGET this password.
Enter KDC database master key: <type the key>
Re-enter KDC database master key to verify: <type it again>
```

The -r option followed by the realm name is not required if the realm name is equivalent to the domain name in the server's namespace.

6. Edit the Kerberos access control list file (*kadm5.acl*). Once populated, the */etc/krb5/kadm5.acl* file should contain all principal names that are allowed to administer the KDC.

```
kws/admin@EXAMPLE.COM *
kiprop/kdc2.example.com@EXAMPLE.COM p
```

The first entry gives the kws/admin principal in the EXAMPLE.COM realm the ability to modify principals or policies in the KDC. The default installation includes a wildcard (*) to match all admin principals. This default could be a security risk, so it is more secure to include a list of all of the admin principals. The second entry allows the master KDC to receive requests for incremental propagation for the kdc2 server.

7. Start the kadmin.local command. The following substeps create principals that are used by SEAM.

```
kdc1 # /usr/sbin/kadmin.local
kadmin.local:
```

   a. Add administration principals to the database. You can add as many admin principals as you need, but you must add at least one admin principal to complete the KDC configuration process. For this example, a kws/admin principal is added. You can substitute an appropriate principal name instead of *kws*.

```
kadmin.local: addprinc kws/admin
Enter password for principal kws/admin@EXAMPLE.COM: <type the password>
Re-enter password for principal kws/admin@EXAMPLE.COM: <type it again>
Principal "kws/admin@EXAMPLE.COM" created.
kadmin.local:
```

b. Create a keytab file for the kadmind service. This command sequence creates a special keytab file with principal entries for kadmin and changepw. These principals are needed for the kadmind service. Note that when the principal instance is a host name, the FQDN must be entered in lowercase letters, regardless of the case of the domain name in the /etc/resolv.conf file.

```
kadmin.local: ktadd -k /etc/krb5/kadm5.keytab kadmin/kdc1.example.com
Entry for principal kadmin/kdc1.example.com with kvno 3, encryption type DES-CBC-CRC
added to keytab WRFILE:/etc/krb5/kadm5.keytab.
kadmin.local: ktadd -k /etc/krb5/kadm5.keytab changepw/kdc1.example.com
Entry for principal changepw/kdc1.example.com with kvno 3, encryption type DES-CBC-CRC
added to keytab WRFILE:/etc/krb5/kadm5.keytab.
kadmin.local: ktadd -k /etc/krb5/kadm5.keytab kadmin/changepw
Entry for principal kadmin/changepw with kvno 3, encryption type DES-CBC-CRC
added to keytab WRFILE:/etc/krb5/kadm5.keytab.
kadmin.local:
```

c. Quit `kadmin.local`. You have added all of the required principals for the next steps.

```
kadmin.local: quit
```

8. Start the Kerberos daemons:

```
kdc1 # /etc/init.d/kdc start
kdc1 # /etc/init.d/kdc.master start
```

9. Add more principals. At this point, you can add principals by using the SEAM Administration Tool. To do so, you must log on with one of the admin principal names that you created earlier in this procedure. However, the following command-line example is shown for simplicity:

```
kdc1 # /usr/sbin/kadmin -p kws/admin
Enter password: <Type kws/admin password>
kadmin:
```

a. Create the master KDC host principal. The host principal is used by Kerberized applications, such as klist and kprop. Note that when the principal instance is a host name, the FQDN must be entered in lowercase letters, regardless of the case of the domain name in the /etc/resolv.conf file.

```
kadmin: addprinc -randkey host/kdc1.example.com
Principal "host/kdc1.example.com@EXAMPLE.COM" created.
kadmin:
```

b. (Optional) Create the master KDC root principal. This principal is used for authenticated NFS mounting, so the principal might not be necessary on a master KDC. Note that when the principal instance is a host name, the FQDN must be entered in lowercase letters, regardless of the case of the domain name in the */etc/resolv.conf* file.

```
kadmin: addprinc root/kdc1.example.com
Enter password for principal root/kdc1.example.com@EXAMPLE.COM: <type the password>
Re-enter password for principal root/kdc1.example.com@EXAMPLE.COM: <type it again>
Principal "root/kdc1.example.com@EXAMPLE.COM" created.
kadmin:
```

c. (Optional) Create the kclient principal. This principal is used by the kclient utility during the installation of a SEAM client. If you do not plan on using this utility, you do not need to add the principal. The users of the kclient utility need to use this password.

```
kadmin: addprinc clntconfig/admin
Enter password for principal clntconfig/admin@EXAMPLE.COM: <type the password>
Re-enter password for principal clntconfig/admin@EXAMPLE.COM: <type it again>
Principal "clntconfig/admin@EXAMPLE.COM" created.
kadmin:
```

d. Create the kiprop principal. The kiprop principal is used to authenticate the master KDC server and to authorize the updates from the master KDC.

```
kadmin: addprinc -randkey kiprop/kdc1.example.com
Principal "kiprop/kdc1.example.com@EXAMPLE.COM" created.
kadmin: addprinc -randkey kiprop/kdc2.example.com
Principal "kiprop/kdc2.example.com@EXAMPLE.COM" created.
kadmin:
```

e. Add the master KDC's host principal to the master KDC's keytab file. Adding the host principal to the keytab file allows this principal to be used automatically.

```
kadmin: ktadd host/kdc1.example.com
kadmin: Entry for principal host/kdc1.example.com with
kvno 3, encryption type DES-CBC-CRC added to keytab
WRFILE:/etc/krb5/krb5.keytab
kadmin:
```

f. Add the kiprop principal to the kadmind keytab file. Adding the kiprop principal to the *kadm5.keytab* file allows the `kadmind` command to authenticate itself when it is started.

```
kadmin: ktadd -k /etc/krb5/kadm5.keytab kiprop/kdc1.example.com
kadmin: Entry for principal kiprop/kdc1.example.com with
kvno 3, encryption type DES-CBC-CRC added to keytab
WRFILE:/etc/krb5/kadm5.keytab
kadmin:
```

g. Quit `kadmin`.

```
kadmin: quit
```

10. Add an entry for each KDC into the propagation configuration file (*kpropd.acl*).

```
kdc1 # cat /etc/krb5/kpropd.acl
host/kdc1.example.com@EXAMPLE.COM
host/kdc2.example.com@EXAMPLE.COM
```

11. (Optional) Synchronize the master KDC's clock by using NTP or another clock synchronization mechanism. Although it is not required that you install and use the NTP, every clock must be within the default time that is defined in the libdefaults section of the *krb5.conf* file in order for authentication to succeed.

How to Configure a Slave KDC

In this procedure, a new slave KDC named kdc3 is configured.

1. Complete the prerequisites for configuring a slave KDC. The master KDC must be configured.

2. On the master KDC, become superuser.

3. On the master KDC, start kadmin. You must log on with one of the admin principal names that you created when you configured the master KDC.

```
kdc1 # /usr/sbin/kadmin -p kws/admin
Enter password: <Enter kws/admin password>
kadmin:
```

a. On the master KDC, add slave host principals to the database, if not already done. For the slave to function, it must have a host principal. Note that when the principal instance is a host name, the FQDN must be entered in lowercase letters, regardless of the case of the domain name in the */etc/resolv.conf* file.

```
kadmin: addprinc -randkey host/kdc3.example.com
Principal "host/kdc3@EXAMPLE.COM" created.
kadmin:
```

b. (Optional) On the master KDC, create the slave KDC root principal. This principal is needed only if the slave will be NFS mounting an authenticated file system. Note that when the principal instance is a host name, the FQDN must be entered in lowercase letters, regardless of the case of the domain name in the */etc/resolv.conf* file.

```
kadmin: addprinc root/kdc3.example.com
Enter password for principal root/kdc3.example.com@EXAMPLE.COM: <type the password>
Re-enter password for principal root/kdc3.example.com@EXAMPLE.COM: <type it again>
Principal "root/kdc3.example.com@EXAMPLE.COM" created.
kadmin:
```

    c. On the master KDC, create the kiprop principal. The kiprop principal is used to authorize incremental updates from the master KDC.

```
kadmin: addprinc -randkey kiprop/kdc3.example.com
Principal "kiprop/kdc3.example.com@EXAMPLE.COM" created.
kadmin:
```

    d. Quit kadmin.

```
kadmin: quit
```

4. On the master KDC, edit the Kerberos configuration file (*krb5.conf*). You need to add an entry for each slave.

```
kdc1 # cat /etc/krb5/krb5.conf .
.[realms]
EXAMPLE.COM = {
kdc = kdc1.example.com
kdc = kdc2.example.com
kdc = kdc3.example.com
admin_server = kdc1.example.com
}
```

5. On the master KDC, add an entry for each slave KDC into the database propagation configuration file (*kpropd.acl*).

```
kdc1 # cat /etc/krb5/kpropd.acl
host/kdc1.example.com@EXAMPLE.COM
host/kdc2.example.com@EXAMPLE.COM
host/kdc3.example.com@EXAMPLE.COM
```

6. On the master KDC, add a kiprop entry to *kadm5.acl*. This entry allows the master KDC to receive requests for incremental propagation for the kdc3 server.

```
kdc1 # cat /etc/krb5/kadm5.acl
*/admin@EXAMPLE.COM *
kiprop/kdc2.example.com@EXAMPLE.COM p
kiprop/kdc3.example.com@EXAMPLE.COM p
```

7. On all slave KDCs, copy the KDC administration files from the master KDC server. This step needs to be followed on all slave KDCs, since the master KDC server has updated information that each KDC server needs. You can use FTP or a similar transfer mechanism to grab copies of the following files from the master KDC:

```
/etc/krb5/krb5.conf
/etc/krb5/kdc.conf
/etc/krb5/kpropd.acl
```

8. On the new slave, change an entry in *krb5.conf*. Replace the sunw_dbprop_master_ulogsize entry with an entry defining sunw_dbprop_slave_poll. The entry sets the poll time to two minutes.

```
kdc3 # cat /etc/krb5/krb5.conf
.
.
[realms]
EXAMPLE.COM = {
kdc = kdc1.example.com
kdc = kdc2.example.com
kdc = kdc3.example.com
admin_server = kdc1.example.com
sunw_dbprop_enable = Y
sunw_dbprop_slave_poll = 2m
}
```

9. On the new slave, issue the kadmin command. You must log on with one of the admin principal names that you created when you configured the master KDC.

```
kdc3 # /usr/sbin/kadmin -p kws/admin
Enter password: <Type kws/admin password>
kadmin:
```

a. Add the slave's host principal to the slave's keytab file by using kadmin. This entry allows kprop and other Kerberized applications to function. Note that when the principal instance is a host name, the FQDN must be entered in lowercase letters, regardless of the case of the domain name in the */etc/resolv.conf* file.

```
kadmin: ktadd host/kdc3.example.com
kadmin: Entry for principal host/kdc3.example.com with
kvno 3, encryption type DES-CBC-CRC added to keytab
WRFILE:/etc/krb5/krb5.keytab
kadmin: quit
```

    b. Add the kiprop principal to the *kadm5.keytab* file. Adding the kiprop principal to this file allows the `kpropd` command to authenticate itself when it is started.

```
kadmin: ktadd -k /etc/krb5/kadm5.keytab kiprop/kdc3.example.com
kadmin: Entry for principal kiprop/kdc3.example.com with
kvno 3, encryption type DES-CBC-CRC added to keytab
WRFILE:/etc/krb5/kadm5.keytab
kadmin:
```

    c. Quit `kadmin`.

```
kadmin: quit
```

10. On the master KDC, back up and propagate the database by using `kprop_ script`. If a backup copy of the database is already available, it is not necessary to complete another backup.

```
kdc1 # /usr/lib/krb5/kprop_script kdc3.example.com
Database propagation to kdc3.example.com: SUCCEEDED
```

11. On the new slave, create a stash file by using `kdb5_util`:

```
kdc3 # /usr/sbin/kdb5_util stash
kdb5_util: Cannot find/read stored master key while reading master key
kdb5_util: Warning: proceeding without master key
Enter KDC database master key: <type the key>
```

12. (Optional) On the new slave KDC, synchronize the master KDC's clock by using NTP or another clock synchronization mechanism. Although it is not required that you install and use the NTP, every clock must be within the default time that is defined in the libdefaults section of the *krb5.conf* file in order for authentication to succeed.

13. On the new slave, start the KDC daemon (krb5kdc).

```
kdc3 # /etc/init.d/kdc start
```

Configuring Cross-Realm Authentication

You can link realms together in several ways so that users in one realm can be authenticated in another realm. Normally, this cross-realm authentication is accomplished by establishing a secret key that is shared between the two realms. The relationship of the realms can be either *hierarchical* or *directional*.

How to Establish Hierarchical Cross-Realm Authentication

The example in this procedure uses two realms, ENG.EAST.EXAMPLE.COM and EAST.EXAMPLE.COM. Cross-realm authentication will be established in both directions. This procedure must be completed on the master KDC in both realms.

1. Complete the prerequisites for establishing hierarchical cross-realm authentication. The master KDC for each realm must be configured. To test the authentication process fully, several clients or slave KDCs must be installed.

2. Become superuser on the first master KDC.

3. Create TGT service principals for the two realms. You must log on with one of the admin principal names that was created when you configured the master KDC.

```
# /usr/sbin/kadmin -p kws/admin
Enter password: <Type kws/admin password>
kadmin: addprinc krbtgt/ENG.EAST.EXAMPLE.COM@EAST.EXAMPLE.COM
Enter password for principal krgtgt/ENG.EAST.EXAMPLE.COM@EAST.EXAMPLE.COM: <type password>
kadmin: addprinc krbtgt/EAST.EXAMPLE.COM@ENG.EAST.EXAMPLE.COM
Enter password for principal krgtgt/EAST.EXAMPLE.COM@ENG.EAST.EXAMPLE.COM: <type password>
kadmin: quit
```

4. Add entries to the Kerberos configuration file to define domain names for every realm (*krb5.conf*).

```
# cat /etc/krb5/krb5.conf
[libdefaults]
  .
  .
[domain_realm]
.eng.east.example.com = ENG.EAST.EXAMPLE.COM
.east.example.com = EAST.EXAMPLE.COM
```

In this example, domain names for the ENG.EAST.EXAMPLE.COM and EAST.EXAMPLE.COM realms are defined. It is important to include the subdomain first, since the file is searched top down.

5. Copy the Kerberos configuration file to all clients in this realm. In order for cross-realm authentication to work, all systems (including slave KDCs and other servers) must have the new version of the Kerberos configuration file (*/etc/krb5/krb5.conf*) installed.

6. Repeat these steps in the second realm.

How to Establish Direct Cross-Realm Authentication

The example in this procedure uses two realms: ENG.EAST.EXAMPLE.COM and SALES.WEST.EXAMPLE.COM. Cross-realm authentication will be established in both directions. This procedure must be completed on the master KDC in both realms.

1. Complete the prerequisites for establishing direct cross-realm authentication. The master KDC for each realm must be configured. To test the authentication process fully, several clients or slave KDCs must be installed.

2. Become superuser on one of the master KDC servers.

3. Create TGT service principals for the two realms. You must log on with one of the admin principal names that was created when you configured the master KDC.

```
# /usr/sbin/kadmin -p kws/admin
Enter password: <Type kws/admin password>
kadmin: addprinc krbtgt/ENG.EAST.EXAMPLE.COM@SALES.WEST.EXAMPLE.COM
Enter password for principal
krgtgt/ENG.EAST.EXAMPLE.COM@SALES.WEST.EXAMPLE.COM: <type the password>
kadmin: addprinc krbtgt/SALES.WEST.EXAMPLE.COM@ENG.EAST.EXAMPLE.COM
Enter password for principal
krgtgt/SALES.WEST.EXAMPLE.COM@ENG.EAST.EXAMPLE.COM: <type the password>
kadmin: quit
```

4. Add entries in the Kerberos configuration file to define the direct path to the remote realm (*krb5.conf*). This example shows the clients in the ENG.EAST .EXAMPLE.COM realm. You would need to swap the realm names to get the appropriate definitions in the SALES.WEST.EXAMPLE.COM realm.

```
# cat /etc/krb5/krb5.conf
[libdefaults]
  .

  .
[capaths]
ENG.EAST.EXAMPLE.COM = {
SALES.WEST.EXAMPLE.COM = .
}
SALES.WEST.EXAMPLE.COM = {
ENG.EAST.EXAMPLE.COM = .
}
```

5. Copy the Kerberos configuration file to all clients in the current realm. In order for cross-realm authentication to work, all systems (including slave KDCs and other servers) must have the new version of the Kerberos configuration file (*krb5.conf*) installed.

6. Repeat these steps for the second realm.

Configuring SEAM Network Application Servers

Network application servers are hosts that provide access using one of the following network applications: ftp, rcp, rlogin, rsh, and telnet. Only a few steps are required to enable the SEAM version of these commands on a server.

How to Configure a SEAM Network Application Server

This procedure uses the following configuration parameters:

- Application server = boston
- Admin principal = kws/admin
- DNS domain name = example.com
- Realm name = EXAMPLE.COM

1. Complete the prerequisites for configuring an application server. This procedure requires that the master KDC has been configured. To test the process fully, several clients must be installed.

2. Install SEAM client software. (The SEAM client software must be installed.)

3. (Optional) Install NTP client or another clock synchronization mechanism.

4. Start kadmin. The following example shows how to add the required principals using the command line. You must log on with one of the admin principal names that you created when configuring the master KDC.

```
kdc1 # /usr/sbin/kadmin -p kws/admin
Enter password: <Enter kws/admin password>
kadmin:
```

a. Create the server's host principal:

```
kadmin: addprinc -randkey host/boston.example.com
Principal "host/boston.example.com" created.
kadmin:
```

b. (Optional) Create a root principal for the host principal:

```
kadmin: addprinc root/boston.example.com
Enter password for principal root/boston.example.com@EXAMPLE.COM: <type the password>
Re-enter password for principal root/boston.example.com@EXAMPLE.COM: <type it again>
Principal "root/boston.example.com@EXAMPLE.COM" created.
kadmin:
```

c. Add the server's host principal to the server's keytab. If the `kadmin` command is not running, restart it with a command such as this:

```
/usr/sbin/kadmin -p kws/admin
kadmin: ktadd host/boston.example.com
kadmin: Entry for principal host/boston.example.com with
kvno 3, encryption type DES-CBC-CRC added to keytab
WRFILE:/etc/krb5/krb5.keytab
kadmin: quit
```

d. Quit `kadmin`.

```
kadmin: quit
```

5. Add principals for the new server and update the server's keytab. The following command reports the existence of the host principal:

```
boston # klist -k |grep host
4 host/boston.example.com@EXAMPLE.COM
```

6. If the command does not return a principal, create new principals using the following steps. You must log on with one of the admin principal names that you created when configuring the master KDC.

```
boston # /usr/sbin/kadmin -p kws/admin
Enter password: <Enter kws/admin password>
kadmin:
```

a. Create the server's host principal:

```
kadmin: addprinc -randkey host/boston.example.com
Principal "host/boston.example.com" created.
kadmin:
```

b. (Optional) Create a root principal for the host principal:

```
kadmin: addprinc root/boston.example.com
Enter password for principal root/boston.example.com@EXAMPLE.COM: <type the password>
Re-enter password for principal root/boston.example.com@EXAMPLE.COM: <type it again>
Principal "root/boston.example.com@EXAMPLE.COM" created.
kadmin:
```

    c. Add the server's host principal to the server's keytab. If the `kadmin` command is not running, restart it with a command such as this:

```
/usr/sbin/kadmin -pkws/admin
kadmin: ktadd host/boston.example.com
kadmin: Entry for principal host/boston.example.com with
kvno 3, encryption type DES-CBC-CRC added to keytab
WRFILE:/etc/krb5/krb5.keytab
kadmin: quit
```

    d. Quit `kadmin`.

```
kadmin: quit
```

Configuring SEAM NFS Servers

NFS services use UNIX user IDs (UIDs) to identify users and cannot directly use principals. To translate the principal to a UID, a credential table that maps user principals to UNIX UIDs must be created. The procedures in this section focus on the tasks that are necessary to configure a SEAM NFS server, to administer the credential table, and to initiate Kerberos security modes for NFS-mounted file systems.

How to Configure SEAM NFS Servers

In this procedure, the following configuration parameters are used:

- Realm name = EXAMPLE.COM
- DNS domain name = example.com
- NFS server = denver.example.com
- Admin principal = kws/admin

1. Complete the prerequisites for configuring a SEAM NFS server. The master KDC must be configured. To test the process fully, you need several clients.

2. (Optional) Install the NTP client or another clock synchronization mechanism. It is not required that you install and use the NTP. However, every clock must be within the default time that is defined in the libdefaults section of the *krb5.conf* file in order for authentication to succeed.

3. Start `kadmin`.

```
denver # /usr/sbin/kadmin -p kws/admin
Enter password: <Type kws/admin password>
kadmin:
```

a. Create the server's NFS service principal. Note that when the principal instance is a host name, the FQDN must be entered in lowercase letters, regardless of the case of the domain name in the *letc/resolv.conf* file.

```
kadmin: addprinc -randkey nfs/denver.example.com
Principal "nfs/denver.example.com" created.
kadmin:
```

b. (Optional) Create a root principal for the NFS server:

```
kadmin: addprinc root/denver.example.com
Enter password for principal root/denver.example.com@EXAMPLE.COM: <type the password>
Re-enter password for principal root/denver.example.com@EXAMPLE.COM: <type it again>
Principal "root/denver.example.com@EXAMPLE.COM" created.
kadmin:
```

c. Add the server's NFS service principal to the server's keytab file:

```
kadmin: ktadd nfs/denver.example.com
kadmin: Entry for principal nfs/denver.example.com with
kvno 3, encryption type DES-CBC-CRC added to keytab
WRFILE:/etc/krb5/krb5.keytab
kadmin:
```

d. Quit `kadmin`.

```
kadmin: quit
```

4. Create the gsscred table. The gsscred credential table is used by an NFS server to map SEAM principals to a UID. In order for NFS clients to mount file systems from an NFS server with Kerberos authentication, this table must be created or made available:

   a. Edit *letc/gss/gsscred.conf* and change the mechanism to files.

   b. Create the credential table by using `gsscred`:

   ```
   # gsscred -m kerberos_v5 -a
   ```

   c. The `gsscred` command gathers information from all sources that are listed with the passwd entry in the *letc/nsswitch.conf* file. You might need to remove the files entry temporarily if you do not want the local password entries included in the credential table.

5. Share the NFS file system with Kerberos security modes.

   a. Become superuser on the NFS server.

   b. Verify that an NFS service principal exists in the keytab file. The `klist` command reports whether a keytab file exists and displays the principals. If the results show that no keytab file or no NFS service principal exists, you need to verify the completion of all of the steps in "How to Configure SEAM NFS Servers" earlier in this chapter.

```
# klist -k
Keytab name: FILE:/etc/krb5/krb5.keytab
KVNO Principal
---- ----------------------------------------------------------
3 nfs/denver.example.com@EXAMPLE.COM
```

c. Enable Kerberos security modes in the /etc/nfssec.conf file. Edit the /etc/nfssec.conf file and remove the # from in front of the Kerberos security modes:

```
# cat /etc/nfssec.conf
 .
 .
 #
 # Uncomment the following lines to use Kerberos V5 with NFS
 #
 krb5 390003 kerberos_v5 default - # RPCSEC_GSS
 krb5i 390004 kerberos_v5 default integrity # RPCSEC_GSS
 krb5p 390005 kerberos_v5 default privacy # RPCSEC_GSS
```

d. Edit the /etc/dfs/dfstab file and add the `sec=` option with the required security modes to the appropriate entries. `share -F nfs -o sec=mode file-system mode` specifies the security modes to be used when sharing. When using multiple security modes, the first mode in the list is used as the default by the automounter. *file-system* defines the path to the file system to be shared. All clients that attempt to access files from the named file system require Kerberos authentication. To access files, both the user principal and the root principal on the NFS client should be authenticated.

e. Make sure that the NFS service is running on the server. The following commands can be used to kill the daemons and restart them if necessary:

```
# /etc/init.d/nfs.server stop
# /etc/init.d/nfs.server start
```

f. (Optional) If the automounter is being used, edit the *auto_master* database to select a security mode other than the default. You need not follow this procedure if you are not using the automounter to access the file system or if the default selection for the security mode is acceptable.

```
file-system auto_home -nosuid,sec=mode
```

g. (Optional) Manually issue the mount command to access the file system by using a nondefault mode. Alternatively, you could use the mount command to specify the security mode, but this alternative does not take advantage of the automounter:

```
# mount -F nfs -o sec=mode file-system
```

Configuring SEAM Clients

SEAM clients include any host, not a KDC server, on the network that needs to use SEAM services. This section provides procedures for installing a SEAM client, as well as specific information about using root authentication to mount NSFs.

How to Create a SEAM Client Installation Profile

This procedure creates a kclient profile that can be used when installing a SEAM client. By using the kclient profile, you reduce the likelihood of typing errors. Also, using the profile reduces the number of manual steps that the installer must complete.

1. Become superuser.

2. Create a kclient profile that has the following entries:

```
client# cat /net/kdc1.example.com/export/install/profile
REALM EXAMPLE.COM
KDC kdc1.example.com
ADMIN clntconfig
FILEPATH /net/kdc1.example.com/export/install/krb5.conf
NFS 1
DNSLOOKUP none
```

How to Configure a SEAM Client Automatically

1. Become superuser.

2. Run the kclient installation script. You need to provide the password for the clntconfig principal to complete the process.

```
client# /usr/sbin/kclient -p /net/kdc1.example.com/export/install/krb5.conf
Starting client setup

-------------------------------------------------
kdc1.example.com
Setting up /etc/krb5/krb5.conf.
Obtaining TGT for clntconfig/admin ...
```

```
Password for clntconfig/admin@EXAMPLE.COM: <type the password>
nfs/client.example.com entry ADDED to KDC database.
nfs/client.example.com entry ADDED to keytab.
root/client.example.com entry ADDED to KDC database.
root/client.example.com entry ADDED to keytab.
host/client.example.com entry ADDED to KDC database.
host/client.example.com entry ADDED to keytab.
Copied /net/kdc1.example.com/export/clientinstall/krb5.conf.
------------------------------------------------------
Setup COMPLETE.
client#
```

How to Configure a SEAM Client Interactively   This procedure uses the
kclient installation utility without an installation profile.

1. Become superuser.

2. Run the kclient installation script. You need to provide the following
   information:

   ■ Kerberos realm name

   ■ KDC master host name

   ■ Administrative principal name

   ■ Password for the administrative principal

```
client# /usr/sbin/kclient
Starting client setup
------------------------------------------------------
Do you want to use DNS for kerberos lookups ? [y/n]: n
No action performed.
Enter the Kerberos realm: EXAMPLE.COM
Specify the KDC hostname for the above realm: kdc1.example.com
Setting up /etc/krb5/krb5.conf.
Enter the krb5 administrative principal to be used: clntconfig/admin
Obtaining TGT for clntconfig/admin ...
Password for clntconfig/admin@EXAMPLE.COM: <type the password>
Do you plan on doing Kerberized nfs ? [y/n]: y
nfs/client.example.com entry ADDED to KDC database.
nfs/client.example.com entry ADDED to keytab.
root/client.example.com entry ADDED to KDC database.
root/client.example.com entry ADDED to keytab.
host/client.example.com entry ADDED to KDC database.
host/client.example.com entry ADDED to keytab.
Do you want to copy over the master krb5.conf file ? [y/n]: y
Enter the pathname of the file to be copied: \
```

```
/net/kdc1.example.com/export/install/krb5.conf
Copied /net/kdc1.example.com/export/install/krb5.conf.
---------------------------------------------------
Setup COMPLETE !
#
```

Synchronizing Clocks Between KDCs and SEAM Clients

All hosts that participate in the Kerberos authentication system must have their internal clocks synchronized within a specified maximum amount of time (known as *clock skew*). This requirement provides another Kerberos security check. If the clock skew is exceeded between any of the participating hosts, client requests are rejected. The clock skew also determines how long application servers must keep track of all Kerberos protocol messages to recognize and reject replayed requests. Therefore, the longer the clock skew value, the more information that application servers have to collect.

The default value for the maximum clock skew is 300 seconds (5 minutes). You can change this default in the lib defaults section of the *krb5.conf* file. Since it is important to maintain synchronized clocks between the KDCs and SEAM clients, you should use the NTP software to synchronize them. NTP public domain software from the University of Delaware is included with Solaris 2.6 and later releases.

NTP enables you to manage precise time, network clock synchronization, or both, in a network environment. NTP is basically a server/client implementation. You pick one system to be the master clock (the NTP server), and you then set up all your other systems (the NTP clients) to synchronize their clocks with the master clock.

To synchronize the clocks, NTP uses the xntpd daemon, which sets and maintains a UNIX system time-of-day in agreement with Internet standard time servers. The following shows an example of this server/client NTP implementation. To ensure that the KDCs and SEAM clients maintain synchronized clocks, implement the following steps:

1. Set up an NTP server on your network (this server can be any system except the master KDC).

2. As you configure the KDCs and SEAM clients on the network, set them up to be NTP clients of the NTP server.

Increasing Security

The following procedures help you increase security on SEAM application servers and on KDC servers.

How to Enable Only Kerberized Applications

This procedure restricts network access to the server using telnet, ftp, rcp, rsh, and rlogin to Kerberos authenticated transactions only.

1. Edit the telnet entry in */etc/inetd.conf*. Add the `-a` user option to the telnet entry to restrict access to those users who can provide valid authentication information.

```
telnet stream tcp nowait root /usr/sbin/in.telnetd telnetd -a user
```

2. Edit the ftp entry in */etc/inetd.conf*. Add the `-a` option to the ftp entry to permit only Kerberos authenticated connections.

```
ftp stream tcp nowait root /usr/sbin/in.ftpd ftpd -a
```

3. Disable Solaris entries for other services in */etc/inetd.conf*. The entries for shell and login need to be commented out or removed:

```
# shell stream tcp nowait root /usr/sbin/in.rshd in.rshd
# login stream tcp nowait root /usr/sbin/in.rlogind in.rlogind
```

How to Restrict Access to KDC Servers

Both master KDC servers and slave KDC servers have copies of the KDC database stored locally. Restricting access to these servers so that the databases are secure is important to the overall security of the SEAM installation.

1. Disable remote services in the */etc/inetd.conf* file. To provide a secure KDC server, all nonessential network services should be disabled by commenting out the entry that starts the service in the */etc/inetd.conf* file. In most circumstances, the only services that would need to run would be *time* and *krdb5_kprop*. In addition, any services that use `loopback tli` (`ticlts`, `ticotsord`, and `ticots`) can be left enabled. After you edit the file, it should look similar to the following (to shorten the example, many comments have been removed):

```
kdc1 # cat /etc/inetd.conf
#
#ident "@(#)inetd.conf 1.33 98/06/02 SMI" /* SVr4.0 1.5 */
.
.
#name dgram udp wait root /usr/sbin/in.tnamed in.tnamed
```

```
#
#shell stream tcp nowait root /usr/sbin/in.rshd in.rshd
#login stream tcp nowait root /usr/sbin/in.rlogind in.rlogind
#exec stream tcp nowait root /usr/sbin/in.rexecd in.rexecd
#comsat dgram udp wait root /usr/sbin/in.comsat in.comsat
#talk dgram udp wait root /usr/sbin/in.talkd in.talkd
#
#uucp stream tcp nowait root /usr/sbin/in.uucpd in.uucpd
#
#finger stream tcp nowait nobody /usr/sbin/in.fingerd in.fingerd
#
# Time service is used for clock synchronization.
#
time stream tcp nowait root internal
time dgram udp wait root internal
#
.
.
.
#
100234/1 tli rpc/ticotsord wait root /usr/lib/gss/gssd gssd
#dtspc stream tcp nowait root /usr/dt/bin/dtspcd /usr/dt/bin/dtspcd
#100068/2-5 dgram rpc/udp wait root /usr/dt/bin/rpc.cmsd rpc.cmsd
100134/1 tli rpc/ticotsord wait root /usr/lib/ktkt_warnd kwarnd
krb5_prop stream tcp nowait root /usr/lib/krb5/kpropd kpropd
```

2. Reboot the KDC server after the changes are made.

3. Restrict access to the hardware that supports the KDC. To restrict physical access, make sure that the KDC server and its monitor are located in a secure facility. Users should not be able to access this server in any way.

4. Store KDC database backups on local disks or on the KDC slaves. Make tape backups of your KDC only if the tapes are stored securely. Follow the same practice for copies of keytab files. It would be best to store these files on a local file system that is not shared with other systems. The storage file system can be on either the master KDC server or any of the slave KDCs.

Restricting access to both master KDC servers and slave KDC servers so that the databases are secure *is important to the overall security of the SEAM installation.*

TWO-MINUTE DRILL

Here are some of the key points from the certification objectives in Chapter 14.

Define the Sun Enterprise Authentication Mechanism and Configuration Issues

❑ SEAM uses strong authentication that verifies the identities of both the sender and the recipient, verifies the validity of data to provide data integrity, and encrypts the data during transmission to guarantee privacy.

❑ SEAM is based on the ticket-based Kerberos. You need to authenticate yourself to SEAM only once per session; therefore, all transactions during the session are automatically secured.

❑ The initial SEAM authentication process begins when a user or service starts a SEAM session by requesting a TGT from the KDC. The KDC creates a TGT and sends it back, in encrypted form, to the user or service. The user or service then decrypts the TGT by using a password. Now in possession of a valid TGT, the user or service can request tickets for all sorts of network operations, for as long as the TGT lasts.

❑ Subsequent SEAM authentication continues when a user or service requests a ticket for a particular service. The KDC sends the ticket for the specific service to the requesting user or service. The user or service sends the ticket to the server that hosts the requested service. The server then allows the user or service access.

❑ A realm is a logical network that defines a group of systems that are under the same master KDC. Issues such as the realm name, the number and size of each realm, and the relationship of a realm to other realms for cross-realm authentication should be resolved before you configure SEAM.

❑ Realm names can consist of any ASCII string (usually using the same name as your DNS domain, in uppercase). This convention helps differentiate problems with SEAM from problems with the DNS namespace, while using a name that is familiar. If you do not use DNS, you can use any string.

❑ The number of realms that your installation requires depends on the number of clients to be supported, the amount of SEAM traffic that each client generates, how far apart the clients are, and the number of hosts that are available to be installed as KDCs (each realm should have at least two KDC servers—a master and a slave).

❑ When you are configuring multiple realms for cross-realm authentication, you need to decide how to tie the realms together. You can establish a hierarchical relationship between the realms that provides automatic paths to the associated domains. You could establish the connection directly, which can be especially helpful when too many levels exist between two hierarchical domains or when there is no hierarchical relationship at all. In this case, the connection must be defined in the *letc/krb5/krb5.conf* file on all hosts that use the connection.

❑ The mapping of host names onto realm names is defined in the domain_ realm section of the *krb5.conf* file.

❑ For the principal names that include the FQDN of a host, it is important to match the string that describes the DNS domain name in *letc/resolv.conf.* SEAM requires that the DNS domain name be in lowercase letters when you are entering the FQDN for a principal. The DNS domain name can include uppercase and lowercase letters, but you should use only lowercase letters when you are creating a host principal.

❑ When you are using SEAM, it is strongly recommended that DNS services already be configured and running on all hosts. If DNS is used, it must be enabled on all systems or on none of them. If DNS is available, then the principal should contain the Fully Qualified Domain Name (FQDN) of each host.

❑ The ports used for KDC are defined in the *letc/services* and *letc/krb5/krb5. conf* files on every client, and in the *letc/krb5/kdc.conf* file on each KDC. They include port 88 and 750 for the KDC, and port 749 for the KDC administration daemon.

❑ Slave KDCs generate credentials for clients just as the master KDC does. The slave KDCs provide backup if the master becomes unavailable. Each realm should have at least one slave KDC. Additionally, you can have too many slave KDCs. Not only does each slave retain a copy of the KDC database, which increases the risk of a security breach, but the KDC database must be propagated to each server, which can cause latency or delay to get the data updated throughout the realm.

❑ The database that is stored on the master KDC must be regularly propagated to the slave KDCs.

❑ All hosts that participate in the Kerberos authentication system must have their internal clocks synchronized within a specified maximum amount of time. This process is known as clock skew.

❑ An encryption type is an identifier that specifies the encryption algorithm, encryption mode, and hash algorithms used in SEAM.

Configure and Administer the Sun Enterprise Authentication Mechanism

❑ SEAM uses strong authentication that verifies the identities of both the sender and the recipient, verifies the validity of data to provide data integrity, and encrypts the data during transmission to guarantee privacy.

❑ To restrict network access to the server using telnet, ftp, rcp, rsh, and rlogin to Kerberos authenticated transactions only, edit the telnet entry in */etc/inetd.conf*. Add the -a user option to the telnet entry to restrict access to those users who can provide valid authentication information:

```
telnet stream tcp nowait root /usr/sbin/in.telnetd telnetd -a user
```

Then edit the ftp entry in */etc/inetd.conf*. Add the -a option to the ftp entry to permit only Kerberos authenticated connections:

```
ftp stream tcp nowait root /usr/sbin/in.ftpd ftpd -a
```

Then disable Solaris entries for other services in */etc/inetd.conf*. The entries for shell and login need to be commented out or removed:

```
# shell stream tcp nowait root /usr/sbin/in.rshd in.rshd
# login stream tcp nowait root /usr/sbin/in.rlogind in.rlogind
```

❑ Restricting access to both master KDC servers and slave KDC servers so that the databases are secure is important to the overall security of the SEAM installation.

SELF TEST

The following questions will help you measure your understanding of the material presented in this chapter. Read all the choices carefully, because there might be more than one correct answer. Choose all correct answers for each question. Some questions are short-answer questions to ensure you have a good understanding of the material.

Define the Sun Enterprise Authentication Mechanism and Configuration Issues

1. Which of the following are security features provided for by SEAM?
   A. Verification of the identities of both the sender and the recipient
   B. Verification of the validity of data
   C. Guaranteed privacy
   D. All of the above

2. Explain the steps taken during the initial SEAM authentication process.

3. What is a SEAM realm?

4. The number of realms that your installation requires depends on which of the following issues?
   A. How far apart the clients are
   B. The amount of SEAM traffic that each client generates
   C. The number of hosts that are available to be installed as KDCs
   D. The number of clients to be supported
   E. All of the above

5. You need to authenticate yourself to SEAM only once per session.
   A. True
   B. False

6. What two elements should be propagated and synchronized between master and slave KDCs?

7. Explain Sun's naming convention for realm names.

8. Why is it important to the overall security of the SEAM installation to restrict access to the KDC servers?

9. Explain the steps taken after the initial SEAM authentication process for all subsequent SEAM authentications.

10. Where are the ports for the KDC and Admin Services defined, and what ports are assigned by default?

11. Explain the purpose of slave KDCs. How many slave KDCs should be implemented per realm? Can you have too many slave KDCs?

Configure and Administer the Sun Enterprise Authentication Mechanism

12. Why is it important to match the string that describes the DNS domain name in */etc/resolv.conf* for the principal names that include the FQDN of a host? Should DNS services be configured and running on all hosts?

13. Realm hierarchy is important when you configure multiple realms for cross-realm authentication. How should you tie the realms together?

14. Where is the mapping of host names onto realm names defined?

15. Explain how to restrict network access to the server using telnet to Kerberos authenticated transactions only.

LAB QUESTION

After the installation of SEAM, you are called in to configure a master KDC and a slave KDC for your client. How would you go about performing these tasks?

SELF TEST ANSWERS

Define the Sun Enterprise Authentication Mechanism and Configuration Issues

1. ☑ **D.** All answers are correct. SEAM uses strong authentication that verifies the identities of both the sender and the recipient, verifies the validity of data to provide data integrity, and encrypts the data during transmission to guarantee privacy.

2. ☑ A user or service begins a SEAM session by requesting a TGT from the KDC. This request often occurs automatically at login. A TGT is needed to obtain other tickets for specific services. The TGT identifies you and allows you to obtain numerous tickets for remote machines or network services. TGTs have limited lifetimes. The KDC creates a TGT and sends it back, in encrypted form, to the user or service. The user or service then decrypts the TGT by using a password. Now in possession of a valid TGT, the user or service can request tickets for all sorts of network operations, for as long as the TGT lasts (usually for a few hours). Each time the user or service performs a unique network operation, it requests a ticket for that operation from the KDC.

3. ☑ A SEAM realm is a logical network that encompasses a group of systems that fall under the same master KDC. Before you configure SEAM, you should consider the realm name, the number and size of each realm, and the relationship of a realm to other realms for cross-realm authentication.

4. ☑ **E.** All of the answers are correct. The number of realms that your installation requires depends on the number of clients to be supported, the amount of SEAM traffic that each client generates, how far apart the clients are, and the number of hosts that are available to be installed as KDCs (each realm should have at least two KDC servers—a master and a slave).

5. ☑ **A.** True. Since SEAM is based on Kerberos, the whole system is ticket-based and, therefore, when a transaction is initiated, a ticket is requested from a Key Distribution Center (KDC) that identifies the user and his or her access privileges. In most cases, for a SEAM session to begin, a user simply logs in and provides a Kerberos password. What's nice about SEAM is that the user needs to authenticate himself or herself to SEAM only once per session; therefore, all transactions during the session are automatically secured.

6. ☑ The database that is stored on the master KDC must be regularly propagated to the slave KDCs. All hosts that participate in the Kerberos authentication system must have their internal clocks synchronized within a specified maximum amount of time. This process is known as clock skew.

7. ☑ Although realm names can be any ASCII string, the realm name is more commonly the same name as your DNS domain name—in uppercase. Not only does this convention help differentiate and facilitate problems with SEAM as opposed to problems with the DNS namespace, you'll be using a recognizable name. On the flipside, if you opt not to use DNS, you can use any ASCII string. Keep in mind, though, that the configuration process will require more work upon doing so. Therefore, the use of realm names that follow the standard Internet naming structure is recommended.

8. ☑ Both master KDC servers and slave KDC servers have copies of the KDC database stored locally; therefore, restricting access to these servers so that the databases are secure is important to the overall security of the SEAM installation.

9. ☑ The user or service requests a ticket for a particular service (say, to `rlogin` into another machine) from the KDC by sending the KDC its TGT as proof of identity. The KDC sends the ticket for the specific service to the user or service. The user or service sends the ticket to the server. When using the NFS service, the NFS client automatically and transparently sends the ticket for the NFS service to the NFS server. The server allows the user or service access. These steps make it appear that the server doesn't ever communicate with the KDC. The server does communicate, though; it registers itself with the KDC, just as the first user or service does.

10. ☑ The ports used for KDC are defined in the *etc/services* and *etc/krb5/krb5.conf* files on every client, and in the *etc/krb5/kdc.conf* file on each KDC. By default, they include port 88 and 750 for the KDC and port 749 for the KDC administration daemon. Different port numbers can be specified and therefore would have to be changed on every client and KDC.

11. ☑ Slave KDCs generate credentials for clients just as the master KDC does. The slave KDCs provide backup if the master becomes unavailable. Each realm should have at least one slave KDC. Be aware that you can have too many slave KDCs. Not only does each slave retain a copy of the KDC database, which increases the risk of a security breach, but the KDC database must be propagated to each server, which can cause latency or delay to get the data updated throughout the realm.

Configure and Administer the Sun Enterprise Authentication Mechanism

12. ☑ For the principal names that include the FQDN of a host, it is important to match the string that describes the DNS domain name in *etc/resolv.conf*. SEAM requires that the DNS domain name be in lowercase letters when you are entering the FQDN for a principal. The DNS domain name can include uppercase and lowercase letters, but use only lowercase letters when you are creating a host principal. When you are using SEAM, it is strongly recommended that DNS services already be configured and running on all hosts. If DNS is used, it must be enabled on all systems or on none of them. If DNS is available, the principal should contain the Fully Qualified Domain Name (FQDN) of each host.

13. ☑   You can establish a hierarchical relationship between the realms that provides automatic paths to the associated domains. Be warned, though, that if there are many levels of domains, you might not want to use the default path because of the amount of transactions it requires. Alternatively, you can establish the connection directly. This can be especially helpful when too many levels exist between two hierarchical domains or when no hierarchical relationship exists at all. In this case, the connection must be defined in the *letc/krb5/krb5.conf* file on all hosts that use the connection; therefore, additional work is required.

14. ☑   The mapping of host names onto realm names is defined in the domain_realm section of the *krb5.conf* file.

15. ☑   To restrict network access to the server using telnet, edit the telnet entry in *letc/inetd.conf*. Add the -a user option to the telnet entry to restrict access to those users who can provide valid authentication information:

```
telnet stream tcp nowait root /usr/sbin/in.telnetd telnetd -a user
```

LAB ANSWER

To configure a Master KDC, assuming the prerequisites have been met, follow these steps:

1. Become superuser on the master KDC.

2. Edit the Kerberos configuration file (*krb5.conf*). You need to change the realm names and the names of the servers.

```
kdc1 # cat /etc/krb5/krb5.conf
[libdefaults]
default_realm = EXAMPLE.COM
[realms]
EXAMPLE.COM = {
kdc = kdc1.example.com
kdc = kdc2.example.com
admin_server = kdc1.example.com
sunw_dbprop_enable = Y
sunw_dbprop_master_ulogsize = 2500
}
[domain_realm]
.example.com = EXAMPLE.COM
#
# if the domain name and realm name are equivalent,
# this entry is not needed
#
[logging]
default = FILE:/var/krb5/kdc.log
kdc = FILE:/var/krb5/kdc.log
[appdefaults]
```

```
gkadmin = {
help_url = http://denver:8888/ab2/coll.384.1/SEAM/@AB2PageView/6956
}
```

In this example, the lines for `default_realm`, `kdc`, `admin_server`, and all `domain_realm` entries were changed. Also, in the realms section, lines to enable incremental propagation and to select the number of updates the KDC master keeps in the log were added. In addition, the line that defines the `help_url` was edited.

3. Edit the KDC configuration file (*kdc.conf*). You need to change the realm name.

```
kdc1 # cat /etc/krb5/kdc.conf
[kdcdefaults]
kdc_ports = 88,750
[realms]
EXAMPLE.COM= {
profile = /etc/krb5/krb5.conf
database_name = /var/krb5/principal
admin_keytab = /etc/krb5/kadm5.keytab
acl_file = /etc/krb5/kadm5.acl
kadmind_port = 749
max_life = 8h 0m 0s
max_renewable_life = 7d 0h 0m 0s
}
```

In this example, the realm name definition in the realms section was changed.

4. Create the KDC database by using the `kdb5_util` command. The `kdb5_util` command creates the KDC database. Also, when used with the `-s` option, this command creates a stash file that is used to authenticate the KDC to itself before the kadmind and krb5kdc daemons are started.

```
kdc1 # /usr/sbin/kdb5_util create -r EXAMPLE.COM -s
Initializing database '/var/krb5/principal' for realm 'EXAMPLE.COM'
master key name 'K/M@EXAMPLE.COM'
You will be prompted for the database Master Password.
It is important that you NOT FORGET this password.
Enter KDC database master key: <type the key>
Re-enter KDC database master key to verify: <type it again>
```

The `-r` option followed by the realm name is not required if the realm name is equivalent to the domain name in the server's namespace.

5. Edit the Kerberos access control list file (*kadm5.acl*). Once populated, the */etc/krb5/kadm5.acl* file should contain all principal names that are allowed to administer the KDC.

```
kws/admin@EXAMPLE.COM *
kiprop/kdc2.example.com@EXAMPLE.COM p
```

6. The first entry gives the kws/admin principal in the EXAMPLE.COM realm the ability to modify principals or policies in the KDC. The default installation includes an asterisk (*) to match all admin principals. This default could be a security risk, so it is more secure to include a list of all of the admin principals. The second entry allows the master KDC to receive requests for incremental propagation for the kdc2 server. Start the kadmin.local command. The next substeps create principals that are used by SEAM.

```
kdc1 # /usr/sbin/kadmin.local
kadmin.local:
```

a. Add administration principals to the database. You can add as many admin principals as you need. You must add at least one admin principal to complete the KDC configuration process. For this example, a kws/admin principal is added. You can substitute an appropriate principal name instead of *kws*.

```
kadmin.local: addprinc kws/admin
Enter password for principal kws/admin@EXAMPLE.COM: <type the password>
Re-enter password for principal kws/admin@EXAMPLE.COM: <type it again>
Principal "kws/admin@EXAMPLE.COM" created.
kadmin.local:
```

b. Create a keytab file for the kadmind service. This command sequence creates a special keytab file with principal entries for kadmin and changepw. These principals are needed for the kadmind service. Note that when the principal instance is a host name, the FQDN must be entered in lowercase letters, regardless of the case of the domain name in the */etc/resolv.conf* file.

```
kadmin.local: ktadd -k /etc/krb5/kadm5.keytab kadmin/kdc1.example.com
Entry for principal kadmin/kdc1.example.com with kvno 3, encryption type DES-CBC-CRC
added to keytab WRFILE:/etc/krb5/kadm5.keytab.
kadmin.local: ktadd -k /etc/krb5/kadm5.keytab changepw/kdc1.example.com
Entry for principal changepw/kdc1.example.com with kvno 3, encryption type DES-CBC-CRC
added to keytab WRFILE:/etc/krb5/kadm5.keytab.
kadmin.local: ktadd -k /etc/krb5/kadm5.keytab kadmin/changepw
Entry for principal kadmin/changepw with kvno 3, encryption type DES-CBC-CRC
added to keytab WRFILE:/etc/krb5/kadm5.keytab.
kadmin.local:
```

c. Quit kadmin.local. You have added all of the required principals for the next steps.

```
kadmin.local: quit
```

7. Start the Kerberos daemons.

```
kdc1 # /etc/init.d/kdc start
kdc1 # /etc/init.d/kdc.master start
```

8. Add more principals. At this point, you can add principals by using the SEAM Administration Tool. To do so, you must log on with one of the admin principal names that you created earlier in this procedure. However, the following command-line example is shown for simplicity.

```
kdc1 # /usr/sbin/kadmin -p kws/admin
Enter password: <Type kws/admin password>
kadmin:
```

a. Create the master KDC host principal. The host principal is used by Kerberized applications, such as klist and kprop. Note that when the principal instance is a host name, the FQDN must be entered in lowercase letters, regardless of the case of the domain name in the */etc/resolv.conf* file.

```
kadmin: addprinc -randkey host/kdc1.example.com
Principal "host/kdc1.example.com@EXAMPLE.COM" created.
kadmin:
```

b. (Optional) Create the master KDC root principal. This principal is used for authenticated NFS mounting. So, the principal might not be necessary on a master KDC. Note that when the principal instance is a host name, the FQDN must be entered in lowercase letters, regardless of the case of the domain name in the */etc/resolv.conf* file.

```
kadmin: addprinc root/kdc1.example.com
Enter password for principal root/kdc1.example.com@EXAMPLE.COM: <type the password>
Re-enter password for principal root/kdc1.example.com@EXAMPLE.COM: <type it again>
Principal "root/kdc1.example.com@EXAMPLE.COM" created.
kadmin:
```

c. (Optional) Create the kclient principal. This principal is used by the kclient utility during the installation of a SEAM client. If you do not plan on using this utility, then you do not need to add the principal. The users of the kclient utility need to use this password.

```
kadmin: addprinc clntconfig/admin
Enter password for principal clntconfig/admin@EXAMPLE.COM: <type the password>
Re-enter password for principal clntconfig/admin@EXAMPLE.COM: <type it again>
Principal "clntconfig/admin@EXAMPLE.COM" created.
kadmin:
```

d. Create the kiprop principal. The kiprop principal is used to authenticate the master KDC server and to authorize the updates from the master KDC.

```
kadmin: addprinc -randkey kiprop/kdc1.example.com
Principal "kiprop/kdc1.example.com@EXAMPLE.COM" created.
kadmin: addprinc -randkey kiprop/kdc2.example.com
Principal "kiprop/kdc2.example.com@EXAMPLE.COM" created.
kadmin:
```

e. Add the master KDC's host principal to the master KDC's keytab file. Adding the host principal to the keytab file allows this principal to be used automatically.

```
kadmin: ktadd host/kdc1.example.com
kadmin: Entry for principal host/kdc1.example.com with
kvno 3, encryption type DES-CBC-CRC added to keytab
WRFILE:/etc/krb5/krb5.keytab
kadmin:
```

  f. Add the kiprop principal to the *kadm5.keytab* file. Adding the kiprop principal to the *kadm5.keytab* file allows the `kadmind` command to authenticate itself when it is started.

```
kadmin: ktadd -k /etc/krb5/kadm5.keytab kiprop/kdc1.example.com
kadmin: Entry for principal kiprop/kdc1.example.com with
kvno 3, encryption type DES-CBC-CRC added to keytab
WRFILE:/etc/krb5/kadm5.keytab
kadmin:
```

  g. Quit `kadmin`.

```
kadmin: quit
```

 9. Add an entry for each KDC into the propagation configuration file (*kpropd.acl*).

```
kdc1 # cat /etc/krb5/kpropd.acl
host/kdc1.example.com@EXAMPLE.COM
host/kdc2.example.com@EXAMPLE.COM
```

10. (Optional) Synchronize the master KDCs clock by using NTP or another clock synchronization mechanism. It is not required that you install and use the NTP. However, every clock must be within the default time that is defined in the libdefaults section of the *krb5.conf* file in order for authentication to succeed.

To configure a slave KDC, assuming the master KDC is configured, follow these steps:

 1. On the master KDC, become superuser.

 2. On the master KDC, start kadmin. You must log on with one of the admin principal names that you created when you configured the master KDC.

```
kdc1 # /usr/sbin/kadmin -p kws/admin
Enter password: <Enter kws/admin password>
kadmin:
```

  a. On the master KDC, add slave host principals to the database, if not already done. In order for the slave to function, it must have a host principal. Note that when the principal instance is a host name, the FQDN must be entered in lowercase letters, regardless of the case of the domain name in the */etc/resolv.conf* file.

```
kadmin: addprinc -randkey host/kdc3.example.com
Principal "host/kdc3@EXAMPLE.COM" created.
kadmin:
```

b. (Optional) On the master KDC, create the slave KDC root principal. This principal is needed only if the slave will be NFS mounting an authenticated file system. Note that when the principal instance is a host name, the FQDN must be entered in lowercase letters, regardless of the case of the domain name in the /etc/resolv.conf file.

```
kadmin: addprinc root/kdc3.example.com
Enter password for principal root/kdc3.example.com@EXAMPLE.COM:
 <type the password>
Re-enter password for principal root/kdc3.example.com@EXAMPLE.COM: <type it again>
Principal "root/kdc3.example.com@EXAMPLE.COM" created.
kadmin:
```

c. On the master KDC, create the kiprop principal. The kiprop principal is used to authorize incremental updates from the master KDC.

```
kadmin: addprinc -randkey kiprop/kdc3.example.com
Principal "kiprop/kdc3.example.com@EXAMPLE.COM" created.
kadmin:
```

d. Quit kadmin.

```
kadmin: quit
```

3. On the master KDC, edit the Kerberos configuration file (krb5.conf). You need to add an entry for each slave.

```
kdc1 # cat /etc/krb5/krb5.conf .
.[realms]
EXAMPLE.COM = {
kdc = kdc1.example.com
kdc = kdc2.example.com
kdc = kdc3.example.com
admin_server = kdc1.example.com
}
```

4. On the master KDC, add an entry for each slave KDC into the database propagation configuration file (kpropd.acl).

```
kdc1 # cat /etc/krb5/kpropd.acl
host/kdc1.example.com@EXAMPLE.COM
host/kdc2.example.com@EXAMPLE.COM
host/kdc3.example.com@EXAMPLE.COM
```

5. On the master KDC, add a kiprop entry to kadm5.acl. This entry allows the master KDC to receive requests for incremental propagation for the kdc3 server.

```
kdc1 # cat /etc/krb5/kadm5.acl
*/admin@EXAMPLE.COM *
kiprop/kdc2.example.com@EXAMPLE.COM p
kiprop/kdc3.example.com@EXAMPLE.COM p
```

6. On all slave KDCs, copy the KDC administration files from the master KDC server. This step needs to be followed on all slave KDCs, because the master KDC server has updated information that each KDC server needs. You can use FTP or a similar transfer mechanism to grab copies of the following files from the master KDC:

```
/etc/krb5/krb5.conf
/etc/krb5/kdc.conf
/etc/krb5/kpropd.acl
```

7. On the new slave, change an entry in *krb5.conf*. Replace the `sunw_dbprop_master_ulogsize` entry with an entry defining `sunw_dbprop_slave_poll`. The entry sets the poll time to two minutes.

```
kdc3 # cat /etc/krb5/krb5.conf
.

.
[realms]
EXAMPLE.COM = {
kdc = kdc1.example.com
kdc = kdc2.example.com
kdc = kdc3.example.com
admin_server = kdc1.example.com
sunw_dbprop_enable = Y
sunw_dbprop_slave_poll = 2m
}
```

8. On the new slave, issue the `kadmin` command. You must log on with one of the admin principal names that you created when you configured the master KDC.

```
kdc3 # /usr/sbin/kadmin -p kws/admin
Enter password: <Type kws/admin password>
kadmin:
```

a. Add the slave's host principal to the slave's keytab file by using kadmin. This entry allows kprop and other Kerberized applications to function. Note that when the principal instance is a host name, the FQDN must be entered in lowercase letters, regardless of the case of the domain name in the */etc/resolv.conf* file.

```
kadmin: ktadd host/kdc3.example.com
kadmin: Entry for principal host/kdc3.example.com with
kvno 3, encryption type DES-CBC-CRC added to keytab
WRFILE:/etc/krb5/krb5.keytab
kadmin: quit
```

b. Add the kiprop principal to the kadmind keytab file. Adding the kiprop principal to the *kadm5.keytab* file allows the kpropd command to authenticate itself when it is started.

```
kadmin: ktadd -k /etc/krb5/kadm5.keytab kiprop/kdc3.example.com
kadmin: Entry for principal kiprop/kdc3.example.com with
kvno 3, encryption type DES-CBC-CRC added to keytab
WRFILE:/etc/krb5/kadm5.keytab
kadmin:
```

c. Quit kadmin.

```
kadmin: quit
```

9. On the master KDC, back up and propagate the database by using kprop_script. If a backup copy of the database is already available, it is not necessary to complete another backup.

```
kdc1 # /usr/lib/krb5/kprop_script kdc3.example.com
Database propagation to kdc3.example.com: SUCCEEDED
```

10. On the new slave, create a stash file by using kdb5_util.

```
kdc3 # /usr/sbin/kdb5_util stash
kdb5_util: Cannot find/read stored master key while reading master key
kdb5_util: Warning: proceeding without master key
Enter KDC database master key: <type the key>
```

11. (Optional) On the new slave KDC, synchronize the master KDCs clock by using NTP or another clock synchronization mechanism. It is not required that you install and use the NTP. However, every clock must be within the default time that is defined in the libdefaults section of the *krb5.conf* file in order for authentication to succeed.

12. On the new slave, start the KDC daemon (krb5kdc).

```
kdc3 # /etc/init.d/kdc start
```

Part VII

Appendixes

A

Final Test Study Guide

F ollowing are the key points from certification objectives in this book that are covered on the exam. It's in your best interest to study this guide until you can answer all questions in Appendix B correctly before taking Sun's exam.

Describe Principles of Information Security

❑ Information security is the confidentiality, integrity, and availability of information.

❑ Confidentiality is the prevention of unauthorized disclosure of information.

❑ Integrity is the means of ensuring that information is protected from unauthorized or unintentional alteration, modification, or deletion.

❑ Availability ensures that information is readily accessible to authorized viewers at all times.

❑ Identification is the means by which a user (human, system, or process) provides a claimed unique identity to a system.

❑ Authentication is a method for proving that you are who you say you are.

❑ Strong authentication is the use of two or more different authentication methods: such as a smart card and PIN, or a password and a form of biometrics such as a fingerprint or retina scan.

❑ Authorization is the process of ensuring that a user has sufficient rights to perform the requested operation, and preventing those without sufficient rights from doing the same.

❑ The principle of least privilege stipulates that users are granted no more privileges than those absolutely necessary to do the required job.

❑ The purpose of the segregation (or separation) of duties is to avoid the possibility of a single person being responsible for different functions within an organization. Rotation of duties is a similar control that is intended to detect abuse of privileges or fraud and is practiced to avoid becoming overly dependent on a single member of staff. By rotating staff, the organization has more chances of discovering violations or fraud.

Identify the Security Life Cycle
and Describe Best Security Practices

❏ A security policy is a high-level document or set of documents that in particular identifies the information assets of the organization, stipulates who owns them and how they may or may not be used, and sets requirements for their use along with sanctions for misuse.

❏ The security life cycle process is intended to prevent, detect, respond, and deter—and repeat the cycle again, keeping in mind the lessons learned.

❏ Preventive controls include firewalls, logical and physical access control systems, and security procedures that are devised to prevent violations of security policy from occurring.

❏ Detection controls include network/host intrusion detection systems, physical movement, alarms, and cryptographic checksums on transmitted information (to detect unauthorized modifications).

❏ Incident response is a subdiscipline of information security; it is the formal set of defined and approved actions based on the information security policy and best practices that are to be taken in response to a security incident.

❏ Deterrent controls include good information security management, regular audits, security-aware staff, well-administered systems, good employee morale, and security certifications.

❏ Security-aware employees are the best partners of the organization and its information security efforts, while staff that have no idea about security practices or simply don't care are the worst enemy. One doesn't need determined adversaries to suffer a security breach—a clueless insider who doesn't understand the consequences may expose the organization to risks that could otherwise have been avoided.

❏ Security policies are one of the mechanisms that define and convey the information security requirements of the organization's management to the staff of the organization. The security policy is the high-level document or set of documents that in particular identifies the information assets of the organization, stipulates who owns them and how they may or may not be used, and sets requirements for their use along with sanctions for misuse.

❑ Security procedures are developed by subject-matter specialists within the organization with the assistance of security professionals and/or information systems auditors. Procedures may be application- and/or version-specific and as such need to be kept current with the current information systems environment of the organization. System and security administrators play a key role in developing and enforcing security procedures.

❑ Security guidelines are nonbinding recommendations on how to develop, define, and enforce security policies and procedures.

❑ Security standards are mandatory either because they are dictated by the security policy, law, or regulations or because the entity in question has decided to adhere to the standard.

❑ Physical security addresses the physical vulnerabilities, threats, and countermeasures necessary to control risks associated with physical destruction, unauthorized access, loss, theft, fire, natural disasters (floods, earthquakes, tornados), environmental issues (air conditioning, ventilation, humidity control), and all associated issues.

❑ Although Sun Certified Security Administrator for Solaris certification candidates are not required to have Sun Certified System or Network Administrator certifications, they are expected to be familiar with subjects covered by their exam objectives and have at least six months of experience administering Solaris systems.

❑ The Solaris operating system complies to EAL4.

Explain Attackers, Motives, and Methods

❑ A secure system is a system that has certain security functionalities and that provides certain assurance that it will function in accordance with and enforce a defined security policy in a known environment provided it is operated in a prescribed manner.

❑ A trusted system or component has the power to break one's security policy. *Trusted path* is the term used to describe the secure communication channel between the user and the software (an application or the operating system itself). A trusted path exists when a mechanism is in place to assure the users that they are indeed interacting with the genuine application or the operating system and not software that impersonates them.

❏ A *threat* describes the potential for attack or exploitation of a vulnerable business asset. This term defines the cost of an attack weighed against the benefit to the attacker that can be obtained through such an attack. It does not describe when an administrator decides to accept a specific risk.

❏ A vulnerability describes how susceptible you are to an attack and how likely you are to succumb to an attack if it occurs.

❏ Risk assessment is a critical element in designing the security of systems and is a key step in the accreditation process that helps managers select cost-effective safeguards.

❏ Attacks from disgruntled employees are most dangerous because they have the closest physical and logical access to the internal infrastructure, applications, and data. Disgruntled employees also have a good understanding of business and technical climate, organization, and capabilities.

❏ A script kiddie is a novice with little experience who has access to tools and documentation that can be used to interfere with a system's assets.

❏ Eavesdropping is a passive attack that affects confidentiality of information. Regular Internet protocols are insecure and prone to eavesdropping attacks, because they transmit information unencrypted. It is relatively easy to defend against eavesdropping attacks by using protocols that encrypt information before transmitting it over the network.

❏ Traffic analysis is a passive attack aimed at such aspects of communication as time, direction, frequency, flow, who sent the communication, and to whom it is addressed. An important issue to note is that encryption does not protect against traffic analysis unless specifically designed and implemented with traffic analysis resistance.

❏ Timing analysis is about measuring time between actions or events in information systems and networks. Timing analysis may be effective when used in concert with other attack types in complex attacks.

❏ Social engineering is used by potential attackers to manipulate people to do what the attacker wants them to do without them realizing the hidden agenda. The only defense against social engineering is having security-aware and risks-aware staff and management.

- ❏ Buffer overflow attacks are perhaps the most primitive and the most effective of attacks. In a buffer overflow attack, the target system or application is sent more data or data different from what it is designed to handle, which usually results in a crash of the target or execution of the part of sent data. The data sent to the target may contain machine code or instructions that may be executed as a result of buffer overflow, thus giving the attacker a way in or making it simpler to gain access.

- ❏ Denial of service (DoS) attacks are directed at the availability of information and information systems. Denial of service attacks exhaust all available resources—be it network bandwidth, number of maximum simultaneous connections, disk space, or RAM—to prevent legitimate users from using the system.

- ❏ Spoofing refers to attacks in which the source of information is falsified with malicious intent. Spoofing attacks are usually used to circumvent filtering and access control based on source addresses. The most effective defense against spoofing is the use of cryptographic authentication and digital signatures.

- ❏ Man-in-the-middle attacks involve an attacker located physically or logically between two or more communicating parties on a network, where the attacker poses as the remote party to communicate and actively engages in masquerading as the remote party. Man-in-the middle attacks are difficult to protect against unless a well-designed and well-implemented cryptographic authentication system is in place.

- ❏ Replay attacks are usually directed against simple authentication mechanisms but may also be used against poorly designed or implemented cryptographic protocols. During a replay attack, the attacker intercepts and records a valid authentication session and later replays whole or part of it again to gain unauthorized access. Replay attacks are active attacks that are usually launched after a successful eavesdropping or man-in-the-middle attack.

- ❏ Connection or session hijacking refers to taking over an already established connection or session with assigned identity and authorizations. Insecure network protocols that do not provide continuous authentication and do not use strong cryptographic algorithms to protect the confidentiality and integrity of data transmissions are especially vulnerable to connection hijacking.

- ❑ Brute-force attacks are usually used against passwords, cryptographic keys, and other security mechanisms. In a brute-force attack the adversary performs an exhaustive search of the set in question to find the correct password or cryptographic key. The defense against brute-force attacks is to make the amount of time and computations required to conduct an exhaustive search impossible to afford by using a sufficiently large set—that is, longer passwords and keys.

- ❑ In a dictionary attack, the adversary uses a list ("dictionary") of possible passwords or cryptographic keys to perform a search of the set to find the correct password or key. The defense against dictionary attacks is to use passwords or keys that are unlikely to be included in such a list.

Identify, Monitor, and Disable Logins

- ❑ Issue the `logins` command and view the *letc/shadow* file to determine which accounts are locked or disabled and which do not currently have assigned passwords. These techniques are useful when identifying user login status.

- ❑ You can disable user logins by either creating a *letc/nologin* file, bringing the system down to single-user mode with the command `init s`, or disabling user accounts from the Solaris Management Console (SMC) interface.

- ❑ Failed login attempts from terminal sessions are stored in the *var/adm/ loginlog* file.

- ❑ Syslog can monitor all unsuccessful login attempts. To do so, edit the *letc/ default/login* file and make sure that the `SYSLOG=YES` and `SYSLOG_FAILED_ LOGINS=0` entries are uncommented.

- ❑ You can customize the System Logging Facility to log failed login access attempts after a predefined number of tries by editing the `SYSLOG_ FAILED_LOGINS=0` entry in the *letc/default/login* file to some number such as `SYSLOG_FAILED_LOGINS=3`. At this point, the system will log access attempts only after the first three failures.

- ❑ You can customize the System Logging Facility to close the login connections after some predefined number of failures by uncommenting the RETRIES entry in the *letc/default/login* file, and making sure the value is set to some number (5 is the default value). By default, after five failed login attempts in the same session, the system will close the connection.

❑ The su program usage is monitored through the *letc/default/su* file as SULOG= / var/adm/sulog, and the syslog logging facility will determine whether or not to log all su attempts with the SYSLOG=YES entry.

❑ In real time, you can display superuser access attempts on the console by uncommenting the CONSOLE=/dev/console entry in the *letc/ default/su* file.

❑ To disable remote superuser login access attempts (disabled by default), simply uncomment the CONSOLE=/dev/console entry in the *letc/default/ login* file.

Configure Solaris Auditing and Customize Audit Events

❑ Events that are capable of creating audit logs include system startup and shutdown, login and logout, identification and authentication, privileged rights usage, permission changes, process and thread creation and destruction, object creation and manipulation, application installation, and system administration.

❑ The *audit_control* file can be modified to preselect audit classes and customize audit procedures.

❑ The audit policy is automatically started in the *audit_startup* script.

❑ The *audit_warn* script generates mail to an e-mail alias called *audit_warn*. You can change the alias by editing the *etc/security/audit_warn* file and changing the e-mail alias in the script at entry ADDRESS=audit_warn, or by redirecting the *audit_warn* e-mail alias to a different account.

❑ When auditing is enabled, the contents of the *etc/security/audit_startup* file determine the audit policy.

❑ To audit efficiently, Sun recommends randomly auditing only a small percentage of users at any one time, compressing files, archiving older audit logs, monitoring in real time, and automatically increasing unusual event auditing.

❑ In the *audit_control* file, the flags and naflags arguments define which attributable and nonattributable events should be audited for all users on the system.

❑ You can manually issue the bsmrecord command to add events that should be audited.

❑ The *audit_event* file is the event database that defines which events are part of classes you can audit.

❑ The audit event numbers—with the exception of 0, which is reserved as an invalid event number—are 1–2047 for Solaris Kernel events, 2048–32767 for Solaris programs (6144–32767 also includes SunOS 5.X user-level audit events), and 32768–65535 for third-party applications.

❑ The *audit_user* file defines specific users and classes of events that should always or never be audited for each user.

❑ Syslog audit files should never be placed in the same locations as binary data.

❑ Syslog files should be monitored and archived regularly to accommodate potentially extensive outputs.

❑ Execute the *bsmconv* script to enable and disable the auditing service.

❑ Issue the `audit -s` command to refresh the kernel and the `auditconfig -conf` command to refresh the auditing service.

❑ To display audit records formats, use the `bsmrecord` command.

❑ To merge audit files into a single output source to create an audit trail, use the `auditreduce` command.

Control Access to Devices by Configuring and Managing Device Policy and Allocation

❑ Device policy is enabled by default and enforced in the kernel to restrict and prevent access to devices that are integral to the system. Device allocation is not enabled by default and is enforced during user-allocation time to require user authorization to access peripheral devices.

❑ To view device policies for all devices or specific ones, use the `getdevpolicy` command.

❑ To modify or remove device policies for a specific device, use the `update_ drv -a -p` *policy device-driver* command; where *policy* is the device policy or policies (separated by a space) for *device-driver*, which is the device driver whose device policy you wish to modify or remove.

❑ The AUE_MODDEVPLCY audit event is part of the `as` audit class by default, which is used to audit changes in device policy. To audit device policies, you'll need to add the `as` class to the *audit_control* file `flags` argument.

❑ Run the *bsmconv* script to enable the auditing service, which also enables device allocation.

❑ The ot audit class is used to audit device allocation. To audit an allocatable device, you'll need to add the ot class to the *audit_control* file flags argument.

❑ Users with the appropriate rights and authorization can allocate and deallocate devices. The authorization required to allocate a device is solaris.device.allocate. The authorization required to forcibly allocate or deallocate a device is solaris.device.revoke.

❑ Users with the appropriate rights and authorization can allocate a device by issuing the allocate *device-name* command and deallocate a device by issuing the deallocate *device-name* command.

Use the Basic Audit Reporting Tool to Create a Manifest and Check System Integrity

❑ The Basic Audit Reporting Tool (BART) can report file-level changes that have occurred on the system.

❑ To compare a control manifest with a new comparison manifest issue the command

```
bart compare options control-manifest compare-manifest > bart-report
```

Differentiate Between the Types of Host-Based Denial of Service Attacks and Understand How Attacks Are Executed

❑ The most common forms of DoS attacks include program buffer overflow, malformed packets (that is, overlapping IP fragments), Teardrop, Ping of Death, Smurf, Bonk, Boink, NewTear, WinNuke, Land, LaTierra, and SYN attacks.

❑ After penetrating a target system, an attacker would typically attempt to erase any traces of the incident by deleting activity logs and leaving backdoors in place to allow later clandestine access to the system.

❑ When default executable stacks with permissions set to read/write/execute are allowed, programs may be targets for buffer overflow attacks. A buffer overflow occurs when a program process or task receives extraneous data that is not properly programmed. As a result, the program typically operates in such a way that an intruder can abuse or misuse it.

❏   During a SYN attack, the attacker abuses the TCP three-way handshake by sending a flood of connection requests (SYN packets) while not responding to any of the replies. To verify that this type of attack is occurring, you can check the state of the system's network traffic with the `netstat` command.

❏   In a Teardrop attack, the attacker modifies the length and fragmentation offset fields in IP packets, which causes the target to crash.

❏   Ping of Death is a malformed ICMP packet attack, in which an attacker sends an oversized ping packet in an attempt to overflow the system's buffer.

❏   A Smurf attack involves a broadcasted ping request to every system on the target's network with a spoofed return address of the target.

Establish Courses of Action to Prevent Denial of Service Attacks

❏   To help prevent DoS attacks against the Solaris operating system, Sun advocates disabling executable stacks, disabling extraneous IP services/ ports, employing egress filtering, using firewalls, monitoring networks, and implementing a patch update program.

❏   Sun recommends that you always monitor programs that are executed with privileges as well as the users that have rights to execute them. You can search your system for unauthorized use of the setuid and setgid permissions on programs to gain superuser privileges using the `find` command:

```
find directory -user root -perm -4000 -exec ls -ldb {} \; >/tmp/filename
```

where `find directory` checks all mounted paths starting at the specified directory, which can be root (/), sys, bin, or mail; `-user root` displays files owned only by root; `-perm -4000` displays only files with permissions set to 4000, `-exec ls -ldb` displays the output of the `find` command in *ls -ldb* format; and `>/tmp/filename` writes results to this file.

❏   To defend against stack smashing, you can configure attributes so that code cannot be executed from the stack by setting the `noexec_user_stack=1` variable in the */etc/system* file. If you disable executable stacks, programs that require the contrary will be aborted, so it's crucial first to test this procedure on a nonproduction system.

❏   The *inetd.conf* defines how the inetd daemon handles common Internet service requests. To disable an unneeded port and prevent unauthorized access to the associated service, comment out the service in the */etc/inetd.conf* file with the hash character and then restart the inetd process or reboot the server if the service started through the inetd daemon.

❑ Use the `showrev -p` command from a terminal session to view your system's current patches.

❑ To install a patch, use the `patchadd` command: `patchadd /dir/ filename`; where `/dir/` is the folder that contains the patch and `filename` is the name of the patch.

Identify, Detect, and Protect Against Trojan Horse Programs and Backdoors

❑ A Trojan horse program is a malicious program that is disguised as some useful software. Trojan examples include a shell script that spoofs the login program and a malicious substitute switch user (su) program.

❑ Device-specific files in the /etc and /devices directories are common targets for attackers to attempt to gain access to the operating system, especially for creating backdoors to the system.

❑ A worm is a self-replicating program that will copy itself from system-to-system, sometimes using up all available resources on infected systems or installing a backdoor on the system.

❑ A logic bomb is code that is inserted into programming code and is designed to execute under specific circumstances.

❑ A fork bomb is a process that replicates itself until it consumes the maximum number of allowable processes.

❑ A rootkit utility can be used not only to provide remote backdoor access to attackers but also to hide the attacker's presence on the system. Some types of rootkit utilities exploit the use of loadable kernel modules to modify the running kernel for malicious intent.

❑ To harden your system and help protect against Trojan horse programs, Sun recommends user awareness education, installing and updating anti-virus software, removing unnecessary compilers, securing file and directory permissions, and monitoring path variables.

❑ Path variables should not contain a parameter indicated with a dot (`.`) that could cause the system to search for executables or libraries within that path, as well as a search path for root that contains the current directory.

❑ To monitor and help prevent unauthorized changes from being made to system files, Sun recommends using the Automated Security Enhancement Tool (ASET), the Basic Security Module (BSM), Tripwire, and the Solaris cryptographic framework.

❑ Automated Security Enhancement Tool (ASET) enables you to monitor and restrict access to system files and directories with automated administration governed by a preset security level (low, medium, or high). The seven tasks that ASET can regularly perform are system files permissions tuning, system files checks, user and group checks, system configuration files check, environment variables check, EEPROM check, and firewall setup.

❑ To run ASET at any given time, simply log in as root or become superuser, and then issue the command `/usr/aset/aset -l level -d pathname`; where `level` is the security level value (either low, medium, or high), and `pathname` is the working directory for ASET (the default is /usr/asset).

❑ To avoid resource encumbrance, ASET tasks should be run during off-peak hours or when system activities are low.

❑ Verify whether files were maliciously altered by using message digest algorithms. A message digest is a digital signature for a stream of binary data used as verification that the data was not altered since the signature was first generated. The MD5 and the Secure Hashing Algorithm (SHA1) are among the most popular message digest algorithms.

❑ Using the `digest` command, you can compute a message digest for one or more files. In the Solaris cryptographic framework environment, you can perform digest computations using the following syntax: `digest -v -a algorithm input-file > digest-listing`; where `-v` displays the output with file information, `-a algorithm` is the algorithm used to compute a digest (that is, MD5 or SHA1), `input-file` is the input file for the digest to be computed, and `digest-listing` is the output file for the `digest` command.

❑ The Solaris Fingerprint Database (sfpDB) is a free tool from Sun that allows you to check the integrity of system files through cryptographic checksums online. By doing so, you can determine whether system binaries and patches are safe in accordance with their original checksums stored at Sun, which includes files distributed with Solaris OE media kits, unbundled software, and patches.

❑ Frequently using integrity checking mechanisms such as checksums and the Solaris Fingerprint Database can help detect maliciously altered programs.

❑ If a rootkit is detected, Sun recommends restoring the operating system from trusted sources, followed by the reinstallation of applications, and finally restoring data from secured backups.

❑ Kernel-level rootkits are not as easily detectable using integrity checking mechanisms given that the kernel itself is involved in the process. Sun recommends building a kernel that monitors and controls the system's treatment of its loadable kernel modules, especially for perimeter security or outside systems operating as gateways, web, and mail agents. If restricting loadable kernel modules is not practical, Sun recommends taking advantage of the Solaris Cryptographic services.

❑ The system file (*/etc/system*) contains commands that are read when the kernel is initialized. These commands can be used to modify the system's operation concerning how to handle loadable kernel modules. Commands that modify the handling of LKMs require you to specify the module type by listing the module's namespace, thus giving you the ability to load a loadable kernel module or exclude one from being loaded.

Describe the Benefits and Capabilities of Role-Based Access Control

❑ With Role-Based Access Control (RBAC), system administrators can delegate privileged commands to non-root users without giving them full superuser access.

❑ The principle of least privilege states that a user should *not* be given any more privilege or permissions than necessary for performing a job.

❑ A rights profile grants specific authorizations and/or privilege commands to a user's role. Privilege commands execute with administrative capabilities usually reserved for administrators.

❑ Sun's best practices dictate that you do not assign rights profiles, privileges, and authorizations directly to users, or privileges and authorizations directly to roles. It's best to assign authorizations to rights profiles, rights profiles to roles, and roles to users.

❑ Applications that check authorizations include audit administration commands, batch job commands, device commands, printer administration commands, and the Solaris Management Console tool suite.

❑ Privileges that have been removed from a program or process cannot be exploited. If a program or process was compromised, the attacker will have only the privileges that the program or process had. Other unrelated programs and processes would not be compromised.

❑ Roles get access to privileged commands through rights profiles that contain the commands.

❏ Commands that check for privileges include commands that control processes, file and file system commands, Kerberos commands, and network commands.

❏ The four sets of process privileges are the *effective privilege set (E)*, which are privileges currently in use; the *inheritable privilege set (I)*, which are privileges a process can inherit; the *permitted privilege set (P)*, which are privileges available for use now; and the *limit privilege set (L)*, which are outside privilege limits of which processes can shrink but never extend.

❏ With RBAC, a user role whose rights profile contains permission to execute specific commands can do so without having to become superuser.

❏ A rights profile can be assigned to a role or user and can contain authorizations, privilege commands, or other rights profiles.

❏ The rights profile name and authorizations can be found in the *prof_attr* database, the profile name and commands with specific security attributes are stored in the *exec_attr* database, and the *user_attr* database contains user and role information that supplements the passwd and shadow databases.

❏ A role is a type of user account that can run privileged applications and commands included in its rights profiles.

Explain How to Configure and Audit Role-Based Access Control

❏ Before implementing Role-Based Access Control (RBAC), you should properly plan by creating profiles and roles that adhere to company policy and abide by the principle of least privilege when assigning permissions.

❏ A right is a named collection, consisting of commands, authorizations to use specific applications (or to perform specific functions within an application), and other, previously created, rights, whose use can be granted or denied to an administrator.

❏ The `roleadd` command can be used to create roles and associates a role with an authorization or a profile from the command line.

❏ From the command line, the `usermod` command associates a user's login with a role, profile, and authorization in the */etc/user_attr* database, which can also be used to grant a user access to a role.

❏ A role is a special user account used to grant rights.

❏ Users can assume only those roles they have been granted permission to assume. Once a user takes on a role, the user relinquishes his or her own user identity and takes on the properties, including the rights, of that role.

❏ To audit a role, you should add the `ua` or the `as` event to the flags line in the *audit_control* file, and then start the auditing service.

Use UNIX Permissions to Protect Files

❑ Access control lists (ACLs) provide better file security by enabling you to define file permissions for each user class.

❑ The `ls` command is used to list files and some information about the files contained within a directory.

❑ The `chown` command is used to change file ownership.

❑ The `chgrp` command is used to change group ownership of a file.

❑ The `chmod` command is used to change permissions on a file. The command changes or assigns the mode of a file (permissions and other attributes), which may be absolute or symbolic.

❑ When setuid permission is set on an executable file, a process that runs this file is granted access on the basis of the owner of the file. This permission presents a security risk as attackers can find a way to maintain the permissions that are granted to them by the setuid process even after the process has finished executing.

❑ You should always monitor the system for unauthorized setuid and setgid permissions to gain superuser privileges.

Use Access Control Lists to Set File Permissions

❑ Unless you have added ACL entries that extend UNIX file permissions, the plus sign (+) does not display to the right of the mode field.

❑ To set an ACL on a file, use the `setfacl` command. Note that if an ACL already exists on a file, the `-s` option replaces the entire ACL with the new one. To verify the file has your ACL, issue the `getfacl filename` command.

Explain How to Protect Files Using the Solaris Cryptographic Framework

❑ Algorithms can be symmetric *secret key* or asymmetric *public key* computational procedures used for encryption. In symmetric algorithms, the same key is used for both encryption and decryption, and in asymmetric algorithms, two keys are used—one to encrypt and another to decrypt a message.

❑ Providers are cryptographic plug-ins that applications, end users, or kernel operations—which are all termed "consumers"—use. The Solaris cryptographic framework allows only three types of plug-ins: user-level plug-ins, kernel-level plug-ins, and hardware plug-ins.

❑ To monitor and help prevent unauthorized changes from being made to system files, Sun recommends using the Automated Security Enhancement Tool (ASET), the Basic Security Module (BSM), Tripwire, and the Solaris cryptographic framework.

❑ Random keys can be generated using the `encrypt` and `mac` commands.

❑ To create a symmetric key, use the `dd` command:

`dd if=/dev/urandom of=keyfile bs=n count=n`

where `if=file` is the input file (for a random key, use the */dev/urandom* file), `of=keyfile` is the output file that holds the generated key, `bs=n` is the key size in bytes (for the length in bytes divide the key length in bits by 8), and `count=n` is the count of the input blocks (the number for *n* should be 1).

❑ To compute a message digest for one or more files, issue the `digest` command:

`digest -v -a algorithm input-file > digest-listing`

where `-v` displays the output with file information, `-a algorithm` is the algorithm used to compute a digest (that is, MD5 or SHA1), `input-file` is the input file for the digest to be computed, and `digest-listing` is the output file for the `digest` command.

❑ To create a MAC of a file, use the command:

`mac -v -a algorithm -k keyfile input-file`

where `-v` displays the output in the following format: `algorithm (input-file) = mac`; `-a algorithm` is the algorithm to use to compute the MAC (type the algorithm as the algorithm appears in the output of the `mac -l` command); `-k keyfile` is the file that contains a key of algorithm-specified length; and `input-file` is the input file for the MAC.

❑ To encrypt and decrypt a file, simply create a symmetric key and then issue the `encrypt` command:

`encrypt -a algorithm -k keyfile -i input-file -o output-file`

where `-a algorithm` is the algorithm to use to encrypt the file (type the algorithm as the algorithm appears in the output of the `encrypt -l` command); `-k keyfile` is the file that contains a key of algorithm-specified length (the key length for each algorithm is listed, in bits, in the output of the `encrypt -l` command); `-i input-file` is the input file that you want to encrypt (this file is left unchanged); and `-o output-file` is the output file that is the encrypted form of the input file. To decrypt the output file, you simply pass the same key and the same encryption mechanism that encrypted the file but to the `decrypt` command.

Administer the Solaris Cryptographic Framework

❑ To display the list of installed providers, issue the `cryptoadm list` command.

❑ To display a list of mechanisms that can be used with the installed providers, issue the `cryptoadm list -m` command.

❑ To display the mechanism policy for the installed providers and the provider feature policy, issue the `cryptoadm list -p` command.

❑ To prevent the use of a user-level mechanism, issue the `cryptoadm disable` *provider* \ *mechanism(s)* command.

❑ To disable a kernel software, issue the `cryptoadm disable` *provider* command; to restore an inactive software provider, issue the `cryptoadm refresh` command; to remove a provider permanently, issue the `cryptoadm uninstall` command.

Explain and Configure Secure RPC to Authenticate a Host and a User Across an NFS Mount

❑ The Secure NFS service uses Secure RPC (Remote Procedure Call) to authenticate users who make requests to the service.

❑ The authentication mechanism (Diffie-Hellman) uses Data Encryption Standard (DES) encryption to encrypt the common key between client and server with a 56-bit key

❑ Normally, a user login password is identical to the Secure RPC password, where the login process passes the secret key to the keyserver. If the passwords are different, then the user must always run the `keylogin` command. When the command is included in the user's environment configuration file (that is, `~/.login`, `~/.cshrc`, or `~/.profile`), the command runs automatically whenever the user logs in.

❑ The process of generating a conversation key when a user initiates a transaction with a server begins with the keyserver randomly generating a conversation key. The kernel uses the conversation key, plus other material, to encrypt the client's timestamp. Next the keyserver looks up the server's public key in the public key database and then uses the client's secret key and the server's public key to create a common key. At that point, the keyserver encrypts the conversation key with the common key.

❏   When decrypting a conversation key after the server receives the transmission from the client, the keyserver that is local to the server looks up the client's public key in the public key database. The keyserver then uses the client's public key and the server's secret key to deduce the common key. The kernel uses the common key to decrypt the conversation key, and then calls the keyserver to decrypt the client's timestamp with the decrypted conversation key.

❏   Returning the verifier to the client and authenticating the server starts when the server returns a verifier, including the index ID, which the server records in its credential cache; and the client's timestamp minus 1, which is encrypted by the conversation key. The client receives the verifier and authenticates the server. The client knows that only the server could have sent the verifier because only the server knows what timestamp the client sent. With every transaction after the first transaction, the client returns the index ID to the server in its next transaction. The client also sends another encrypted timestamp. The server sends back the client's timestamp minus 1, which is encrypted by the conversation key.

❏   By requiring authentication for use of mounted NFS file systems, you increase the security of your network.

Use the PAM Framework to Configure the Use of System Entry Services for User Authentication

❏   The Pluggable Authentication Module (PAM) framework lets you plug in new authentication technologies without changing system entry services, and configure the use of system entry services (ftp, login, telnet, or rsh, for example) for user authentication.

❏   The PAM software consists of a library, various service modules, and a configuration file. The *pam.conf* file defines which modules to use and in what order the modules are to be used with each application. The PAM library provides the framework to load the appropriate modules and to manage the stacking process. The PAM library provides a generic structure to which all of the modules can plug in. The PAM framework provides a method for authenticating users with multiple services by using stacking. Depending on the configuration, the user can be prompted for passwords for each authentication method. The order in which the authentication services are used is determined through the PAM configuration file.

❑ If the PAM configuration file is misconfigured or the file becomes corrupted, all users might be unable to log in. Since the `sulogin` command does not use PAM, the root password would then be required to boot the machine into single-user mode and fix the problem.

❑ For security reasons, PAM module files must be owned by root and must not be writable through group or other permissions. If the file is not owned by root, PAM does not load the module. To load the module, ensure that the ownership and permissions are set so that the module file is owned by root and the permissions are 555. Then edit the PAM configuration file, /etc/ pam.conf, and add this module to the appropriate services. Then you must reboot the system before you can verify that the module has been added.

❑ To prevent rhost-style access from remote systems with PAM, remove all of the lines that include `rhosts_auth.so.1` from the PAM configuration file. This prevents unauthenticated access to the local system from remote systems. To prevent other unauthenticated access to the ~/.rhosts files, remember to disable the rsh service by removing the service entry from the /etc/inetd.conf file.

❑ Changing the PAM configuration file does not prevent the service from being started.

Explain the Simple Authentication and Security Layer (SASL) in Solaris

❑ SASL adds authentication support to network protocols so applications can utilize optional security services by calling the SASL library as a security layer inserted between the protocol and the connection.

❑ SASL mechanisms are named by strings, from 1 to 20 characters in length, consisting of uppercase letters, digits, hyphens, and/or underscores.

❑ During the authentication protocol exchange, the mechanism performs authentication, transmits an authorization identity (that is, userid) from the client to the server, and negotiates the use of a mechanism-specific security layer.

❑ The security layer takes effect immediately following the last response of the authentication exchange for data sent by the client and the completion indication for data sent by the server. Once the security layer is in effect, the protocol stream is processed by the security layer into buffers of cipher-text.

❑ SASL provide services including plug-in support, determining the necessary security properties from the application to aid in the choice of a security mechanism, listing available plug-ins to the application, choosing the best mechanism for a particular authentication attempt, routing the authentication data between the application and the chosen mechanism, and providing information about the SASL negotiation back to the application.

Use Solaris Secure Shell to Access a Remote Host Securely Over an Unsecured Network

❏ In Solaris Secure Shell, authentication is provided by the use of passwords, public keys, or both, where all network traffic is encrypted. Some of the benefits of Solaris Secure Shell include preventing an intruder from being able to read an intercepted communication as well as from spoofing the system.

❏ The standard procedure for generating a Solaris Secure Shell public/private key pair is by using the key generation program `ssh-keygen -t rsa`.

❏ To change your passphrase, type the `ssh-keygen` command with the `-p` option, and answer the prompts.

❏ To start a Solaris Secure Shell session, type the `ssh` command and specify the name of the remote host.

❏ You can avoid providing your passphrase and password whenever you use Solaris Secure Shell by automatically starting an agent daemon, ssh-agent. You can start the agent daemon from the *.dtprofile* script.

❏ You can specify that a local port be forwarded to a remote host. The connection from this port is made over a secure channel to the remote host. Similarly, a port can be specified on the remote side.

❏ Use the `scp` command to copy encrypted files between hosts. You can copy encrypted files either between a local host and a remote host, or between two remote hosts. The command operates similarly to the `rcp` command, except that the `scp` command prompts for passwords.

❏ You can use Solaris Secure Shell to make a connection from a host inside a firewall to a host on the other side of the firewall. This task is done by specifying a proxy command for ssh either in a configuration file or as an option on the command line. In general, you can customize your ssh interactions through a configuration file. You can customize either your own personal file in *$HOME/.ssh/config* or you can customize an administrative configuration file in */etc/ssh/ssh_config*. The files can be customized with two types of proxy commands: one for HTTP connections and another for SOCKS5 connections.

Define the Sun Enterprise Authentication Mechanism and Configuration Issues

❑ The Sun Enterprise Authentication Mechanism (SEAM) uses strong authentication that verifies the identities of both the sender and the recipient, verifies the validity of data to provide data integrity, and encrypts the data during transmission to guarantee privacy.

❑ SEAM is based on the ticket-based Kerberos. You only need to authenticate yourself to SEAM once per session; therefore, all transactions during the session are automatically secured.

❑ The initial SEAM authentication process begins when a user or service starts a SEAM session by requesting a ticket-granting ticket (TGT) from the Key Distribution Center (KDC). The KDC creates a TGT and sends it back, in encrypted form, to the user or service. The user or service then decrypts the TGT by using their password. Now in possession of a valid TGT, the user or service can request tickets for all sorts of network operations, for as long as the TGT lasts.

❑ Subsequent SEAM authentication continues when a user or service requests a ticket for a particular service. The KDC sends the ticket for the specific service to the requesting user or service. The user or service sends the ticket to the server that hosts the requested service. The server then allows the user or service access.

❑ A realm is a logical network which defines a group of systems that are under the same master KDC. Issues such as the realm name, the number and size of each realm, and the relationship of a realm to other realms for cross-realm authentication should be resolved before you configure SEAM.

❑ Realm names can consist of any ASCII string (usually the same as your DNS domain name, in uppercase). This convention helps differentiate problems with SEAM from problems with the DNS namespace, while using a name that is familiar. If you do not use DNS or you choose to use a different string, then you can use any string.

❑ The number of realms that your installation requires depends on the number of clients to be supported, the amount of SEAM traffic that each client generates, how far apart the clients are, and the number of hosts that are available to be installed as KDCs (each realm should have at least two KDC servers—a master and a slave).

❑ When you configure multiple realms for cross-realm authentication, you need to decide how to tie the realms together. You can establish a hierarchical relationship between the realms that provides automatic paths to the associated domains. You could establish the connection directly, which can be especially helpful when too many levels exist between two hierarchical domains or when there is no hierarchal relationship at all. In this case the connection must be defined in the /etc/krb5/krb5.conf file on all hosts that use the connection.

❑ The mapping of host names onto realm names is defined in the domain_realm section of the krb5.conf file.

❑ For the principal names that include the FQDN of an host, it is important to match the string that describes the DNS domain name in /etc/resolv.conf. SEAM requires that the DNS domain name be in lowercase letters when you are entering the FQDN for a principal. The DNS domain name can include uppercase and lowercase letters, but only use lowercase letters when you are creating a host principal.

❑ When you are using SEAM, it is strongly recommended that DNS services already be configured and running on all hosts. If DNS is used, it must be enabled on all systems or on none of them. If DNS is available, the principal should contain the Fully Qualified Domain Name (FQDN) of each host.

❑ The ports used for KDC are defined in the /etc/services and /etc/krb5/krb5.conf files on every client, and in the /etc/krb5/kdc.conf file on each KDC. They include port 88 and 750 for the KDC, and port 749 for the KDC administration daemon.

❑ Slave KDCs generate credentials for clients just as the master KDC does. The slave KDCs provide backup if the master becomes unavailable. Each realm should have at least one slave KDC. Additionally, you can have too many slave KDCs. Not only does each slave retain a copy of the KDC database, which increases the risk of a security breach, but the KDC database must be propagated to each server which can cause latency or delay to get the data updated throughout the realm.

❑ The database that is stored on the master KDC must be regularly propagated to the slave KDCs.

❏ All hosts that participate in the Kerberos authentication system must have their internal clocks synchronized within a specified maximum amount of time. This process is known as clock skew.

❏ An encryption type is an identifier that specifies the encryption algorithm, encryption mode, and hash algorithms used in SEAM.

Configure and Administer the Sun Enterprise Authentication Mechanism

❏ To restrict network access to the server using telnet, ftp, rcp, rsh, and rlogin to Kerberos-authenticated transactions only, edit the telnet entry in /etc/inetd.conf. Add the -a user option to the telnet entry to restrict access to those users who can provide valid authentication information:

```
telnet stream tcp nowait root /usr/sbin/in.telnetd telnetd -a user
```

Edit the ftp entry in /etc/inetd.conf. Add the -a option to the ftp entry to permit only Kerberos-authenticated connections:

```
ftp stream tcp nowait root /usr/sbin/in.ftpd ftpd -a
```

Disable Solaris entries for other services in /etc/inetd.conf. The entries for shell and login need to be commented out or removed:

```
# shell stream tcp nowait root /usr/sbin/in.rshd in.rshd
# login stream tcp nowait root /usr/sbin/in.rlogind in.rlogind
```

❏ Restricting access to both master KDC servers and slave KDC servers so that the databases are secure is important to the overall security of the SEAM installation.

B

Final Test

T he following questions will help you measure your understanding of the material presented in this book. Read all the choices carefully, because there might be more than one correct answer. Choose, and in some cases explain, all correct answers for each question. It's in your best interest to retake this test until you can answer all questions correctly before taking Sun's exam. The answers are provided in Appendix C.

1. In the Solaris cryptographic framework, which of the following best explains providers?
   A. Applications, end users, or kernel operations
   B. User-level plug-ins, kernel-level plug-ins, and hardware plug-ins
   C. Cryptographic plug-ins that consumers use
   D. All of the above

2. Which of these databases contains role information?
   A. *prof_attr*
   B. *exec_attr*
   C. *user_attr*
   D. *passwd*
   E. *shadow*
   F. All of the above

3. How would you set the minimum free disk space for an audit file before a warning is sent?

4. Which of these techniques is used to actively detect and display superuser access attempts on the console?
   A. By commenting out the `CONSOLE=/dev/console` entry in the */etc/default/login* file
   B. By uncommenting the `CONSOLE=/dev/console` entry in the */etc/default/su* file
   C. By uncommenting the `CONSOLE=/dev/console` entry in the */etc/default/login* file
   D. By commenting out the `CONSOLE=/dev/console` entry in the */etc/default/su* file
   E. All of the above

5. Why is a process life cycle–based approach to information security management appropriate?
   A. Because it is the only existing approach
   B. Because it is a good practice
   C. Because it takes into account changing environment
   D. Because it is business-oriented
   E. All of the above

6. What is the rationale behind nondisclosure of software version numbers and other details of systems used?

   A. Making attackers spend more time and effort

   B. To avoid easy identification of bugs and vulnerabilities of deployed software

   C. To avoid or minimize script kiddie attacks

   D. To comply with principles of minimization and least privilege

   E. All of the above

7. When executable stacks with permissions set to read/write/execute are allowed, programs by default will be vulnerable to buffer overflow attacks.

   A. True

   B. False

8. Which of the following is a form of denial of service acting as a system process that replicates itself until it exceeds the maximum number of allowable processes?

   A. Trojan horse

   B. Worm

   C. Logic bomb

   D. Fork bomb

   E. Rootkit

   F. All of the above

9. Which of the following are benefits of Role-Based Access Control (RBAC)?

   A. Privilege commands can execute with administrative capabilities usually reserved for administrators.

   B. System administrators can delegate privileged commands to non-root users without giving them full superuser access.

   C. Rights profiles, privileges, and authorizations can be assigned directly to users.

   D. Users can be assigned only the exact privileges and permissions necessary for performing a job.

   E. All of the above

10. What is the purpose of audit trail and logs?

   A. They record events as they happen.

   B. Audit trail can be used in court proceedings but logs cannot.

   C. They serve to establish accountability.

   D. They may be used in place of deterrent controls.

   E. All of the above

11. Security life cycle includes which of the following?
- **A.** Preventive controls
- **B.** Detection
- **C.** Controls that deter potential attackers
- **D.** Incident response
- **E.** All of the above

12. Which of these tools can be used to check the integrity of system files?
- **A.** MD5
- **B.** The Solaris Fingerprint Database
- **C.** sfpDB
- **D.** SHA1
- **E.** System files checks
- **F.** All of the above

13. Explain the meaning of a "right" as it pertains to Role-Based Access Control (RBAC).

14. List and explain the providers supported by the Solaris cryptographic framework.

15. Fingerprints can be used for:
- **A.** *What you have* authentication
- **B.** *What you are* authentication
- **C.** Biological identification
- **D.** Keeping things simple
- **E.** All of the above

16. Which of the following can be used to check the integrity of the system's files?
- **A.** Access control lists (ACLs)
- **B.** Device policy
- **C.** Device allocation
- **D.** Basic Audit Reporting Tool (BART)
- **E.** All of the above

17. Half-open connections are commonly initiated by an attacker in which of these types of attacks?
- **A.** Program buffer overflow
- **B.** Ping of Death
- **C.** Executable stacks
- **D.** SYN flooding
- **E.** Smurf attacks
- **F.** All of the above

18. Which of the following is a self-replicating program that will copy itself from system-to-system?

    A. Trojan horse

    B. Worm

    C. Logic bomb

    D. Fork bomb

    E. Rootkit

    F. All of the above

19. Which command can be used to create roles and associates a role with an authorization or a profile from the command line?

    A. `ppriv`

    B. `smc &`

    C. `usermod`

    D. `roleadd`

    E. All of the above

20. In the Solaris cryptographic framework, which of the following best explains consumers?

    A. Applications, end users, or kernel operations

    B. User-level plug-ins, kernel-level plug-ins, and hardware plug-ins

    C. Cryptographic plug-ins that consumers use

    D. All of the above

21. Which of the following can be assigned to a role or user as a collection of administrative functions and can contain authorizations and privilege commands or rights profiles?

    A. Authorization

    B. Privilege

    C. Privileged application

    D. Rights profile

    E. Role

    F. All of the above

22. Which of these is a code that is inserted into programming code that is designed to execute under specific circumstances?

    A. Trojan horse

    B. Worm

    C. Logic bomb

    D. Fork bomb

    E. Rootkit

    F. All of the above

23. Which of these is an ASET task that is used to verify the integrity of user accounts, their passwords, and their groups?

    A. System files permissions tuning

    B. System files checks

    C. User and group checks

    D. System configuration files check

    E. Environment variables check

    F. EEPROM check

    G. Firewall setup

    H. All of the above

24. Assuming the syslog kern facility is set to notice level, when you disallow executable stacks, programs that attempt to execute code on their stack will likely do which of these?

    A. Execute the program with privileges.

    B. Display a warning message with the name of the program, its process ID, and the UID of the user who ran the program.

    C. Monitor executable stacks.

    D. Log a message by syslog.

    E. All of the above

25. Which type of attack occurs when a broadcasted ping request is sent to every system on the target's network?

    A. Program buffer overflow

    B. Ping of Death

    C. Executable stacks

    D. SYN flooding

    E. Smurf attacks

    F. All of the above

26. A backdoor can be a legitimate remote access portal to perform debugging and troubleshooting tasks.

    A. True

    B. False

27. Which of the following can be used to restrict and prevent access to peripheral devices?

    A. AUE_MODDEVPLCY event

    B. Device policy

    C. Running the *bsmconv* script

    D. Device allocation

    E. Issuing the `update_drv -a -p` *policy device-driver* command

    F. All of the above

28. Which of the following can be used to restrict and prevent access to devices integral to the system?

    A. AUE_MODDEVPLCY event

    B. Device policy

    C. Running the bsmconv script

    D. Device allocation

    E. Issuing the `update_drv -a -p` *policy device-driver* command

    F. All of the above

29. Which of the following can be used to merge audit files into a single output source to create an audit trail?

    A. `audit -s`

    B. `auditconfig -conf`

    C. `bsmconv`

    D. `bsmrecord`

    E. `auditreduce`

    F. All of the above

30. To perform system maintenance, you must bring system resources down to minimum levels. Which of these techniques can be used to disable user logins?

    A. Bring the system down to single-user mode.

    B. Issue the `shutdown -g 120 -y` command.

    C. Issue the `init S` command.

    D. Create a */etc/nologin* file.

    E. Disable user accounts individually with the Solaris Management Console.

    F. All of the above

31. Which of the following statements are true?

    A. Certification is the technical evaluation of systems.

    B. Certification is done by an organization's management.

    C. Accreditation is the formal acceptance of the system and its risks.

    D. Certification requires accreditation.

    E. All of the above

32. How can you protect systems against brute-force attacks?
  A. Use strong authentication.
  B. Make the amount of time and computations required unaffordable.
  C. Use longer passwords and keys.
  D. Use Role-Based Access Control.
  E. All of the above

33. What is the benefit of cost-benefit analysis?
  A. Cost-benefit analysis is necessary because organizations cannot reduce all risks to zero.
  B. Cost-benefit analysis increases an organization's return on investment.
  C. Cost-benefit analysis prevents denial of service attacks.
  D. Cost-benefit analysis is a good governance practice.
  E. All of the above

34. What is a trusted system?
  A. A trusted system is another name for a high-security system.
  B. A trusted system is a system that can break a security policy if compromised.
  C. Trusted system refers to operating systems like Trusted Solaris.
  D. Trusted systems are more rigorously designed and tested.
  E. All of the above

35. Continuous authentication protects against:
  A. Hacking
  B. Script kiddies
  C. Hijacking attacks
  D. Sniffing
  E. All of the above

36. By commenting out extraneous inetd services, the operating system will disable the service from being available and potentially vulnerable to an attack.
  A. True
  B. False

37. Which of these can be used not only to provide remote backdoor access to attackers but also to hide the attacker's presence on the system?
  A. Trojan horse
  B. Loadable Kernel Module
  C. Logic bomb
  D. Fork bomb
  E. Rootkit
  F. All of the above

38. Explain the meaning of a "role" as it pertains to Role-Based Access Control (RBAC).

39. In the Solaris cryptographic framework, which of the following commands can be used to generate random keys?

A. `dd`

B. `digest`

C. `encrypt`

D. `mac`

E. All of the above

40. What command displays the mechanism policy for the installed providers?

41. Which of the following can be used to display audit record formats?

A. `audit -s`

B. `auditconfig -conf`

C. `bsmconv`

D. `bsmrecord`

E. `auditreduce`

F. All of the above

42. Which of the following commands would you issue to view device policies for all devices or just for specific devices?

A. `list_devices`

B. `getdevpolicy`

C. `allocate` *device-name*

D. All of the above

43. What type of control is intended to offset deficiencies of other controls?

A. Preventive

B. Defensive

C. Compensating

D. Recovery

E. All of the above

44. If A trusts B, and B trusts C, then:

A. A trusts C.

B. A does not automatically trust C.

C. C trusts A.

D. The trust relationship is symmetric and bidirectional.

E. All of the above

45. Why is detection an important part of the security process?
   A. Because it shows which preventive controls work and which don't.
   B. Because it serves as a quality/reliability control.
   C. Because no usable preventive control is perfect.
   D. Detection is not necessary in low-security environments.
   E. All of the above

46. The switch user (su) program usage (by default) is monitored.
   A. True
   B. False

47. Which configuration file specifies the primary and secondary audit directories?
   A. *Audit_control*
   B. *Audit_startup*
   C. *Audit_warn*
   D. *Audit_user*
   E. All of the above

48. Which of the following can be executed to disable the auditing service?
   A. `audit -s`
   B. `auditconfig -conf`
   C. The *bsmconv* script
   D. `bsmrecord`
   E. `auditreduce`
   F. All of the above

49. Which of the following can be used to report file-level changes that have occurred on the system?
   A. Access control lists (ACLs)
   B. Device policy
   C. Device allocation
   D. Basic Audit Reporting Tool (BART)
   E. All of the above

50. To prevent and defend against DoS attacks, Sun recommends which of the following mechanisms?
   A. Using egress filtering
   B. Installing recommended patches from SunSolve

    C. Disabling unnecessary service ports

    D. Using TCP wrappers

    E. Network monitoring and deploying a firewall

    F. All of the above

51. Which of these is an ASET task that automatically sets system file permissions according to the security level you choose?

    A. System files permissions tuning

    B. System files checks

    C. User and group checks

    D. System configuration files checks

    E. Environment variables checks

    F. EEPROM check

    G. Firewall setup

    H. All of the above

52. What is the principle of least privilege?

53. Which of the following are shared objects that provide services by using PKCS #11 libraries?

    A. Hardware plug-ins

    B. Kernel-level plug-ins

    C. User-level plug-ins

    D. All of the above

54. What commands would you issue to disable temporarily and then later restore the use of a kernel software provider?

55. What is strong authentication?

    A. Strong authentication uses long passwords.

    B. Strong authentication requires smart cards.

    C. Strong authentication requires the use of at least two different authentication methods.

    D. Biometrics provides strong authentication.

    E. All of the above

56. What is the purpose of authentication?

    A. To obtain proof of claimed identity

    B. To implement access control

    C. To establish accountability

    D. To allow use of different authorizations

    E. All of the above

57. User trust is
- **A.** Guaranteed by trusted systems
- **B.** Defined in security policy
- **C.** Gained and maintained by definition and enforcement of good security policies and their professional implementation
- **D.** Transitive and bidirectional
- **E.** All of the above

58. What is the purpose of deterrent controls?
- **A.** To back up detective controls
- **B.** To prevent attacks from happening
- **C.** To discourage attackers
- **D.** To compensate for preventive controls
- **E.** All of the above

59. Which of the following techniques is used to identify user login status with regard to logins without assigned passwords?
- **A.** Issue the command `logins`
- **B.** Issue the command `logins -x`
- **C.** Issue the command `logins -p`
- **D.** Access the *\/var\/adm\/loginlog* file with superuser privileges
- **E.** All of the above

60. When auditing is enabled, the contents of the *etc\/security\/audit_startup* file determine the _____.

61. Which of the following can be executed to refresh the auditing service?
- **A.** `audit -s`
- **B.** `auditconfig -conf`
- **C.** `bsmconv`
- **D.** `bsmrecord`
- **E.** `auditreduce`
- **F.** All of the above

62. You can create a manifest of more than one file by separating the files with a comma.
- **A.** True
- **B.** False

63. From within a terminal session, which command would you execute to view the system's current installed patches?

   A. `grep` *filename*
   B. `showpatch -p`
   C. `showrev -p`
   D. `vi system`
   E. All of the above

64. Which type of attack occurs when an attacker sends an oversized ICMP packet in an attempt to overflow the target system's buffer?

   A. Program buffer overflow
   B. Ping of Death
   C. Executable stacks
   D. SYN flooding
   E. Smurf attacks
   F. All of the above

65. To harden your system and help protect against Trojan horse programs, Sun recommends that path variables do not contain which of these?

   A. A parameter indicated with a dot (.)
   B. A search path for root that contains the current directory
   C. A parameter indicated with a forward slash (/)
   D. A search path for superuser that contains the current directory
   E. All of the above

66. Which of these is used to produce a cyclical-redundancy-check (CRC) and block count for files that can help prevent backdoor attacks?

   A. ASET
   B. Message digest
   C. Checksum
   D. EEPROM check
   E. All of the above

67. Which of these are privileges in common with every process?

   A. E
   B. I
   C. D
   D. P
   E. G
   F. All of the above

68. Which of the following is inherently provided for by using cryptography?

   A. Authenticity

   B. Confidentiality

   C. Integrity

   D. RBAC

   E. Checksum

   F. All of the above

69. What command displays the list of installed providers?

70. In which of the following are two cryptographic keys used: one to encrypt a message and another to decrypt it?

   A. Asymmetric algorithm

   B. Public key

   C. Secret key

   D. Symmetric algorithm

   E. All of the above

71. Which command can be used to check the privileges available to your current shell's process?

   A. `ppriv`

   B. `smc &`

   C. `usermod`

   D. `roleadd`

   E. All of the above

72. Which of these is an ASET task that performs a file comparison check from a master file that is created when the task is first executed?

   A. System files permissions tuning

   B. System files checks

   C. User and group checks

   D. System configuration files checks

   E. Environment variables checks

   F. EEPROM check

   G. Firewall setup

   H. All of the above

73. The principle of least privilege applies only to user accounts.

   A. True

   B. False

74. What is a threat?

    A. A threat is the absence of security mechanisms.

    B. A threat is the opposite of assurance.

    C. A threat is anything that can exploit vulnerabilities.

    D. Threats may be natural, physical, and logical.

    E. All of the above

75. Which of the following may protect against spoofing attacks?

    A. Encryption

    B. Cryptographic initiation

    C. Cryptographic authentication

    D. Secret addresses

    E. All of the above

76. Why is incident response capability necessary?

    A. Because any organization may have a security incident.

    B. Because detection is useless without response.

    C. Because it is required by law.

    D. Because correct reaction to a security incident is important.

    E. All of the above

77. Which of the following are part of Sun's required password policy?

    A. The password should be at least 8 characters long.

    B. The password must consist of between 6 and 15 letters, numbers, and special characters.

    C. The password must have at least 2 alphabetic characters and at least one numeric or special character within the first 6 characters.

    D. The first 8 characters of the password should not be the same as the previous password.

    E. All of the above

78. Which of these is a common run level used to go into single-user state for administrative functions?

    A. S

    B. 0

    C. 2

    D. 5

    E. 6

    F. All of the above

79. How would you manually set the minimum free disk space for an audit file before a warning is sent?

80. Syslog audit files should be placed in the same locations as binary data?

A. True

B. False

81. What command would you execute to verify that you have the appropriate rights to forcibly deallocate a device?

82. In which of these files would you find the list that specifies the ports used by the server processes as contact ports (also known as *well-known ports*)?

A. /usr/sbin/in.telnetd

B. /tmp/patch

C. /etc/services

D. /etc/inetd.conf

E. All of the above

83. Which of the following does Sun recommend for hardening your system and helping to protect against Trojan horse programs?

A. Removing unnecessary compilers

B. Securing file and directory permissions

C. Anti-virus software

D. Monitoring path variables

E. User awareness education

F. All of the above

84. Which of these is an ASET task that checks the integrity of, inspects, and makes modifications to system files mostly found in the /etc directory?

A. System files permissions tuning

B. System files checks

C. User and group checks

D. System configuration files check

E. Environment variables check

F. EEPROM check

G. Firewall setup

H. All of the above

85. To audit a role, which event(s) should be added to the flags line in the *audit_control* file?

86. Explain the usage of a Message Authentication Code (MAC).

87. The principle of isolating process spaces from each other is known as

    A. Virtualization

    B. Separation

    C. Defense in depth

    D. Compartmentalization

    E. All of the above

88. What is the purpose of choke points?

    A. Choke points are used to isolate firewalls.

    B. Choke points protect confidentiality of information.

    C. Choke points may be used only on TCP/IP networks.

    D. Choke points are for control and monitoring of dataflows.

    E. All of the above

89. Vulnerabilities are weaknesses which can be exploited by

    A. Risks

    B. Threats

    C. Hackers

    D. Software bugs

    E. All of the above

90. Why is risk management important?

    A. Because it is impossible to eliminate all risks

    B. Because it is not cost effective to eliminate all risks

    C. Because it is a good governance practice

    D. Because it improves business performance

    E. All of the above

91. Why should security awareness training be an ongoing concern?

    A. Because security risks and vulnerabilities change and evolve

    B. Because people need to refresh their knowledge periodically

    C. Because an organization's information systems change over time

    D. Because people may become complacent with time

    E. All of the above

92. Which of the following security domains are covered by ISO 17799?

- **A.** Security policy
- **B.** Access control
- **C.** Physical security
- **D.** Solaris security
- **E.** All of the above

93. Failed login attempts from terminal sessions are stored in which file?

- **A.** */etc/default/login*
- **B.** */etc/nologin*
- **C.** */etc/shadow*
- **D.** *var/adm/loginlog*
- **E.** All of the above

94. Surveys show that most organizations are at which level of the information security maturity model?

- **A.** Nonexistent
- **B.** Defined
- **C.** Detective
- **D.** Repeatable
- **E.** All of the above

95. Risk is a product of

- **A.** Threats – Vulnerabilities + Asset value
- **B.** Threats × Vulnerabilities + Asset value
- **C.** Threats × Vulnerabilities × Asset value
- **D.** Threats + Vulnerabilities × Asset value
- **E.** All of the above

96. Documents that set high-level goals, requirements, and priorities are called:

- **A.** Guidelines
- **B.** Procedures
- **C.** Standards
- **D.** Policies
- **E.** All of the above

97. Which of the following techniques can be used to identify current user login status?

- **A.** Access the */etc/shadow* file with superuser privileges
- **B.** Issue the command `logins`
- **C.** Issue the command `init s`

    D.   Access the */var/adm/loginlog* file with superuser privileges

    E.   All of the above

98. Which of these techniques can be used to capture unsuccessful login attempts?

    A.   Edit the */etc/default/login* file and uncomment the RETRIES entry

    B.   Create a *var/adm/loginlog* file

    C.   Edit the */etc/default/login* file and uncomment the SYSLOG=YES and SYSLOG_FAILED_LOGINS=0 entries

    D.   All of the above

99. You can specify events that should be audited by using the bsmrecord command.

    A.   True

    B.   False

100. With regard to classes of events, the *audit_event* file is the event database that can be read to find out which events are part of classes you can audit. Which event numbers are reserved for the Solaris Kernel events?

    A.   1–2047

    B.   2048–32767

    C.   6144–32767

    D.   32768–65535

    E.   All of the above

101. Which of the following can be used to control access to devices on a Solaris system?

    A.   Access control lists (ACLs)

    B.   Device policy

    C.   Device allocation

    D.   Basic Audit Reporting Tool (BART)

    E.   All of the above

102. When viewing your system's current patches from a terminal session, the output will display which of the following useful information?

    A.   A list of current installed patches

    B.   Whether a patch obsoletes a previous patch

    C.   Whether a patch is incompatible with other patches

    D.   What packages are directly affected by a patch

    E.   If there are any prerequisite patches for a current patch

    F.   All of the above

103. Which of the following directories are the most common targets for attackers to attempt to gain access to the operating system, especially for creating backdoors to the system?

    A. /etc

    B. /usr/aset

    C. /usr/local

    D. /devices

    E. All of the above

104. Which of the following is an example of the principle of least privilege?

    A. Programs—using privileges—that do not require making calls to `setuid`.

    B. System administrators can delegate privileged commands to non-root users without giving them full superuser access.

    C. A user should be given only the privileges or permissions necessary for performing a job.

    D. Privilege commands execute with administrative capabilities usually reserved for administrators.

    E. All of the above

105. Which command associates a user's login with a role, profile, and authorization in the /etc/user_attr database, which can also be used to grant a user access to a role?

    A. `ppriv`

    B. `smc &`

    C. `usermod`

    D. `roleadd`

    E. All of the above

106. To monitor and help prevent unauthorized changes from being made to system files, which of the following does Sun recommend using?

    A. Automated Security Enhancement Tool (ASET)

    B. Basic Security Module (BSM)

    C. Solaris cryptographic framework

    D. Tripwire

    E. All of the above

107. What command is used to display a list of mechanisms that can be used with the installed providers?

108. Which rights profile database contains the profile name and commands with specific security attributes?

   A. *prof_attr*

   B. *exec_attr*

   C. *user_attr*

   D. *passwd*

   E. *shadow*

   F. All of the above

109. Which of these can be deployed to monitor and help prevent unauthorized changes from being made to system files?

   A. Tripwire

   B. BSM

   C. Solaris cryptographic framework

   D. ASET

   E. All of the above

110. Which command would display the following output in a terminal session that could indicate that the system is being attacked?

```
10.16.3.11.22      10.16.3.100.21834      0      0   9112      0 SYN_RECEIVED
10.16.3.11.22      10.16.3.100.22090      0      0   9112      0 SYN_RECEIVED
10.16.3.11.22      10.16.3.100.22346      0      0   9112      0 SYN_RECEIVED
10.16.3.11.22      10.16.3.100.22602      0      0   9112      0 SYN_RECEIVED
10.16.3.11.22      10.16.3.100.22858      0      0   9112      0 SYN_RECEIVED
```

   A. `find directory -user root`

   B. `netstat -a -f inet`

   C. `showrev -p`

   D. `grep inetd.conf`

   E. All of the above

111. Who must be ultimately responsible for information security within organizations?

   A. Information security professionals

   B. Information systems auditors

   C. Top management

   D. Stockholders

   E. All of the above

112. Do insiders pose a threat to information security, and if so why?

    A. No, because they are bound by employment and confidentiality agreements.

    B. Yes, because they are not subject to access control.

    C. No, because they already have access to information.

    D. Yes, because they have more authorizations and knowledge.

    E. All of the above

113. Documents that are usually technical, detailed, and implement security policies are called

    A. Guidelines

    B. Normative acts

    C. Procedures

    D. Standards

    E. All of the above

114. Nonbinding recommendations on how to develop, define, and enforce security policies and procedures are known as

    A. Standards

    B. Auditing regulations

    C. Guidelines

    D. Control objectives

    E. All of the above

115. The syslog daemon is located in which directory?

    A. */etc*

    B. */etc/init.d*

    C. */usr/local*

    D. */usr/asset*

    E. */devices*

    F. All of the above

116. In the *audit_control* file, which arguments define which attributable and nonattributable events should be audited for the entire system?

    A. `flags`

    B. `minfree`

    C. `dir:`

    D. `naflags`

    E. All of the above

117. Which of these techniques can be used to set up a warning alias, which is the e-mail account that will receive warnings generated from the *audit_warn* script, such as when the minimum free-space level is reached?

   A. Redirect the *audit_warn* e-mail alias to the appropriate account

   B. Edit the *etc/security/audit_warn* file by changing the e-mail alias in the script at entry: `ADDRESS=audit_warn`

   C. Edit the *audit_control* file in your text editor and modify the `minfree` entry by specifying the *audit_warn* e-mail alias

   D. All of the above

118. Which of the following is a type of information commonly found in a BART manifest?

   A. Group ID

   B. Content

   C. User ID

   D. Permissions

   E. Size

   F. All of the above

119. By comparing BART manifests over time, which of the following can you accomplish?

   A. Detect corrupt files.

   B. Verify the integrity of files.

   C. Detect security breaches.

   D. Troubleshoot the system.

   E. All of the above

120. Which of the following should be added to the */etc/system* file manually to disable programs from using executable stacks?

   A. `set noexec_user_stack=1`

   B. `set noexec_user_stack_log=1`

   C. `set noexec_program_stack=0`

   D. `set noexec_user_stack_log=0`

   E. All of the above

121. Which type of attack occurs when a program process or task receives extraneous data that is not properly programmed?

   A. Program buffer overflow

   B. Ping of Death

   C. Executable stacks

    D. SYN flooding

    E. Smurf attacks

    F. All of the above

122. It is advisable not to assign rights profiles, privileges, and authorizations directly to users.

    A. True

    B. False

123. Which of the following types of applications comply with RBAC and therefore can check a user's authorizations before giving the user access?

    A. Audit administration commands

    B. The Solaris Management Console tool suite

    C. Printer administration commands

    D. Batch job commands

    E. Device commands

    F. All of the above

124. Explain the usage of message digest with regard to file integrity.

125. What command would you issue to remove a kernel software provider permanently?

126. Which rights profile database contains user and role information that supplements the *passwd* and *shadow* databases?

    A. *prof_attr*

    B. *exec_attr*

    C. *user_attr*

    D. *passwd*

    E. *shadow*

    F. All of the above

127. Which of the following are common forms of DoS attacks against Solaris operating systems?

    A. Program buffer overflow

    B. Extraneous IP ports

    C. Teardrop

    D. Executable stacks

    E. SYN flooding

    F. All of the above

128. Users with the appropriate rights and authorization can allocate and deallocate devices. Which of these authorizations is required to forcibly allocate a device?

    A. *solaris.device.allocate*

    B. *solaris.device.revoke*

    C. Both *solaris.device.allocate* and *solaris.device.revoke*

    D. All of the above

129. With regard to classes of events, the *audit_event* file is the event database that can be read to find out which events are part of classes you can audit. Which event numbers are available for third-party TCB applications?

    A. 1–2047

    B. 2048–32767

    C. 6144–32767

    D. 32768–65535

    E. All of the above

130. Which configuration file specifies classes of events that should always or never be audited for each user?

    A. *audit_control*

    B. *audit_startup*

    C. *audit_warn*

    D. *audit_user*

    E. All of the above

131. Which of these is a common run level used to stop the operating system and then reboot?

    A. S

    B. 0

    C. 2

    D. 5

    E. 6

    F. All of the above

132. Which of the following commands can be executed to switch between run levels on, and to perform functions such as halting and rebooting the Solaris operating system?

    A. `shutdown -y`

    B. `init (Run Level #)`

    C. `shutdown -i init-level -g grace-period -y`

    D. All of the above

133. Which of the following are events that are capable of creating audit logs?

   A. Privileged rights usage

   B. Object creation and destruction

   C. Permission changes

   D. Process creation and destruction

   E. Thread creation and destruction

   F. All of the above

134. Which of the following can be used to control access to files on a Solaris system?

   A. Access control lists (ACLs)

   B. Device policy

   C. Device allocation

   D. Basic Audit Reporting Tool (BART)

   E. All of the above

135. To disable an extraneous service and associated IP port, which file would you edit?

   A. */usr/sbin/in.telnetd*

   B. */tmp/patch*

   C. */etc/services*

   D. */etc/inetd.conf*

   E. All of the above

136. It is advisable to assign privileges and authorizations directly to roles.

   A. True

   B. False

137. What command displays the provider feature policy? If a provider is specified, this command will display the name of the provider with the mechanism policy enforced on it only.

138. Which of the following can check for user IDs (UIDs), group IDs (GIDs), privileges, or authorizations via an application or command?

   A. Authorization

   B. Privilege

   C. Privileged application

   D. Rights profile

   E. Role

   F. All of the above

139. Which of these techniques can be implemented for the most efficient auditing while still adhering to security prioritizations?

A. Auditing only a small percentage of users at any one time

B. Compressing files

C. Archiving older audit logs

D. Monitoring in real time

E. Automatically increasing unusual event auditing

F. All of the above

140. Which of these commands can be executed to display only the extended user login status for Becky Blake, whose login name is *b_blake*?

A. `logins`

B. `logins b_blake`

C. `logins -p`

D. `logins -x -l b_blake`

E. All of the above

141. With regard to the Solaris auditing subsystem, what is the directory of last resort?

142. What is the highest evaluation assurance level under Common Criteria that may be reached using commonly accepted best practices in systems/software development?

A. EAL7

B. EAL5

C. EAL4

D. EAL3

E. All of the above

143. Information security policies and procedures are a(n):

A. Technical control

B. Administrative control

C. Form of access control

D. Operational control

E. All of the above

144. Which of the following are applications or commands that check for privileges?

A. `prof_attr`

B. Commands that control processes

C. File commands

D. `ifconfig`

E. `user_attr`

F. All of the above

145. Which of the following provide for implementations of algorithms in software?

A. Hardware plug-ins

B. Kernel-level plug-ins

C. User-level plug-ins

D. All of the above

146. What command is used to prevent the use of a user-level mechanism?

147. Which of the following can be granted to a command, user, role, or system, and gives a process the ability to perform an operation and therefore enforces security policy in the kernel?

A. Authorization

B. Privilege

C. Privileged application

D. Rights profile

E. Role

F. All of the above

148. In which of the following is the same cryptographic key used for both encryption and decryption?

A. Asymmetric algorithm

B. Public key

C. Secret key

D. Symmetric algorithm

E. All of the above

149. For an attack to take place and succeed, which of the following should be present?

A. Opportunity

B. Means

C. Motives

D. All of the above

150. If a provider is specified, what command will display the name of the specified provider and the mechanism list that can be used with that provider?

C

Final Test Answers

1. ☑ **B** and **C.** Providers are cryptographic plug-ins that consumers use. According to Sun. the framework allows only three types of plug-ins: user-level plug-ins that are shared objects that provide services by using PKCS #11 libraries, kernel-level plug-ins that provide for implementations of algorithms in software, and hardware plug-ins that are device drivers and their associated hardware accelerators.

☒ **A** is wrong because consumers, not providers, can be applications, end users, or kernel operations.

2. ☑ **C, D,** and **E.** Role information can be found in the *passwd, shadow,* and *user_attr* databases. The *user_attr* database contains user and role information that supplements the *passwd* and *shadow* databases. This database also contains extended user attributes such as authorizations, rights profiles, and assigned roles.

☒ **A** and **B** are wrong because the rights profile name and authorizations can be found in the *prof_attr* database, while the rights profile name and commands with specific security attributes are stored in the *exec_attr* database.

3. ☑ To set the minimum free disk space for an audit file before a warning is sent, you need to modify the */etc/security/audit_control* file by adding the `minfree` argument followed by a percentage.

4. ☑ **B.** To actively detect and display superuser access attempts on the console in real time, uncomment the `CONSOLE=/dev/console` entry in the */etc/default/su* file.

☒ **A** is wrong because you will enable remote superuser login access. **C** is wrong because by uncommenting the `CONSOLE=/dev/console` entry in the */etc/default/login* file you will disable remote superuser login access. **D** is wrong because that will simply turn off the detection and display of superuser access attempts directly on the console.

5. ☑ **B, C,** and **D.** A process life cycle–based approach to information security management is appropriate because it takes into account changing information systems environments, it is business-oriented, and is considered a good practice.

☒ **A** is incorrect because the process life cycle-based approach is not the only existing approach to information security management.

6. ☑ **E.** All of the answers are correct. It is important to protect software version numbers and other details of your systems in order to make attackers spend more time and effort on an attack, to avoid easy identification of bugs and vulnerabilities of deployed software, to avoid or minimize script kiddie attacks, and to comply with principles of minimization and least privilege.

7. ☑ **B.** False. When default executable stacks with permissions set to read, write, and execute are allowed, programs *may* be inherently vulnerable to buffer overflow attacks.

☒ **A** is incorrect because by default programs are not inherently vulnerable to stack smashing. This is especially true when the latest patches have been applied.

8. ☑   **D.** A fork bomb is a system process that replicates itself until it exceeds the maximum number of allowable processes.

☒   **A** is wrong because a Trojan horse program is a malicious program that is disguised as some useful software. **B** is incorrect because a worm is a self-replicating program that will copy itself from system to system. **C** is wrong because a logic bomb is code that is inserted into programming code designed to execute under specific circumstances. **E** is incorrect because a rootkit is used not only to provide remote backdoor access to attackers but also to hide the attacker's presence on the system.

9. ☑   **B** and **D.** RBAC allows system administrators to delegate privileged commands to non-root users without giving them full superuser access to the system. Similarly, users can be assigned only the exact privileges and permissions necessary for performing a job.

☒   **A** is wrong because, although it's true that privilege commands execute with administrative capabilities usually reserved for administrators, that statement does not describe a benefit to RBAC. **C** is wrong because Sun's best practices dictate that you do not assign rights profiles, privileges, and authorizations directly to users, or privileges and authorizations directly to roles. It's best to assign authorizations to rights profiles, rights profiles to roles, and roles to users.

10. ☑   **C.** The purpose of audit trails and logs is to provide accountability in information systems.

☒   **A** is correct but is not the best answer; choices **B** and **D** are wrong. The issue of whether audit trails and logs can be used in court proceedings would depend on the particular jurisdiction and is outside the scope of this book; audit trail and logs are detective controls but may function as deterrent controls as well when their existence is known to potential attackers.

11. ☑   **E.** All answers are correct. The security life cycle process consists of prevention, detection, response, and deterrence.

12. ☑   **F.** All answers are correct. A message digest is a digital signature for a stream of binary data as verification that the data was not altered since the signature was first generated. The MD5 (for shorter message digests) and the Secure Hashing Algorithm (SHA1, for larger message digests) are among the most popular message digest algorithms. The Solaris Fingerprint Database (sfpDB) is a free tool from Sun that allows you to check the integrity of system files online through cryptographic checksums stored in the database. System files checks is an ASET task used as a file comparison check from a master file that is created when the task is first executed.

13. ☑   A right is a named collection, consisting of commands, authorizations to use specific applications (or to perform specific functions within an application), and other, previously created, rights, whose use can be granted or denied to an administrator.

14. ☑   Providers are cryptographic plug-ins that applications, end users, or kernel operations— which are all termed "consumers"—use. The Solaris cryptographic framework allows only three types of plug-ins: user-level plug-ins that are shared objects that provide services by using PKCS #11 libraries, kernel-level plug-ins that provide for implementations of algorithms in software, and hardware plug-ins that are device drivers and their associated hardware accelerators.

15. ☑ **B.** Fingerprints can be used for *what you are*, or biometric, authentication.
☒ **A** is wrong because *what you have* authentication refers to token-based authentication mechanisms. **C** is wrong because there is no such term as biological identification in information security. **D** is wrong because the use of fingerprints does not simplify authentication or identification since it requires additional configuration and tuning.

16. ☑ **D.** The Basic Audit Reporting Tool (BART) is used to check the integrity of files.
☒ **A** is wrong because access control lists (ACLs) are used to control access to files. **B** and **C** are wrong because device policy and device allocation are used to control access to devices.

17. ☑ **D.** During a SYN attack, the attacker sends a flood of connection requests but does not respond to any of the replies. This is referred to as a half-open connection, because during a normal connection between a client and a server, the connection is considered to be "open" after the handshake process. When the server has not received an ACK from the client, the connection is considered to be half-open.
☒ **A** is incorrect because a program buffer overflow occurs when a program process or task receives unwarranted and/or an abundance of data that is not properly programmed. **B** is incorrect because Ping of Death is a malformed ICMP packet attack in which an attacker sends an oversized ping packet in an attempt to overflow the system's buffer. **C** is incorrect because executable stacks involve program buffer overflows. **E** is incorrect because a Smurf attack involves a broadcasted ping request to every system on the target's network with a spoofed return address of the target.

18. ☑ **B.** A worm is a self-replicating program that will copy itself from system to system, sometimes using up all available resources on a target or installing a backdoor on the system.
☒ **A** is incorrect because a Trojan horse program is a malicious program that is disguised as some useful software. **C** is wrong because a logic bomb is code that is inserted into programming code designed to execute under specific circumstances. **D** is incorrect because a fork bomb is a system process that replicates itself until it exceeds the maximum number of allowable processes. **E** is incorrect because a rootkit is used not only to provide remote backdoor access to attackers but also to hide the attacker's presence on the system. Some types of rootkit utilities exploit the use of loadable kernel modules to modify the running kernel for malicious intent.

19. ☑ **D.** The `roleadd` command can be used to create roles and associates a role with an authorization or a profile from the command line.
☒ **A** is wrong because to check the privileges available to your current shell's process, you would use the `ppriv -v pid $$` command. **B** is wrong because in order to start the management console you would issue the `/usr/sbin/smc &` command. **C** is wrong because the `usermod` command associates a user's login with a role, profile, and authorization in the */etc/user_attr* database, which can also be used to grant a user access to a role.

20. ☑ **A.** Consumers can be applications, end users, or kernel operations.

☒ **B** and **C** are wrong because providers are cryptographic plug-ins that consumers use. According to Sun, the framework allows only three types of plug-ins: user-level plug-ins that are shared objects that provide services by using PKCS #11 libraries, kernel-level plug-ins that provide for implementations of algorithms in software, and hardware plug-ins that are device drivers and their associated hardware accelerators.

21. ☑ **D.** A rights profile can be assigned to a role or user as a collection of administrative functions. Rights profiles can contain authorizations, privilege commands, or other rights profiles.

☒ **A** is wrong because authorization can be assigned to a role or user but is typically included in a rights profile. **B** is wrong because a privilege can be granted to a command, user, role, or system. Privilege gives a process the ability to perform an operation and therefore enforces security policy in the kernel. **C** is wrong because a privileged application can check for user IDs (UIDs), group IDs (GIDs), privileges, or authorizations via an application or command. **E** is wrong because a role is a predefined identity that can run privileged applications.

22. ☑ **C.** A logic bomb is code that is inserted into programming code designed to execute under specific circumstances.

☒ **A** is wrong because a Trojan horse program is a malicious program that is disguised as some useful software. **B** is incorrect because a worm is a self-replicating program that will copy itself from system-to-system. **D** is wrong because a fork bomb is a system process that replicates itself until it exceeds the maximum number of allowable processes. **E** is incorrect because a rootkit is used not only to provide remote backdoor access to attackers but also to hide the attacker's presence on the system.

23. ☑ **C.** The user and group checks task is used to verify the integrity of user accounts, their passwords, and their groups. The primary check is made from the *passwd* and *group* files, and the passwords in *local*, and *NIS*, and *NIS+* files.

☒ **A** is wrong because the system files permissions tuning task automatically sets system file permissions according to the security level you choose. **B** is incorrect because system files checks is a file comparison check from a master file that is created when the task is first executed. For each security level a list of directories that contains files to check is automatically defined; however, this list can be modified. **D** is incorrect because during the system configuration files check, ASET checks the integrity of, inspects, and makes modifications to system files mostly found in the */etc* directory, and then reports problems in the *sysconf.rpt* file. **E** is incorrect because the environment variables check task inspects the PATH and UMASK environment variables. These are found in the */.profile*, */.login*, and */.cshrc* files. **F** is incorrect because the EEPROM check inspects the eeprom security parameter to ensure that it is set to the appropriate security level and has not been tampered with. **G** is incorrect because the firewall setup task simply ensures that the system can be safely used as a perimeter gateway or secure network relay.

24. ☑ **B** and **D.** When you disallow executable stacks, programs that attempt to execute code on their stack will abort with a core dump. At that time, a warning message will be displayed with the name of the program, its process ID, and the UID of the user who ran the program. In addition, the message can be logged by syslog when the syslog kern facility is set to notice level.
    ☒ **A** is incorrect because when a program attempts to execute code on its stack when you disallow executable stacks, the program will abort. **C** is incorrect because whether or not you are monitoring executable stacks has nothing to do with the results of a program that attempts to execute code on its stack.

25. ☑ **E.** A Smurf attack involves a broadcasted ping request to every system on the target's network with a spoofed return address of the target.
    ☒ **A** is incorrect because a program buffer overflow occurs when a program process or task receives unwarranted and/or an abundance of data that is not properly programmed. **B** is incorrect because Ping of Death is a malformed ICMP packet attack by which an attacker sends an oversized ping packet in an attempt to overflow the system's buffer. **C** is incorrect because executable stacks involve program buffer overflows. **D** is incorrect because during a SYN attack the attacker sends a flood of connection requests but does not respond to any of the replies.

26. ☑ **A.** True. A popular form of permissible backdoor that can potentially be exploitable is a program setup by a programmer to provide remote access to the system to perform debugging and troubleshooting tasks.

27. ☑ **C** and **D.** The *bsmconv* script is used to enable the auditing service, which also enables device allocation, which is enforced during user allocation to require user authorization to access a peripheral device such as a CD-ROM or printer.
    ☒ **A** is wrong because the AUE_MODDEVPLCY audit event is part of the as audit class by default, and is used to audit changes in device policy. **B** is incorrect because device policy is a default kernel-level mechanism that restricts and prevents access to devices integral to the system. **E** is wrong because to modify or update a device policy for a specific device to restrict or prevent access, you would use the update_drv -a -p *policy device-driver* command.

28. ☑ **B** and **E.** Device policy is a default kernel-level mechanism that restricts and prevents access to devices integral to the system by mandating that processes that open such a device require certain privileges such as reading and writing. To modify or update a device policy for a specific device to restrict or prevent access, you would use the update_drv -a -p *policy device-driver* command.
    ☒ **A** is wrong because the AUE_MODDEVPLCY audit event is part of the as audit class by default, which is used to audit changes in device policy. **C** is incorrect because the *bsmconv* script is used to enable the auditing service, which also enables device allocation. **D** is wrong because device allocation is enforced during user allocation to require user authorization to access a peripheral device such as a CD-ROM or printer.

29. ☑ **E.** The `auditreduce` command can be used to merge audit files into a single output source to create an audit trail.

☒ **A** is wrong because that command is used to refresh the kernel. **B** is wrong because that command is used to refresh the auditing service. **C** is wrong because you would run the *bsmconv* script to enable and disable the auditing service. **D** is wrong because the `bsmrecord` command can be used to display record formats.

30. ☑ **F.** All answers are correct. Disabling user logins can be accomplished by creating a */etc/nologin* file, bringing the system down to single-user mode (by issuing the `init S` or `shutdown` command with the default init state), and disabling user accounts individually with the Solaris Management Console (SMC) interface.

31. ☑ **A** and **C.** Certification is the technical evaluation of systems, and it is granted by independent and qualified third parties. Certification does not require accreditation. Certification is a basis for accreditation, but the responsibility for the accredited system lies mainly with the management of the organization which accredits the system.

☒ **B** is incorrect because certification is not done by an organization's management. **D** is incorrect because certification does not require accreditation.

32. ☑ **B** and **C.** The defense against brute-force attacks is to make the amount of time and computations required to conduct an exhaustive search impossible to afford by using a sufficiently large set—that is, longer passwords and keys.

☒ **A** and **D** are incorrect. The use of strong authentication alone would not guarantee protection against brute-force attacks, and Role-Based Access Control does not address the risk of brute-force attacks.

33. ☑ **A, B,** and **D.** Cost-benefit analysis is necessary because organizations cannot reduce all risks to zero, it increases an organization's return on investment, and it is a good governance practice.

☒ **C** is wrong because cost-benefit analysis is not related to, and does not prevent, denial of service attacks.

34. ☑ **B** and **D.** A trusted system or component has the power to break a security policy. This may seem like an oxymoron—how do you trust a component that can break your security policy? Although it is a good engineering practice to have as few trusted components as possible (remember the principles of least privilege and minimization), it is impossible to eliminate them altogether. Because of this, trusted systems are subject to more testing and verification than non-trusted systems.

☒ **A** and **C** are incorrect because a high security system is not necessarily a trusted system, and trusted systems do not refer to operating systems only.

35. ☑ **C.** Continuous authentication protects against hijacking attacks but does not protect against sniffing unless all traffic is encrypted.

☒ Answers **A** and **B** are too general. **D** is incorrect because continuous authentication does not protect against sniffing unless all traffic is encrypted.

36. ☑ **A.** True. To disable a service that is defined in inetd, you simply comment it out in the */etc/inetd.conf* file by inserting a hash character in the very first character position before the service. To activate the change, simply restart the process or reboot the operating system.
☒ **B** is incorrect because unless the service is enabled in inetd, the port and service will not be listening for connection attempts.

37. ☑ **B and E.** A rootkit is used not only to provide remote backdoor access to attackers but also to hide the attacker's presence on the system. Some types of rootkit utilities exploit the use of loadable kernel modules to modify the running kernel for malicious intent.
☒ **A** is wrong because a Trojan horse program is a malicious program that is disguised as some useful software. **C** is wrong because a logic bomb is code that is inserted into programming code designed to execute under specific circumstances. **D** is wrong because a fork bomb is a system process that replicates itself until it exceeds the maximum number of allowable processes.

38. ☑ A role is a special user account used to grant rights. Users can assume only those roles they have been granted permission to assume. Once a user takes on a role, the user relinquishes his or her own user identity and takes on the properties, including the rights, of that role. With RBAC each user is assigned one or more roles, and each role is assigned one or more privileges that are permitted to users in that role. Security administration with RBAC consists of determining the operations that must be executed by persons in particular jobs, and assigning employees to the proper roles. Complexities introduced by mutually exclusive roles or role hierarchies are handled by the RBAC software, making security administration easier.

39. ☑ **C and D.** Random keys can be generated using the `encrypt` and `mac` commands.
☒ **A** is wrong because you can generate the symmetric key with the `dd` command. **B** is wrong because you can issue the `digest` command to compute a message digest for one or more files.

40. ☑ The `cryptoadm list -p` command displays the mechanism policy for the installed providers. It also displays the provider feature policy. If a provider is specified, the command will display the name of the provider with the mechanism policy enforced on it only.

41. ☑ **D.** The `bsmrecord` command can be used to display record formats.
☒ **A** is wrong because that command is used to refresh the kernel. **B** is wrong because that command is used to refresh the auditing service. **C** is wrong because you would run the *bsmconv* script to enable and disable the auditing service. **E** is wrong because the `auditreduce` command can be used to merge audit files into a single output source to create an audit trail.

42. ☑ **B.** To view device policies for all devices or specific ones, you would use the `getdevpolicy` command.
☒ **A** is wrong because `list_devices` is used to display information about allocatable devices. **C** is wrong because a user with the appropriate rights and authorization can allocate a device by issuing the `allocate` *device-name* command.

43. ☑ **C.** Compensating controls offset deficiencies of other controls.
☒ There is no such term as defensive controls in information security, so that rules out **B.** Choices **A** and **D** are incorrect because preventive controls aim to prevent security violations and recovery controls are not intended to offset deficiencies of other controls.

44. ☑ **B.** This answser is correct because even if A trusts B, and B trusts C, it does not mean that A automatically trusts C.
☒ **A** and **C** are wrong because trust is not transitive: if A trusts B, and B trusts C, it does not mean that A automatically trusts C, or vice versa. **D** is wrong because trust is not symmetric: if A trusts B, it doesn't mean that B trusts A.

45. ☑ **A, B,** and **C.** Detection is important because it shows whether or not preventive controls work, because it serves as a quality and reliability control, and because no usable preventive control is perfect.
☒ **D** is incorrect because the security level of the environment has no bearing on the need for detective controls.

46. ☑ **A.** True. The su program usage, by default, is already monitored through the *etc/default/su* file as `SULOG=/var/adm/sulog`, and the syslog logging facility will determine whether or not to log all su attempts with the `SYSLOG=YES` entry.

47. ☑ **A.** The primary and secondary audit directories are specified in the *audit_control* file.
☒ **B** is wrong because the audit policy is established by the `auditconfig` command, which is automatically started in the *audit_startup* script. **C** is incorrect because the *audit_warn* script generates mail to an e-mail alias called *audit_warn*. **D** is wrong because the *audit_user* file defines specific users and classes of events that should always or never be audited for each user.

48. ☑ **C.** Run the *bsmconv* script to enable and disable the auditing service.
☒ **A** is wrong because that command is used to refresh the kernel. **B** is wrong because that command is used to refresh the auditing service. **D** is wrong because the `bsmrecord` command can be used to display record formats. **E** is wrong because the `auditreduce` command can be used to merge audit files into a single output source to create an audit trail.

49. ☑ **D.** The Basic Audit Reporting Tool (BART) is used to check the integrity of files by reporting file-level changes that have occurred on the system.
☒ **A** is wrong because access control lists (ACLs) are used to control access to files. **B** and **C** are wrong because device policy and device allocation are used to control access to devices.

50. ☑ **F.** All of the answers are correct. To prevent DoS attacks against the Solaris operating system, Sun advocates disabling executable stacks, disabling extraneous IP ports, using egress filtering, monitoring the network, using firewalls, and implementing a patch update program.

51. ☑ **A.** The system files permissions tuning task automatically sets system file permissions according to the security level you choose. At the high level setting, permissions are assigned to restrict access; at the medium level, permissions are tightened just enough for most normal operating environments; and at the low level setting, permissions are set for open sharing.

☒ **B** is incorrect because system files checks is a file comparison check from a master file that is created when the task is first executed. For each security level a list of directories that contains files to check is automatically defined; however, this list can be modified. **C** is incorrect because the user and group checks task is used to verify the integrity of user accounts, their passwords, and their groups. **D** is incorrect because during the system configuration files check, ASET checks the integrity of, inspects, and makes modifications to system files mostly found in the */etc* directory and reports problems in the *sysconf.rpt* file. **E** is incorrect because the environment variables check task inspects the PATH and UMASK environment variables. These are found in the */.profile*, */.login*, and */.cshrc* files. **F** is incorrect because the EEPROM check inspects the eeprom security parameter to ensure that it is set to the appropriate security level and has not been tampered with. **G** is incorrect because the firewall setup task simply ensures that the system can be safely used as a perimeter gateway or secure network relay.

52. ☑ The principle of least privilege asserts that a user should not be granted any more privileges or permissions than those necessary for performing a specific job.

53. ☑ **C.** User-level plug-ins are shared objects that provide services by using PKCS #11 libraries.
☒ **A** is wrong because hardware plug-ins are device drivers and their associated hardware accelerators. **B** is wrong because kernel-level plug-ins provide for implementations of algorithms in software.

54. ☑ To disable a kernel software provider, issue the cryptoadm disable *provider* command; to restore an inactive software provider, issue the cryptoadm refresh command.

55. ☑ **C.** At least two different authentication methods are necessary for strong authentication.
☒ Long passwords do not provide strong authentication on their own, so answer **A** is not correct. Strong authentication does not necessarily require the use of smart cards, as stated in **B**. And **C** is wrong because biometrics does not necessarily provide strong authentication on its own.

56. ☑ **E.** All of the answers are correct. Authentication is needed to obtain proof of claimed identity, to implement access control, to establish accountability, and to allow for different users with different authorizations.

57. ☑ **C.** User trust refers to users' expectations of reasonable security of systems, which in practical terms is the responsibility of security administrators who enforce security policy set by the management. User trust may also refer to expectations of reasonable operation of systems (hardware and software), which is closely linked to the issue of assurance. User trust is gained and maintained by definition of sound security policies and their professional implementation and enforcement.
☒ **A, B,** and **D** are incorrect because user trust is not guaranteed by trusted systems, it is not defined in security policy, and it is not transitive and bi-directional.

58. ☑ **C.** Deterrent controls are created to discourage potential attackers. Deterrent controls may potentially be confused with preventive controls, and although both types of controls aim to preclude security violations from happening, they try to do so at different times.

☒ **A** and **B** are incorrect because deterrent controls are not a backup for detective controls and they do not necessarily prevent attacks from happening. **D** is incorrect because, while preventive security controls try to prevent a breach of security after the adversary has decided to attack but before the attack has succeeded, deterrent controls try to discourage the attacker from attacking in the first place by demonstrating that the attack is not going to succeed and even if it does, it will be detected and dealt with.

59. ☑ **C.** The `logins` command with the `-p` option is used to display which users do not have assigned passwords.

☒ **A** is wrong because the `logins` command will display general information concerning all login accounts organized in ascending order by user ID. **B** is incorrect because the `-x` argument will display extended information regarding all login accounts. **D** is wrong because Solaris keeps track of each user login and records login attempts in the *var/adm/loginlog* file.

60. ☑ Audit policy determines the characteristics of the audit records. When auditing is enabled, the contents of the *etc/security/audit_startup* file determine the *audit policy*.

61. ☑ **B.** After you start the auditing service in a production environment, there may be times when you'll need to tweak the configuration to audit more classes or perhaps audit specific users more closely. After making changes, you'll need to update the auditing service. This restarts the auditd daemon, which in effect will apply the new configuration changes to the service. To refresh the auditing service, issue the command `auditconfig -conf`.

☒ **A** is wrong because that command is used to refresh the kernel. **C** is wrong because you would run the *bsmconv* script to enable and disable the auditing service. **D** is wrong because the `bsmrecord` command can be used to display record formats. **E** is wrong because the `auditreduce` command can be used to merge audit files into a single output source to create an audit trail.

62. ☑ **B.** False. You can create a manifest of more than one file by separating the files with a space, not a comma.

63. ☑ **C.** To verify that a patch was successfully installed, issue the `shorev` command `showrev -p`, or to verify a specific individual patch, use `showrev -p | grep filename`, where *filename* is the name of the patch.

☒ **A** is incorrect because `grep filename` is an option to the `showrev` command when verifying that a specific patch was successfully installed. **B** is incorrect because the command `showpatch -p` does not exist. **D** is incorrect because vi is the system's visual editor, which is used to create and modify text within files. Depending on where you executed the command `vi system`, the editor would either create a new file entitled *system* or open the current system file for editing.

64. ☑ **B.** Ping of Death is a malformed ICMP packet attack in which an attacker sends an oversized ping packet in an attempt to overflow the system's buffer.

☒ **A** is incorrect because a program buffer overflow occurs when a program process or task receives unwarranted and/or an abundance of data that is not properly programmed. **C** is incorrect because executable stacks involve program buffer overflows. **D** is incorrect because during a SYN attack, the attacker sends a flood of connection requests but does not respond to any of the replies. **E** is incorrect because a Smurf attack involves a broadcasted ping request to every system on the target's network with a spoofed return address of the target.

65. ☑ **A, B,** and **D.** To harden your system and help protect against Trojan horse programs, Sun recommends that path variables do not contain a parameter indicated with a dot (.) that could cause the system to search for executables or libraries within that path, as well as a search path for root or superuser that contains the current directory.

☒ **C** is wrong because a forward slash is legitimately used in the search path to indicate root and subdirectories.

66. ☑ **C.** Checksum uses the `sum` command to produce a cyclical-redundancy-check (CRC) and block count for files that can help prevent backdoor attacks.

☒ **A** is incorrect because ASET enables you to monitor and restrict access to system files and directories with automated administration governed by a preset security level (low, medium, or high). **B** is wrong because a message digest is a digital signature for a stream of binary data as verification that the data was not altered since the signature was first generated. **D** is incorrect because the EEPROM check is an ASET task that inspects the `eeprom` security parameter to ensure that it is set to the appropriate security level and has not been tampered with.

67. ☑ **A, B,** and **D.** Every process has four sets of privileges: the effective privilege set (E), which are privileges currently in use (note that processes can add permitted privileges to the set); the inheritable privilege set (I), which are privileges a process can inherit; the permitted privilege set (P), which are privileges available for use now; and the limit privilege set (L), which are outside privilege limits of which processes can shrink but never extend.

☒ **C** and **E** are wrong because they do not represent any known existing privileges.

68. ☑ **A, B** and **C.** Cryptography provides for the integrity, confidentiality, and authenticity of information.

☒ **D** is wrong because RBAC is a system of controlling which users have access to resources based on the role of the user. **E** is wrong because checksum is a simple error-detection scheme.

69. ☑ The `cryptoadm list` command displays the list of installed providers.

70. ☑ **A** and **B.** With asymmetric (public key) algorithms, two keys are used: one to encrypt a message and another to decrypt it.

☒ **C** and **D** are wrong because in symmetric (secret key) algorithms, the same key is used for both encryption and decryption—anyone knowing the key can both encrypt and decrypt messages.

71. ☑ **A.** To check the privileges available to your current shell's process, you would use the `ppriv -v pid $$` command.

☒ **B** is wrong because to start the management console, you would issue the `/usr/sbin/smc & command.` **C** is wrong because the `usermod` command associates a user's login with a role, profile, and authorization in the /etc/user_attr database, which can also be used to grant a user access to a role. **D** is wrong because the `roleadd` command can be used to create roles and associates a role with an authorization or a profile from the command line.

72. ☑ **B.** A system files check is a file comparison check from a master file that is created when the task is first executed. For each security level, a list of directories that contains files to check is automatically defined; however, this list can be modified.

☒ **A** is incorrect because the system files permissions tuning task automatically sets system file permissions according to the security level you choose. **C** is incorrect because the user and group checks task is used to verify the integrity of user accounts, their passwords, and their groups. **D** is incorrect because during the system configuration files check ASET checks the integrity of, inspects, and makes modifications to system files mostly found in the /etc directory, and reports problems in the *sysconf.rpt* file. **E** is incorrect because the environment variables check task inspects the PATH and UMASK environment variables. These are found in the /.*profile*, /.*login*, and /.*cshrc* files. **F** is incorrect because the EEPROM check inspects the `eeprom` security parameter to ensure that it is set to the appropriate security level and has not been tampered with. **G** is incorrect because the firewall setup task simply ensures that the system can be safely used as a perimeter gateway or secure network relay.

73. ☑ **B.** False. The principle of least privilege does not only apply to user accounts but is a universally applicable principle.

74. ☑ **C** and **D.** A threat is anyone or anything that can exploit a vulnerability. Threats to information systems may be grouped into natural, physical, and logical threats.

☒ **A** and **B** are incorrect because the absence of security mechanisms is not a threat, and threat is not the opposite of assurance.

75. ☑ **C.** The most effective defense against spoofing is the use of cryptographic authentication and digital signatures.

☒ **A** is incorrect because encryption does not necessarily protect against spoofing. There is no such term as cryptographic initiation (**B**), and secret addresses don't make sense (**D**).

76. ☑ **A, B,** and **D.** Depending on the jurisdiction and industry, incident response capability may be required but it is not required in all cases.

☒ **C** is wrong because incident response capability is not required by law.

77. ☑ **B** and **C.** Sun's policy mandates that passwords must be composed of between 6 and 15 letters, numbers, and special characters, and must have at least 2 alphabetic characters and at least 1 numeric or special character within the first 6 characters.

☒ **A** and **D** are wrong because they are part of industry-recognized security recommendations for creating passwords and are not mandated by Sun's password policy.

78. ☑ **A.** By issuing `init S` you will go into single-user mode.

☒ **B** is wrong because `init 0` is used to go into firmware maintenance mode. **C** is wrong because `init 2` is used to go into multi-user state where NFS is not running. **D** is wrong because `init 5` is used to shut down the operating system altogether. **E** is incorrect because by issuing `init 6` you will stop the operating system and reboot.

79. ☑ To set the minimum free disk space for an audit file before a warning is sent, you need to modify the */etc/security/audit_control* file by adding the `minfree` argument followed by a percentage. It's important to first save a backup of the original file before making changes. For example, to set the minimum free-space level for all audit file systems so that a warning is sent when 15 percent of the file system is available, edit the *audit_control* file and modify the following line item: `minfree:xx`, where *xx* is a percentage less than 100.

80. ☑ **B.** False. The syslog text logs can generate massive log files so be sure to monitor and archive them regularly. In addition, you should never store syslog audit files in the same location as binary data.

81. ☑ To verify that you have the appropriate rights to forcibly deallocate a device (for example, `solaris.device.revoke`), you can issue the `auths` command.

82. ☑ **C.** The */etc/services* file specifies the ports used by the server processes as contact ports, which are also known as well-known ports.

☒ **A** is incorrect because that file is used with the telnet service. **B** is incorrect because the file does not typically exist. **D** is incorrect because the *inetd.conf* file defines how the inetd daemon handles common Internet service requests.

83. ☑ **F.** All of the answers are correct. To harden your system and help protect against Trojan horse programs, Sun recommends user awareness education, installing and updating anti-virus software, removing unnecessary compilers, securing file and directory permissions, and monitoring path variables.

84. ☑ **D.** During the system configuration files check, ASET checks the integrity of, inspects, and makes modifications to system files mostly found in the */etc* directory, and reports problems in the *sysconf.rpt* file.

☒ **A** is incorrect because the system files permissions tuning task automatically sets system file permissions according to the security level you choose. **B** is incorrect because system files checks is a file comparison check from a master file that is created when the task is first executed. **C** is incorrect because the user and group checks task is used to verify the integrity of user accounts, their passwords, and their groups. **E** is incorrect because the environment variables check task inspects the `PATH` and `UMASK` environment variables. These are found in the */.profile*, */.login*, and */.cshrc* files. **F** is incorrect because the EEPROM check inspects the `eeprom` security parameter to ensure that it is set to the appropriate security level and has not been tampered with. **G** is incorrect because the firewall setup task simply ensures that the system can be safely used as a perimeter gateway or secure network relay.

85. ☑   To audit a role, you should add the ua or the as event to the flags line in the *audit_control* file, and then start the auditing service.

86. ☑   Without altering the original file and to protect a digest, you can compute a message authentication code (MAC) of a file.

87. ☑   **D.** Compartmentalization is the isolation of process spaces from each other in order to minimize the effect of a security violation in one compartment on another.
☒   Answer **A,** virtualization, is a related concept but is not the correct answer. **B** is wrong because compartmentalization is the correct term. **C** is wrong because defense in depth is about using several types and/or layers of defense.

88. ☑   **D.** Choke points are logical "narrow channels" that can be easily monitored and controlled.
☒   **A** is wrong because choke points are not used to isolate firewalls. Choke points do not affect confidentiality of information, so **B** is wrong. And **C** is not the answer because choke points are not protocol-dependent.

89. ☑   **B** and **C.** Vulnerabilities can be exploited by threats, and malicious hackers can pose a threat.
☒   **A** and **D** are incorrect because risks and software bugs do not exploit vulnerabilities—risk is the possibility of an exploit and software bugs are vulnerabilities.

90. ☑   **F.** All of the answers are correct. Risk is the likelihood and cost of a threat exploiting a vulnerability. Information security management is about risk management because in the absolute majority of cases it is either impossible or cost-ineffective to eliminate all risks. In these cases, risk management comes to the rescue and helps us to understand risks and decide what risks to minimize, what risks to transfer (insure against), and what risks to accept.

91. ☑   **E.** All of the answers are correct. To address all of these concerns, security awareness training should be held regularly.

92. ☑   **A, B,** and **C.** ISO 17799 is a *Code of Practice for Information Security Management* and does not cover any specific products or systems such as Solaris.
☒   **D** is incorrect because ISO 17799 does not cover the Solaris operating environment specifically but is an information security management standard.

93. ☑   **D.** Solaris keeps track of each terminal session login attempts in the *var/adm/loginlog* file.
☒   **A** is wrong because */etc/default/login* involves syslog and monitoring *all* unsuccessful login attempts. **B** is wrong because */etc/nologin* is used to disable user logins. **C** is incorrect because the */etc/shadow* file can be accessed to determine which accounts are locked or disabled and which do not currently have assigned passwords.

94. ☑   **D.** Most organizations are at the repeatable level of the information security maturity model.
☒   **C** is inappropriate because it refers to a type of control. Other choices are wrong because surveys show that most organizations are at the repeatable level.

95. ☑ **C.** This simple formula conveniently shows the relationship between threats, vulnerabilities, and risk.
☒ **A, B,** and **D** are incorrect because the correct formula is Threats × Vulnerabilities × Asset value = Risk.

96. ☑ **D.** Security policies are set by management and are high-level in nature. They specify what should and should not happen, without going into detail on how to reach these goals. Security policies should be sufficiently specific to convey their meaning and objectives unambiguously but at the same time be general enough not to require modification every month or after introduction of a new system or application in the organization.
☒ **A, B,** and **C** are incorrect because guidelines are recommendations for consideration, procedures are detailed step-by-step instructions, and standards are general in nature.

97. ☑ **A** and **B.** Identifying user login status—by issuing the `logins` command and viewing the */etc/shadow* file—is important to determine which accounts are locked or disabled and which do not currently have assigned passwords.
☒ **C** is wrong because the `init S` command is used to bring down the system to run level S (single-user mode). **D** is wrong because the */var/adm/loginlog* file is used to log failed terminal session user login attempts.

98. ☑ **B** and **C.** Capturing unsuccessful terminal session login attempts is accomplished by creating a *var/adm/loginlog* file. To monitor all failed login attempts, edit the */etc/default/login file* and make sure that the `SYSLOG=YES` and `SYSLOG_FAILED_LOGINS=0` entries are uncommented.
☒ **A** is incorrect because by uncommenting the `RETRIES` entry in the */etc/default/login* file and editing the `SYSLOG_FAILED_LOGINS=`*some number*, you'll force the system to close the login connection after some predefined number of unsuccessful login attempts.

99. ☑ **A.** True. In the *audit_control* file, the `flags` and `naflags` arguments define which attributable and nonattributable events (the *na* preceding the second `flags` argument specifies nonattributable events) should be audited for the entire system—that is, all users on the system. Incidentally, you can specify events by using the `bsmrecord` command.

100. ☑ **A.** The event numbers (with the exception of 0, which is reserved as an invalid event number) reserved for the Solaris Kernel events are 1–2047.
☒ **B** is incorrect because 2048–32767 are reserved for the Solaris TCB programs. **C** is incorrect because 6144–32767 is used for SunOS 5.X user-level audit events. **D** is wrong because 32768–65535 are available for third-party TCB applications.

101. ☑ **B** and **C.** Controlling access to devices on a Solaris operating system is accomplished by two mechanisms: *device policy* and *device allocation*. Device policy is a default kernel-level mechanism that restricts and prevents access to devices integral to the system by mandating that processes that open such a device require certain privileges such as reading and writing. Device allocation, which is not enabled by default, is enforced during user allocation to require user authorization to access a peripheral device.

⊠ **A** is wrong because access control lists (ACLs) are mechanisms used to control access to files. **D** is incorrect because the Basic Audit Reporting Tool (BART) is used to check the integrity of files.

102. ☑ **F.** All of the answers are correct. Viewing your system's current patches using the `showrev -p` command will display all installed patches, patch numbers, whether a patch obsoletes a previous patch, if any prerequisite patches exist for a current patch, whether a patch is incompatible with other patches, and what packages are directly affected by a patch.

103. ☑ **A** and **D.** Device-specific files in the */etc* and */devices* directories are common targets for attackers to attempt to gain access to the operating system, especially for creating backdoors to the system.
⊠ **B** is incorrect because */usr/asset* is the working directory for ASET. **C** is incorrect because */usr/local* is simply an example of a typical download directory used to store files and programs by the current user.

104. ☑ **A, B,** and **C.** Examples of the principle of least privilege include programs—using privileges—that do not require making calls to `setuid`, when system administrators delegate privileged commands to non-root users without giving them full superuser access, and users that are only given privilege or permission necessary for performing their jobs.
⊠ **D** is incorrect because it is simply a factual statement regarding privileged commands and not an example of the principle of least privilege.

105. ☑ **C.** The `usermod` command associates a user's login with a role, profile, and authorization in the */etc/user_attr* database, which can also be used to grant a user access to a role.
⊠ **A** is wrong because to check the privileges available to your current shell's process, you would use the `ppriv -v pid $$` command. **B** is wrong because to start the management console you would issue the `/usr/sbin/smc &` command. **D** is wrong because the `roleadd` command can be used to create roles and associates a role with an authorization or a profile from the command line.

106. ☑ **E.** All of the answers are correct. Protecting files is a core component in Sun's Solaris security strategy. Although MD5 and SHA1, part of the Solaris cryptographic framework, were developed to help detect corrupt or maliciously altered files, Sun also recommends using a more comprehensive package as well called Tripwire. In addition to Tripwire, to help prevent unauthorized changes from being made to system files, Sun also recommends using ASET (discussed in Chapter 8) and the Basic Security Module (BSM), which is discussed in Chapter 5.

107. ☑ The `cryptoadm -m` command displays a list of mechanisms that can be used with the installed providers. If a provider is specified, the command will display the name of the specified provider and the mechanism list that can be used with that provider.

108. ☑ **B.** The rights profile name and commands with specific security attributes are stored in the *exec_attr* database.

    ☒ **A** is incorrect because the rights profile name and authorizations can be found in the *prof_attr* database. **C, D,** and **E** are incorrect because the *user_attr* database contains user and role information that supplements the *passwd* and *shadow* databases. This database also contains extended user attributes such as authorizations, rights profiles, and assigned roles.

109. ☑ **E.** All of the answers are correct. To monitor and help prevent unauthorized changes from being made to system files, Sun recommends using the Automated Security Enhancement Tool (ASET), the Basic Security Module (BSM), Tripwire, and the Solaris cryptographic framework.

110. ☑ **B.** The `netstat` command with `-a` and `-f inet` switches can be used to show the state of all sockets and all routing table entries for the AF_INET address family showing IPv4 information only.

    ☒ **A** is incorrect because `find directory -user root` is used to check all mounted paths starting at the specified directory and to display files owned by root. **C** is incorrect because the command `showrev -p` is used for viewing the system's current installed patches. **D** is incorrect because `grep inetd.conf` as it stands will produce nothing.

111. ☑ **C.** Top management is ultimately responsible for information security.

    ☒ **A** is incorrect because information security professionals advise management and implement management's decisions, but they do not make the decisions. **B** is incorrect because information systems auditors report on an organization's security to the board of directors and/or the stockholders, but they do not make decisions. **D** is incorrect because while stockholders appoint management, they are not responsible for making security decisions.

112. ☑ **D.** Employees, managers, contractors, consultants, and other insiders constitute a higher threat than a person on the street because they have more authorized network access and sensitive knowledge than outsiders. In fact, risks posed by insider attacks are more substantial, require less means to mount, and may result in larger losses than risks posed by outside attackers—they may also be more difficult to detect and recover from.

    ☒ **A, B,** and **C** are incorrect because although insiders are usually bound by employment and confidentiality agreements, that alone doesn't remove the threat. Insiders are subject to access controls, and access to information is not a threat in itself.

113. ☑ **C.** Security procedures are developed by subject-matter specialists within the organization with the assistance of security professionals and/or information systems auditors. Because security procedures are usually highly specific and technical in nature, they should be developed by those who appreciate these considerations.

    ☒ **A, B,** and **D** are incorrect because guidelines, normative acts, and standards only influence procedures.

114. ☑ **C.** Security guidelines are nonbinding recommendations that deal with how to develop, define, and enforce security policies and procedures. Although guidelines are nonbinding, it is customary to require explanation from those who choose not to follow them.

☒ **A, B,** and **D** are incorrect because standards, auditing regulations, and control objectives are not non-binding recommendations.

115. ☑ **B.** The syslog daemon that controls the logging facilities is located in the */etc/init.d* directory as *syslog*.

☒ **A** and **E** are wrong because device-specific files are located in the */etc* and */devices* directories, which are common targets for attackers to attempt to gain access to the operating system, especially for creating backdoors to the system. **C** is wrong because */usr/local* is an example of a typical download directory used to store files and programs by the current user. **D** is wrong because */usr/asset* is the working directory for ASET.

116. ☑ **A** and **D.** In the *audit_control* file, the `flags` and `naflags` arguments define which attributable and nonattributable events (the *na* preceding the second `flags` argument specifies nonattributable events) should be audited for the entire system—that is, all users on the system.

☒ **B** is wrong because the `minfree` argument is used to set the free-space warning threshold. **C** is incorrect because the `dir:` attribute is used to specify primary and secondary audit directories.

117. ☑ **A** and **B.** Setting up a warning alias can be accomplished in two ways. The easiest method is to edit the *etc/security/audit_warn* file by changing the e-mail alias in the script at entry: `ADDRESS=audit_warn`:

```
#-----------------------------------------------------------------------
send_msg() {
        MAILER=/usr/bin/mailx
        SED=/usr/bin/sed
        LOGCMD="$LOGGER -p daemon.alert"
        ADDRESS=audit_warn                    # standard alias for audit alerts
```

The second way is a little more complicated and requires redirecting the *audit_warn* e-mail alias to the appropriate account. To do so, add the *audit_warn* e-mail alias to the new alias file—in */etc/mail/aliases* or the *mail_aliases* database in the namespace—such as `audit_warn:` `alertadmin`.

☒ **C** is wrong because that procedure is used to set the free-space warning threshold manually.

118. ☑ **F.** All of the answers are correct. Each line in a BART manifest contains the following types of file information: size, content, user ID, group ID, and permissions.

119. ☑ **E.** All of the answers are correct. The most useful feature of BART is to compare manifests over time to monitor file-level changes. By doing so, you can verify the integrity of files, and detect corrupt files and security breaches, all of which help troubleshoot the system.

120. ☑ **A.** If the `noexec_user_stack` variable is set to non-zero, the operating system will apply non-executable but readable and writable attributes to every process stack.
☒ **B** and **D** are incorrect because these settings are used to disable or enable executable stack message logging. **C** is incorrect because that option does not exist.

121. ☑ **A.** A program buffer overflow occurs when a program process or task receives unwarranted and/or an abundance of data that is not properly programmed.
☒ **B** is incorrect because Ping of Death is a malformed ICMP packet attack where an attacker sends an oversized ping packet in an attempt to overflow the system's buffer. **C** is incorrect because executable stacks involve program buffer overflows. **D** is incorrect because during a SYN attack the attacker sends a flood of connection requests but does not respond to any of the replies. **E** is incorrect because a Smurf attack involves a broadcasted ping request to every system on the target's network with a spoofed return address of the target.

122. ☑ **A.** True. Sun's best practices dictate that you do not assign rights profiles, privileges, and authorizations directly to users, or privileges and authorizations directly to roles. It's best to assign authorizations to rights profiles, rights profiles to roles, and roles to users.

123. ☑ **F.** All of the answers are correct. Applications that comply with RBAC can check a user's authorizations before giving the user access. These applications include the following: audit administration commands (that is, `auditconfig` and `auditreduce`), batch job commands (that is, `at`, `atq`, `batch`, and `crontab`), device commands (that is, `allocate`, `deallocate`, `list_devices`, and `cdrw`), printer administration commands (that is, `lpadmin` and `lpfilter`), and the Solaris Management Console (includes all tools).

124. ☑ A message digest is a one-way function for a stream of binary data as verification that the data was not altered since the message digest was first generated, such as from when a file was compiled or modified. With regard to checking the integrity of files, you can use the Solaris Fingerprint Database (sfpDB), which is a free tool from Sun that allows you to check the integrity of system files through online cryptographic checksums. By doing so, you can determine whether system binaries and patches are safe in accordance with their original checksums among a huge database stored at Sun.

125. ☑ To remove a provider permanently, issue the `cryptoadm uninstall` command (for example: `cryptoadm uninstall des`).

126. ☑ **C.** The *user_attr* database contains user and role information that supplements the *passwd* and *shadow* databases. This database also contains extended user attributes such as authorizations, rights profiles, and assigned roles.
☒ **A** is incorrect because the rights profile name and authorizations can be found in the `prof_attr` database. **B** is wrong because the rights profile name and commands with specific

security attributes are stored in the exec_attr database. **D** and **E** are incorrect because the passwd and shadow databases do not contain user and role information that supplement themselves.

127. ☑ **A, C,** and **E.** A buffer overflow occurs when a program process or task receives extraneous data that is not properly programmed. As a result, the program typically operates in such a way that an intruder can abuse or misuse it. In a Teardrop attack, the attacker modifies the length and fragmentation offset fields in IP packets, which causes the target to crash. Finally, during a SYN attack, the attacker sends a flood of connection requests but does not respond to any of the replies thus leaving the connection half-open. The SYN messages will usually flood the server and as a result the target system will fill up with requests until it is unable to accommodate any new requests. In some cases, the system could consume available memory, crash, or be rendered inoperative.

☒ **B** is incorrect because although extraneous IP ports and services could be potential targets for denial of service attacks, they're not forms of attacks in and of themselves. **D** is incorrect because although when default executable stacks with permissions set to read/write/execute are allowed, programs may be targets for buffer overflow attacks, but executable stacks alone are not an attack. It's also important to note that some software may require executable stacks. Therefore, if you disable executable stacks, programs that require the contrary will be aborted.

128. ☑ **B.** The authorization required to allocate or deallocate a device forcibly is *solaris.device.revoke*.

☒ **A** is wrong because *solaris.device.allocate* is the authorization required to allocate a device.

129. ☑ **D.** The event numbers 32768–65535 are available for third-party TCB applications.

☒ **A** is incorrect because 1–2047 are reserved for the Solaris Kernel events. **B** is incorrect because 2048–32767 are reserved for the Solaris TCB programs. **C** is incorrect because 6144–32767 are used for SunOS 5.X user-level audit events.

130. ☑ **D.** The *audit_user* file defines specific users and classes of events that should always or never be audited for each user.

☒ **A** is wrong because general configuration specifications such as the primary and secondary audit directories are specified in the *audit_control* file. **B** is wrong because the audit policy is established by the auditconfig command, which is automatically started in the *audit_startup* script. **C** is incorrect because the *audit_warn* script generates mail to an e-mail alias called *audit_warn*.

131. ☑ **E.** By issuing the init 6 command, you will stop the operating system and reboot.

☒ **A** is incorrect because init S is used to go into single-user state for administrative functions. **B** is wrong because init 0 is used to go into firmware maintenance mode. **C** is wrong because init 2 is used to go into a multi-user state where NFS is not running. **D** is wrong because init 5 is used to shut down the operating system altogether.

132. ☑ **D.** All of the answers are correct. By issuing the `init` (`Run Level #`) command, you can switch between run levels and perform functions such as halting and rebooting the Solaris operating system. Additionally, you can shut down the system with the command `shutdown -i init-level -g grace-period -y`; where `init-level` is 0, 1, 2, 5, 6, or S (which is the default), and `grace-period` is the time (in seconds) before the system is shut down (default is 60 seconds). For example, to shut down the system to run level S and therefore disable all logins, use the command `shutdown -y`.

133. ☑ **F.** All of the answers are correct. Events that are capable of creating audit logs include system startup and shutdown, login and logout, identification and authentication, privileged rights usage, permission changes, process and thread creation and destruction, object creation and manipulation, application installation, and system administration.

134. ☑ **A.** Access control lists (ACLs) are mechanisms used to control access to files.
☒ **B** and **C** are wrong because device policy and device allocation are used to control access to devices. **D** is incorrect because the Basic Audit Reporting Tool (BART) is used to check the integrity of files.

135. ☑ **D.** The *etc/inetd.conf* defines how the inetd daemon handles common Internet service requests.
☒ **A** is incorrect because that file is used with the telnet service. **B** is incorrect because the file does not typically exist. **C** is incorrect because the */etc/services* file specifies the ports used by the server processes as contact ports which are also known as well-known ports.

136. ☑ **B.** False. Sun's best practices dictate that you do not assign rights profiles, privileges, and authorizations directly to users, or privileges and authorizations directly to roles. It's best to assign authorizations to rights profiles, rights profiles to roles, and roles to users.

137. ☑ The `cryptoadm list -p` command displays the mechanism policy for the installed providers. It also displays the provider feature policy. If a provider is specified, the command will display the name of the provider with the mechanism policy enforced on it only.

138. ☑ **C.** A privileged application can check for user IDs (UIDs), group IDs (GIDs), privileges, or authorizations via an application or command.
☒ **A** is wrong because authorization can be assigned to a role or user but is typically included in a rights profile. **B** is wrong because a privilege can be granted to a command, user, role, or system. Privilege gives a process the ability to perform an operation and therefore enforces security policy in the kernel. **D** is wrong because a rights profile can be assigned to a role or user as a collection of administrative functions. **E** is wrong because a role is a predefined identity that can run privileged applications.

139. ☑ **F.** All of the answers are correct. Sun recommends the following techniques for the most efficient auditing while still adhering to security prioritizations: For large networks with limited storage capacity, try randomly auditing a percentage of users at any one time. Perform routine audit file maintenance by reducing the disk-storage requirements by combining, removing, and compressing older log files. It's good practice to develop procedures for archiving the files, for transferring the files to removable media, and for storing the files offline. Monitor the audit data for unusual events in real time. Set up procedures to monitor the audit trail for certain potentially malicious activities. Adhere to company policy and immediately execute mitigations with regard to substantiated malicious findings. Deploy a script to trigger an automatic increase in the auditing of certain users or certain systems in response to the detection of unusual or potentially malicious events.

140. ☑ **D.** To display the extended user login status for a particular user, issue the `logins - x -l` *user* command.
☒ **A** is incorrect because the `logins` command will display general information concerning all login accounts organized in ascending order by user ID. **B** is incorrect because the `logins` *user* command will only display general information about a particular user account. **C** is wrong because the `logins -p` command will display user accounts that currently do not have assigned passwords.

141. ☑ A directory of last resort is a local audit directory that is used if the primary and all secondary audit directories become unavailable.

142. ☑ **C.** EAL4 is the highest practical level of assurance that may be gained using good commercial development practices.
☒ **A** and **B** are wrong because higher levels (EAL5–7) require special development methodologies and procedures which are expensive and not commonplace. **D** is incorrect, of course, because it is a lower level of assurance than EAL4.

143. ☑ **B.** Information security policies and procedures are an administrative control.
☒ **A** is wrong because policies and procedures are not a technical control. **C** is wrong because policies and procedures are not a form of access control. **D** is wrong because, although policies and procedures address operational controls, **B** is a better answer.

144. ☑ **B, C,** and **D.** Applications and commands that check for privileges include commands that control processes (such as `kill`, `pcred`, `rcapadm`), file and file system commands (such as `chmod`, `chgrp`, `mount`), Kerberos commands (such as `kadmin`, `kprop`, `kdb5_util`), and network commands (such as `ifconfig`, `route`, `snoop`).
☒ **A** and **E** are wrong because they represent databases.

145. ☑   **B.** Kernel-level plug-ins provide for implementations of algorithms in software.
  ☒   **A** is wrong because hardware plug-ins are device drivers and their associated hardware accelerators. **C** is wrong because user-level plug-ins are shared objects that provide services by using PKCS #11 libraries.

146. ☑   To prevent the use of a user-level mechanism, issue the `cryptoadm disable provider \ mechanism(s)` command.

147. ☑   **B.** A privilege can be granted to a command, user, role, or system. Privilege gives a process the ability to perform an operation and therefore enforces security policy in the kernel.
  ☒   **A** is wrong because authorization can be assigned to a role or user but is typically included in a rights profile. **C** is wrong because a privileged application can check for user IDs (UIDs), group IDs (GIDs), privileges, or authorizations via an application or command. **D** is wrong because a rights profile can be assigned to a role or user as a collection of administrative functions. **E** is wrong because a role is a predefined identity that can run privileged applications.

148. ☑   **C and D.** In symmetric (secret key) algorithms, the same key is used for both encryption and decryption—anyone knowing the key can both encrypt and decrypt messages.
  ☒   **A and B** are wrong because with asymmetric (public key) algorithms, two keys are used: one to encrypt a message and another to decrypt it.

149. ☑   **D.** All answers are correct. For an attack of any type to take place and to succeed, three factors must be present: the attacker must have a motive, an opportunity, and the means to carry out the attack.

150. ☑   The `cryptoadm -m` command displays a list of mechanisms that can be used with the installed providers. If a provider is specified, the command will display the name of the specified provider and the mechanism list that can be used with that provider.

D

Hands-On Exercises and Solutions

T he following exercises will help you measure your understanding of the material presented in this book. Be sure that you fully understand and can implement a solution for each exercise before taking Sun's exam. The solutions to the exercises are included after the "Exercises" section.

Exercises

Exercise 1   What steps would you take to disable user logins manually and set up the *loginlog* file to monitor failed logins?

Exercise 2   Explain the steps you would take when manually changing the free-space threshold to 30 percent before a warning is sent for all audit file systems.

Exercise 3   What steps should you take to check device allocation authorization and then allocate a CD-ROM?

Exercise 4   What steps could you take to create file digests manually with the `digest` command using both MD5 and SHA1 mechanisms within the cryptographic framework?

Exercise 5   Explain the steps for manually disabling programs from using executable stacks.

Exercise 6   Explain how to restrict network access to the server using telnet to Kerberos authenticated transactions only.

Exercise 7   What can you do to disable the FTP service?

Exercise 8   To check file-level changes, explain how you would create and then compare BART manifests.

Exercise 9   How would you encrypt and decrypt a file using a symmetric key?

Exercise 10   What steps would you perform to set up syslog to monitor all failed login attempts?

Exercise 11 What steps should you take to select users and classes of events manually to audit?

Exercise 12 How would you use BART to create a control manifest of every file installed on the system?

Exercise 13 Explain how you would install, verify, and remove patches on the system.

Exercise 14 Explain how to set up default connections to hosts outside a firewall using Solaris Secure Shell.

Exercise 15 Create a role for the System Administrator Rights Profile.

Exercise 16 Explain how you would enable stack message logging.

Exercise 17 What are the steps for scheduling ASET to run tasks automatically?

Exercise 18 Explain the steps required to run the Automated Security Enhancement Tool (ASET) manually at the high security level using the current parameters on a perimeter Solaris system. Note that off-peak system utilization hours are from 11 P.M. to 3 A.M. Also explain how to configure ASET to run periodically—every day at midnight.

Exercise 19 How would you compute a MAC with the MD5_HMAC and SHA1_HMAC mechanisms?

Exercise 20 Explain and demonstrate how to create a symmetric key, how to compute a digest of a file, and how to encrypt and decrypt a file using the AES algorithm.

Exercise 21 How would you prevent Rhost-style access from remote systems with PAM?

Exercise 22 Explain the procedure for generating a Solaris Secure Shell public/private key pair.

Solutions

Exercise 1 To disable user logins manually:

1. Log in with an account that has root privileges or use the su command to become superuser.

2. Create the */etc/nologin* file in your text editor by issuing the command vi /etc/nologin.

3. Insert a notification message (by pressing the I key on the keyboard) to be displayed when users attempt access by typing: *****Performing System Maintenance. The system will be unavailable until 10pm.*****

4. End insert mode by pressing the ESC key, and then save the file and exit the editor with the command :wq.

To set up the *loginlog* file to monitor failed logins:

1. Log in with an account that has root privileges or use the su command to become superuser.

2. Create the *var/adm/loginlog* file with your vi text editor or by issuing the command touch /var/adm/loginlog.

3. Make the *loginlog* file part of the sys group with the command chgrp sys /var/adm/loginlog.

4. Set both read and write permissions for only the root user on the *loginlog* file with the command chmod 600 /var/adm/loginlog.

5. Test that the system is logging failed login attempts by unsuccessfully logging in to the system from terminal windows (at least five times), and then view the *loginlog* file contents by issuing the command more /var/adm/loginlog.

Exercise 2 Following are steps for manually changing the free-space threshold to 30 percent before a warning is sent for all audit file systems:

1. Log in with an account that has root privileges or use the su command to become superuser.

2. Save a backup copy of the original *audit_control* file: *cp /etc/security/audit_ control /etc/security/audit_control.bak.*

3. Edit the *audit_control* file in your text editor by issuing the command vi /etc/security/audit_control.

4. Modify the minfree entry (by pressing the I key on the keyboard at the current percentage): minfree:30.

5. End insert mode by pressing the ESC key, and then save the file and exit the editor with the command :wq.

Exercise 3 Following are steps for checking whether or not you have the appropriate allocation authorization, and if you do, allocating CD-ROM(0):

1. Log in with your user account.

2. From a terminal session, issue the auths command and verify that you have solaris.device.allocate device allocation authorization rights.

3. Allocate the CD-ROM by issuing the allocate sr0 command.

Exercise 4 Following are steps for manually creating file digests with the digest command using both MD5 and SHA1 mechanisms within the cryptographic framework:

1. To compute an MD5 digest for file *solpatch* into output file *solpatchmd5*, issue the command

   ```
   digest -v -a md5 solpatch >> $HOME/solpatchmd5
   ```

2. We can then concatenate or display the resulting file with the cat command, cat ~/solpatchmd5, to view the following output:

   ```
   md5 (solpatch) = 83c0e53d1a5cc71ea42d9ac8b1b25b01
   ```

3. To compute an SHA1 digest for file *solpatch* into output file *solpatchsha1*, issue the command

   ```
   digest -v -a sha1 solpatch >> $HOME/solpatchsha1
   ```

4. We can then issue the cat command, cat ~/solpatchsha1, to view the following output:

   ```
   sha1 (solpatch) = 1ef50e5ad219e34f0b911a097b7b588e31f9b438
   ```

Exercise 5 Although most programs will run smoothly without running code from the stack, it's important to note that some software may require executable stacks. Therefore, if you disable executable stacks, programs that require the contrary will be aborted; that's why it's crucial to test this procedure first on a nonproduction system. Following are steps for manually disabling programs from using executable stacks:

1. Assume the role of superuser.

2. Change the directory to the */etc* folder and edit the system file (*/etc/system*) by adding `set noexec_user_stack=1`. To do so, type **cd /etc**, press ENTER, and then type **vi system** and press ENTER again. In the visual editor press the I key (to switch to edit mode and insert text) and type **set noexec_ user_stack=1**, and then press ENTER. Next, press the ESC key (to enter into command mode) and simply type **:wq** and then press ENTER to save and exit.

3. At the terminal prompt, reboot the system by typing the command **init 6** and then pressing ENTER.

Exercise 6　To restrict network access to the server using telnet, edit the telnet entry in */etc/inetd.conf*. Add the `-a user` option to the telnet entry to restrict access to those users who can provide valid authentication information:

```
telnet stream tcp nowait root /usr/sbin/in.telnetd telnetd -a user
```

Exercise 7　To disable an unneeded port and prevent unauthorized access to the associated service, comment out the service in the */etc/inetd.conf* file and then restart the inetd process or reboot the server if the service started through the inetd daemon. To disable the FTP services that is defined in inetd, simply comment it out in the */etc/inetd.conf* file by inserting a hash character in the very first character position before the service. Next, identify the process ID (PID) for inetd, and then restart the process by following these steps:

1. Log in with an account that has root privileges or use the switch user (`su`) command to become superuser.

2. Traverse to the */etc* folder and edit the *inetd.conf* file (*/etc/inetd.conf*), or open a terminal session and use vi.

3. Disable the ftp service by inserting a hash character before the service as shown here:

```
# ftp    stream      tcp6    nowait    root    /usr/sbin/in.ftpd
```

Then save the change to the modified inetd.conf file, and exit.

4. From a terminal session, identify the PID for inetd with the following command: `ps -eaf | grep inetd`. For example, the following output with the process for inetd could be shown as:

   ```
   root  181   1 0 08:46:02   ?   0:00 /usr/bin/inetd -s
   ```

5. Restart the inetd process with the command `kill -1 (PID)`—for example, `kill -1 181`, where 181 is the PID for inetd, as shown in the example output in number 4 above; otherwise, simply reboot the server (although this may not always be appropriate).

Exercise 8   Following are steps for creating and then comparing BART manifests to check file-level changes:

1. Log in as superuser or assume the Primary Administrator Role.

2. Create a BART control manifest of, for example, the password files:

   `bart create -I /etc/passwd /etc/shadow > passwd.control.071204.`

   The file name can be anything you prefer to use. In this case, we are specifying a manifest of the password files (`passwd.`) and that it's a control manifest (`control.`) and the date (`071204`).

3. After some period of time, create a comparison manifest to compare with the control manifest to detect any file-level changes:

   `bart create -I /etc/passwd /etc/shadow > passwd.compare.071904`

   Compare the control and compare manifests:

   `bart compare passwd.control.071204 passwd.compare.071904`

   or parse the information into a report file with

   `bart compare passwd.control.071204 passwd.compare.071904 > bart-report`

   The output will display any changes since the control manifest was created.

Exercise 9   To encrypt and decrypt a file, simply create a symmetric key, and then issue the `encrypt` command,

   `encrypt -a algorithm -k keyfile -i input-file -o output-file`

where `-a algorithm` is the algorithm to use to encrypt the file (type the algorithm as the algorithm appears in the output of the `encrypt -l` command);

-k *keyfile* is the file that contains a key of algorithm-specified length (the key length for each algorithm is listed, in bits, in the output of the encrypt -l command); -i *input-file* is the input file that you want to encrypt (this file is left unchanged); and -o *output-file* is the output file that is the encrypted form of the input file. To decrypt the output file, you simply pass the same key and the same encryption mechanism that encrypted the file but to the decrypt command.

Exercise 10   To set up syslog to monitor all failed user logins attempts:

1. Log in with an account that has root privileges or use the su command to become superuser.

2. Edit the */etc/default/login* file by uncommenting the SYSLOG=YES and SYSLOG_FAILED_LOGINS=0 entries:

```
#
# SYSLOG determines whether the syslog(3) LOG_AUTH facility should be used
# to log all root logins at level LOG_NOTICE and multiple failed login
# attempts at LOG_CRIT.
#
SYSLOG=YES
#
# These entries were clipped for brevity.
#
# The SYSLOG_FAILED_LOGINS variable is used to determine how many failed
# login attempts will be allowed by the system before a failed login
# message is logged, using the syslog(3) LOG_NOTICE facility.  For example,
# if the variable is set to 0, login will log -all- failed login attempts.
#
SYSLOG_FAILED_LOGINS=0
#
```

3. Create the log file in the */var/adm* directory: touch /var/adm/authlog.

4. Assign the appropriate read/write permissions for root to the log file: chmod 600 /var/adm/authlog.

5. Change the *authlog* file group membership to *sys*: chgrp sys /var/adm/authlog.

6. Edit the *syslog.conf* file to send all failed login attempts to the *authlog* file with this entry: auth.notice /var/adm/authlog.

7. Stop and start the syslog daemon: `/etc/init.d/syslog stop` and `/etc/init.d/syslog start`.

8. Test that the system is logging failed login attempts by unsuccessfully logging in to the system and then viewing the *var/adm/authlog* file contents by issuing the command `more /var/adm/authlog`.

Exercise 11 The *audit_user* file defines specific users and classes of events that should always or never be audited for each user. By default the root account is included; however, additional user accounts can be added in the following format: `username:always-audit:never-audit`; where `username` is the name of the user to be audited, `always-audit` is the list of classes of events that should be always audited, and `never-audit` is the list of classes of events that should never be audited. Following are steps for manually selecting users and classes of events to audit:

1. Log in with an account that has root privileges or use the `su` command to become superuser.

2. Save a backup copy of the original *audit_user* file. *cp /etc/security/audit_user /etc/security/audit_user.bak*.

3. Edit the *audit_user* file in your text editor by issuing the command `vi /etc/security/audit_user`.

4. Add user entries, one per line, in the following format: `username:classes-to-audit:classes-not-to-audit`. Separate multiple classes with commas. As a reference, the *audit_event* file defines which events are part of classes you can audit. You can use the `more /etc/security/audit_event` command in a terminal session to view the entire database.

5. End insert mode by pressing the ESC key and then save the file and exit the editor with the command `:wq`.

Exercise 12 Creating a manifest with BART is accomplished by issuing the `bart create` *options* > *control-manifest* command; where *options* can be `-R` to specify the root directory for the manifest, and all paths specified by the rules will be interpreted relative to this directory, and all paths reported in the manifest will be relative to this directory; `-I` accepts a list of individual files to be cataloged, either on the command line or read from standard input; `-r` is the name of the rules file for this manifest (note that –, when used with the `-r` option, will be read the rules file from standard input); `-n` turns off content signatures for all regular files in the file list (this option can be used to improve performance, or you can use this option if the contents of the file list are expected to change, as in the case of system log files);

and the `control manifest` is an optional control file name. Therefore, to create a manifest of every file installed on the system, you would issue the `bart create` command without any options.

Exercise 13　To install a patch simply use the `patchadd` command: `patchadd /dir/filename`; where `/dir/` is the folder that contains the patch and `filename` is the name of the patch. To install a group of patches in succession, simply add the additional file names to your command sequence separated by a space: `patchadd /dir/filename1 filename2 filename3 filename4`. To verify that a patch was successfully installed, issue the *showrev* command: `showrev -p`. To verify a specific individual patch: `showrev -p | grep filename`; where `filename` is the name of the patch. Once a patch is installed, if necessary, you can remove it using the `patchrm` command: `patchrm filename`; where `filename` is the name of the patch or patch cluster.

Exercise 14　You can use Solaris Secure Shell to make a connection from a host inside a firewall to a host on the other side of the firewall. This task is done by specifying a proxy command for ssh either in a configuration file or as an option on the command line. In general, you can customize your ssh interactions through a configuration file. You can customize either your own personal file in *$HOME/ .ssh/config* or you can customize an administrative configuration file in */etc/ssh/ssh_config*. The files can be customized with two types of proxy commands. One proxy command is for HTTP connections. The other proxy command is for SOCKS5 connections.

1. Specify the proxy commands and hosts in a configuration file. Use the following syntax to add as many lines as you need:

```
[Host outside-host]
ProxyCommand proxy-command [-h proxy-server] \
[-p proxy-port] outside-host|%h outside-port|%p
```

   ■ `Host outside-host`　Limits the proxy command specification to instances when a remote host name is specified on the command line. If you use a wildcard for outside-host, you apply the proxy command specification to a set of hosts.

   ■ `proxy-command`　Specifies the proxy command. The command can be either `/usr/lib/ssh/ssh-http-proxy-connect` for HTTP connections or `/usr/lib/ssh/ssh-socks5-proxy-connect` for SOCKS5 connections.

■ -h *proxy-server* and -p *proxy-port* These options specify a proxy server and a proxy port, respectively. If present, the proxies override any environment variables that specify proxy servers and proxy ports, such as HTTPPROXY, HTTPPROXYPORT, SOCKS5_PORT, SOCKS5_SERVER, and http_proxy. The http_proxy variable specifies a URL. If the options are not used, the relevant environment variables must be set. For more information, see the ssh-socks5-proxy-connect(1) and ssh-http-proxy-connect(1) man pages.

■ *outside-host* Designates a specific host to connect to. Use the %h substitution argument to specify the host on the command line.

■ *outside_port* Designates a specific port to connect to. Use the %p substitution argument to specify the port on the command line. By specifying %h and %p without using the Host outside_host option, the proxy command is applied to the host argument whenever the ssh command is invoked.

2. Run Solaris Secure Shell, specifying the outside host. For example, use the following:

```
myLocalHost% ssh myOutsideHost
```

This command looks for a proxy command specification for myOutsideHost in your personal configuration file. If the specification is not found, the command looks in the system-wide configuration file, */etc/ssh/ssh_config*. The proxy command is substituted for the ssh command.

Exercise 15 Follow these steps to create a role for the System Administrator Rights Profile:

1. Log in as superuser.
2. Start the management console and click the Administrative Roles icon.
3. Enter the role name: **sysadmin. 4.** Enter the role full name: **System Administrator**.
4. Enter the role description: **Performs non-security admin tasks**.
5. Enter the role password.
6. Assign the role rights: **System Administrator**.
7. Enter the home directory or accept the default.
8. Add the user names of users who will be permitted to assume this role.

Exercise 16 To enable stack message logging, we need to make changes in the */etc/system* file, and then reboot the operating system to initiate the changes:

1. Log in with an account that has root privileges or use the su command to become superuser.
2. While editing the */etc/system* file, add set noexec_user_stack_log=1.
3. Save the changes and exit the editor.
4. Issue the command init 6 to restart the server.

Exercise 17 Following are steps for scheduling ASET to run tasks automatically:

1. Log in with an account that has root privileges or use the switch user (su) command to become superuser. For example, to switch to root simply open a terminal session and type **su root**, press ENTER, and then enter root's password at the prompt.
2. Edit the PERIODIC_SCHEDULE variable in the */usr/aset/asetenv* file to an appropriate start time (by default, it's set to run every day at midnight: PERIODIC_SCHEDULE="0 0 * * *").
3. Inserts a line in the crontab file to start ASET at the time determined by the PERIODIC_SCHEDULE environment variable, using /usr/aset/aset -p.

Exercise 18 To avoid resource encumbrance and knowing that ASET tasks should be run during off-peak hours or when system activities are low as well as the user load, you'll execute ASET promptly at 11 P.M. To do so, log in as root or become superuser and then issue the /usr/aset/aset -l high -d /usr/asset command. The reports are stored in the */usr/aset/reports* directory. Next, to have ASET run every day at midnight, log in with an account that has root privileges and verify that the PERIODIC_SCHEDULE variable in the */usr/aset/asetenv* file is correctly set by default to run every day at midnight as shown here: PERIODIC_SCHEDULE="0 0 * * *". Next, insert a line in the crontab file to start ASET at the time determined by the PERIODIC_SCHEDULE environment variable with the command /usr/aset/aset -p.

Exercise 19 To create a MAC of a file, use the command mac -v -a *algorithm* -k *keyfile input-file*; where -v displays the output in the following format: *algorithm* (*input-file*) = mac; -a *algorithm* is the algorithm to use to compute the MAC (type the algorithm as the algorithm appears in the output of the mac -l command); -k *keyfile* is the file that contains a key of algorithm-specified length; and *input-file* is the input file for the MAC.

Exercise 20 The first part of the lab requires you to explain and demonstrate how to create a symmetric key. To create a symmetric key, use the dd command:

```
dd if=/dev/urandom of=keyfile bs=n count=n
```

where if=file is the input file (for a random key, use the /dev/urandom file); of=keyfile is the output file that holds the generated key; bs=n is the key size in bytes (for the length in bytes, divide the key length in bits by 8), and count=n is the count of the input blocks (the number for n should be 1). The first step in creating a symmetric key is to determine the length (in bytes) required by your encryption algorithm. To do so, simply list the *bit range* of all supported algorithms with the encrypt -l and mac -l commands shown here:

```
encrypt -l
Algorithm          Keysize:   Min   Max (bits)
----------------------------------------------
aes                          128   128
arcfour                        8   128
des                           64   64
3des                         192   192
mac -l
Algorithm          Keysize:   Min   Max (bits)
----------------------------------------------
des_mac                       64   64
sha1_hmac                      8   512
md5_hmac                       8   512
```

The next step is to determine the key length *in bytes* by dividing the minimum and maximum key sizes by 8. Then you can generate the symmetric key with the dd command:

```
dd if=/dev/urandom of=keyfile bs=n count=n
```

where if=file is the input file (for a random key, use the /dev/urandom file); of=keyfile is the output file that holds the generated key; bs=n is the key size in bytes (for the length in bytes, divide the key length in bits by 8); and count=n is the count of the input blocks (the number for n should be 1).

For example, to create a key for the AES algorithm in a file for later decryption you can issue the command (note AES uses a mandatory 128-bit key or 16 bytes):

```
dd if=/dev/urandom of=$HOME/aeskey/aeskey16 bs=16 count=1
```

The second part of the lab requires you to create a digest of a file. To compute a message digest for one or more files issue the digest command:

```
digest -v -a algorithm input-file > digest-listing
```

where -v displays the output with file information; -a *algorithm* is the algorithm used to compute a digest (that is, MD5 or SHA1); *input-file* is the input file for the digest to be computed; and *digest-listing* is the output file for the digest command.

Following is an example of creating a file digest using the SHA1 mechanism within the cryptographic framework:

1. To compute an MD5 digest for file *testfile.tar.Z* into output file *testfilesha1*, issue the command

   ```
   digest -v -a md5 testfile.tar.Z >> $HOME/testfilemd5
   ```

2. We can then issue the cat command

   ```
   cat ~/testfilemd5
   ```

   to view the following output:

   ```
   md5 (testfile.tar.Z) = 1ab89e5ad217e34f0a977a091a1b588b31f9b588
   ```

If *testfile.tar.z* was a system file, we could compare the output to that stored in the online Solaris Fingerprint Database (sfpDB) to determine whether system binaries and patches are safe in accordance with their original checksums. MD5 software binaries that can be used with sfpDB for Intel and SPARC architectures can be freely downloaded from Sun at SunSolve.Sun.COM/md5/md5.tar.Z.

The third part of our lab requires us to encrypt and decrypt a file using the AES algorithm. To encrypt and decrypt a file, simply create a symmetric key, and then issue the encrypt command:

```
encrypt -a algorithm -k keyfile -i input-file -o output-file
```

where -a *algorithm* is the algorithm to use to encrypt the file (type the algorithm as the algorithm appears in the output of the encrypt -l command); -k *keyfile* is the file that contains a key of algorithm-specified length (the key length for each algorithm is listed, in bits, in the output of the encrypt -l command); -i *input-file* is the input file that you want to encrypt (this file is left unchanged); and -o *output-file* is the output file that is the encrypted form of the input file. To decrypt the output file, you simply pass the same key and the same encryption mechanism that encrypted the file but to the decrypt command.

In the following example, a file is encrypted with the AES algorithm. Remember that AES mechanisms use a key of 128 bits, or 16 bytes:

```
encrypt -a aes -k ~/keyf/10.09.aes16 \ -i my.file -o ~/enc/e.my.file
```

The input file, *my.file*, will still exist in its original form. To decrypt the output file, pass the same key and the same encryption mechanism that encrypted the file to the decrypt command:

```
decrypt -a aes -k ~/keyf/10.09.aes16 \ -i ~/enc/e.my.file -o ~/my.file
```

Exercise 21   To Prevent Rhost-style access from remote systems with PAM, remove all of the lines that include `rhosts_auth.so.1` from the PAM configuration file. This prevents unauthenticated access to the local system from remote systems. To prevent other unauthenticated access to the ~/*.rhosts* files, remember to disable the rsh service by removing the service entry from the */etc/inetd.conf* file.

Exercise 22   The standard procedure for generating a Solaris Secure Shell public/ private key pair is as follows:

1. Start the key generation program:

   ```
   ssh-keygen -t rsa
   Generating public/private rsa key pair.
   ```

   where `-t` is the type of algorithm—one of `rsa`, `dsa`, or `rsa1`.

2. Enter the path to the file that will hold the key. By default, the filename *id_rsa*, which represents an RSA v2 key, appears in parentheses. You can select this file by pressing the RETURN key. Or, you can type an alternative filename.

   ```
   Enter file in which to save the key (/home/jdoe/.ssh/id_rsa): <Press Return>
   ```

   The filename of the public key is created automatically by appending the string *.pub* to the name of the private key file.

3. Enter a passphrase for using your key. This passphrase is used for encrypting your private key. A good passphrase is 10–30 characters long, mixes alphabetic and numeric characters, and avoids simple prose and simple names. A null entry means no passphrase is used. A null entry is strongly discouraged for user accounts. Note that the passphrase is not displayed when you type it in.

   ```
   Enter passphrase (empty for no passphrase): <Type passphrase>
   ```

4. Retype the passphrase to confirm it.

   ```
   Enter same passphrase again: <Type passphrase>
   Your identification has been saved in /home/jdoe/.ssh/id_rsa. Your public key
   has been saved in /home/jdoe/.ssh/id_rsa.pub. The key fingerprint is:
   0e:fb:3d:57:71:73:bf:58:b8:eb:f3:a3:aa:df:e0:d1 jdoe@myLocalHost
   ```

5. Check the results. Check that the path to the key file is correct. In the example, the path is */home/jdoe/.ssh/id_rsa.pub*. At this point, you have created a public/private key pair.

6. Set up the *authorized_keys* file on the destination host.

   Copy the *id_rsa.pub* file to the destination host. Type the command on one line with no backslash:

   ```
   cat $HOME/.ssh/id_rsa.pub | ssh myRemoteHost \
   'cat >> .ssh/authorized_keys && echo "Key uploaded successfully"'
   ```

   When you are prompted, supply your login password. After the file is copied, the message "Key uploaded successfully" is displayed.

INDEX

B

C

E

S

T

INTERNATIONAL CONTACT INFORMATION

AUSTRALIA
McGraw-Hill Book Company
Australia Pty. Ltd.
TEL +61-2-9900-1800
FAX +61-2-9878-8881
http://www.mcgraw-hill.com.au
books-it_sydney@mcgraw-hill.com

CANADA
McGraw-Hill Ryerson Ltd.
TEL +905-430-5000
FAX +905-430-5020
http://www.mcgraw-hill.ca

**GREECE, MIDDLE EAST, & AFRICA
(Excluding South Africa)**
McGraw-Hill Hellas
TEL +30-210-6560-990
TEL +30-210-6560-993
TEL +30-210-6560-994
FAX +30-210-6545-525

MEXICO (Also serving Latin America)
McGraw-Hill Interamericana Editores
S.A. de C.V.
TEL +525-1500-5108
FAX +525-117-1589
http://www.mcgraw-hill.com.mx
carlos_ruiz@mcgraw-hill.com

SINGAPORE (Serving Asia)
McGraw-Hill Book Company
TEL +65-6863-1580
FAX +65-6862-3354
http://www.mcgraw-hill.com.sg
mghasia@mcgraw-hill.com

SOUTH AFRICA
McGraw-Hill South Africa
TEL +27-11-622-7512
FAX +27-11-622-9045
robyn_swanepoel@mcgraw-hill.com

SPAIN
McGraw-Hill/
Interamericana de España, S.A.U.
TEL +34-91-180-3000
FAX +34-91-372-8513
http://www.mcgraw-hill.es
professional@mcgraw-hill.es

**UNITED KINGDOM, NORTHERN,
EASTERN, & CENTRAL EUROPE**
McGraw-Hill Education Europe
TEL +44-1-628-502500
FAX +44-1-628-770224
http://www.mcgraw-hill.co.uk
emea_queries@mcgraw-hill.com

ALL OTHER INQUIRIES Contact:
McGraw-Hill/Osborne
TEL +1-510-420-7700
FAX +1-510-420-7703
http://www.osborne.com
omg_international@mcgraw-hill.com

Sound Off!

Visit us at **www.osborne.com/bookregistration** and let us know what you thought of this book. While you're online you'll have the opportunity to register for newsletters and special offers from McGraw-Hill/Osborne.

We want to hear from you!

Sneak Peek

Visit us today at **www.betabooks.com** and see what's coming from McGraw-Hill/Osborne tomorrow!

Based on the successful software paradigm, Bet@Books™ allows computing professionals to view partial and sometimes complete text versions of selected titles online. Bet@Books™ viewing is free, invites comments and feedback, and allows you to "test drive" books in progress on the subjects that interest you the most.

OSBORNE DELIVERS RESULTS!

OSBORNE
www.osborne.com

MAKE A MARK ON YOUR CAREER.

Get Sun certified and get ahead in the IT world. Sun's certification programs provide clear, hard evidence of your skills and dedication— which is essential for career growth. What's more, Sun certifications are recognized industry-wide and are consistently ranked among the highest, from entry level to advanced programs including Java™ and Solaris™ OS technologies.

The Network is the Computer™

TAKE A STEP TOWARD ADVANCING YOUR CAREER
BY VISITING sun.com/training/certification